Pink
Jewels

Pink
Jewels

Arthur W. Pink

Sovereign Grace Publishers, Inc.
P.O. Box 4998
Lafayette, IN 47903
2001

ISBN 1-878442-30-9

Printed In the United States of America
By Lightning Source, Inc.

CONTENTS

OLD THINGS PASSED AWAY

Some of our older readers may recall a book which made quite a stir in the religious world, especially the Arminian sections of it, some forty years ago. It was entitled "Twice-born Men", and was written in a somewhat racy and sensational style by a well-known journalist, Har. Begbie. It purported to describe some startling "conversions" of notorious profligates and criminals under the evangelistic efforts of the Salvation Army and City Missions. Whether or no the reader is acquainted with that particular book, he has probably read similar accounts of reformations of character. He may, as this writer, have personally heard the "testimonies" of some unusual cases. We recall listening unto one in New York city some twenty-five years ago: a man past middle age who had "spent twenty Christmas days in prison", who had been delivered from a life of crime, attributing his deliverance to the amazing grace of God and the efficacy of the redeeming blood of Christ, and who, to use one of his Scriptural quotations, had been given "beauty for ashes, the oil of joy for mourning, the garment of praise for the spirit of heaviness".

Many, if not all, of those reformed characters, testify that so thorough was the work of grace wrought in them that their old habits and inclinations had been completely taken away, that they no longer had the slightest desire to return to their former ways, that all longing for the things which once enthralled them was gone, declaring that God had made them new creatures in Christ, that old things were passed away, and all things had become new (2 Cor. 5:17). Personally we do not deem ourself competent to pass an opinion on such cases. Certainly we would not dare assign any limit to the wonder-working power of God; nevertheless, we should need to be in close contact with such people for some considerable time and closely observe their daily walk, in order to be assured that their goodness was something less evanescent than "a morning cloud and as the early dew" which quickly vanishes (Hos. 6:4). On the one hand we should keep in mind the miraculous transformation wrought in the fierce persecutor of Tarsus, and on the other we would not forget Matt. 12:43-45.

But this we may safely affirm, that such cases as those alluded unto above are not general or even common, and certainly must not be set up as the standard by which we should ascertain the genuineness of conversion, be it our own or another's. Though it be blessedly true that in His saving operations God communicates subduing and restraining grace to the soul—to some a greater measure, to others a lesser; yet it is equally true that He does not remove the old nature at regeneration or eradicate "the flesh". Only One has ever trodden this earth who could truthfully aver "the Prince of this world (Satan) cometh, and hath nothing in me" (John 14:30) — nothing combustible which his fiery darts could ignite. The godliest saint who has ever lived had reason to join with the apostle in sorrowfully confessing "when I would do good, evil is present in me" (Rom. 7:21). It is indeed the Christian's duty and privilege to keep himself from

7

all outward sins: "walk in the spirit and ye shall not fulfil the lusts of the flesh" (Gal. 5:16), yet as the very next verse tells us, the flesh is *there*, operative, and opposing the spirit.

But we will go further. When such persons as those referred to above appropriate 2 Cor. 5:17 to describe their "experience", no matter how well suited its language may seem to their case, they are making an unwarrantable and misleading use of that verse; and the consequence has been that many of God's dear children were brought into sad bondage. Countless thousands have been led to believe that, if they truly received Christ as their personal Lord and Savior, such a radical change would be wrought in them that henceforth they would be immune from evil thoughts, foul imaginations, wicked desires and worldly lusts. But after they *did* receive Christ as their Lord and Saviour, it was not long ere they discovered that things inside them were very different from what they expected: that old inclinations were still present, that internal corruptions now harassed them, and in some instances more fiercely than ever before. Because of the painful consciousness of "the plague of his own heart" (3 Kings 8:38) many a one has drawn the conclusion that he was never soundly converted, that he was mistaken in believing he had been born of God, and great is their distress.

Now one very important and necessary part of the work to which God has called His servants is "take up the stumblingblock out of the way of My people" (Isa. 57:14 and cf. 62:10), and if he would faithfully attend unto this part of his duty, then he must make it crystal clear to his hearers, believers and unbelievers, that God has nowhere promised to eradicate indwelling sin from the one who believes the Gospel. He *does* save the penitent and believing sinner from the love, the guilt, the penalty, and the reigning power of sin; but He does not in this life deliver him from the presence of sin. The miracle of God's saving grace does indeed effect a real, a radical, and a lasting change in all who are the subjects of it—some being more conscious of the same and giving clearer evidence of it, and some (who previously led a moral, and perhaps religious, life) less so; but in no single instance does He remove from the being of that person "the flesh" or evil principle which he brought with him when he entered this world. That which was born of the flesh is still flesh: though that which has born of the Spirit is spirit (John 3:6).

Not that the minister of the Gospel must swing to the opposite extreme and teach, or even convey the impression, that the Christian can expect nothing better than a life of defeat while he be left in this scene; that his foes, both internal and external, are far too mighty for him to successfully cope with. God does not leave His dear child to cope with those foes in his own power, but strengthens him with might by His Spirit in the inner man; yet he is required to be constantly on his guard lest he grieve the Spirit and give occasion for Him to suspend His operations. God tells the saint "My grace is sufficient for thee", but that grace must be *sought* (Heb. 4:16) and *used* (Luke 8:18), and if it be sought humbly and used aright, then "He giveth more grace" (James 4:6), so that he is enabled to fight the good fight of faith. Satan is indeed mighty, but there is one yet mightier: "greater is He that is in you than he that is in the world" (1 John 4:4), and therefore is the Christian called upon to "be strong in the Lord and in the power of *His* might" (Eph. 6:10); and though while severed from Christ he can produce no fruit (John 15:5), yet strengthened by Christ, he "can do all things" (Phil. 4:13). Christians are "overcomers" (1 John 2:13; 5:4; Rev. 2:7). Thus we see once more that there is a balance to be preserved: avoiding at the one extreme the error of sinless perfectionism, and at the other that of spiritual defeatism. Truth is to be presented in its Scriptural proportions, and not dwelt unduly on either its gloomy or its bright side. When one is regenerated he is effectually called "out of darkness into God's marvelous light" (1 Pet. 2:9), yet if an unconverted soul reading those words forms the idea that should God quicken him, all ignorance and error will be immediately dispelled from his soul, he draws an unwarrantable conclusion and will soon discover his mistake. The Lord Jesus promises to give rest unto the heavily-laden soul which comes to Him, but He does not thereby signify that such an one will henceforth enjoy perfect serenity of heart and mind. He saves His people from their sins (Matt. 1:21), yet not in such a way that they will have no occasion to ask for the daily forgiveness of their transgressions (Luke 11:4). It is not that His salvation is an imperfect one, but that it is not completely experienced or entered into in *this* life, as such passages as Rom. 13:11, 1 Pet. 1:5 show. The "best wine" is reserved unto the last. Glorification is yet future.

Above we have said that when such characters as those mentioned in the opening paragraph appropriate 2 Cor. 5:17 to describe their "experience", they make an unwarrantable and misleading use of that verse. They are not the only ones who do so, and since many have been stumbled by toiling to understand that verse aright, a careful exposition of it is called for. "If any man be in Christ, he is a new creature: old things are passed away; behold, all things are become new". It must be admitted in all fairness that the sound of those words decidedly favours those who claim that such a miracle of grace has been wrought in them that the old nature with its evil propensities was eradicated when they were born again. But in view of the very different experience of the vast majority of God's children of the last two thousand years of whom we have any reliable knowledge, must we not pause and ask, Is *that* really the *sense* of the verse? Probably there are few of our readers who have not been perplexed by its language.

The careful student will observe that we have *omitted* the opening word of 2 Cor. 5:17, which is done eight times out of ten by those who quote it; nor are we acquainted with any exposition that satisfactorily explains its force. "*Therefore* if any man be in Christ he is a new creature." Obviously that "therefore" is where we must begin in any critical examination of the verse. It indicates that a conclusion is here drawn from a foregoing premise, and tells us this verse is not to be regarded as a thing apart, complete in itself, but rather as intimately related to something preceding. On turning back to v. 16 we find that it, in turn, opens with "Wherefore" (The same Greek word being used), which at once serves to *classify* the passage, indicating that it is a didactic or doctrinal one, wherein the apostle is presenting an argument, or a reasoned-out train of thought; and not a hortatory passage wherein a call unto duty is made, or a biographical passage in which an experience of the soul is delineated. Unless that key be used, the passage remains locked to us.

The key is hung upon the door by the presence of its introductory "therefore" or "wherefore", and if it be ignored, and instead we force the door, then its lock is strained or its panels and hinges broken; in other words, the interpretation given to it will be a strained and unsatisfactory one. And such has indeed been the case with those who sought to explain its meaning *without* giving any due weight to — using — the very word on which the verse turns. Disregarding the opening "therefore", it has been commonly assumed that 2 Cor. 5:17 is speaking of the miracle of regeneration and describing what is thereby effected in the one experiencing the same. But those who gave the verse that meaning at once felt themselves faced with difficulties, and were obliged to whittle down its terms or qualify its language, for it is an undeniable fact, a matter of painful consciousness to Christians, that though some of the "old things" which characterised them in their unregeneracy have "passed away," yet others of them have *not* done so, nor have *"all"* things" yet become new within them.

In his commentary on 2 Cor. one otherwise excellent expositor tells us, "In the O. T. (Isa. 43:18,19; 65:17) the effects to be produced by the coming of the Messiah are described as a making all things new. The final consummation of the Redeemer's kingdom in heaven is described in the same terms, 'He that sat upon the throne said, Behold, I make all things new' (Rev. 21: 5). *The inward spiritual change* in every believer is set forth in the same words, because it is the type and necessary condition of this great cosmical change. What would avail any conceivable change in things external, if the heart remained a cage of unclean birds? The apostle therefore says that if any man be in Christ he experiences a change *analogous* to that predicted by the prophet, and like to that which we still anticipate when earth shall become heaven. 'Old things are passed away: behold, all things have become new'. Old opinions, plans, desires, principles and affections are passed away; new views of truth, new principles, new apprehensions of the destiny of man, and new feelings and purposes fill and govern the soul".

It is accrediting just such extravagant statements as the above — which is a fair example of those made by many other good men, who have held influential positions in the churches — that have brought so many of God's little ones into cruel bondage, for they know full well that no such great change has been wrought in them as like unto that which will obtain on the new earth, concerning which God assures us "there shall in nowise enter into it any thing that defileth, neither worketh abomination or maketh a lie", and where "there shall be no more death, neither sorrow nor crying, neither shall there be any more pain; for the former things are passed away" (Rev. 21:27,4). We make so bold as to say that the Christian experience of that expositor falsified his own assertions. "Old opinions and plans" many indeed pass away when a person is soundly converted, but it is *not true* that old "desires, principles, and affections" pass away: on the contrary, they remain, are active, and plague him to the end of his course; otherwise there would be no corruptions for him to resist, no lusts which he is exhorted to mortify.

It is really surprising to find some excellent men, whose writings are generally most helpful and whose memories we revere, uttering such absurdities when interpreting 2 Cor. 5:17 (The explanation is that, like ourself, they too were compassed with infirmity). Another of them wrote of the Christian: "He concludes that he is in Christ, because he is 'a new creature.' He finds old things passed away, and all things become new. His old secure, benumbed, unfaithful conscience is passed away. His old perverse, stubborn, rebellious will; he has a new will. His old strong, sensual, corrupt, unbelieving, impenitent heart is gone. . .his old disordered, misplaced, inordinate affections,. . .He has new thoughts, new inclinations, new desires, new delights, new employments." True, he closes his paragraph by saying "sometimes (i.e. formerly) carnal, but now in some measure spiritual; sometimes worldly, but now in some degree has his conversation in heaven; sometimes profane, but now in part holy," which not only virtually contradicts his previous sentences, but serves to illustrate what we said above, about men creating their own difficulties when ignoring the key to a passage, and being obliged to tamper with its terms to make them fit their interpretations.

The Greek word for "passed away" is a very strong one, as may be seen from such passages as Matt. 5:18; 24, 34; James 1:10; 2 Pet. 3:10, and signifies (not from its etymology, but its *usage*) a removal, a making an end of. Whatever be the "old things" referred to in 2 Cor. 5:17, they are not merely subdued, or temporarily put to sleep, only to waken again with fresh vigour but are "passed away" — *done with*. Therefore to define those "old things" as "old affections, old dispositions of Adam" as still another theologian does, is utterly misleading, and one had supposed his own spiritual history had taught him better than to make such an assertion. An older writer is somewhat more satisfactory, when he says, "By old things he means all those corrupt principles, self ends, and fleshly lusts belonging to the carnal state, or the old man; all these are 'passed away', not simply and perfectly, but only in part at present, and wholly in hope and expectation hereafter". The very fact that such a frittering of "passed away" was deemed necessary makes us highly suspicious of his definition of the "old things"; and should make us search for an alternative one.

THE DISPENSATIONAL CHANGE

To say that the "old things" which are " passed away" when a person becomes a new creature in Christ refer to "old desires, principles and appetites" is flatly contradicted by Rom. 7:14 - 25. The old nature, the "flesh" or evil principle, most certainly does not pass away, either wholly or in part, neither at the new birth nor at any subsequent stage of his life while the Christian is left here on earth. Instead, the "flesh" remains in the saint, and "lusteth against the spirit" (Gal. 5:17), producing a continual conflict as he seeks to walk with and please the Lord. That a real and radical change takes place in the soul when a miracle of grace is wrought within him, is indeed blessedly true, but to describe that miraculous change as consisting of or being accompanied by the removal of the old sinful nature or indwelling corruption, is totally unwarranted and utterly unscriptural. And it is just because so many have been confused by this error, and sufficiently affected by it, as to have their assurance undermined and their peace disturbed, that we are now writing upon the subject.

It should be carefully noted that 2 Cor. 5:17 is not describing some exceptional experience which is attained unto only by a favoured few from among the children of God, but rather is it postulating that which is common to the whole family: "Therefore if *any man* be in Christ he is a new creature". The "if any man" shows that we have here a proposition which is general, one which is of universal application unto the regenerate, — as much so as though it said "if any man be in Christ his sins are pardoned". This at once assures the Christian that it is not through any fault of his that he comes short of such a standard as some would appear to measure unto. Nor is our verse giving an account of that which is gained as he reaches christian maturity, still less that which will characterise him only when he reaches Heaven: instead it predicates a present fact the moment one is vitally united to Christ. It is true the substantive "he is" (or "there is" — R.V.) is supplied by the translators, yet the legitimacy or rather the necessity of it is evident from what follows: "old things are passed away; behold all things are become new".

The opening "Therefore" bids us ponder the context. Upon turning to the verse immediately preceding, here is what we read: "Wherefore, henceforth know we no man after the flesh, yea, though we have known Christ after the flesh, yet now henceforth know we (Him so) no more". We wonder how many of our readers understand that verse, have even formulated any idea of what it is speaking about. If they consult the commentators, instead of finding help they are likely to be the more perplexed, for no two of them are agreed as to its meaning, and some of them had been more honest if they frankly owned they did not understand it instead of darkening counsel by a multitude of meaningless words. Now is it not obvious that, in order to a right perception of its significance we must seek answers to the following questions. Whom was the apostle here instructing? Upon what particular subject was he writing? What required his taking up *this* subject? or, in other words, what was his special *design* on this occasion? This alone will afford us the true perspective.

As we have pointed out before in these pages, it is necessary to know something of the circumstances *which occasioned* the writing of the Corinthian epistles if we are to obtain an insight of many of their details. Soon after Paul departed from Corinth (Acts 18) false teachers assailed the saints there, seeking to undermine the apostle's influence and discredit his ministry. The result was that the believers became divided into opposing classes engaged in disputes and being guilty of carnal walking (1Cor. 1: 11,12). Those who said "I am of Paul, and I am of Apollos" were in all probability the Gentile converts; whereas those who boasted "I am of Cephas and I am of Christ" (glorying in a fleshly relation to Him which the Gentiles could not lay claim unto), were undoubtedly the converted Jews. Thus the enemies of the Gospel had succeeded in sowing the seeds of discord in the Corinthian assembly, creating jealousies and animosities by an appeal to *racial* prejudices, seeking to perpetuate the ancient enmities of Semitism and anti-Semitism.

Those false teachers had come to Corinth with "letters of commendation" (2 Cor. 3:1), issued most likely by the temple authorities. They were "Hebrews" (11:22), professing to be "ministers of Christ" — i.e. of the Messiah (11:23), yet in fact they were "false apostles, deceitful workers", the ministers of Satan (11:13-15). They had attempted to *Judaise* the Gentile saints, insisting that such could not participate in the covenant blessings and privileges of God's people unless they be circumcised and become the proselytes of the Mosaic religion. It was because of this the apostle had written to them, "Circumcision is nothing, and uncircumcision is nothing, but the keeping of the commandments of God" (1 Cor. 7:19). *That* was indeed a startling thing to affirm, for it was *God* who had instituted circumcision (Gen. 17:10), and for many centuries it had entailed peculiar privileges (Ex. 12:48). The Lord Jesus Himself had been circumcised (Luke 2:21). But now it was "nothing" — useless, worthless. Why so? Because of the *great change* which had taken place *dispensationally* in the kingdom or economy of God upon earth. Judaism had become effete, a thing of the past. Something new and better had displaced it.

Those false teachers had evidently denied that Paul was a true apostle of Christ, arguing (on the basis of what is recorded in Acts 1:21,22) that he could not be such, since he had not (as the Eleven) accompanied Him during the days of His flesh. This had obliged him to write unto the saints vindicating the Divine authority of his apostleship (1 Cor. 9:1 - 3). That his first epistle had produced a salutary effect upon them is clear from 2 Cor. 1 and 2, yet it had neither silenced the "false apostles" nor completely established those whose faith they had shaken; hence the need for his second epistle to them. On the one hand, the major part of the assembly had expressed the warmest affection for him (1:14;7:7); but on the other, the boldness and influence of his adversaries had increased, and their false charges and determined efforts to repudiate his apostolic authority (10: 2; 11: 2 - 7, 12 - 15) moved him to indignation. Those two adverse elements at Corinth is what serve to explain the sudden change from one subject to another, and the noticeable variations of language in this second epistle.

In the third chap. of 2 Cor. the apostle vindicated his apostleship in a manner which demonstrated the irrelevancy and worthlessness of the objections of his detractors and which placed the faith of his converts on an unshakeable foundation, by affirming that God had made him and his companions "able (or "sufficient") ministers of the *new* testament" (v. 6), or as it should be rendered "of the new covenant". Therein he struck the keynote to all that follows, for unto the end of the chapter he proceeded to draw a series of contrasts between the old and new covenants, and exhibited the immeasurable superiority of the latter over the former. By so doing he entirely cut away all ground from under the feet of those who were troubling the Corinthian saints, for what mattered it whether or no Paul had companied with Christ during the three and a half years of His public ministry, or whether his converts were circumcised or not, seeing that the old order of things, Judaism, had been "done away" (v. 7)! Who would complain at the absence of the stars when the sun was shining in its meridian splendour?

With unmistakable wisdom from on High, Paul wove into the texture of his personal vindication a lovely picture of the various respects in which Christianity excelled Judaism. The one was founded upon what was written on "the tables of stone" and the ceremonial law which accompanied the same; the other is rendered valid and vital by "the Spirit of the living God" writing in fleshly tables of the heart" (v. 3). The one was "of the letter" which "killeth"; the other "of the spirit" which "giveth life" (v. 6), those expressions denoting the leading characteristics of the two covenants or economies — cf. Rom. 7:6. Judaism is likened unto "the letter" because it was something external and objective, for it presented a rule of Divine duty though it conveyed neither disposition nor power to obey: Christianity has to do with the soul and is made effectual — Rom. 1:16. "The one was external, the other spiritual; the one was an outward precept, the other an inward power. In the one case the law was written on

14

stone, in the other on the heart. The one was therefore letter, the other spirit" (C. Hodge).

In vv. 7-11 the apostle contrasts the ministrations of the two dispensations or economies. It is *not*— as the Dispensationalists erroneously teach — that he here opposes Grace (a word never occurring in this chapter!) to the Moral Law, but that Christianity is set over against Judaism. It is a great mistake to suppose that Paul was here speaking of the Ten Commandments as such: rather is it the whole Mosaic system which he has in view — "when Moses is *read*" (v.15) the reference is primarily to the ceremonial law, wherein there was much that pointed forward to Christ and typified His work of redemption, but which, because of their carnality the Jews discerned not. Judaism was a "ministration of death": the Moral Law is designed to slay all self-righteousness, for it condemns and brings in the whole world guilty before God, thereby revealing the sinner's dire need of salvation. The ceremonial law, with its priesthood and ritual, likewise exhibited both the guilt and pollution of man, as well as the ineffable holiness and inexorable justice of God, so that without shedding of blood is no remission. The brazen altar in the outer court, where the sacrificial victims were slain, testified loudly to this fact that Judaism is "a ministration of *death*".

Though the ministration of the old covenant was one of "death", nevertheless it was "*glorious*". Judaism was not of human invention but of Divine institution. In it there was a solemn and yet glorious revelation of the moral perfections of God. In it there was a wondrous and blessed foreshadowing of the person, office and work of the Redeemer. In it there was a wise and necessary paving of the way for the introduction and establishment of Christianity. That "glory" was adumbrated on the countenance of the mediator of that covenant (Deut. 5:5; Gal. 3:19) when he returned to the people after speaking with Jehovah in the mount, for the "skin of his face shone" (Ex. 34:19). That radiance of his features was emblematic of the glory pertaining to the old covenant, and that, in two noticeable respects. First, it was only an *external* one, whereas a glorious work of grace is wrought *within* the beneficaries of the new covenant. Second, it was but a *transcient* glory, as the quickly-fading brightness of Moses' face symbolized; whereas that connected with the new covenant is one that "fadeth not away" (1 Pet. 1:4). Christians, beholding the glory of the Lord, are "changed into the same image from glory to glory, as by the Spirit of the Lord" (2 Cor. 3:18).

Any one who gives an attentive reading to 2 Cor. 3 and 4 should have no difficulty at all in understanding what the apostle was referring to when he said in 5:17 "old things are passed away". First, he tells us in 3:7 that the glory connected with the old covenant "was *to be* done away." But he went further, saying, second, "For if that which *is done away* was glorious much more that which remaineth is glorious" (v. 11): the old economy and its ministry were but temporary and had even then been set aside. The sacrificing of bulls and goats was no longer valid now the Antitype had appeared. Third, in v. 13 he uses still stronger language: "that which is abolished" or "destroyed". In the former epistle (13:10) Paul had laid down the maxim that "when that which is perfect is come, then that which is in part shall be done away", so here he declares the new covenant annulled the old; for that was never designed to have anything more than a transcient existence. The "old things" which are "passed away" are circumcision, the temple ritual, the Levitical priesthood, the whole of the ceremonial law; in a word, Judaism and all that marked it as a system.

In 2 Cor. 4 the apostle continues the same subject. The "this ministry" of v. 1 is that of "the new covenant" spoken of in 3:6 and termed "the ministration of the spirit" and "of righteousness" (vv. 8,9). In 3:14, speaking of the great body of the Jewish nation, he said, "But their minds were blinded" and in 4:3,4 declares "But if our Gospel be hid, it is hid to them that are lost: in whom the god of this world (i.e. Satan, as the director of its religions) hath *blinded* the minds of them that believe not". In 3:9, 10 he affirmed that while indeed there was a "glory" connected with the old covenant, yet that of the new "excelled" it. Amplification of that is made in 4:6. The pillar of cloud and of fire which guided Israel during their journeyings was but external and temporary, but Jehovah has now "shined in *our hearts* unto the light of the knowledge of the glory of God in the face of Jesus Christ": that inward illumination abides in the believer forever — immeasurably superior are the "new things" which have displaced the old! In vv. 8-18 the apostle mentioned some of the trials which a faithful discharge of his commission had entailed.

After a characteristic digression, in which the apostle described the rich compensations God has provided for His servants — and His people in general (vv. 1-10), he returns to the subject of his ministerial labours, making known the springs from which they issued (vv. 11-14). As in chap. 3, when vindicating his apostleship, he had interwoven important doctrinal instruction, so here. First, it should be carefully noted that Paul was still engaged in closing the mouths of his detractors, yea, furnishing his converts with material to silence them (*see* v. 12), speaking of his adversaries as those who "glory in appearance, and not in heart". In what follows, he adduces that which could not be gainsaid. "Because we thus judge (or "reason") that if one died for all, then were all dead" (v. 14) — a most misleading translation, which is corrected in the R.V.: "one died for all, therefore all died". It is quite true that those for whom Christ died were spiritually dead, but that is not what is here referred to — their being unregenerate was a fact *without* Christ dying for them! Rather was Paul showing the legal *effect* or what follows as the consequence of Christ's having died for them.

"Having judged this, that if one died for all, then the all died"(Bag. Int.). The apostle there enunciates a theological axiom: it expresses the principle of federal representation. The act of one is, in the sight of the law, the act of all those on whose behalf he transacts. The whole election of grace "died" *judicially* in the death of their Surety. Christ's death, so far as the claims of the Divine Law or the end of the Divine government were concerned, is the same as though they had all personally died. "Died" *unto what?* The consequences of their sins, the curse of the Law? Yes, though that is *not* the main thing which is here in view. What then? This, rather that they had "died" to their old standing in the flesh: they no longer had any status in that realm where such distinctions as Jew and Gentile obtained. They had not only died unto sin, but unto all *natural relations.* Death levels all distinctions!

But that is only negative; the apostle goes further, and brings in the positive side: "And He died for all, that they that live should not henceforth live unto themselves, but unto Him" who has fulfilled all its requirements. It is the legal oneness of Christ and His Church on resurrection-ground. Having borne the curse, they are dead in law; living now through Christ's resurrection, they cannot but "live unto Him", because judicially one with Him. His resurrection was as vicarious as His death, and the same individuals were the objects of both. The pertinency of this reasoning, this blessed truth and fact, to the apostle's case, should at once be apparent. Christ's own relation to Judaism terminated at His death, and when He came forth from the grave it was onto resurrection — entirely *new* — ground; and thus it is with all those He legally represented.

What has just been pointed out above is made yet clearer in v. 16, where the apostle shows the conclusion which must be drawn from what he had just proved: "Wherefore henceforth know we no man after the flesh: yea, though we have known Christ after the flesh, yet now henceforth know we (Him so) no more". To know a man after the flesh is to own him according to his *natural state* his racial distinction. To know Christ "after the flesh" was to approve Him as the "Seed of David", the Jewish Messiah. But the death of Christ annulled such relations: His resurrection brought Him a new and higher relationship. Therefore in the exercise of his ministry, Paul showed no respect to a man merely because he was a Jew, nor did he esteem Christ on account of His being the Son of David — rather did he adore Him as being the Saviour of Jew and Gentile alike. Thus the sinful partiality of those who were seeking to Judaise the Corinthian saints was conclusively exposed. V. 17 states the grand conclusion to be drawn from what has been established in the context.

THE GREAT CHANGE

"Therefore if any man be in Christ he is a new creature; old things are passed away; behold, all things are become new" (2 Cor. 5:17). Familiar as are those words, simple and plain as their meaning appears to be, yet like almost every verse in the Epistles this one can only be rightly understood by ascertaining its connection with the context. Nay, we go further: unless this verse be interpreted in strict accord with its setting, we are certain to err in our apprehension of it. The very fact that it is introduced with "therefore" shows it is inseparably connected with what goes before, that it introduces an inference, or draws a conclusion therefrom, and if we ignore it we reject the key which alone will open its contents. We have already taken up the preceding verses, though we have by no means attempted to give a full exposition of the same. Our design has been simply to supply a sufficient explanation of their terms as would enable the reader to perceive the apostle's drift. That required us to point out the general conditions prevailing in the Corinthian assembly (so that it might appear *why* Paul wrote to them as he did) and then to indicate the trend of what he said in chapters 3 and 4.

In 5:12 the apostle tells them, "For we commend not ourselves again unto you (see 3:1,2), but give you occasion to glory on our behalf, that ye may have somewhat to answer them which glory in appearance, and not in heart". Those who gloried in appearance were the Judaizers, who boasted of their lineage from Abraham and of belonging to the Circumcision. In what follows Paul furnishes his converts with arguments which the false teachers could not answer, employing language which set aside the exclusivism of Judaism. First he pointed out that " if one died for *all* then the all died; and he died for all" (vv. 14,15). That thrice repeated "all" emphasised the international scope of Christ's federal work: He died as truly on the behalf and in the stead of God's elect among the Gentiles as for the elect Jews, and as v. 15 goes on to show, the one benefits therefrom as much as does the other. The cross of Christ effected and introduced a great change in the kingdom of God. Whatever peculiar position of honour the Jews had previously occupied, whatever special privileges had been theirs under the Mosaic economy, they obtained no longer. The glorious inheritance which Christ purchased was to be the portion *of all* for whom He endured the curse and of all for whom He earned the reward of the Law.

Next the apostle showed the logical inferences which must be drawn forth from what he had established in vv. 14,15. First, "Therefore *henceforth* know we no man after the flesh: yea, though we have known Christ after the flesh, yet *now* henceforth know we (Him so) no more" (v. 16). Notice first the words which we have placed in italics: they are timemarks defining the revolutionary transition, calling attention to the great dispensational change which the redemptive work of Christ had produced. That change consisted of the complete setting aside of the old order of things which had held sway during the fifteen centuries preceding, under which a fleshly relation had predominated. Christ had ushered in an order of things wherein such distinctions as Jew and Gentile, bond and free, male and female, had no virtue and conferred no special privilege. For one who had been redeemed it mattered nothing whether his brethren and sisters in Christ were formerly members of the Jewish nation or aliens from the commonwealth of Israel. He knew or esteemed no man according to his natural descent. The true Circumcision are they "which worship God in the spirit and rejoice in Christ Jesus, and have no confidence in the flesh" — or their genealogy (Phil. 3:3).

Not only had the death and resurrection of Christ resulted in the setting aside of Judaism, which was based upon a fleshly descent from Abraham, and whose privileges could only be enjoyed by those bearing in their bodies the covenant sign of circumcision (Judaism being displaced by Christianity, which is based upon a spiritual relation to Christ, the privileges of which are enjoyed by those who are indwelt by the Holy Spirit — the sign and seal of the new covenant), but Christ Himself is now known or esteemed after a different and higher manner. It was as their promised Messiah He had appeared unto the Jews, and it was as such His disciples had believed on Him (Luke 24:21; John 1: 41,45). Accordingly, He had bidden His apostles "Go not into the way of the Gentiles, and into any city of the Samaritans enter ye not; but go rather to the lost sheep of the house of Israel" (Matt. 10:5,6) — contrast 28:19 after His resurrection! So far from knowing Christ as the Jewish Messiah, they worship Him as exalted above all principality and power. "Jesus Christ *was* a Minister of the circumcision" (Rom. 15:8), but He is *now* seated "on the right hand of the throne of the Majesty in the heavens, a Minister of the (heavenly) Sanctuary" (Heb. 8:1,2).

In v. 17 the apostle draws a further conclusion from what he had stated in v. 15, "Therefore if any man be in Christ he is a new creature" — yes, "any man", be he a Jew or Gentile. Before we can ascertain the force of " a new creature" we have to carefully weigh the opening word, for its absence or presence entirely changes the character of the sentence: "if any man be in Christ he *is* a new creature" is a simple statement of fact, but "therefore if" is a conclusion drawn from something preceding. That one consideration should be sufficient to show our verse is not treating of regeneration, for if it signified "any person who is vitally united to Christ has been born again", the "therefore" would be entirely superfluous — he either is or he is not a spiritually-quickened soul and no reasoning, no inference, can alter the fact. Nor is there anything in the context from which regeneration can be deduced, for the apostle is not treating of the gift and operations of the Spirit, but of the judicial consequences of Christ's federal work. Instead of describing Christian experience in this 17th verse Paul is stating one of the *legal effects* which necessarily results from what Christ did for His people.

In vv. 13, 14 Christ is set forth as the federal Head of His Church, first in death, then in resurrection. From that doctrinal statement of fact a twofold inference is pointed. First and negatively (v. 16) those whom Christ represented *died in Him* to their old status or natural standing, so that henceforth they are no longer influenced by fleshly relationships. Second and positively (v. 17) those whom Christ represented *rose in Him* and were inducted into a new status or spiritual standing. Christ was transacting as the Covenant Head of His people, and He rose as the Head of the New creation (as Adam was the head of the old), and therefore if I be federally in a risen Christ I must legally be "a new creature", having *judicially* "passed from death unto life" As Rom. 8:1 declares "There is therefore now no condemnation to them which are in Christ Jesus", and why? Because being legally one with Him they died in Him. In like manner, they are therefore new creatures in Christ, and why? Because being legally one with Him they rose in Him "Who is the Beginning (i.e. of the new creation, cf. Rev. 3:14), the Firstborn from the dead" (Col. 1:18). Judicially they are "risen *with* Christ" (Col. 3:1).

Not only does the context and its opening "therefore" preclude us from regarding 2 Cor. 5:17 as describing what takes place in a soul at regeneration, but the contents of the verse itself forbid such an interpretation. It is indeed true that such a miracle of grace effects a most blessed transformation in the one who is the subject of it, yet *not* such as comes up to the terms here used. What is the principal thing which affects the character and conduct of a person *before* he is born again? Is it not "the flesh"? Beyond dispute it is. Equally indubitable is it that the old nature does *not* "pass away" when God quickens a spiritually — dead soul. It is also true that regeneration is an entrance upon a new life, yet it certainly is not the case that *"all* things become new", for he receives neither a new memory nor a new body. If v. 17 be describing some aspect of Christian experience then it is glorification, for most assuredly its language does not suit regeneration.

"And all things are of God, who hath reconciled us to Himself by Jesus Christ, and hath given to us (the ministers of the new covenant — 3:6) the ministry of reconciliation" (18). This also is quite against the popular interpretation of the foregoing. Let it be duly noted that v. 18 opens with "And", which indicates it continues the same line of thought. "All ("the" — Greek) things" which are of God refer not to the universe as proceeding from Him, nor to His providential agency by which all events are controlled, but rather to those particular things spoken of from v. 13 onwards: all that Christ accomplished, the great dispensational change which has resulted from His death and resurrection, the preaching of the ministers of the new covenant, have God for their Author. The outcome of what Christ did is, that those for whom He transacted are "reconciled to God", and reconciliation, be it particularly noted is, like justification, entirely *objective* and not subjective as is regeneration! Reconciliation is, as we have fully demonstrated in our articles on that doctrine, wholly a matter of *relationship* — God's laying aside His wrath and being at peace with us.

"And hath given to us (His ambassadors) the ministry of reconciliation: to wit, that God was in Christ reconciling a (Gk.) world unto Himself, not imputing their trespasses unto them" (vv. 88, 19). From there to the end of 6: 10 the apostle informs us what this "ministry" consisted of. First, it was that God "was in Christ reconciling" not merely an apostate Judaism, but an alienated "world", that is, the whole election of grace, the "all" of vv. 14, 15. Then he states the negative side of "reconciliation", namely, "not imputing their trespasses unto them", which again brings in the *legal* side of things. The positive side of reconciliation is given in v. 21: "that we might be made the righteousness of God in Him", which is entirely objective and judicial, and in no sense subjective and experimental. How vastly different is that than if he had said "reconciling a world unto Himself, imparting unto them a new nature" or "subduing their iniquities"! It is not what God works *in* His people, but what by Christ He has done *for* them, that the whole passage treats of.

Turning back again to v. 17. "Therefore": in view of what has been established in the preceding verses, it necessarily follows that — "if any man be in Christ he is a new creature": he has a new standing before God; being representatively one with Christ, he has been brought onto resurrection ground, he is a member of that new creation of which Christ is the federal Head, and consequently he is under an entirely *new Covenant*. This is the grand and incontrovertible conclusion which must be drawn: "the old things are passed away: behold, all things are become new". The natural and national distinctions which obtained under the old covenant find no place on resurrection ground: *they* were connected with the flesh, whereas the relationship which obtains and the privileges which are enjoyed under the new covenant are entirely spiritual. Once that was clearly apprehended and laid hold of by faith it rendered nugatory the contentions of the Judaizers.

It is by no means easy for us at this late date to conceive of what that revolutionary transaction from Judaism to Christianity involved, to Jew and Gentile alike. It was the greatest change this world has ever witnessed. For fifteen centuries God's kingdom on earth had been confined unto one favoured nation, during which time all others had been left to walk in their own ways. The gulf which divided Judaism from Paganism was far more real and very much wider than that which exists between Romanism and orthodox Christianity. The devisive spirit between Jew and Gentile was more intense than that which obtains between the several castes in India. But at the Cross the Mosaic economy "passed away", the middle wall of petition was broken down, and upon Christ's resurrection the "Go not into the way of the Gentiles" gave place to "Go ye into all the world, and preach the Gospel to every creature." Fleshly relationships which had so markedly characterised Judaism, now gave place to spiritual ones; yet it was only with the greatest difficulty that converted Jews could be brought to realise that fact, and much in the N. T. is devoted unto a proving of the same.

The principal design of the entire epistle to the Hebrews was to demonstrate that "old things are passed away; behold, all things are become new"! In it the apostle makes it manifest that the "old covenant" which Jehovah had entered into with Israel, at Sinai, with all its ordinances of worship and the peculiar privileges connected therewith, was disannulled, that it was superceded by a new and better economy. Therein it is declared that Christ hath "obtained a more excellent ministry" in proportion to His being "the Meditator of a better covenant, which was established upon better promises"; and after quoting from Jer. 31 where the new covenant was announced, pointed out that the former one was "waxed old are ready to vanish away" (8:6-13). The transcendent superiority of the new above the old is brought out in many details: the former was but temporary, the latter is eternal; the one contained only the shadow of good things to come, the latter the substance. The Aaronic priesthood has been displaced by Christ's; an earthly inheritance by an heavenly. The blessed contrast between them is set forth most fully in Heb. 12:18-24.

Not only did the converted Jews find it difficult to adjust themselves to the great change produced by the covenant displacing the old, but unconverted Jews caused much trouble in the Christian assemblies, insisting that their descent from Abraham conferred special privileges upon them, and that Gentiles could only participate in them by being circumcised and becoming subject to the ceremonial law. Not a little in Paul's epistles is devoted to a refutation of such errors. That the Corinthians were being harassed by such Judaizers we have already shown — further evidence is supplied by 2 Cor. 11:18, where the apostle refers to "many glory after the flesh", i.e. their natural lineage. But all ground had been cut from under their feet by what he had declared in 2 Cor. 3 and his unanswerable argument in 5:13-18. Christ's death and resurrection had caused "old things" to pass away: the old covenant, the Mosaic economy, Judaism was no more. "*All* things had become new": a new covenant, Christianity, with better relationships and privileges, a superior standing before God, different ordinances of worship, had been introduced.

The same is true of the epistle to the Galatians, wherein there are many parallels to what has been before us in Corinthians. The churches of Galatia were also troubled by teachers of error, who were seeking to Judaise them, and Paul uses much the same method in exposing their sophistries. "There is neither Jew nor Greek . . . bond or free . . . for ye are all one in Christ" (Gal. 3:28) is an echo of "henceforth know we no man after the flesh". In several respects the contents of 4:21-31 are similar to what is found in 2 Cor. 3, for in both the two covenants are contrasted in Gal. 4, under the allegory of Hagar and Sarah and their sons, the superiority of the latter is shown. "Ye that desire to be under the law" (4:21) means under the old covenant. "Born after the flesh" in v. 23 signifies according to nature, "by promise" equals supernaturally. "These are" means "*represent* the two covenants" (v. 24). "Cast out the bond woman and her son" of 4:30 has the force of act in accordance with the fact that the old things are "passed away". While the "For in Christ Jesus neither circumcision availeth anything, nor uncircumcision, but a new creature" (the only other place in the N. T. that expression occurs!!) of 6:15 is enforcing the same truth as 2 Cor. 5:17.

Once the meaning of 2 Cor. 5:16 be perceived there is no place for any dispute as to the signification of what immediately follows. In the light of 5:12; 10:7; 11:18 it is unmistakably clear that the apostle was dissuading the Corinthian saints from a carnal and sinful partiality, namely, of regarding men according to "outward appearance" or fleshly descent; bidding them to esteem their brethren by their relation *to Christ* and not to Abraham, and to view Christ Himself not as "a Minister of the circumcision" but as "the Mediator of a better covenant" who has made "all things new". The old covenant was made with one nation only; the new with believers of all nations. Its sacrifices made nothing perfect, our Sacrifice has perfected us forever (Heb. 10:1, 14). Circumcision was for the natural seed of Jacob; baptism is for the spiritual children of Christ. Only the Levites were permitted to enter the holy place, all the children of God have the right of immediate access to Him. The seventh day was the Sabbath under the Siniatic constitution; the first day celebrates the order of things introduced by a risen Christ. "Old things are passed away; behold *all* things are become new"!

CHANGE OF HEART

We turn next to Romans 5:5, where we read, "the love of God is shed abroad in our hearts by the Holy Spirit which is given unto us." By nature no man has any love for God. To those Jews who contended so vehemently for the unity of God and abhorred all forms of idolatry, and who in their mistaken zeal sought to kill the Saviour because of "making Himself equal with God," He declared, "I know you, that ye have not the love of God in you" (John 5:18, 42). Not only loveless, the natural man is filled with enmity against God (Rom. 8:7). But when a miracle of grace is wrought within him by the Holy Spirit, his heart experiences a great change Godwards, so that the One he formerly dreaded and sought to banish from his thoughts is now the Object of his veneration and joy, the One upon whose glorious perfections he delights to meditate, and for whose honour and pleasure he now seeks to live.

That great change which is wrought within the regenerate does not consist in the annihilation of the evil principle, "the flesh," but in freeing the mind from its dominion, and in the communication of a holy principle which conveys a new propensity and disposition to the soul: God is no longer hated but loved. That freeing of the mind from the evil dominion of the flesh is spoken of in Ezekiel 36:26, as God's taking away "the stony heart," and that shedding abroad of His love within the heart by His Spirit is termed giving them "a heart of flesh." Such strong figurative language was used by the prophet to intimate that the change wrought is no superficial or transient one. Through regarding too carnally ("literally") the terms used by the prophets, dispensationalists and their adherents have created their own difficulty and failed to understand the purport of the passage. It is not that an inward organ or faculty is removed and replaced by a different one, but rather that a radical change for the better had been wrought upon the original faculty − not by changing its essential nature or functions, but by bringing to bear a new and transforming influence upon it.

It ought not to be necessary for us to labour what is quite simple and obvious to the spiritually-minded, but in view of the fearful confusion and general ignorance prevailing, we feel that a further word (for the benefit of the perplexed) is called for. Perhaps a simple illustration will serve to elucidate still further. Suppose that for a long time I have cherished bitter animosity against a fellow creature and treated him with contempt, but that God has now made me to repent deeply of the injustice I have done him, so that I have humbly confessed my sin to him, and henceforth shall esteem him highly and do all in my power to amend the wrong I did him; surely no one would have any difficulty in understanding what was meant if I said that I had undergone a real "change of heart" toward that person, nor would it be misleading to say that a "heart of bitterness" had been removed from me and "a heart of good will" be given to me. Though we do not pretend to explain the *process* yet something very much like that are the *nature* and *effect* of God's taking away the heart of stone and giving a heart of flesh or freeing the mind of enmity against God and shedding abroad His love in the heart.

"But God be thanked, that ye were the servants of sin, but ye have obeyed from the heart that form of doctrine which was delivered you ("whereunto ye were delivered" — margin). Being then made free from (the guilt and dominion of) sin, ye became the servants of righteousness" (Rom. 6:17,18). In this passage the Holy Spirit is describing that wondrous transformation whereby the servants of sin became the servants of righteousness. That transformation is effected by their being delivered unto that form of doctrine which requires hearty obedience. To aid our feeble understanding another similtude is used. "The Truth which is after godliness" (Titus 1:1) is called "that form ("type or impress," Young; rendered "fashion, pattern" in other passages) of doctrine" or "teaching": the figure of a mould or seal being used wherein the hearts of the regenerate (softened and made pliable by the Holy Spirit) are likened to molten metal which receives and retains the exact impress of a seal, answering to it line for line, conformed to the shape and figure of it. The quickened soul is "delivered unto" (the Greek word signifies "given over to," as may be seen in Matthew 5:25; 11:27; 20:19) the Truth, so that it is made answerable or conformable unto it.

In their uncoverted state they had been the willing and devoted servants of sin, uniformly heeding its promptings and complying with its behests, gratifying their own inclinations without any regard to the authority and glory of God. But now they cordially yielded submission to the teaching of God's Word whereunto they had been delivered or cast into the very fashion of the same. They had been supernaturally renewed into or conformed unto the holy requirements of Law and Gospel alike. Their minds, their affections, their wills had been formed according to the tenor of God's Standard. Thus, from still another angle, we are informed of what the great change consists; it is God's bringing the soul from the love of sin to the love of holiness, a being transformed by the renewing of the mind — such a transformation as produces compliance with the Divine will. It is an inward agreement with the Rule of righteousness into which the heart is cast and after which the character is framed and modelled, the consequence of which is an obedience from the heart — in contrast from forced or feigned obedience which proceeds from fear or self-interest.

"For I was alive without the Law once: but when the commandment came, sin revived, and I died" (Rom. 7:9). As the last-considered passage describes the positive side of the great change experienced in the child of God, this one treats more of its negative aspect. The commentators are generally agreed that in Romans 7:7-11, the apostle is narrating one of the experiences through which he passed at his conversion. First, he says, there had been a time when he was "without the Law" — words which cannot be taken absolutely. In his unregenerate days he had been a proud pharisee. Though he had received his training under the renowned rabbi, Gamaliel, where his chief occupation was the study of the Law, yet being totally ignorant of its spirituality he was, vitally and experimentally speaking, as one "without" it — without a realization of its design or an inward acquaintance of its power. Supposing that a mere external conformity unto its requirements was all that was necessary, and strictly attending to the same, he was well pleased with himself, satisfied with his righteousness, and assured of his acceptance with God.

Second, "but when the commandment came": verse seven informs us it was the tenth commandment which the Holy Spirit used as the arrow of conviction. When those words, "thou shalt not covet," were applied to him, when they came in the Spirit's illuminating and convicting power to his conscience, the bubble of his self-righteousness was pricked and his self-complacency was shattered. Like a thunderbolt out of a clear sky that Divine prohibition, "thou shalt not (even) *desire* that which is forbidden, brought home to his heart with startling force the strictness and spirituality of the Divine Law. As those words, "thou must have no self-will," pierced him, he realized the Law demanded inward as well as outward conformity to its holy terms. Then it was that "sin revived": he was conscious of his lusts rising up in protest against the holy and extensive requirements of the Divine Rule. The very fact that God has said "thou shalt not lust" only served to aggravate and stir into increased activity those corruptions of which previously he was unconscious, and the more he attempted to bring them into subjection the more painfully aware did he become of his own helplessness.

Third, "and I died": in his own apprehensions, feelings, and estimate of himself. Before he became acquainted with his inward corruptions and was made to feel something of the plague of his heart, living a morally upright life and being most punctilious in performing the requirements of the cermonial law, the apostle deemed himself a good man. He was in his own opinion "alive" uncondemned by the Law, having no dread of punishment and judgment to come. But when the tenth commandment smote his conscience, he perceived the spirituality of the law and realized that hitherto he had only a notional knowledge of it. Convicted of his inward depravity, of his sinful desires, thoughts and imaginations, he felt himself to be a condemned criminal, deserving eternal death. *That* is another essential element in the great change — which we should have introduced much earlier had we followed a theological order rather than tracing out the various references to it as recorded in the Scriptures. That essential element consists of a personal conviction of sin, of one's lost estate, and *such* a conviction that its subject completely despairs of any self-help and dies to his own righteousness.

"And such were some of you: but ye are washed, but ye are sanctified, but ye are justified in the name of the Lord Jesus and by the Spirit of our God" (1 Cor. 6:11). The "such were some of you" refers to the licentious and vicious characters mentioned in verses nine and ten, of whom Matthew Henry said they were "very monsters rather than men. Note, some that are eminently good after conversion have been as remarkable for wickedness before." What a glorious alteration does grace effect in reclaiming persons from sins so debasing and degrading! That grand transformation is here described by three words: "washed, sanctified, justified." It may appear very strange to some of our readers to hear that quite a number of those who regard themselves as the champions of orthodoxy, if they do not explicitly repudiate the first, yet give it no place at all in their concept of what takes place at regenerations. They so confine their thoughts to that which is newly created and communicated to the Christian that any change and cleansing of his *original* being is quite lost sight of. God's children are as truly "washed" as they are sanctified and justified. Literally so? Yes; in a material sense. No, *morally*.

"But ye are washed" was the fulfilment of that Old Testament promise, "Then will I sprinkle clean water upon you, and ye shall be clean; from all your filthiness and your idols will I cleanse you" (Ezek. 36:25). Titus 3:5, makes it clear that the new birth consists of something more than the communication of a new nature, namely, "the washing of regeneration" — cf. Ephesians 5:26. It is further to be noted that "ye are washed" is distinct from "justified," so it cannot refer to the removal of guilt. Moreover it is effected by the Spirit and therefore must consist of something which He does *in* us. The foul leper is purged: by the Spirit's agency he is cleansed from his pollutions and his heart is made "pure" (Matt. 5:8). It is a moral cleansing or purification of character from the love and practice of sin. First, "washed," then "sanctified" or set apart and consecrated to God as vessels meet for His use. Thereby we obtain evidence of our justification — the cancellation of guilt and the imputation of righteousness to us. Justification is here attributed to the Holy Spirit because He is the Author of that faith which justifies a sinner.

"But we all with open (it should be "with *unveiled*") face beholding as in a glass (better "mirror") the glory of the Lord, are changed into the same image from glory to glory, as by the Spirit of the Lord" (2 Cor. 3:18). In the unveiled face there is a double reference and contrast. First, to the veil over the face of Moses (verse 13), which symbolized the imperfection and transitoriness of Judaism: in contrast, Christians behold God as He is fully and finally revealed in the person and work of His Son. Second, to the veil which is over the hearts of unconverted Jews (verse 16): in contrast with them, those who have turned to the Lord have the blinding effects of error and prejudice removed from them, so that they can view the Gospel without any medium obscuring it. The "glory of the Lord, " the sum of His perfections, is revealed and shines forth in the Word, and more particularly in the Gospel. As His glory is beheld by that faith which is produced and energized by the Spirit, its beholder is changed gradually from one degree to another into the "same image," becoming more and more conformed unto Him in character and conduct. The verb "changed" ("*metamorphoo*") is rendered "transformed" in Romans 12:2, and "transfigured" in Matthew 17:2! The "mirrors" of the ancients were made of burnished metals, and when a strong light was thrown on them they not only reflected images with great distinctness but the rays of light were cast back upon the face of one looking into them, so that if the mirror were of silver or brass a white or golden glow suffused his or her countenance. The "mirror" is the Scriptures in which the glory of the Lord is discovered, and as the Spirit shines upon the soul and enables him to act faith and love thereon, he is changed into the same image. The glory of the Lord is irradicated by the Gospel, and as it is received into the heart is reflected by the beholder, through the transforming agency of the Spirit. By the heart's being occupied with Christ's perfection, the mind's meditating thereon, the will's subjection to His precepts, we drink into His spirit, become partakers of His holiness, and are conformed to His image. As our view of Christ is imperfect, the transformation is incomplete in this life: only when we "see Him" face to face shall we be made perfectly "like Him" (1 John 3:2).

"For God, who commanded the light to shine out of darkness, hath shined in our hearts, unto the light of the knowledge of the glory of God in the face of Jesus Christ" (2 Cor. 4:6). Had we been following a strictly logical and theological order, this is another aspect of our subject we should have brought in earlier, for the spiritual illumination of the understanding is one of the first works of God when He begins to restore a fallen creature. By nature he is in a state of complete spiritual ignorance of God, and therefore of his own state before Him, sitting in "darkness" and "in the region and shadow of death" (Matt. 4:16). That "darkness" is something far more dreadful than a mere intellectual ignorance of spiritual things: it is a positive and energetic "power" (Luke 22:53), an evil principle which is inveterately opposed to God, and with which the heart of fallen man is in love (John 3:19), and which no external means or illumination can dispel (John 1:5). Nothing but the sovereign fiat and all-mighty power of God is superior to it, and He alone can bring a soul "out of darkness into His *marvellous* light."

As God commanded the light to shine out of that darkness which enveloped the old creation (Gen. 1:2, 3), so He does in the work of new creation within each of His elect. That supernatural enlightenment consists not in dreams and visions, nor in the revelation to the soul "of anything which has not been made known in the Scripture of Truth, for it is "The entrance of Thy words (which) giveth light" (Psa. 209:130). Yes, the *entrance*: but ere that takes place, the blind eyes of the sinner must first be miraculously opened by the Spirit, so that he is made capable of receiving the light: it is only in God's light we "see light" (Psa. 36:9). The shining of God's light in our hearts partially and gradually dissipates the awful ignorance, blindness, error, prejudice, unbelief of our souls, thereby preparing the mind to (in measure) apprehend the Truth and the affections to embrace it. By this supernatural illumination the soul is enabled to see things as they really are (1 Cor. 2:10-12), perceiving his own depravity, the exceeding sinfulness of sin, the spirituality of the Law, the excellency of truth, the beauty of holiness, the loveliness of Christ.

We repeat: the Spirit communicates no light to the quickened soul which is not to be found in the written Word, but removes those obstacles which precluded its entrance, disposes the mind to attend unto the Truth (Acts 16:14) and receive it in the *love* of it (2 Thess. 2:10). When the Divine light shines into his heart the sinner perceives something of his horrible plight, is made conscious of his guilty and lost condition, feels that his sins are more in number than the hairs of his head. He now *knows* that there is "*no* soundness" (Isa. 1:6) in him, that all his righteousnesses are as filthy rags, and that he is utterly unable to help himself. But the Divine light shining in his heart also reveals the all-sufficient remedy. It awakens hope in his breast. It makes known to him "the glory of God" as it shines in the face of the Mediator, and the sun of righteousness now arises upon his benighted soul with healing in His wings or beams. Such knowledge of sin, of himself, of God, of the Saviour, is not obtained by mental effort but is communicated by the gracious operations of the Spirit.

"For the weapons of our warfare are not carnal, but mighty through God to the pulling down of strongholds; casting down imaginations, and every high thing that exalteth itself against the knowledge of God, and bringing into captivity every thought to the obedience of Christ" (2 Cor. 10:4, 5). The apostle is here alluding to his ministry: its nature, difficulties and success. He likened it unto a conflict between truth and error. The "weapons" or means he employed were not such as men of the world depended upon. The Grecian philosophers relied upon the arguments of logic or the attractions of rhetoric. Mohammed conquered by the force of arms. Rome's appeal is to the senses. But the ambassadors of Christ use nought but the Word and prayer, which are "mighty through God." Sinners are converted by the preaching of Christ crucified, and not by human wisdom, eloquence, or debate. The Gospel of Christ is the power of God unto salvation (Rom. 1:16).

Sinners are here pictured as sheltering in "strongholds." By hardness of heart, stubbornness of will, and strong prejudices they have fortified themselves against God and betaken themselves to a "refuge of lies" (Isa. 28:15). But when the Truth is effectually applied to their hearts by the Spirit those strongholds are demolished and their haughty imaginations and proud reasonings are cast down. They no longer exclaim, "I cannot believe that a just God will make one a vessel unto honour and another to dishonour," or "I cannot believe a merciful God will consign any one to eternal torments." All objections are now silenced, rebels are subdued, lofty opinions of self cast down, pride is abased, and reverential fear, contrition, humility, faith and love take their place. Every thought is now brought into captivity to the obedience of Christ: they are conquered by grace, taken captives by love, and Christ henceforth occupies the throne of their hearts. Every faculty of the soul is now won over to God. Such is the great change wrought in a soul who experiences the miracle of grace: a worker of iniquity is made a loving and loyal child of obedience.

GOD'S WORKMANSHIP

"My little children, of whom I travail in birth again until Christ be formed in you" (Gal. 4:19). In the past the apostle had laboured hard in preaching the Gospel to the Galatians, and apparently his efforts had met with considerable success. He had plainly set before them "Christ crucified" (3:1) as the sinner's only hope, and many had professed to receive Him as He was offered in the Gospel. They had abandoned their idolatry, seemed to be soundly converted, and had expressed great affection for their spiritual father (4:15). For a time they had "run well," but they had been "hindered" (5:7). After Paul's departure, false teachers sought to seduce them from the Faith and persuade them that they must be circumcised and keep the ceremonial law in order to salvation. They had so far given ear unto those Judaisers that Paul now stood in doubt of them (4:20), being fearful lest after all they had never been truly regenerated (4:11). It is to be carefully noted that he did not take refuge in fatalism and say, If God has begun a good work in them He will certainly finish it, so there is no neeed for me to be unduly worried. Very much the reverse.

No, the apostle was much exercised over their state and earnestly solicitous about their welfare. By this strong figure of speech "I travail in birth again," the apostle intimated both his deep concern and his willingness to labour and suffer ministerially after their conversion, to spare no pains in seeking to deliver them from their present delusion and get them thoroughly established in the truth of the Gospel. He longed to be assured that the great change had taken place in them, which he speaks of as "Christ be formed in you." By which we understand that they might be genuinely evangelized by a saving knowledge of Christ. First, that by spiritual apprehension of the Truth He might be revealed in their understandings. Second, that by the exercise of faith upon Him, He might "dwell in their hearts" (Eph. 3:17): faith gives a subsistence and reality in the soul of that object on which it is acted (Heb. 9:1). Third, that He might be so endeared to their affections that neither Moses nor anyone else could be admitted as a rival. Fourth, that by the surrender of their wills He might occupy the throne of their hearts and rule over them. Christ thus "formed in" us is the proof of His righteousness imputed to us.

"For we are His workmanship, created in Christ Jesus unto good works, which God hath before ordained that we should walk in them" (Eph. 2:10). In those words the apostle completes the blessed declaration he had made in verses 8 and 9, thereby preserving the balance of Truth. Verses 8 and 9 present only one side of the Gospel and ought never to be quoted without adding the other side. None so earnest as Paul in proclaiming sovereign grace; none more insistent in maintaining practical godliness. Has God chosen His people in Christ before the foundation of the world? It was that they "should be holy" (Eph. 1:4). Did Christ give Himself for us? It was that "He might redeem us from all iniquity and purify unto Himself a peculiar people zealous of good works" (Titus 2:14). So here, immediately after magnifying free grace, Paul states with equal clearness the moral results of God's saving power, as they are exhibited with more or less distinctness in the lives of His people. Salvation by grace is evidenced by holy conduct: unless our lives are characterized by "good works" we have no warrant to regard ourselves as being the children of God.

"We are His workmanship"; He, and not ourselves, has made us what we are spiritually. "Created in Christ Jesus" means made vitally one with Him. "In Christ" always has reference to *union* with Him: in Ephesians 1:4, to a mystical or election union; in 1 Corinthians 15:22, to a federal or representative one; in 1 Corinthians 6:17, and 2 Corinthians 5:17, to a vital or living one. Saving faith (product of the Spirit's quickening us) makes us branches of the living Vine, from whom our fruit proceeds (Hos. 14:8). "Created in Christ Jesus *unto* good works" expresses the design and efficacy of God's workmanship, being parallel with "This people have I formed for Myself: they shall show forth My praise" (Isa. 43:21). God fits the thing for which He creates it: fire to burn, the earth to yield food, His saints to walk in good works — God's work in their souls inclining and propelling thereunto. He creates us in Christ or gives us vital union with Him that we should walk in newness of life, He being the Root from which all the fruits of righteousness proceed. United to the Holy One, holy conduct marks us. Those who live in sin have never been savingly joined to Christ. God saves that we may glorify Him by a life of obedience.

"Put on the new man, which after God is created in righteousness and true holiness" (Eph. 4:24). Those words occur in the practical section of the epistle, being part of an exhortation which begins at verse 22, the passage as a whole being similar to Romans 13:12-14. Its force is, Make it manifest by your conduct that you are regenerate creatures, exhibiting before your fellows the character of God's children. That which most concerns us now is the particular description which is here given of the great change effected in the regenerate, namely, "a new man which after God is created in righteousness and true holiness." With our present passage should be carefully compared the parallel one in Colossians, for the one helps to explain and supplements the other. There we read "And have put on the new man, which is renewed in knowledge after the image of Him that created him." In both we find the expression "the new man," by which we are *not* to understand that a new individual has been brought into existence, that a person is now brought forth who previously had no being. Great care needs to be taken when seeking to understand and explain the meaning of terms which are taken from the material realm and applied to spiritual objects and things.

A regenerated sinner is the same individual he was before, though a great change has taken place in his soul. How different the landscape when the sun is shining than when darkness of a moonless night is upon it — the same landscape and yet not the same! How different the condition of one who is restored to fullness of health and vigour after being brought very low by serious illness — yet it is the same person. How different will be the body of the saint on the resurrection morning from its present state — the same body which was sown in the grave, and yet not the same! So too with those saints alive on earth at the Redeemer's return: "Who shall change our vile body that it may be fashioned like unto His glorious body" (Phil. 3:21). Thus it is, in measure, at regeneration: the soul undergoes a Divine work of renovation and transformation: a new light shines into the understanding, a new Object engages the affections, a new power moves the will. It is the same individual, and yet not the same. "Once I was blind, but now I see" is his blessed experience.

In Ephesians 4:24, we read of the new man "which after God is created in righteousness and true holiness," while in Colossians 3:10, it is said "which is renewed in knowledge after the image of Him that created him." i.e. originally. By comparing the two passages, we understand the "which after God" to signify conformity to Himself, for it is parallel with "after the image of Him." That the new man is said to be "created" denotes that this spiritual transformation is a Divine work in which the human individual plays no part, either by contribution, co-operation, or concurrence. It is wholly a supernatural operation, in which the subject of it is entirely passive. The "which is *renewed*" of Colossians 3:10, denotes that it is not something which previously had no existence, but the spiritual quickening and renovating of the soul. By regeneration is restored to the Christian's soul the moral image of God, which image he lost in Adam at the fall. That "image" consists in "righteousness and true holiness" being imparted to the soul, or, as Colossians 3:10, expresses it, in the spiritual "knowledge" of God. God is now known, loved, revered, loyally served. It is now fitted for communion with Him.

"Being confident of this very thing, that He which hath begun a good work in you will finish it" (Phil. 1:6). This verse contains a manifest warning, if an indirect or implied one, against our pressing too far the figure of a "new creation." "Creation" is an act and not a "work," a finished or completed object and not an incomplete and imperfect one. God speaks and it is done, wholly and perfectly done in an instant. The very fact that the Holy Spirit has employed such figures as "begetting" and "birth" to describe the saving work of God in the soul, intimates that the reference is only to the *initial* experience of Divine grace. A new life is then imparted, but it requires nurturing and developing. In the verse now before us we are informed that the great change produced in us is not yet fully accomplished, yea, that it is only just begun. The work of grace is called "good" because it is so in itself and because of what it effects: it conforms us to God and fits us to enjoy God. It is termed a "work" because it is a *continuous process*, which the Spirit carries forward in the saint as long as he is left in this scene.

This good work within the soul is commenced by God, being wrought neither by our will nor our agency. That was the ground of the apostle's persuasion or confidence: that He who had begun this good work would perform or finish it — had it been originated by man, he could have had no such assurance. Not only did God initate this good work, but He alone continues and perfects it — were it left to unto us, it would quickly come to nought. "Will finish it until the day of Jesus Christ" tells us it is not complete in this life. With that should be compared "them that believe to the saving of the soul" (Heb. 10:39): observe carefully, not "have believed" (a past act) to the salvation (a completed deliverance) of the soul, but "who believe (a present act) to the *saving* of the soul" — a continuous process. As Christ ever liveth to make intercession for us, so the Spirit ever exercises an effectual influence within us. The verb for "finish" is an intensive one, which means to carry forward unto the end. "The Lord *will perfect* that which concerneth me" (Psa. 138:8) enunciates the same promise.

"According to His mercy He saved us by the washing of regeneration and renewing of the Holy Spirit, which He shed on us abundantly through Jesus Christ" (Titus 3:5, 6). If we followed our inclination, we should essay an exposition of the whole passage (verses 4,7), but unless we keep within bounds and confine ourself to what bears directly on our present theme, these articles will be extended too much to suit some of our readers. In this passage we are shown how the three Persons of the Godhead co-operate in the work of salvation, and that salvation itself has both an experimental and legal side to it. Here we are expressly said to be "saved by" the effectual operations of the Holy Spirit, so that the Christian owes his personal salvation unto *Him* as truly as he does unto the Lord Jesus. Had not the blessed Spirit taken up His abode in this world, the death of Christ would have been in vain. It is by the meditation and merits of His redemptive work that Christ purchased the gift and graces of the Spirit, which are here said to be "shed on us abundantly *through* Jesus Christ our Saviour."

The will of the father is the originating cause of our salvation, the worth of the Son's redemption its meritorious cause, and the work of the Spirit, its effectual cause. Experimental salvation is begun in the soul by "the washing of regeneration," when the heart is cleansed from the prevailing love and power of sin and begins to be restored to its pristine purity. And by the "renewing of the Holy Spirit," that is, the renewing of the soul in the Divine image: or, more particularly, "the renewing of the *spirit of* the mind" (Eph. 4:23), that is in the *disposition* of it. The whole of which is summed up in the expression, God has given us "a sound mind" (2 Tim. 1:7), "an understanding, that we may know Him" (1 John 5:20). The mind is renovated and reinvigorated, so that it is capacitated to "spiritually discern" the things of the Spirit, which the natural man cannot do (1 Cor. 2:14), no matter how well he be educated or religiously instructed.

But that to which we would specially direct the attention of the reader is the present tense of the verbs: "the washing and renewing (not "renewal") of the Holy Spirit." Like 2 Corinthians 3:18, and Philippians 1:6, this is another verse which shows the great change is not completed at the new birth, but is a *continual process*, in course of effectuation. The "good work" which God has begun in the soul, that washing and renewing of the Holy Spirit, proceeds throughout the whole course of our earthly life, and is not consummated until the Redeemer's return, for it is only then that the saints will be perfectly and eternally conformed to the image of God's Son. God says of His heritage, "I the Lord do keep it: I will *water it every moment*" (Isa. 27:3): it is only by the continuous and gracious influences of the Spirit that the spiritual life is nurtured and developed. The believer is often conscious of his need thereof, and under a sense of it cries, "quicken me according to Thy Word." And God does: for "Though our outward man perish, yet the inward is renewed day by day" (2 Cor. 4:16). That "inner man" is termed "the hidden man of the heart" (1 Peter 3:4).

"For this is the covenant that I will make with the house of Israel after those days, saith the Lord. I will put My laws into their minds, and I will write them in their hearts" (Heb. 8:10 — quoted from Jer. 31:31-34). Without entering into the prophetic bearings of this passage (about which none should speak without humble diffidence,) suffice it to say that by the "house of Israel" we understand "the Israel of God" (Gal. 6:16), the whole election of grace, to be here in view. The "I will put" and "I will write" refer to yet another integral part of the great change wrought in God's people, the reference being to that invincible and miraculous operation of the Spirit which radically transforms the favoured subjects of it. "God articles with His people. He once wrote His laws *to* them, now He writes His laws *in* them. That is, He will give them understanding to know and believe them; He will give them courage to profess and power to put them into practice: the whole habit and frame of their souls shall be a table and transcript of His laws" (Matthew Henry).

"I will put My laws into their minds, and I will write them in their hearts." We are shown how rebels are made amendable to God. "God calls to us without effect as long as He speaks to us in no other way than by the voice of man. He indeed teaches us and commands what is right, but He speaks to the deaf; for when we seem to hear aright, our ears are only struck by an empty sound, and the heart, being full of depravity and perverseness rejects every wholesome doctrine. In short, the Word of God never penetrates into our hearts, for they are iron and stone until they are softened by Him; nay they have engraved on them a contrary law, for perverse passions reek within, which lead us to rebellion. In vain then does God proclaim His Law by the voice of men until He writes it by His spirit on our hearts, that is until He frames and prepares us for obedience" (Calvin).

"And I will write them in their hearts." The "heart." as distinguished from the "mind," comprises the affections and the will. This is what renders actually effective the former. The heart of the natural man is alienated from God and opposed to His authority. That is why God wrote the Ten Words upon tables of stone: not so much to secure the outward letter of them, as to represent the hardness of heart of the people into whom they were given. But at regeneration God takes away "the heart of stone" and gives "a heart of flesh" (Ezek. 36:26). Just as the tables of stone received the impression of the finger of God, of the letter and words wherein the Law was contained, so "the heart of flesh" receives a durable impression of God's laws, the affections and will being made answerable unto the whole revealed will of God and conformed to its requirements: a principle of obedience is imparted, subjection to the Divine authority is wrought in us.

Here, then, is the grand triumph of Divine grace: a lawless rebel is changed into a loyal subject, enmity against the Law (Rom. 8:7) is displaced by love for the Law (Psa. 119:97). The heart is so transformed that it now loves God and has a genuine desire and determination to please Him. The renewed heart *"delights* in the Law of God" and *"serves* the Law of God" (Rom. 7:22, 25), it being its very "nature" to do so! Let each reader sincerely ask himself, Is there now that in me which responds to the holy Law of God? Is it truly my longing and resolve to be wholly regulated by the Divine will? Is it the deepest yearning of my soul and the chief aim of my life to honour and glorify Him? Is it my daily prayer for Him to "work in me both to will and to do of His good pleasure"? Is my acutest grief occasioned when I feel I sadly fail to fully realize my longing? If so, the great change *has been* wrought in me.

"According as His Divine power has given unto us all things that pertain unto life and godliness, through the knowledge of Him that hath called us by glory and virtue. Whereby are given unto us exceeding great and precious promises, that by these ye might be partakers of the Divine nature, having escaped the corruption that is in the world through lust" (2 Peter 1:3, 4). That is more of a general description of experimental salvation than a delineation of any particular part thereof, yet since there be in it one or two expressions not found elsewhere, it calls for a separate consideration. The opening "According as" should be rendered "Forasmuch as" or "Seeing that" (R.V.), for it indicates not so much a standard of comparison, as that verses 3 and 4 form the ground of the exhortation of verses 5 to 7. First, we have their spiritual enduement. This was by "Divine power," or as Ephesians 1:19, expresses it, "the exceeding greatness of His power to usward, who believe according to the working of His mighty power," for nothing less could quicken souls dead in trespasses and sins or free the slaves of sin and Satan.

That Divine power "hath given unto us (not merely offered them in the Gospel, but hath graciously bestowed, actually communicated) all things that pertain unto life and godliness": that is, whatever is needful for the production, preservation and perfecting of spirituality in the souls of God's elect. Yet though the recipients be completely passive, yea, unconscious of this initial operation of Divine grace, they do not continue so, for, second, their enduement is accompanied by and accomplished "through the knowledge of Him that hath (effectually) called us by glory and virtue" or "energy." That "knowledge of Him" consists of such a personal revelation of Himself to the soul as imparts a true, spiritual, affecting, transforming perception of and acquaintance with His excellency. It is such a knowledge as enables its favoured recipient in adoring and filial recognition to say, "I have heard of Thee by the hearing of the ear; but now mine eye seeth Thee" (Job 42:5). God has now become an awe producing, yet a living and blessed reality to the renewed soul.

Third, through that spiritual "knowledge" which God has imparted to the soul is received all the gracious benefits and gifts of His love: "Whereby are given unto us exceeding great and precious promises, that by these ye might be partakers," etc. The "whereby" has reference to "His glory and virtue," or better "His glory and energy" or "might." The "promises" are "given unto us" not simply in words but in their actual fulfilment: just as the "by His glory and might" is the same thing as "His Divine power" in the previous verse, so "are given unto us exceeding great and precious promises, that by these ye might be partakers of the Divine nature" corresponds with "hath given unto us all things that pertain unto life and godliness," the one amplifying the other. The "exceeding great and precious promises" were those made in the Old Testament — the original (Gen. 3:15), fundamental, central, and all-pervading one being that of a personal Saviour; and those made by Christ, which chiefly respected the gift and coming of the Holy Spirit, which He expressly designated as *"the promise of the Father"* (Acts 1:4).

Now those two promises — that of a Divine Saviour and that of a Divine Spirit — were the things that the prophets of old "ministered not unto themselves, but unto us" (1 Peter 2:12), and they may indeed most fitly be termed "exceeding great and precious promises," for they who are given this Saviour and this Spirit do in effect receive "all things that pertain unto life and godliness," for Christ becomes their Life and the Spirit their Sanctifier. Or, as verse 3 expresses it, the end for which this knowledge (as well as its accompanying blessings) are bestowed is first "that by these (i. e. the promises are fulfilled and fulfilling in your experience) ye might be partakers of the Divine nature." Here we need to be on our guard against forming a wrong conclusion from the bare sound of those words: "Not the essence of God, but His communicable excellencies, such moral properties as may be imparted to the creature, and those not considered in their absolute perfection, but as they are agreeable to our present state and capacity" (Thos. Manton).

That "Divine nature," or "moral properties," is sometimes called "the life of God" (Eph. 4:18), because it is a vital principle of action; sometimes the "image of Him" (Col. 3:10), because they bear a likeness to Him — consisting essentially of "righteousness and true holiness" (Eph. 4:24); or in verse 3, "life and godliness" — spiritual life, spiritual graces, abilities to perform good works. It is here called "the Divine nature because it is the communication of a vital principle of operation which God transmits unto His children. The second end for which this saving knowledge of God is given is expressed in the closing words: "having escaped the corruption which is in the world through lust." Personally we see no need for taking up this expression *before* "partakers of the Divine nature" as that eminent expositor Thos. Manton did, and as did the most able John Lillie (to whom we are indebted for part of the above), for the apostle is not here enforcing the human-responsibility side of things (as he *was* in Rom. 13:12; Eph. 4:22-24), but treats of the Divine operations and their effects. It is quite true that *we* must put off the old man before we can put on the new man in a practical way, that we must first attend to the work of mortification ere we can make progress in our sanctification, but this is not the aspect of Truth which the apostle is *here* unfolding. When the Gospel call is addressed unto our moral agency the promise is *"that whosoever believeth in Him should not perish, but have eternal life"* (John 3:15,16). But where spiritual things are concerned, the unregenerate man never discharges his moral agency. A miracle of grace must take place before he does that, and therefore God in a sovereign manner (unsought by us) imparts life, that he may and will believe (John 1:12,13; 1 John 5:1) — the "sanctification of the Spirit" precedes the saving "and belief of the Truth" (2 Thess. 2:13)! In like manner, our becoming "partakers of the Divine nature" precedes (not in time, but in order of nature and of actual experience, though not of consciousness) our escaping "the corruption that is in the world through lust."

Let not the young preacher be confused by what has been pointed out in the last paragraph. His marching orders are plain: when addressing the unsaved he is to enforce their responsibility, press upon them the discharging of their duties, bidding them forsake their "way" and "thoughts" *in order to* pardon (Isa. 55:7), calling upon them to "repent" and "believe" if they would be saved. But if God be pleased to own his preaching of the Word and pluck some brands from the burning, it is quite another matter (or aspect of Truth) for the preacher (and, later on, his saved hearer, by means of doctrinal instruction) to understand something of the nature of that miracle of grace which God wrought in the hearer, which caused him to savingly receive the Gospel. It is *that* which we have endeavoured to deal with in the above paragraphs, namely, explain something of the operations of Divine grace in a renewed soul, so far as those operations are described in 2 Peter 1:3,4.

"Having escaped the corruption that is in the world through lust." First, by the Divine operation, and then by our own agency, for it is ever "God which worketh in you both *to* will and *to* do of His good pleasure" (Phil. 2:13). Indwelling sin (depravity) is here termed "corruption" because it blighted our primitive purity, degenerated our original state, and because it continues both in its nature and effects to pollute and waste. That "corruption" has its source, or is seated in, our "lusts" — depraved affections and appetites. This "corruption" is what another apostle designated "evil concupiscence" (Col. 3:5), for it occupies in the heart that place which is due alone unto the love of God as the Supreme Good. "Lust" always follows that "nature": as is the nature, so are its desires — if corrupt, then evil; if holy, then pure. All the corruption that is in the world is "through lust," i.e. through inordinate desire: lust lies at the bottom of every unlawful thought, every evil imagination.

The world could harm no man were it not for "lust" in his heart — some inordinate desire in the understanding or fancy, a craving for something which sets him a-work after it. The fault is not in the gold, but in the spirit of covetousness which possesses men; not in the wine, but in their craving to excess. "But every man is tempted when he is drawn away of *his own* lust" (James 1:14) — the blame lies on us rather than Satan! It is remarkable that when the apostle explained his expression "all that is in the world," he defined it as "the lust of flesh, and the lust of the eye, and the pride of life" (1 John 2:16). Now of Christians our passage says, "having escaped the corruption that is in the world through lust," and that by the interposition of the Divine hand, as Lot escaped from Sodom; yet not through a simple act of omnipotence, but by the gracious bestowments which that hand brings, but that holiness which He works in the heart, or, as a passage already reviewed expresses it, "by the washing of

34

regeneration and renewing of the Holy Spirit." We escape from the dominion of inward corruption by the "Divine nature in us" causing us to hate and resist our evil lusts.

Thus it is by adhering closely to the Divine order of this passage that we are enabled to understand the meaning of its final clause. When we become partakers of "the Divine nature," that is, when we are renewed after the image of God, a principle of grace and holiness is communicated to the soul, which is called "spirit" because "born of the Spirit" (John 3:6), and that principle of holiness (termed by many "the new nature") is a vital and operating one, which offers opposition to the workings of "corruption" or indwelling sin, for not only does the flesh lust against the spirit, but "the spirit lusteth against the flesh" (Gal. 5:17). The "Divine nature" has wrought "godliness" in us, drawing off the heart of its recipient from the world to heaven, making him to long after holiness and pant for communion with God. Herein lies the radical difference between those described in 2 Peter 1:3,4, and the ones in 2 Peter 2:20 — nothing is said of the latter being "partakers of the Divine nature!" Their "escaping from the pollutions of the world" was merely a temporary reformation from *outward* defilements and gross sins, as their *turning again* to the same makes clear (verse 22).

"We know that we have passed from death unto life because we love the brethren" (1 John 3:14). Here is set before us still another criterion by which the Christian may determine whether the great change has been wrought in him. First, let us point out that it seems to be clearly implied here (as in other places in this epistle: e.g. 2:3; 4:13) that the miracle of grace is *not* perceptible to our senses at the moment it occurs, but is cognizable by us afterward from its effects and fruits. We cannot recall a single statement in Scripture which expressly declares or even plainly implies that the saint is conscious of regeneration during the moment of quickening. There are indeed numbers (the writer among them) who can recall and specify the very hour when they were first convicted of sin, realized their lost condition, trusted in the atoning blood, and felt the burden of their hearts roll away. Nevertheless, they knew not when life was imparted into their spiritually dead souls — life which prompted them *to* breathe, feel, see, hear and act in a way they never had previously. Life must be present before there can be any of the functions and exercises of life. One dead in sin cannot savingly repent and believe.

Now it is one of the designs for which the first epistle of John was written that the regenerate may have assurance that eternal life has been imparted to them (5:13), several different evidences and manifestations of that life being described in the course of the apostle's letter. The one specified in 3:14, is "love for the brethren." By nature we were inclined to hate the children of God. It could not be otherwise: since we hated God, and that because He is holy and righteous, we despised those in whom the image of His moral perfections appeared. Contrariwise, when the love of God was shed abroad in our hearts and we were brought to delight ourselves in Him, His people became highly esteemed by us, and the more evidently they were conformed unto His likeness, the more we loved them. That "love" is of a vastly superior nature from any natural sentiment, being a holy principle. Consequently, it is something very different from mere zeal for a certain group or party spirit, or even an affection for those whose sentiments and temperaments are like our own. It is a Divine, spiritual and holy love which goes out unto the whole family of God: not respect to this or that brother, but which embraces "the brethren" at large.

That of which 1 John 3:14, treats is a peculiar love for those saved by Christ. To love the Redeemer and His Redeemed is congenial to the spiritual life which has been communicated to their renewed soul. It is a fruit of that holy disposition which the Spirit has wrought in them. It must be distinguished from what is so often mis-termed "love" in the natural realm, which consists only of sentimentality and amiability. The regenerate "love the brethren" not because they are affable and genial, or because they give them a warm welcome to their circle. They "love the brethren" not because they deem them wise and orthodox, but because of their *godliness,* and the more their godliness is evidenced the more will they love them; and hence they love *all* the godly — no matter what be their denominational connections. They love those whom Christ loves, they love them for His sake — because they belong to Him. Their love is a spiritual, disinterested and faithful one which seeks the good of its objects, which sympathizes with them in their spiritual trials and conflicts, which bears them up in their prayers before the throne of grace, which unselfishly shows kindness unto them, which admonishes and rebukes when that be necessary.

But that to which we would here direct particular attention is the language employed by the Spirit in describing the great change, namely, "passed from death unto life." The same expression was used by our Lord in John 5:24, though there its force is rather different. "Verily, verily, I say unto you, He that heareth (with an inward or spiritual ear) My word, and (savingly) believeth on Him that sent Me, *hath everlasting life* (the very fact he so heareth and believeth is proof he has it) and shall not come into condemnation, but is passed from death unto life." The "shall not come into condemnation," brings in the forensic side of things, and therefore the "hath passed from death unto life" (which, be it duly noted, is in addition to "hath everlasting life" in the preceding clause) is *judicial.* The one who has had "everlasting life" sovereignly imparted to him, and who in consequence thereof "hears" or heeds the Gospel of Christ and savingly believes, has for ever emerged from the place of condemnation, being no longer under the curse of the Law, but now entitled to its award of "life," by virtue of the personal obedience or meritorious righteousness of Christ being imputed unto him; for which reason he is exhorted "reckon ye also yourself to be dead indeed unto sin but alive unto God through (in) Jesus Christ our Lord" (Rom. 6:11).

But 1 John 3:14, is not treating of the forensic or legal side of things, but the experimental, that of which God's elect are made the subjects of in their own persons. Here it is not a relative change (one in relation to the Law), but an actual one that is spoken of. They have "passed from" that fearful state in which they were born — "alienated from the life of God" (Eph. 4:18): a state of unregeneracy. They have been supernaturally and effectually called forth from the grave of sin and death. They have entered "into life," which speaks of the state which they are now in before God as the consequence of His quickening them. They have for ever left that sepulchre of spiritual death in which by nature they lay, and have been brought into the spiritual sphere to "walk in newness of life." And "love for the brethren" is one of the effects and evidences of the miracle of grace of which they have been favored subjects. They evince their spiritual resurrection by this mark: they love the beloved of Christ; their hearts are spontaneously drawn out unto and they earnestly seek the good of all who wear Christ's yoke, bear His image and seek to promote His glory, 1 John 3:14, is not an exhortation but a factual statement of Christian experience.

Now let the reader most diligently note that in 1 John 3:14, the Holy Spirit has employed the figure of *resurrection* to set forth the great change, and that *it* also must be given due place in our thoughts as we endeavour to form something approaching an adequate conception of what the miracle of grace consists. Due consideration of this figure should check us in pressing too far that of the new birth. The similitude of resurrection brings before us something distinct and in some respects quite different from that which is connotated by "new creation," "begetting" (Jas. 1:18) or being "born again" (1 Peter 1:23). Each of the latter denotes the bringing into existence of something which previously existed not; whereas "resurrection" is the quickening of what is there already. The miracle of grace consists of far more than the communication of a new life or nature: it also includes the renovation and purification of the original soul. Because it is a "miracle," an act of omnipotence, accomplished by the mere fiat of God, it is appropriately likened unto "creation," yet it needs to be carefully borne in mind that it is not some *thing* which is created in us: for "*we* (ourselves) are His workmanship created in Christ Jesus" (Eph. 2:10). It is the person himself, and not merely a nature, which is born again.

We have now reviewed not less than twenty-five passages from God's Word, wherein a considerable variety of terms and figures are used to set forth the *different aspects of* the great change which takes place in a person when the miracle of grace is wrought within him: all of which passages, in our judgment, treating of the same. We have not sought to expound or comment upon them at equal length, but, following our usual custom, have rather devoted the most space in an attempt to explain those which are least understood, which present the most difficulty to the average reader, and upon which the commentators often supply the least help. A comparison of those passages will at once show that what theologians generally speak of as "regeneration" or "the effectual call" is very far from being expressed by the Holy Spirit in uniform language, and therefore that those who restrict their ideas to what is connoted by being born again, or, even on the other hand, "a change of heart," are almost certain to form a very one-sided, inadequate and faulty conception of what experimental salvation consists. Regeneration is indeed a new birth, or the beginning of a new life; but that it is not *all* it is — there is also something resurrected and renewed, and something washed and transformed!

The Bible is not designed for lazy people. Truth has to be *bought* (Prov. 23:23), but the slothful and worldly minded are not willing to pay the price required. That "price" is intimated in Prov. 2:1-5: there must be a diligent applying of the heart, a crying after knowledge, a seeking for an apprehension of spiritual things with that ardour and determination as men employ when seeking for silver; and a searching for a deeper and fuller knowledge of the Truth as men put forth when searching for hid treasures — persevering until their quest is successful; if we would really understand the things of God. Those who complain that these articles are "too difficult" or "too deep" for them, do but betray the sad state of their souls and reveal how little they really value the Truth; otherwise they would ask God to enable them to concentrate, and reread these pages perseveringly until they made its contents their own. People are willing to work and study hard and long to master one of the arts or sciences, but where spiritual and eternal things are concerned it is usually otherwise.

"Search the Scriptures" (John 5:39), "comparing the spiritual things with spiritual" (1 Cor. 2:13). *That* is what we sought to heed. Twenty-five different passages have been collated — all of which we are persuaded treat of some aspect or other of "the miracle of grace" or the great change — and in varying measure engaged our attention. It will be observed that in some of them it is the illumination of the understanding which is in view (Acts 26:18), in others the searching and convicting of the conscience (Rom. 7:9), and in others the renovation of the heart (Ezek. 36:26). In some it is the subduing of the will (Psa. 110:3) which is emphasized, in others casting down reasonings and bringing our thoughts into subjection (2 Cor. 10:5), and in others the writing of God's laws in our minds and hearts. In some the miracle of grace appears to be a completed thing (1 Cor. 6:11), in others the great change is seen as a gradual process (2 Cor. 3:18; Phil. 1:6). In one something is communicated (Rom. 5:5), In different passages the figures of creation (Eph. 2:10), of renewing (Titus 3:5), and of resurrection (1 John 3:14) are employed.

If it be asked, Why has it pleased the Holy Spirit to describe His work so diversely and use such a variety of terms and figures? Several answers may be suggested. First, because the work itself, though one, is so many-sided. Its subject is a complex creature and the process of salvation radically affects every part of his composite being. Just as sin has marred each part of our constitution and has corrupted every faculty the Creator gave us, so grace renews and transforms every part of our constitution and purifies every faculty we possess. When the apostle prayed, "The very God of peace sanctify you *wholly*, and your whole spirit and soul and body be preserved blameless unto the coming of the Lord Jesus Christ" (1 Thess. 5:23), he was asking that God would graciously preserve and perfect that which He had already wrought in His people, and the terms he there used intimated the comprehensiveness and entirety of the grand miracle of grace. This is a gem possessing many facets and our estimate of it is certain to be most faulty if we confine our view to only one of them.

Second, because God would thereby warn us from supposing that He acts according to a stereotyped plan or method in His saving of sinners. Variety rather than uniformity marks all the ways and workings of God, in creation, providence, and grace. No two seasons are alike — no field or tree yields the same crop in any two years. Every book in the Bible is equally the inspired Word of God, yet how different in character and content is Leviticus from the Psalms, Ruth from Ezekiel, Romans from the Revelation! How varied the manner in which the Lord Jesus gave sight to different ones who were blind: different in the means used and the effect produced — one, at first, only seeing men as though they were trees walking (Mark 8:24)! How differently He dealt with religious Nicodemus in John 3 and the adulterous woman of John 4, pressing on the one his imperative need of being born again, convicting the other of her sins and telling her of "the gift of God!" The great God is not confined to any rule and we must not restrict His operations in our thoughts: if we do, we are certain to err.

Third, because God would thereby teach us that, though the work of grace be essentially and substantially the same in all its favored subjects, yet in no two of them does it appear identical in all its circumstantials — neither in its operations nor manifestations. Not only does endless variety mark all the ways and workings of God, but it does so equally in His *workmanship*. This is generally recognized and acknowledged in connection with the material world, where no two blades of grass or two grains of sand are alike. But in the spiritual realm it is very far from being perceived and owned: rather is it commonly supposed that all truly regenerate persons conform strictly unto one particular pattern, and those who differ from it are at once suspected of being counterfeits. This should not be. The twelve foundations of the new and holy Jerusalem, in which are the names of the twelve apostles of the Lamb, are all composed of "precious" stones, but how diverse is each! The first jasper, the second sapphire, the third a chalcedony, the fourth emerald, etc. (Rev. 21) — different in color, size and brilliancy. Each Christian has his own measure of faith and grace "according to the measure of the gift of Christ" (Eph. 4:7).

REVERSAL OF THE FALL

Since we are seeking to write these articles for the benefit of young preachers as well as the rank and file of God's people, let us point out that the nature of this great change may also be determined by contemplating it as *the begun reversal of the Fall*: "begun reversal," for what is commenced at regeneration is continued throughout our sanctification and completed only at our glorification. While it be true that those who are renewed by the Holy Spirit gain *more* than Adam lost by the Fall, yet we have clear Scripture warrant for affirming that the workmanship of the new creation is *God's answer* to man's ruination of his original creation. Great care needs to be taken in cleaving closely to the Scriptures in developing this point, particularly in ascertaining exactly what was the moral and spiritual condition of man originally, and precisely what happened to him when he fell. We trust that a patient perusal of what follows will convince the reader of both the importance and value of our discussion of these details at this stage — the more so since the children have sadly departed from the teaching of the fathers thereon.

Even those sections of Christendom which boast the most of their soundness in the Faith are defective here. Mr. Darby and his followers hold that Adam was merely created innocent (a negative state), and not in (positive) holiness. Mr. Philpot said, "I do not believe that Adam was a spiritual man, that is, that he possessed those spiritual gifts and graces which are bestowed upon the elect of God, for they are new covenant blessings in which he had no share" (*Gospel Standard*, 1861, page 155). One error ever involves another. Those who deny that fallen man possesses any responsibility to perform spiritual acts (love God, savingly believe in Christ) must, to be consistent, deny that unfallen man was a spiritual creature. Different far was the teaching of the Reformers and Puritans. "And where Paul treats of the restoration of this image (2 Cor. 3:18), we may readily infer from his words that man was conformed to God not by an influx of His substance, but by the grace and power of His Spirit." And again, "As the *spiritual life* of Adam consisted in a union to his Maker, so an alienation from Him was the death of his soul" (Calvin, *Institutes*).

"Adam had the Spirit as well as we: the Holy Spirit was at the making of him and wrote the image of God upon his heart, for where holiness was, we may be sure the Spirit of God was too . . .the same Spirit was in Adam's heart to assist *his graces* and cause them to flow and bring forth, and to move him to live according to those principles of life given him" (Goodwin, 6/54). And again, commenting on Adam's being made in the image and likeness of God, and pointing out that such an "image" imports a thing "permanent and inherent," he asked, "what could this be but habitual inclinations and dispositions unto whatsover was holy and good, insomuch as *all holiness* radically *dwelt in him*" (page 202). So too Charnock: "The righteousness of the first man evidenced not only a sovereign power, as the Donor of his being, but a holy power, as the pattern of His work. . . . The law of love to God, with his whole soul, his whole mind, his whole heart and strength, was originally writ upon his nature. All the parts of his nature were framed in a moral conformity with God, to answer His Law and imitate God in His purity" (vol. 2, page 205).

In his *Discourse on the Holy Spirit* (chapter 4, His "Peculiar works in the first creation"), when treating of "the image of God" after which Adam was created (namely, "an ability to discern the mind and will of God," an "unentangled disposition to every duty" and "a readiness of compliance in his affections"), J. Owen said, "For in the *restoration* of these abilities unto our minds in our renovation unto the image of God in the Gospel, it is plainly asserted that the Holy Spirit is the imparter of them, and He doth thereby restore His own work. For in the new creation the Father, in the way of authority, designs it and brings all things unto a head in Christ (Eph. 1:10), which *retrieves* His original work. And thus Adam may be said to have had the Spirit of God in his innocency: he had Him in those peculiar effects of His power and goodness, and he had Him according to the tenor of that covenant whereby it was possible that he should utterly lose Him, as accordingly it came to pass." The superiority of the new covenant lies in its gifts being unforfeitable, because secured in and by Christ.

"God made man *upright*" (Eccl. 7:29) – the same Hebrew word as in Job 1:8, and Psalm 25:8: "This presupposes a law to which he was conformed in his creation, as when anything is made regular or according to rule, of necessity the rule itself is presupposed. Whence we may gather that this law was no other than the eternal indispensable law of righteousness, observed in all points by the second Adam. . . . In a word, this law is the very same which was afterwards summed up in the Ten Commandments . . . called by us the Moral Law, and man's righteousness consisted in conformity to this law or rule" (Thomas Boston, *Human Nature in its Fourfold State*). "When God created man at first, He gave him not an outward law, written in letters or delivered in words, but an inward law put into his heart and concreated with him, and wrought in the frame of his soul . . .*spiritual* dispositions and inclinations, in his will and affections, carrying him on to pray, love God and fear Him, to seek His glory in a spiritual and holy manner" (Goodwin). The external command of Genesis 2:17, was designed as the *test* of his responsibility, and at the same time it served to make manifest that his "uprightness" was mutable.

When Adam left the Creator's hand the law of God was in his heart, for he was endowed with holy instincts and inclinations, which tended unto his doing that

which was pleasing unto God and an antipathy against whatever was displeasing
to Him. That "law of God" within him was his original *character* or constitution
of his soul and spirit — as it is the "law" or character of beasts to care for their
young and of birds to build nests for theirs. Should it be asked, Is there any
other Scripture which teaches that God placed His law in the heart of unfallen
Adam? we answer, Yes, by clear and necessary implication. Christ declared "Thy
Law is within My heart" (Psalm 40:8), and Romans 5:14, tells us that Adam was
"the figure of Him that was to come." Again, just as we may ascertain what
grain a certain field bore from the stubble in it, so we may discover what was in
unfallen man by the ruins of what is still discernible in fallen humanity: "the
Gentiles do *by nature* the things contained in the Law" (Rom. 2:14) — their
consciences informing them that immorality and murder are crimes: there is still
a shadow in his descendants of the character originally possessed by Adam.

But Adam did not continue as God created him. He fell, and terrible were the
consequences. But it is only by adhering closely to the terms used in the Word
that we can rightly apprehend the nature of those consequences; yea, unless we
allow Scripture itself to interpret those terms for us, we are certain to err in our
understanding of them. Possibly the reader is ready to exclaim, There is no need
to make any mystery out of it: the matter is quite simple — those
"consequences" may all be summed up in one word — "death." Even so, we
must carefully inquire what is meant there by "death." "Spiritual death," you
answer. True, and observe well that presupposes spiritual life, and that in turn
implies a spiritual person, for surely one endowed with spiritual life must be so
designated. However, our inquiry must be pressed back a stage farther, and the
question put, Exactly what is connoted by "spiritual death"? It is at this point
so many have gone wrong and, departing from the teaching of Holy Writ, have
landed in serious error.

It is to be most carefully noted that God did not say to Adam, "In the day that
thou eatest thereof thy spirit or thy soul shall surely die," but rather *"thou* shalt
surely die" (Gen. 2:17). It was not some *thing* in or some part of Adam which
died, but Adam himself! That is very, very far from being a distinction without
any difference: it is a real and radical difference, and if we tamper with Scripture
and change what it says, we depart from the Truth. Nor is "death" an extinction
or annihilation; instead, it is a *separation*. Physical death is the severance or
separation of the soul from the body, and spiritual death is the separation of the
soul from God. The prodigal son was "dead" so long as he remained in "the far
country" (Luke 15:24), because away from his Father. 1 Timothy 5:6, tells us,
"she that liveth in pleasure is dead while she liveth"; that is, she is spiritually
dead, dead Godwards, while alive and active in sin. For the same reason, "the
lake which burneth with fire and brimstone" is called "the Second Death" (Rev.
21:8), because those cast into it are "punished with everlasting destruction *from
the presence of the Lord"* (2 Thess. 1:9).

Man was created a tripartite being, composed of "spirit and soul and body" (1
Thess. 5:23). That is unmistakably implied in the Divine account of his creation:
"God said, Let *Us* make man in *Our* image, after *Our* likeness" (Gen. 1:26); the
Triune God made man a trinity in unity! And when man fell, he *continued to be*
a tripartite being: no part of his being was extinguished, no faculty was lost
when he apostatized from God. It cannot be insisted upon too strongly that no
essential element of man's original constitution was forfeited, no component

part of his complex make-up was annihilated at the Fall, for multitudes are seeking to hide behind a misconception at this very point. They would fain believe that man lost some vital part of his nature when Adam ate of the forbidden fruit, and that it is the absence of this part in his descendants which explains (and excuses!) all their failures. They console themselves that they are more to be pitied than blamed: the blame rests on their first parents, and they, forsooth, are to be pitied because he deprived them of the faculty of working righteousness. Much preaching encourages that very delusion.

The truth is that fallen man today possesses identically the same faculties as those with which Adam was originally created, and his accountability lies in his making good use of those faculties, and his criminality consists in the evil employment of them. Others seek to evade the onus of man by affirming that he *received a nature* which he did not possess before the Fall, and all the blame for his lawless actions is thrown upon that evil nature: equally erroneous and equally vain is such a subterfuge. No material addition was made to man's being at the Fall, any more than some intrinsic part was taken from it. That which man lost at the Fall was his primitive *holiness*, and that which then entered into his being was *sin*, and sin has defiled every part of his person; but for *that* we are to be blamed and not pitied. Nor has fallen man become so helplessly the victim of sin that his accountability is cancelled; rather does God hold him responsible to resist and reject every inclination unto evil, and will justly punish him because he fails to do so. Every attempt to negative human responsibility and undermine the sinner's accountability, no matter by whom made, must be steadfastly resisted by us.

It is by persuading men that the spirit died at the Fall, or that some concrete but evil thing was then communicated to the human constitution, that Satan succeeds in deceiving so many of his victims: and it is the bounden duty of the Christian minister to expose his sophistries, drive the ungodly out of their refuge of lies, and press continually upon them the solemn fact that they are without the vestige of an excuse for their own rebellion against God. In the day of his disobedience Adam himself died, died spiritually, and so did all his posterity in him. But that spiritual death consisted not of the extinction of anything in them, but of their separation from God: no part of Adam's being was annihilated, but every part of him was *vitiated*. It was not the essence but the rectitude of man's soul and spirit which sin destroyed. By the Fall man relinquished his honour and glory, lost his holiness, forfeited the favour of God, and was severed from all communion with Him; but he still retained *his human nature*. All desire Godwards, all love for his Maker, all real knowledge of Him was gone. Sin now possessed him, and to the love and exercise of it he devoted himself. Such too is *our* natural condition.

Writing upon "A *Persisting* Sinner being an *unpardoned* sinner," the Puritan, Jos. Caryl, said: "There is abundant mercy for returning sinners, but I know of none for those who resolve to go on in sin. There is a promise *of* repentance, and a promise *to* repentance, but there is no promise that doth not either offer or require repentance. 'Repent, and thou shalt be saved' is the tenor of the Gospel, as well as 'believe and thou shalt be saved.' Though many who are going on in their sins are overtaken by grace, yet there is no grace promised to those who go on in their sins. The holiest are threatened with wrath if they do: surely then none are put into an expectation of mercy if they do. The promises either find us repenting, or they cause us to repent. No sinner is pardoned *for* repentance, nor *without* it. Job speaks that language more clearly in the words that follow: 'If I be wicked, woe unto me' (Job 5:15)."

Let none conclude from the last few paragraphs that we do not believe in the "total depravity" of man, or that we do so in such a manner as practically to evacuate that expression of any real meaning. Most probably the writer believes more firmly in the utter ruin of fallen human nature than do some of his readers, and views the plight of the natural man as being more desperate than they do. We hold that the state of every unregenerate soul is such that he *cannot* turn his face Godward or originate a single spiritual thought, and that he has not even so much as the wish or will to do so. Nor let it be inferred from our preceding remarks that we deny the evil principle or "the flesh" as being existent and dominant in the natural man: we most emphatically believe — both on the testimony of the Word of Truth and from personal experience of its awful potency and horrible workings — that it is. But we also hold that great care should be taken when seeking to visualize or define in our minds what "the flesh" consists of. It is a principle of evil and not a concrete or tangible entity. The moment we regard it as something material, we confuse ourselves.

It is because all of us are so accustomed to thinking in the terms of matter that we find it difficult to form a definite concept of something which though immaterial is *real*. Nor is it by any means a simple task for one to express himself thereon so that he will be coherent unto others. Man lost no part of his tripartite nature when he fell, nor was a fourth part then communicated to him. Instead, sin — which is not a material entity — entered into him, and vitiated and corrupted his entire being. He was stricken with a loathsome disease which defiled all his faculties and members, so that his entire spirit and soul became precisely like one whose body is thus described: "From the sole of the foot even unto the head there is no soundness in it; but wounds, and bruises, and putrefying sores" (Isa. 1:5). A potato is still a potato even when frozen, though it is no longer edible. An apple remains an apple when decayed within. And man still retained his human nature when he apostatized from God, died spiritually, and became totally depraved. He remained all that he was previously minus only his holiness.

When man fell he died spiritually and, as we have shown, death is not annihilation, but separation. Yet that word "separation" does not express the full meaning of what is signified by "spiritual death." Scripture employs another term — *"alienation,"* and that too we must take fully into account. "Alienation" includes the thought of severance, but it also imparts an *opposition*. A dear friend may be separated from me physically, but a cruel enemy is bitterly antagonistic to me. Thus it is with fallen man: he is not only cut off from all communion with the Holy One, but he is innately and inveterately hostile to Him — "alienated" in his affections. We are not here striving about mere "words," but calling attention to a most solemn truth and fact. It is thus that the Scripture depicts the condition of fallen mankind: "Having the understanding darkened, being alienated from the life of God, through the ignorance that is in them, because of the hardness of their heart" (Eph. 4:18); yea, it solemnly declares that "the carnal mind is enmity against God" (Rom.

8:7), and "enmity" is not a negative and passive thing, but a positive and active one.

"Dead in trespasses and sins" (Eph. 2:1) is the fearful diagnosis made of fallen man by the Divine Physician. Yet though that language be true to fact and is no exaggeration, still it is a *figure*, and unless we interpret it in strict accord with Scripture, we shall falsify its meaning. It is often said that the spiritual state of the natural man is analogous to that of a corpse buried in the cemetery. From one standpoint that is correct; from another it is utterly erroneous. The natural man is a putrefying creature, a stench in the nostrils of the Holy One, and he can no more perform a spiritual act Godwards than a corpse can perform a physical act manwards. But there the analogy ends! There is a contrast between the two cases as well as a resemblance. A corpse has no responsibility, but the natural man *has*! A corpse can perform no actions; different far is the case of the sinner. He *is* active, active against *God*! Though he does not love Him (and he ought!), yet he is filled with enmity and hatred against Him. Thus spiritual death is not a state of passivity and inactivity, but one of aggressive hostility against God.

Here then, as everywhere, there is a balance to be preserved; yet it is rarely maintained. Far too many Calvinists, in their zeal to repudiate the free-willism of Arminians, have at the same time repudiated man's moral agency; anxious to enforce the utter helplessness of fallen men in spiritual matters, they have virtually reduced him to an irresponsible machine. It has not been sufficiently noted that in the very next verse after the statement"who were dead in trespasses and sins," the apostle added, "Wherein (i.e. that state of spiritual death) ye *walked* (which a corpse in the grave could not!) according to the course of this world, according to the spirit of the power of the air, the spirit that now worketh in the children of disobedience. Among whom also we all had our conversation ("conduct") in times past in the lusts of our flesh, fulfilling the desires of the flesh and of the mind" (Eph. 2:1-3). So that in one sense they were dead (i.e. Godward) while they lived (i.e. in sin), and in another sense they *lived* (a life of self-seeking and of enmity against God), while *dead* to all spiritual things.

By the fall man both lost something and acquired something. Term that something a "nature" if you will, so long as you do not conceive of it as something material. That which man lost was holiness, and that which he acquired was sin, and neither the one nor the other is a substance, but rather a moral quality. A "nature" is not a concrete entity, but instead that which characterizes and impells an entity or creature. It is the "nature" of gravitation to attract; it is the nature of fire to burn. A "nature" is not a tangible thing, but a power impelling to action, a dominating influence — an "instinct" for want of a better term. Strictly speaking a "nature" is that which we have by our *origin*, as our partaking of *human nature* distinguishes us from the celestial creatures who are partakers of angelic nature. Thus we speak of a lion's "nature" (ferocity), a vulture's nature (to feed on carrion), a lamb's nature (gentleness). A "nature," then, describes more what a creature is by birth and disposition, and therefore we prefer to speak of holiness or imparted grace as a *"principle* of good," and indwelling sin or "the flesh" as a principle of evil — a prevalent disposition which moves its subjects to ever act in accord with its distinguishing quality.

If it be kept in mind that, strictly speaking, a "nature" is that which we have *by our origin*, as partaking of human nature distinguishes us from the celestial creatures on the one hand and from the beasts of the field (with their animal nature) on the other, much confusion of thought will be avoided. Furthermore, if we distinguish carefully between what our nature intrinsically consists of and what it "accidentally" (non-essentially) became and becomes by virtue of the changes passing upon it at the fall and at regeneration, then we should have less difficulty in understanding what is signified by the Lord's assuming *our nature*. When the Son of God became incarnate He took unto Himself human nature. He was, in every respect, true Man, possessed of spirit (Luke 23:46), soul (John 12:27), and body (John 19:40): "in *all* things it behoved Him to be made like unto His brethren" (Heb. 2:17) — otherwise He could not be their Surety and Mediator. This does not explain the miracle and mystery of the Divine incarnation, for that is incomprehensible, but it states the fundamental fact of it. Christ did not inherit our corruption, for *that* was no essential part of manhood! He was born and ever remained immaculately pure and holy; nevertheless, He took upon Him our nature intrinsically considered, but *not* as it had been defiled by sin; and therefore is denominated "the son *of Adam*" (Luke 3:38).

When, then, we say that by the fall man became possessed of a "sinful nature" it must not be understood that something comparable to his spirit or soul was *added to* his being, but instead that a principle of evil entered into him, which defiled every part of his being, as frost entering into fruit ruins it. Instead of his faculties now being influenced and regulated by holiness, they became defiled and dominated by sin. Instead of spiritual propensities and properties actuating his conduct, a carnal disposition became the law of his being. The objects and things man formerly loved, he now hated; and those which he was fitted to hate, he now desires. Therein lies both his depravity and his criminality. God holds fallen man responsible to mortify every inclination unto evil, to resist and reject every solicitation unto sin, and will justly punish him because he fails to do so. Nay more, God requires him and holds him accountable to love Him with all his heart and to employ each of his faculties in serving and glorifying Him: his failure so to do consists solely in a voluntary refusal, and for that He will righteously judge him.

Now the miracle of grace is *God's answer* to man's ruination of himself, His begun reversal of what happened to him at the fall. Let us now establish that fact from the Scriptures and show this concept is no invention of ours. The very fact that Christ is denominated "the last Adam" implies that He came to right the wrong wrought by the first Adam — tough only so far as God's elect are concerned. Hence we find Him saying by the Spirit of prophecy, "I *restored* that which I took not away" (Psa. 69:4). A lengthy article might well be written on those comprehensive words: suffice it now to say that He recovered both unto God and His people what had been lost by Adam's defection — to the One His manifestative honour and glory; to the other, the Holy Spirit and holiness in their hearts. What Christ did for His people is the meritorious ground of what the Spirit works in them, and at regeneration they begin to be restored to their pristine purity or brought back to their original state. Therefore it is that the great change is spoken of as the "*renewing* of the Holy Spirit" (Titus 3:5), that is, a renovating and restoring of spiritual life to the soul.

"Lie not one to another, seeing that ye have put off the old man with his deeds, and have put on the new man, which is renewed in knowledge after the image of Him that created him" (Col. 3:9). Those to whom the apostle was writing had, by their profession and practice, "put off" or renounced "the old man," and by lip and life had avowed and exhibited the new. That new man is here said to be *"renewed* in knowledge," which cannot be the obtaining of a knowledge which man never had previously but rather the recovery and restoration of that spiritual knowledge of God which he had originally. That is confirmed by what follows: *"after* the image of Him that created him," i.e. at the beginning. Man was originally made "in the image of God" (Gen. 1:27), which imported at least three things. First, he was constituted a tripartite being by the Triune God; and this he continued to be after the Fall. Second, he was created in His *natural* image, being made a moral agent, endowed with rationality and freedom of will; this too he retained. Third, God's *moral* image, being "made upright," endued "with righteousness and true holiness"; which was lost when man became a sinner, but is restored to him by the miracle of grace.

That which takes place in the elect at regeneration is the *reversing* of the effects of the Fall. The one born again is, through Christ, and by the Spirit's operations, restored to union and communion with God (1 Pet. 3:18). The one who previously was spiritually dead, alienated from God, is now spiritually alive, reconciled to God. Just as spiritual death was brought about by the entrance into man's being of a principle of evil, which darkened his understanding and hardened his heart (Eph. 4:18), so spiritual life is the introduction of a principle of holiness into man's soul, which enlightens his understanding and softens his heart. God communicates a *new principle* one which is as real and potent unto good as indwelling sin is unto evil. Grace is now imparted, a holy disposition is wrought in the soul, a new temper of spirit is bestowed upon the inner man. But no new faculties are communicated unto him: rather are his original faculties (in measure) purified, enriched, elevated, empowered. Just as man did not become less than a threefold being when he fell, neither does he become more than a threefold being when he is renewed. Nor will he in heaven itself: his spirit and soul and body will then be *glorified* — completely purged from every taint of sin, and perfectly conformed unto the image of God's Son.

But is not a "new nature" received by us when we are born again? If that term (in preference to "another principle") be admitted and used, we must be careful lest we carnalize our conception of what is connoted by that expression. Much confusion has been caused at this point through failure to recognize that is a *person*, and not merely a "nature," who is born of the Spirit: *"he* is born of God" (1 John 3:9). The selfsame person who was spiritually dead Godwards (separated and alienated from Him) is now spiritually alive Godwards — reconciled and brought back into union and communion with Him. The same person whose entire being (and not merely some part of him!) was dead in trespasses and sins, wherein he walked according to the course of this world, according to the evil spirit who worketh in the children of disobedience, fulfilling the lusts of the flesh; his entire being is now alive in holiness and righteousness, and he walks according to the course of God's Word, according to the power and promptings of the Holy Spirit, who worketh in the children of obedience, moving them to fulfil the dispositions and develop the graces of the spirit or "new nature."

This must be so, or otherwise there would be no preservation of the *identity* of the individual: we repeat, it is the individual himself who is born again, and not merely something *in* him. The person of the regenerate is constitutionally the same as the person of the unregenerate, each having a spirit and soul and body. But just as in fallen man there is *also* a principle of evil which has corrupted each part of his threefold being — which principle may be styled his "sinful nature" (if by that be meant his evil disposition and character), as it is the "nature" of swine to be filthy; so when a person is born again another and new principle is introduced into his being, which may be styled a "new nature," if by it be meant a disposition which propels him in a new direction — Godwards. Thus, in both cases, "nature" is a moral principle rather than a tangible entity. "That which is born of the Spirit is spirit" — spiritual and not material, and must not be regarded as something substantial, distinct from the soul of the regenerate, like one part of matter added to another; rather is it that which *spiritualizes* his inward faculties as the "flesh" had carnalized them.

When treating of regeneration under the figure of the new birth some writers (ourself included in earlier days) have introduced analogies from natural birth which Scripture by no means warrants, and which, by its employment of *other* figures it disallows. Physical birth is the bringing forth into this world of a creature, a complete personality which before conception had no existence whatever. But the one regenerated by God *had* a complete personality before he was born again! To that statement it may be objected, Not a *spiritual* personality. True, but keep steadily in mind that spirit and matter are opposites, and we only confuse ourselves if we think or speak of that which is "spiritual" as being something concrete. Regeneration is not the creating of a person who hitherto had no existence, but the spiritualizing of one who had — the renewing and renovating of one whom sin had unfitted for communion with God, and this by the imparting to him of a principle, or "nature," or *life*, which gives a new and different bias to all his faculties. Ever beware of regarding the Christian as made up of two distinct personalities.

A century ago a booklet was published in England purporting to prove that "A child of God cannot backslide," and many in a reputedly orthodox circle were evilly affected by it. Its author argued "a regenerated man possesses two natures: an old man of sin, and a new man of grace; that the old man of sin never made any progress in the Divine life nor ever can, consequently he can never go back or imbibe the least taint or particle of sin. How then can the child of God backslide?" A reviewer exposed this sophistry by mentioning a Papist in Germany who was a royal bishop that was very fond of hunting, and who was friendly admonished of the inconsistency of the chase with the mitre. His reply was, "I do not hunt as bishop, but as prince," to which it was answered, "If the prince should break his neck while a-hunting and went to hell, what would become of the bishop!" That was answering a fool according to his folly!

The "old man" and the "new man" indwell and belong to the same individual, and can no more be divorced from *his person* than the bishop could be separated from the prince. It is not merely something *in* the Christian but the Christian *himself* who backslides. What we have called attention to above is but the corollary, a carrying out to its logical conclusion of another error, equally mischievous and reprehensible, though not so fully developed, namely, wherein the "two natures" in the believer are made so prominent and dominant that the person possessing them is largely lost sight of and his responsibility repudiated. Thus, it is just as much an idle quibble to reason that neither "the flesh" or old nature, nor "the spirit" or new nature, is capable of backsliding. It is the person possessing those two natures (or principles) who backslides, and for that God holds him accountable and chastens him accordingly. Unless believers are much on their guard, they will eagerly snatch at any line of teaching which undermines their accountability and causes them to slur over the exceeding sinfulness of *their* sins, by finding a pretext for supposing they are more to be pitied than blamed.

The youth differs much from the infant, and the adult from the immature youth; nevertheless, it is *the same individual*, the same human person, who passes through those stages. Human beings we are; moral agents, responsible creatures we shall ever remain, no matter what be the precise nature of the internal change we experienced at regeneration (nor how the character of that experience be defined or expressed), or whatever change awaits the body at resurrection: we shall never lose our essential personality or *identity* as God created us at the first. Let that be clearly understood and firmly grasped: we remain *the same persons* all through our history. Neither the deprivation of spiritual life at the Fall, nor the communication of spiritual life at the new birth, affects the reality of our being in possession of *human nature*. By the Fall we did not become less than men; by regeneration we do not become more than men — though our relation to God is altered. That which essentially constitutes our manhood was not lost, and no matter what be imparted to us at regeneration, our individuality and personal identity as a responsible being remains unchanged.

We will now endeavour to summarize all that has been set before the reader concerning the great change which takes place in one who is born again, renewed spiritually, resurrected, by the operations of the Spirit of God. Perhaps this can best be accomplished by making some epitomized statements and then offering some further remarks on those against which certain of our readers may be most inclined to take issue. *Negatively*, that great change does not consist of any constitutional alteration in the make-up of our being, no essential addition being made to our persons. We regard it as a serious mistake to consider the natural man as possessed of but soul and body, and as only having a "spirit" communicated to him when he is regenerated. Again, it is a still worse error to suppose that indwelling sin is eradicated from the being of a born-again person: not only does Scripture contain no warrant to countenance such an idea, but the uniform experience of God's children repudiates it. Nor does the great change effect any improvement in the evil principle. The "flesh," with its vile properties and lusts, its deceiving and debasing inclinations, its power to promote hypocrisy, pride, unbelief, opposition unto God, remains unchanged unto the end of our earthly course.

Yet it would be utterly wrong for us to conclude from those negatives that regeneration is not entitled to be designated a "miracle of grace" or that the change effected in its subject is far from being a *great* one. A real, a radical, a stupendous, a glorious change *is* wrought, yet the precise nature of it can only be discovered in the light of Holy Writ. While it is indeed an experimental change, yet the subject of it must interpret the same by the teaching of Scripture, and not by either his own reason or feelings. Nor should that statement be either surprising or disappointing. The miracle of grace effects a great change Godwards in the one who experiences it, and God is not an Object of sense nor can He be known by any process of reasoning. We may then summarize by saying the great change, positively considered, consists first of a radical *change of heart Godwards*. God discovers Himself unto the soul, makes Himself a living reality unto it, reveals Himself both as holy and gracious, clothed with authority and yet full of mercy. That personal and powerful revelation of God unto the soul produces an altered disposition and attitude toward Him: the one alienated is reconciled, the one who shrank from and was filled with enmity against Him, now desires His presence and longs for communion with Him.

Such a vital and radical change in the disposition and attitude of a soul Godwards is indeed a miracle of grace, and cannot be described as anything less than a great change. It is as real and great as was the change when man apostasized from his Maker, as vivid and blessed a change spiritually as the resurrection will effect physically: when that which was sown in corruption, in dishonour, in weakness, shall be raised in incorruption, glory and power; when our vile body shall be changed, "that it may be fashioned like unto His glorious God to now become experimentally and savingly acquainted with Him, for one who sought to banish Him from his thoughts to now find his greatest delight in meditating upon His perfections, for one who lived in total disregard of His righteous claims upon him to be made a loyal and loving subject, is a transformation which human language — with all its adjectives and superlatives — cannot possibly do justice unto. In the words of Divine inspiration, it is a "passing from death unto life," a being "called out of darkness into God's marvellous light," a being "created in Christ Jesus unto good works."

Second, that great change consists in a *moral purification of the inner man*. Though this be the most difficult aspect of it for us to understand, yet the teaching of the Word thereon is too clear and full to leave us in any uncertainty as to the same. Such expressions as "Then will I sprinkle clean water upon you, and ye shall be clean: from all your filthiness and from all your idols will I cleanse you" (Ezek. 36:25), "but ye are washed, but ye are sanctified" (1 Cor. 6:11), "Ye have purified your souls in obeying the Truth" (1 Pet. 1:22) would be meaningless if there had been no internal transformation. Our characters are formed by the Truth we receive: our thoughts are more or less moulded, our affections directed, and our wills regulated by what we heartily believe. Truth has a vital, effectual, elevating influence. Any man who professes to take the Word of God for his Guide and Rule and is not altered by it, both internally and externally, is deceiving himself. "The Truth will make you free" (John 8:32): from the dominion of sin, from the snares of Satan, from the deceits of the world. The tastes, the aims, the ways of a Christian are assimilated to and fashioned by the Word.

A radical change Godwards which is accompanied by a moral purification within, necessarily consists, in the third place, of a thoroughly altered attitude toward the *Divine Law*. It cannot be otherwise. "The carnal mind is enmity against God"; it is completely dominated by ill will unto Him. The evidence adduced by the Spirit in demonstration of that fearful indictment is this, "and is not subject unto the law of God, neither indeed can be" (Rom. 8:7): the one is the certain outcome of the other — hatred for the Lawgiver expresses itself in contempt for and defiance of His Law. Before there can be any genuine respect for and subjection to the Divine Law the heart's attitude towards its Governor and Administrator must be completely changed. Conversely, when the heart of any one has been won unto God, His authority will be owned, His government honoured, and his sincere language will be, "I delight in the Law of God after the inward man" — i.e. the soul as renewed by the Spirit (Rom. 7:22). Thus, while the unregenerate are denominated "the children of disobedience" (Eph. 2:2) the regenerate are called "obedient children" (1 Pet. 1:14), for obedience is one of their characteristic marks, evidencing as it does the general tenor and course of their lives.

After all that has been said, it ought not to be necessary for us to interrupt our train of thought at this point and consider a question which can only prove wearisome unto the well-taught reader; but others who have drunk so deeply from the foul pools of error need a word thereon. Are there not two "minds" in a born-again person: the one carnal and the other spiritual? Certainly not, or he would have a dual personality, and a divided responsibility. By nature his mind was, spiritually speaking, *deranged* — how else can a mind which is "enmity against God" be described? But by grace his mind has been restored to sanity: illustrated by the demoniac healed by Christ, "sitting, and clothed, and in his right mind" (Mark 5:15); or as 2 Timothy 1:7, expresses it, "For God hath not given us the spirit of fear, but of power, and of love, and of *a sound mind.*" It is true his original carnality ("the flesh") still remains, ever seeking to regain complete control of his mind; but Divine grace suffers it not to *so* succeed that his mind ever becomes "enmity against God." There will be risings of rebellion against His providences, but a renewed person will nevermore hate God.

A real and radical change of heart Godwards will, in the fourth place, be marked by a thoroughly altered attitude *towards sin.* And again we say, it cannot be otherwise. Sin is that "abominable thing" which God "hates" (Jer. 44:4), and therefore that heart in which the love of God is shed abroad will hate it too. Sin is "the transgression of the Law" (1 John 3:4), and therefore each one who has been brought to "delight in the Law" will detest sin and earnestly seek to resist its solicitations. That which formerly was his native element has become repugnant to his spiritual inclinations. Sin is now his heaviest burden and acutest grief. Whereas the giddy worldling craves after its pleasures and the covetous seek after its riches, the deepest longing of the renewed soul is to be completely rid of the horrible activities of indwelling sin. He has already been delivered from its reigning power, for God has dethroned it from its former dominion over the heart, but it still rages within him, frequently gets the better of him, causes him many a groan, and makes him look forward with eager longing to the time when he shall be delivered from its polluting presence.

Another important and integral part of the great change consists in the soul's deliverance from the toils of Satan. Where the heart has really undergone a radical change of disposition and attitude toward God, toward His Law, and toward sin, the great Enemy has lost his hold on that person. The Devil's power over mankind lies in his keeping them in ignorance of the true God, in the scorning of His Law, in holding them in love with sin; and hence it is that he "hath blinded the minds of them that believe not, lest the light of the glorious Gospel of Christ. . . should shine unto them" (2 Cor.4:4). While God permits him to succeed therein, men are his captives, his slaves, his prisoners, held fast by the cords of their lusts. But it was announced of the coming Saviour that He would "proclaim liberty to the captives and the opening of the prison to them that are bound" (Isa. 61:1). Accordingly when He appeared we are told that He not only healed the sick, but also "all that were oppressed of the Devil" (Acts 10:38). The regenerate have been delivered "from the power of Satan" (Acts 26:18; Col. 1:13) and made "the Lord's free men." True, he is still suffered to harass and tempt them from without, but cannot succeed without their consent; and if they steadfastly resist him, he flees from them.

In those five aspects of the great change we may perceive the *begun reversal* of what took place at man's apostasy from God. What were the leading elements in the Fall? No doubt they can be expressed in a variety of ways, but do they not consist, essentially, of these? First, in giving ear unto Satan and heed to the senses of the body, instead of to the Word of God. It was in parleying with the Serpent that Eve came under his power. Second, in preferring the pleasures of sin (the forbidden fruit which now made such a powerful appeal to her affection — Gen. 3:6) rather than communion with her holy Maker. Third, in transgressing God's Law by an act of deliberate disobedience (Rom. 5:19). Fourth, in the loss of their primitive purity: "and the eyes of them both were opened, and they knew that they were naked, and they sewed figleaves together and made them aprons" (Gen. 3:7). Their physical eyes were open previously (!) but now they had a discovery of the consequences of their sin: a guilty sense of shame crept over their souls, their innocence was gone, they perceived what a miserable plight they were now in — stripped of their original righteousness, condemned by their own conscience.

Fifth, in becoming alienated from God: "And they heard the voice of the Lord God walking in the garden in the cool of the day" (Gen. 3:8). And what was their response? Did they rejoice at His gracious condescension in thus paying them a visit? Did they welcome their opportunity to cast themselves upon His mercy? Or did they even fall down before Him in brokenhearted confession of their excuseless offence: Far otherwise. When the Serpent spoke, Eve promptly gave ear to and conferred with him; but now that the voice of the Lord God was audible, she and her guilty partner fled from Him. "Adam and his wife hid themselves from the presence of the Lord among the trees of the garden." A guilty conscience warned them that it was the approach of that Judge whose Law they had broken, and they were terror-stricken at the prospect of having a face-to-face meeting with the One against whom they had rebelled. They dared not look upon Holiness incarnate, and therefore sought to escape from His presence. Thereby they evidenced they had *died spiritually* — their hearts being separated and alienated from Him! Their understanding was "darkened" and their hearts in a condition of "blindness" (Eph. 4:18); a spirit of madness now possessed them, as appears in their vain attempt to hide among the trees from the eyes of Omniscience.

resulting in the loss of their primitive purity and their consequent alienation from God. The attentive reader will observe those things are in the inverse order of those mentioned above as constituting the five leading characteristics of the great change wrought in those who are the favoured subjects of the miracle of grace. Nor is the reason for that far to seek: *conversion* is a turning round, a right-about face, a being restored to a proper relation and attitude toward God. Let us employ a simple illustration. If I journey five miles from a place and then determine to return to it, must I not re-traverse the fifth mile before coming to the fourth, and tread again the fourth before I arrive at the third, and so on until I reach the original point from which I departed? Was it not thus with the ragged and famished prodigal, who had journeyed into the far country: he must return unto the Father's House if he would obtain food and clothing.

If the great change be the *reversing* of what occurred at the Fall, then the order of its constituents should necessarily be viewed *inversely*. First, being restored to our original relation unto God, which was one of spiritual union and communion with Him. That is made possible and actual by the renewing us after His image, which consists of "righteousness and true holiness," a saving and experimental knowledge of His ineffable perfections; or in other words, by the renovation and moral purification of our souls, for it is only the "pure in heart" (Matt. 5:8) who see God as He actually is — our rightful Lord, our everlasting Portion. Only then does the Divine Law have its due and true place in our hearts: its authority being owned, its spirituality esteemed, the fulfilling of its holy and just requirements being our sincere and resolute aim. Obviously it cannot be until we have a right attitude toward God, until our hearts truly love Him, until after His Law becomes the rule and director of our lives, that we can perceive the exceeding sinfulness of sin, and consequently loathe, resist and mourn over it. And just so far as *that* be the case with us, and we morally delivered from the power of Satan: while the heart beats true to God the solicitations of His enemy will be repellent to us rather than attractive.

But let us point out once more that this great change is not completed by a single act of the Spirit upon or within the soul, but occurs in distinct *stages*: it is commenced at regeneration, continues throughout the whole process of our experimental sanctification, and is only consummated at our glorification. Thus, regeneration is only the *begun* reversing of what occurred at the Fall. The very fact that regeneration is spoken of as a Divine begetting and birth at once intimates there is there only the beginning of the spiritual life in the soul, and that there is need for the growth and development of spiritual life in the soul, and that there is need for the growth and development of the same. "He which hath begun a good work in you will finish it" (Phil. 1:6) is the plain declaration and blessed assurance of what is implied by the "birth," and such statements as "the inward man is renewed day by day" (2 Cor. 4:16) and our being "changed into the same image *from* glory *to* glory as by the Spirit of the Lord" (2 Cor. 3:18) tell us something of the Divine operations within the souls of the regenerate while the great change is continued and brought, little by little, unto completion. That miracle of grace which was begun at regeneration is gradually carried forward in us by the process of sanctification, which appears in our growth in grace or the development of our graces.

If the reader desires a more detailed analysis and description of what that process consists of, how the great change is carried forward in us by sanctification, we may delineate it thus. First, by the illumination of the understanding which enables the believer to grow "in the knowledge of the

Lord" and gives him a clearer and fuller perception of His will. Second, by the elevation and refining of the affections, the Spirit drawing them forth unto things above, fixing them on holy objects, assimilating the heart thereto.Third, by the emancipation of the will, God working in the soul "both to will and to do of His good pleasure," giving us both the desire and the power to concur with Him, for He deals with us not as mere automatons but ever as moral agents. Thus it is our responsibility to *seek* illumination, to prayerfully study His Word for the same, to occupy our minds (by constant meditation) and exercise our hearts with spiritual objects, and to diligently seek his enablement to avoid everything which would hinder and use all the means appointed for the promotion of our spiritual growth. As we do so, that process will issue and appear, fourth, in the rectification of our life.

From what has just been pointed out it plainly appears that they err greatly who suppose that regeneration consists of nothing more than the communication of a new nature or principle to an individual, leaving everything else in him just as it was before. It is the person himself who is regenerated, his whole soul which is renewed, so that all its faculties and powers are renovated and enriched thereby. How can everything else in him be unchanged, how otherwise can we designate the blessed transformation which the miracle of grace has wrought in him, than by styling it "a great change" — a real, radical and thorough one; since his understanding (which was previously darkened by ignorance, error and prejudice) is now spiritually enlightened, since his affections (which formerly were fixed only on the things of time and sense) are now set upon heavenly and eternal objects, and since his will (which hitherto was enslaved by sin, being "free *from* righteousness" — Rom. 6:20) is now emancipated from its bondage, being "free *from sin*" (Rom. 6:18). That glorious transformation, that supernatural change, is what we chiefly have in mind when we speak of "the moral purification" of the soul.

Just as the Fall introduced the principle of sin into man's being, which resulted in the death of his soul Godwards — for death is ever the wages of sin — so in the reversing of the Fall, a principle of holiness is conveyed to man's soul, which results in his again being spiritually alive unto God. Just as the introduction of sin vitiated and corrupted all the faculties of the soul, so the planting of a principle of holiness within vitalizes and purifies all its faculties. We say again that man lost no portion of his original tripartite nature by the Fall, nor was he deprived of any of his faculties, but he did lose all *power* to use them Godwards and for His glory, because they came completely under the dominion of sin and were defiled by it. And again we say that man receives no addition to his original constitution by regeneration, nor is any new faculty then bestowed upon him, but he *is* now empowered (to a considerable degree) to use his faculties Godwards and employ them in His service; because so long as he maintains communion with God they are under the dominion of grace and are ennobled, elevated, and empowered by the renewing of the Spirit.

Those then were the essential elements in the Fall, or the several steps in man's departure from God. A parleying with and coming under the power of the Devil, sin's being made attractive in their sight, inclining unto the act of disobedience,

CONCLUSION

That which occasions the honest Christian the most difficulty and distress as he seeks to ascertain whether a miracle of grace has been wrought within him is the discovery that so much remains what it always was, yea, often his case appears to be much *worse* than formerly — more risings of opposition to God, more surgings of pride, more hardness of heart, more foul imaginations. Yet that very consciousness of and grief over indwelling corruptions is, itself, both an effect and an evidence of the great change. It is proof that such a person *has* his eyes open to see and a heart to feel evils which previously he was blind unto and insensible of. An unregenerate person is not troubled about the weakness of his faith, the coldness of his affections, the stirrings of self within. *You* were not yourself while you were dead Godwards! But if such things now exercise you deeply, if your eyes be open to and you mourn over that within to which no fellow creature is privy, must you not be very different now from what you once were?

But, asks the exercised reader, if I have been favoured with a supernatural change of heart, how can such horrible experiences consist therewith? Surely if my heart had been made pure there would not still be a filthy and foul sea of iniquity within me! Dear friend, that filth has been in you from birth, but it is only since you were born again that you have beocme increasingly *aware* of its presence. A pure heart is not one from which all sin has been removed, as is clear from the histories of Abraham, Moses, David. The heart is not made wholly pure in this life: as the understanding is only enlightened in part (much ignorance and error still remaining), so at regeneration the heart is cleansed but in part. Observe that Acts 15:9, does not say "purified their hearts by faith," but "purifying" — a continued process. A pure heart is one which is attracted by "the beauty of holiness" and longs to be fully conformed thereunto, and therefore one of the surest proofs I possess a pure heart is my abhorring and grieving over impurity — as Lot dwelling in Sodom *"vexed* his righteous soul" by what he saw and heard there.

Then are we not obliged to conclude that the Christian has *two* "hearts" — the one pure and the other impure? Perhaps the best way for us to answer that question is to point out what is imported by the "heart" as that term is used in Scripture. In a few passages, where it is distinguished from the "mind" (1 Sam. 2:35; Heb. 8:10) and from the "soul" (Deut. 6:5), the heart is restricted to the affections; but generally it has reference to *the whole inner man,* for in other places it is the seat of the intellectual faculties too, as in "I gave my heart to know wisdom," etc. (Eccl. 1:17) — I applied my *mind* unto its investigation. In its usual and wider signification the "heart" connotes the one indwelling the body. "The heart in the Scriptures is variously used: sometimes for the mind and understanding, sometimes for the will, sometimes for the affection, sometimes for the conscience.. *Generally* it denotes the whole soul of man and all the faculties of it" (J. Owen). We have carefully tested that statement by the Word and confirmed it. The following passages make it clear that the "heart" has reference to the man himself as distinguished from his body.

Its first occurrence is, "God saw that the wickedness of man was great in the earth and every imagination of the *thoughts of* his heart was only evil

53

continually" (Gen. 6:5). "Before I had spoken in my heart" (Gen. 24:45) plainly means "within myself." It does so in "Esau said in his heart" — determined in himself (Gen. 27:41). "Now Hannah, she spake in her heart" (1 Sam. 1:13). "Examine *me*, O Lord, prove me: try my reins [motives] and my *heart*" (Psa. 26:2) — my inner man. "With my whole heart [my entire inner being] have I sought Thee" (Psa. 26:2). In the New Testament the "mind" often has the same force. On Romans 12:2, C. Hodge pointed out, "The word *nous* ["mind"] is used, as it is here frequently in the New Testament (Rom. 1:28; Eph. 4:17, 23; Col. 2:18, etc.). In all these and similar cases it does not differ from the heart, i.e. in its wider sense, for *the whole soul*." Ordinarily, then, the "heart"signifies the whole soul, the "inner man," the "hidden man of the heart" (1 Pet. 3:4) at which God ever looks (1 Sam. 16:7).

Now "the heart" of the natural man (that is, his entire soul — understanding affections, will, conscience) is "deceitful above all things, and desperately wicked" (Jer. 17:9), which is but another way of saying he is "totally depraved" — the whole of his inner being is corrupt. And therefore God bids us "Circumcise yourselves to the Lord and take away the foreskins of your hearts . . . *wash thine heart* from wickedness [in true repentance from the love and pollution of sin] that thou mayest be saved" (Jer.4:4, 14). Yea He bids men "Cast away from you all your transgressions . . . and make you a new heart" (Ezek. 18:31), and holds them responsible so to do. That man cannot effect this change in himself by any power of his own is solely because he is bound by the cords of his sins: the very essence of his depravity consists in being of the contrary spirit. So far from excusing him, that only aggravates his case, and compliance with those precepts is as much man's duty and as proper a subject for exhortation as is faith, repentance, love to God. So in the New Testament, "purify your hearts ye double minded" (James 4:8).

"Make you a new heart." But, says the awakened and convicted sinner, that is the very thing which I am unable to produce: alas, what shall I do? Why, cast yourself upon the mercy and power of the Lord, and say to Him as the leper did, "If Thou wilt, Thou canst make me clean." Beg Him to work *in* you what He requires *of* you. Nay, more, lay hold of His Word and plead with Him: Thou hast made promise "A new heart also will I give you" (Ezek. 36:26), so "do as Thou hast said" (2 Sam. 7:25). It is a blessed fact that God's promises are as large as His exhortations, and for each of the latter there is one of the former exactly meeting it. Does the Lord bid us circumcise our hearts (Deut. 10:16)? Then He assures His people "I will circumcise thine heart" (Deut. 30:16). Does He bid us purify our heart (James 4:8)? He also declares "From all your filthiness and from all your idols will I cleanse you" (Ezek. 36:25). Are Christians told to cleanse themselves "from all filthiness of the flesh and spirit, perfecting holiness in the fear of God" (2 Cor. 7:1)? Then they are promised "He which hath begun a good work in you will finish it."

God, then, does not leave the hearts of His people as they were born into this world, and as they are described in Jeremiah 17:9. No, blessed be His name, He works a miracle of grace within them, which changes the whole of their inner man. Spiritual life is communicated to them, Divine light illumines them, a principle of holiness is planted within them. That principle of holiness is a fountain of purity, from which issue streams of godly desires, motives, endeavours, acts. It is a supernatural habit residing in every faculty of the soul, giving a new direction to them, inclining them Godwards. Divine grace is imparted to the soul subjectively, so that it has entirely new propensities unto God and holiness and newly created antipathies to sin and Satan, making us willing to endure suffering for Christ's sake rather than to retain the friendship of the world. To make us partakers of His *holiness* is the substance and sum of God's purpose of grace for us, both in election (Eph. 1:4), regeneration (Eph. 4:24), and all His dealings with us afterwards (Heb. 12:10). Not that finite creatures can ever be participants of the essential holiness of God, either by imputation or transubstantiation, but only by fashioning us in the *image* thereof.

It is the communication of Divine grace, or the planting within us of the principle and habit of holiness, which both purifies the heart or soul, and which gives the death-wound unto indwelling sin. Grace is not only a Divine attribute of benignity and free favour that is exercised *unto* the elect, but it is also a powerful influence that works *within* them. It is in this latter sense the term is used when God says "My grace is sufficient for thee," and when the apostle decalred "by the grace of God, I am what I am." That communicated grace makes the heart "honest" (Luke 8:15), "tender" (2 Kings 22:10), "pure" (Matt. 5:8). An *honest* heart is one that abhors hypocrisy and pretence, that is fearful of being deceived, that desires to know the truth about itself at all costs, that is sincere and open, that bares itself to the Sword of the Spirit. A "tender" heart is one that is *pliant* Godwards: that of the unregenerate is likened unto the "nether" millstone" (Job 41:24), but that which is wrought upon by the Spirit resembles wax — receptive to His impressions upon it (2 Cor. 3:3). It is *sensitive* — like a tender plant — shrinking from sin and making conscience of the same. It is compassionate, gentle, considerate.

In addition to our previous remarks thereon, we would add that a heart (or "soul") which has been made inchoately yet radically pure, and which is being continually purified, is one in which the love of God has been shed abroad, and therefore it loathes what He loathes; one wherein the fear of the Lord dwells, so that evil is hated and departed from. It is one from which the corrupting love of the world has been cast out. A pure heart is one wherein faith is operative (Acts 15:9), attracting and conforming it unto a Holy Object, drawing the affections unto things above. It is one from which self has been deposed and Christ enthroned, so that it sincerely desires and earnestly endeavours to please and honour Him in all things. It is one that is purged, progressively, from ignorance and error by apprehending and obeying the Truth (1 Peter 1:22). A pure heart is one that makes conscience of evil thoughts, unholy desires, foul imaginations, which grieves over their prevalency and weeps in secret for indulging them. The purer the heart becomes, the more is it aware of and distressed by inward corruptions.

The Puritans were wont to say that at regeneration sin receives its "death-wound." We are not at all sure what exactly they meant by that expression, nor do we know of any Scripture which expressly warrants it — certainly such passages as Romans 6:6,7, and Galatians 5:24, do not; yet we have no objection to it providing it be understood something like this. When faith truly lays hold of the atoning sacrifice of Christ the soul is for ever delivered from the condemnation and guilt of sin, and it can never again obtain legal "dominion" over him. By the moral purification of the soul it is cleansed from the prevailing love and power of sin, so that the lusts of the flesh are detested and resisted. Sin is divested of its reigning power over the faculties of the soul, so that full and willing subjection is no longer rendered to it. Its dying struggles are hard and long, powerfully felt within us, and though God grants brief respites from its ragings, it breaks forth with renewed force and causes us many a groan.

In our earlier days we rejected the expression "a change of heart" because we confounded it with "the flesh." The heart *is* changed at regeneration, but "the flesh" is *not* purified or spiritualized, though it ceases to have uncontrolled and undisputed dominion over the soul. Indwelling sin is not eradicated, but its reign is broken and can no longer produce hatred of God. The appetites and tendencies of "the flesh" in a Christian are precisely the same after he is born again as they were before. They are indeed "subdued" by grace, and conversion is often followed by such inward peace and joy it appears as though they were dead, but they soon seek to reassert themselves, as Satan left Christ "for a season" (Luke 4:13), but later renewed his assaults. Nevertheless, grace opposes sin, the "spirit" or principle of holiness strives against the flesh, preventing it from having full sway over the soul. As life is opposed to death, purity to impurity, spirituality to carnality, so there is henceforth experienced within the soul a continual and sore conflict between sin and grace, each striving for the mastery.

While then it be true that there are two distinct and diverse springs of action in the Christian, the one prompting to evil and the other unto good, it is better to speak of them as two "principles" than "natures." To conceive of there being two minds, two wills, or two hearts in him, is no more warrantable than to affirm he has two souls, which would mean two moral agents, two centres of responsibility, which would destroy the identity of the individual and involve us in hopeless confusion of thought. "Take heed, brethren, lest there be in any of you an evil heart of unbelief, in departing from the living God" (Heb 3:12) would be meaningless if the saint possessed *two* "hearts" — the one incapable of anything *but* unbelief the other incapable of unbelief. The Christian is a unit, a person with one heart or soul, and he is responsible to watch and be sober, to be constantly on his guard against the workings of his corruptions, to prevent sin hardening his heart so that he comes under the power of unbelief and turns away from God.

"Incline my heart [my whole soul] unto Thy testimonies and not to covetousness" (Psa. 119:36). This is another one of many verses which expose the error of a Christian's having two "hearts," the one carnal and the other spiritual, and making them synonymous with "the flesh" and "the spirit." It would be useless my asking God to incline "the flesh" (indwelling sin) unto His testimonies for it is radically opposed unto them. Equally necessary is it for me to ask God *not* to incline "the Spirit" (indwelling grace) unto covetousness, for it is entirely holy. But no difficulty remains if we regard the "heart" as the inner man: "incline *me* unto Thy testimonies," etc. The saint longs after complete conformity unto God's will but is conscious of much within him that is prone to disobedience, and therefore he prays that the habitual bent of his thoughts and affections may be unto heavenliness rather than worldliness: let the reasons and motives unto godliness Thou hast set before me in Thy Word be made effectual by the powerful operations of Thy Spirit.

The heart of man must have an object unto which it is inclined or whereto it cleaves. The thoughts and affections of the soul cannot be idle or be without some object on which to place them. Man was made for God, to be happy in the enjoyment of Him, to find in Him a satisfying portion, and when he apostatized from God he sought satisfaction in the creature. While the heart of fallen man be devoid of grace it is wholly carried out to the things of time and sense. As soon as he is born, he follows his carnal appetites and for the first few years is governed entirely by his senses. Sin occupies the throne of his heart, and though conscience may interpose some check, it has no power to incline the soul Godwards, and sin cannot be dethroned by anything but a miracle of grace. That miracle consists in giving the soul a prevailing and habitual bent Godwards. The heart is taken off from the *love of* base objects and set upon Christ, yet *we* are required to keep our hearts with all diligence, mortify our lusts, and seek the daily strengthening of our graces.

Great as is the change effected in the soul by the miracle of grace, yet, as said before, it is neither total nor complete, but is carried forward during the whole subsequent process of sanctification, a process that involves a daily and lifelong conflict within the believer, so that his "experience" is like that described in Romans 7:13-25. The Christian is not the helpless slave of sin, for he resists it — to speak of a "helpless victim" *fighting* is a contradiction in terms. So far from being helpless, the saint can do all things through Christ strengthening him (Phil. 4:13). As a new object has won his heart, his duty is to serve his new Master: "yield yourselves unto God as those that are alive from the dead, and your members as instruments of righteousness unto God" (Rom. 6:13) — use to His glory the same faculties of soul as you as you formerly did in the pleasing of self. The Christian's responsibility consists in resisting his evil propensities and acting according to his inclinations and desires after holiness.

The great change in and upon the Christian will be completed when dawns that "morning without clouds," when the Day breaks "and the shadows flee away." For then shall he not only see the King in His beauty, see Him face to face, but he shall be made "like Him," fashioned unto the body of His glory, fully and eternally conformed unto the image of God's Son.

ENJOYING GOD'S BEST

Since God has foreordained whatsoever comes to pass, to speak of an enjoying of His best (rather than His second or third best) and *missing* His best, strikes him as meaningless if not erroneous expressions. Before proceeding farther let us explain what we intend by "enjoying God's best." We mean (as we wrote two years ago) for the saint to have daily communion with God, to walk in the light of His countenance, for His Word to be sweet unto our taste, light to our understanding, strength to the inner man. It is for prayer to be a delight, for answers of peace to be received without intermission, for the channel of supplies to remain unchoked, open. It is to have the mind stayed upon Him, to have a conscience void of offence, to have full assurance of our acceptance in Christ. It is for our graces to be kept healthy and vigorous, so that faith, hope, love, meekness, patience, zeal, are in daily exercise. And such *should be* the experience of every Christian.

By God's "best" we mean a personal experience of His approbation; a manifest enjoyment of His favour in grace, in providence, and in nature. It is not to be limited unto the receiving of His special favours in a spiritual way, but includes as well His interpositions on our temporal behalf. It is to have the blessing of the Lord upon our lives, in all their varied aspects and relations, upon the soul and body alike. It is to enjoy the sense of His approval, and have Him showing Himself strong in our behalf. Though it does not mean that such a one will be exempted from the ordinary vicissitudes and trials of life, but rather that such will be sanctified unto him and result in increased blessing, for they not only make a way for God to put forth His power in delivering him from them or elevating his heart above them, but they also serve for the developing of his graces and provide opportunities for him to "glorify Him in the fire"; nevertheless, it *does* mean that such a one will escape those troubles and afflictions in which the follies of so many Christians involve them: it does mean that he will be immune from those sore chastisements which disobedience and a course of backsliding necessarily entail.

Before considering those just requirements of God which must be met if we are to enjoy His best, let us point out that the particular aspect of truth which is here engaging our attention concerns not the Divine decrees, but rather the Divine *government*: for the one consists solely of the exercise of God's sovereign will, whereas the other is concerned also with the discharge of our responsibility. In no sense whatever is there the slightest failure in God's accomplishment of His eternal purpose, either as a whole, or in any of its parts; but in many respects God's people fail to possess their possessions and enjoy those privileges and blessings to which the blood of Christ entitles them. This subject presents no difficulty to the writer, except the finding of suitable language to accurately express his thoughts; nor should it to the reader. The formation and the effectuation of God's eternal decrees are in no wise affected by man: he can neither delay nor hasten the same. But the present government of this world by God *is*, in large measure, affected and determined by the actions of men (His own people included), so that in this life they are, to a very considerable extent, made to reap according as they sow, both in spirituals and in temporals.

It is not sufficiently realized that the Bible has far, very far, more to say about this *present life* than it has about the future one, that it makes known the secrets of temporal felicity as well as everlasting bliss. Granted that the latter is of immeasurably more importance than the former, yet the one is the prelude to the other, and unless God be our satisfying Portion here, He certainly will not be so hereafter. In their zeal to tell men how to escape from Hell and make sure of Heaven, many evangelical preachers have had all too little to say upon our conduct on earth, and consequently many who entertain no doubt whatever that they will inhabit a mansion in the Father's house, are not nearly so much concerned about their present walk and warfare as they should be; and even though they reach their desired haven, such slackness results in great loss to them now and will do so for ever. The teaching of Holy Writ is the very reverse of the plan followed by many an "orthodox pulpit": it not only gives much prominence to, but in Old and New Testament alike its main emphasis is on, our life in *this* world, giving instruction how we are to conduct ourselves here now.

In like manner, there has been a grievous departure from the Analogy of Faith in the presentation of the attitude of God and His conduct towards men. Few indeed who have stressed the sovereignty of God have given even a proportionate place to His governmental dealings, either with nations or with individuals, the elect or the reprobate. Yet for every passage in His Word which speaks of God's eternal counsels, there are scores which describe His time dealings, and for every verse which alludes to God's secret or decretive will, there is a hundred which describe His revealed or preceptive will. Blessed indeed is it to ponder God's predestinating grace; equally important is it that we study those principles which regulate His providential dealings with us. The governmental ways of God, that is His dealings with us in this life, both in our spiritual and temporal affairs, are determined by something more than an arbitrary sovereignty. God has established an inseparable connection between our conduct and its consequences, and He acts in such a way toward us as to make manifest the pleasure He takes in righteousness and to give encouragement to those performing it; as He evidences His displeasure against the unrighteous and makes us to smart for the same.

It is a very great and serious mistake to conceive of the sovereignty of God as swallowing up all His perfections, and to attribute all His actions unto the mere exercise of His imperial will. Holy Writ does not; nor should we do so. Instead, much is said therein of God's acting both in mercy and righteousness, for *they* are the chief principles which regulate His governmental ways. It is true that mercy is shown by mere prerogative (Rom. 9:18), but not so with righteousness. God can no more suspend the operation of His righteousness than He can cease to be. "The righteous Lord loveth righteousness" (Psa. 11:7); "the Lord is righteous in all His ways" (Psa. 145:17); "Righteousness and judgment are the habitation of His throne" (Psa. 97:2). It was predicted of the Messiah that "righteousness should be the girdle of His loins" (Isaiah 11:5), and we are told that since He loved righteousness and hated iniquity "*therefore* God, Thy God, hath anointed Thee with the oil of gladness above Thy fellows" (Psa. 45:7). Alas that so many have completely lost the balance between God's sovereignty and God's righteousness. It is His *righteousness* which regulates all His dealings with the sons of men now, as it is "in righteousness He will judge" them in the Day to come. It is His righteousness which *requires* God to punish vice and reward virtue, and therefore does He bless His obedient children and chasten His refractory ones.

The central thing which we wish to make clear and to impress upon the reader is that God has established an inseparable connection between holiness and happiness, between our pleasing of Him and our enjoyment of His richest blessing; that since we are always the losers by sinning, so we are always the gainers by walking in the paths of righteousness, and that there will be an exact ratio between the measure in which we walk therein and our enjoyment of "the peaceable fruits of rightousness." God has declared "them that honour Me, I will honour" (1 Sam. 2:30),, and *that* expresses the general principle which we are here seeking to explain and illustrate, namely that God's governmental dealings with us are regulated by our attitude toward Him and our conduct before Him: for in proportion as we honour the Lord, so will He honour us. But suppose we fail to honour God, suppose we do not obtain from Him that grace which He is ever ready to give unto those who earnestly seek it in a right way — what then? Why, we shall not enter into His best for us; we shall miss it. For as the same verse goes on to tell us, "and they that despise Me shall be lightly esteemed."

"This Book of the Law shall not depart out of thy mouth, but thou shalt meditate therein; for *then* thou shalt make thy way prosperous, and then thou shalt have good success" (Joshua 1:8). That expresses in plain and simple language the basis on which we may enter into and enjoy God's best for us. The believer is not to be regulated by his own inclinations or lean unto his own understanding; he is not to be governed by any consideration of expediency or the pleasing of his fellows, but seek to please God in all things, being actuated by a "thus saith the Lord" in everything he does. Nothing less than full and constant obedience to God is what is required of him. However distasteful to the flesh, whatever sneers it may produce from professing Christians, the saint must rigidly and perpetually act by the Rule that God has given him to walk by. In so doing he will be immeasurably the gainer, for the path of *obedience* is the path of *prosperity*. Conformity unto the revealed will of God may indeed entail trial, nevertheless it will be richly compensated in this life, both in spiritual and temporal bounties.

It cannot be too strongly insisted upon that the path of God's precepts is the way of *blessing*. Though the treading thereof incurs the frowns of the profane world, and the criticisms of not a few in the professing world, yet it ensures the smile and benediction of our Master! Those words "for then shalt thou make thy way *prosperous*" are from the mouth of "the God of Truth" and are to be received by us without the slightest quibbling, and treasured in our hearts. The "prosperity" does not always immediately appear, for faith has to be tried and patience developed, yet in the long run it will most surely be found that in keeping the Divine commandments "there is great reward" (Psa. 19:11). So Joshua found it: he adhered strictly to the Divine Law, and God crowned his labours with success; and that, dear reader, is recorded for our encouragement. Yet if we would prosper as Joshua did, then we must act as he did! That conditional promise made to Joshua was very far from being a special one made to him only — rather does it belong equally to every servant and child of God, for His governmental ways have been the same in all dispensations. From the beginning of human history it has always been true, and to the very end of history it will continue so to be, that "no good thing will He withhold from them that walk uprightly" (Psa. 84:11).

Long before Joshua was born Elihu had affirmed "If they obey and serve Him they shall spend their days in prosperity and their years in pleasure" (Job 36:11); and centuries after Joshua's death, the Holy Spirit declared through Zechariah "Thus saith God, why transgress ye the command of the Lord, that ye cannot prosper?" (2 Chron. 24:30). Nor is there any justification to insist that such statements pertained only to the Mosaic economy. If we unhesitatingly apply to our own day that precious word in Isaiah 1:18, "Come now, let us reason together, saith the Lord: though your sins be as scarlet, they shall be as white as snow, though they be red like crimson, they shall be as wool," is it honest to refuse taking unto ourselves the very next verse "If *ye* be willing and obedient ye shall eat the good of the Land"? The principles which regulate God's providential dealings with His people are in no way altered by any change made in the outward form of His kingdom upon earth. The teaching of the New Testament is equally express: that "Godliness is profitable for *all* things: having promise of the life that *now is* and of that which is to come" (1 Tim. 4:8), yet the fulfilment of that promise is conditional upon our keeping of the Divine precepts, upon our personal piety.

There is a definite *proviso* on which we are warranted to hope for an enjoyment of God's best. That was announced by Joshua and Caleb when they said unto Israel, *"If* the Lord delight in us then He will bring us into this land and give it us" (Num. 14:8). That term "delight" has no reference there unto that Divine love unto the souls of believers which is the source of their salvation, but rather to His complacency in their character and conduct. So also is it to be understood in the words used by David when he was fleeing from the conspiracy of Absalom: "Carry back the ark of God into the city: if I shall find favour in the eyes of the Lord, He will bring me again and show me both it and His habitation. But if He thus say, I have *no delight* in thee; behold, here am I, let Him do to me as seemeth good unto Him" (2 Sam. 15:25, 26). David certainly could not mean by that language, If God have no love for my soul, I am willing to be for ever banished from Him; for such submission is required of none who lives under a dispensation of mercy. Rather did he signify, If God approve not of me as I am the head of His people, let Him take away my life if that so pleaseth Him.

As we must distinguish between the twofold "will," the twofold "counsel" and the twofold "pleasure" of God (see the "Prayers of the Apostles" article in this issue), so we must between His eternal love for and His present delight in us, between His acceptance of us in Christ and the acceptableness of our character and conduct unto Him — it is the *latter* which determines His governmental smile upon us. If any reader deems that distinction an artificial and forced one, then we ask him, Is no differentiation to be made between those words of Christ unto the Father "Thou lovedst Me before the foundation of the world" (John 17:24) and His declaration "Therefore doth My Father love Me because I lay down My life . . . This commandment have I received of My Father" (John 10:17, 18)? Is not one the Father's love of Christ's person, and the other His approbation of His obedience? So again, must we not avoid confounding "I have loved thee with an everlasting love" (Jer. 31:3) and "For the Father loveth you *because* ye have loved Me and have believed that I came out from God" (John 16:27)? Of Enoch it is said "before his translation he had this testimony, that he pleased God" (Heb. 11:5), whereas of Israel in the wilderness He declared "I was grieved with that generation" (Heb. 3:10)!

It must not be inferred from what has been said above that the one who walks in the paths of righteousness brings God into his debt or that he merits favour at His hands. Not so, for nothing that we can do profits *God* anything. and if we rendered perfect obedience unto His every precept, we had merely performed our duty and rendered unto God what is His rightful due. On the other hand, it is very plain that *we* profit from and are the gainers by our obedience. Scripture has not a little to say upon the subject of *rewards*. It goes so far as to teach that the joys of the future will bear a definite relation and proportion to our conduct in the present, such as obtains between sowing and reaping (Gal. 6:7, 8). If then the future rewarding of the saints according to their work (Rev. 22:12) clashes neither with the grace of God nor the merit of Christ, then the *present* rewarding of them cannot do so, for no difference in place or condition can make any difference as to the nature of things. Deity does not hesitate to take as one of His titles "The Lord God of recompenses" (Jer. 51:56), and many are the passages which show Him recompensing righteousness even in this world.

We have already alluded to Psalm 19:11, where we are told of God's statutes and judgments that "in keeping of them there is great reward" and we simply call attention now to the tense of that statement: not "shall be," but *is so* now. A part of that present "reward" is described in such verses as "Great peace have they which love Thy Law, and nothing shall offend [be a "stumbling-block" to] them" (Psa. 119:165); "the work of righteousness [right doing] shall be peace, and the effect of righteousness, quietness and assurance for ever" (Isaiah 32:17). Such too is the testimony of Psalm 58:11, "So that a man shall say, Verily there *is* a reward for the righteous; verily He is a God that judgeth in [governs, administers the affairs of] the earth." "The righteous [i.e. the one whose practices conform to the Rule of Righteousness] shall flourish like the palm tree, he shall grow like a cedar in Lebanon . . . to show that the Lord is upright" (Psa. 92:12-15), i.e. to make it evident that He takes notice of and richly blesses such. "Behold, the righteous shall be recompensed in the earth" (Prov. 11:31). On the other hand, "The Lord will punish Jacob according to his *ways*, according to his doings will He recompense him" (Hosea 12:2).

It is an unalterable law of the Divine government that as we sow, so shall we reap. That principle is enunciated and illustrated all through the Scriptures. On the one hand, "they have sown the wind, and they shall reap the whirlwind" (Hosea 8:7); on the other, "sow to yourselves in righteousness, reap in mercy" (Hosea 10:12). "Even as I have seen, they that plough iniquity and sow wickedness, reap the same" (Job 4:8). "Therefore shall they eat of the fruit of their own way" (Prov. 1:31). "But to him that soweth righteousness shall be a sure reward" (Prov. 11:18). Our Lord taught precisely the same thing when He said, "There is no man that hath left house, or parents or brethren, or wife, or children, for the kingdom of God's sake, who shall not receive manifold more in this *present* time and in the world to come life everlasting" (Luke 18:29, 30). So too the apostles: "He which soweth sparingly, shall reap also sparingly; and he which soweth bountifully shall reap also bountifully" (2 Cor. 9:6). "The fruit of righteousness is sown in peace of them that make peace" (James 3:18). It is lamentable that such passages are so rarely heard from the pulpit.

It is right here that we have the key to a class of passages which has puzzled and perplexed not a few, namely, those which speak of the Lord's *repenting*. To say that such an expression is a figure of speech, God's condescending to employ our language, though true, really *explains* nothing. But the difficulty is at once removed when it be seen that the reference is not to the modifying of God's eternal decrees, but rather unto His governmental ways; signifying that when men alter their attitude and conduct toward Him, the Lord changes in His *dealings* with them — withholding the judgment threatened, or bestowing the blessing which their sins had kept back. The general principle is clearly expressed in, "At what instant I shall speak concerning a nation and concerning a kingdom, to pluck up and to pull down, and to destroy it, *If* that nation against whom I have pronounced turn from their evil, I will repent of the evil that I thought to do unto them. And at what instant I shall speak concerning a nation and concerning a kingdom, to build and to plant it, *If* it do evil in My sight, that it obey not My voice, then I will repent of the good wherewith I said I would benefit them" (Jer. 18:7-10).

There is no "if" whatever about the Divine foreordination, but there *is* in connection with human responsibility. Necessarily so, for in the enforcing thereof the alternatives of recompense must be stated. Many of the woes which God pronounces against kingdoms are not declarations of His eternal decrees or infallible predictions of what is about to take place, but rather ethical intimations of His sore displeasure against sin, and solemn threatenings of what must inevitably follow if there be no change for the better in those denounced: whether or no those impending judgments are to become historic realities is contingent upon their readiness to heed those warnings, or their refusal to do so. The passage quoted above enunciates that basic moral law by which God governs the world, telling us that He approves of obedience and righteousness wherever it be found, and rewards the same; whereas He hates the opposite and punishes it (see Prov. 14:34). Jeremiah 18 sets not before us God as the Determiner of human destiny, but as the Dispenser of temporal awards, governing in equity and in accordance with the discharge of human accountability, showing He is ever ready to prosper the righteous.

The same principle pertains unto the individual. "Then came the sword of the Lord unto Samuel, saying, It repenteth Me that I have set up Saul to be king: for he is turned back from following Me and hath not performed My commandments" (1 Sam. 15:11). That does not mean God *regretted* His former act of enthroning Saul, but that because of his defection the Lord would *reverse* it and depose him (verse 26). Thus we see that God's governmental actions are determined — in part, at least — by man's conduct. We say "in part," for God does not act uniformly, and some of His ways in providence are "past finding out," as when He suffers the righteous to be severely afflicted, and the wicked to flourish like a green bay tree. If righteousness were always visibly rewarded and wickedness punished in this life, there would be no room for the exercise of faith in God's justice, for the Day of Judgment would be anticipated instead of presaged. Nevertheless, if we strike a balance and take the history of each nation or individual as a whole, God's moral government is now apparent, for we are daily made to see and feel that we are the losers by sinning and the gainers by holiness.

If the balance is to be duly preserved here and a proper concept formed of God's moral government, then it requires to be pointed out that His justice is tempered with *mercy*, as well as patience. Therefore does He grant "space to repent," and where that clemency be availed of, God acts accordingly. For, as many of those Divine promises which respect earthly good are conditional upon the performance of obedience, so many of the Divine judgments threatened are averted upon a reformation of manners. "If so be they will hearken, and turn every man from his evil way, that I may repent Me of the evil, which I purpose [better, "think"] to do unto them because of the evil of their doings" (Jer. 26:3). Perhaps the most remarkable example of that is seen in the case of wicked Ahab, who, when he heard the sentence of woe pronounced, "rent his clothes, and put sackcloth upon his flesh, and fasted, and lay in sackcloth, and went softly." And we are told that the Lord said, "*Because* he humbleth himself before Me, I will not bring the evil in his days, but in his son's days" (1 Kings 21:20-29).

Let us now consider more definitely a few of those Scriptures which make known what God requires of us if we are to enter into and enjoy His best. Some of them have already been before us in a general way, but they require to be examined from a more particular viewpoint. "This Book of the Law shall not depart out of thy mouth, but thou shalt meditate therein day and night, that thou mayest observe to do according to all that is written therein; for *then* thou shalt make thy way prosperous, and *then* thou shalt have good success" (Joshua 1:8). That is so plain no interpreter is needed. "Then," first, when our speech is ordered by God's Word, all of our converse being consonant thereto. "The mouth of the righteous speaketh wisdom and his tongue talketh of judgment." And why? "The Law of God is in his heart" (Psa. 31:30, 31). Second, in order thereto, it must be made our constant "meditation." It is by daily pondering the words of Scripture that we obtain a better understanding of them, fix the same in our memories, and become more fully conformed to them in our souls. Third, that our meditation must be with a definite design and practical end: to "do," to walk obediently.

"For the eyes of the Lord run to and fro throughout the whole earth, to show Himself strong in the behalf of those whose heart is perfect toward Him" (2 Chron. 16:9). The word generally used for "perfect" (*tamim*) signifies sincere, but here a different one (*shalem*) is employed, meaning *whole*. A "whole heart' is in contrast with a "divided" one (Hosea 10:2), which pertains to him who vainly seeks to serve two masters, the "double-minded man" who is "unstable in all his ways" (James 1:8). Those with a whole heart love the Lord their God with all their mind, soul and strength. They make Him their Portion, find their delight in Him, constantly seek to please and glorify Him. Their affections are undivided, their aim in life is one, like Caleb they *"wholly* follow the Lord" (Deut. 1:36). And such receive distinctive favours from Him. The "eyes of the Lord" speaks of His knowledge, and their "running to and fro throughout the earth" means that He governs this world in infinite wisdom. The reference is to His *providential* dealings: His eye directs His hand, and both are employed in His giving special supplies and support to those who make Him their All in all. "And he shall be like a tree planted by the rivers of water, that bringeth forth his fruit in his season; his leaf also shall not wither and whatsoever he doeth shall prosper" (Psa. 1:3). *There* is what we intend by one's enjoying God's *best."* But to whom does the "he" refer? Why, to the "blessed man" described in the context. The one who has completely broken with the world: "who walketh not in the counsel of the ungodly, nor standeth in the way of sinners, nor sitteth in the seat of the scornful." Observe that the man whom God pronounces "blessed" is one that is careful about his *walk*. He refuses to follow the advice of the unregenerate. They will urge him to be broad-minded and warn him against being too strict, and press upon him the maxims of the world, but he heeds them not. He is very particular about his associates, knowing that those with whom he is intimate will either be a help or a hindrance to him spiritually. Evil communications corrupt good manners, and therefore he refuses to fraternize with the Christless. And so must you, young Christian, if you desire the smile of God to be upon you.

This opening Psalm strikes the keynote of the whole Psalter, and has for its theme the blessedness of the righteous, i.e. those who tread the paths of righteousness; and contrasts the portion and doom of the ungodly. And the first thing emphasized of that righteous one is that he has turned his back upon the world, for it is at *that* point practical godliness begins. There can be no walking with God, no real communing with Christ, no treading of "the way of peace," until that word is heeded: "Come out from among them and be ye separate, saith the Lord," (2 Cor. 6:17). Second, it is said of this blessed man, "But his delight is in the Law of the Lord, and in His Law doth he meditate day and night." He is completely subject to God's authority and makes His revealed will the rule of his life. Nor does he force himself to do so against his inclinations, for his *delight* is in the same. That is evidenced by its constantly engaging his thoughts, for "where your treasure is, there will your heart be also" (Matt. 6:21). The mind is regulated by the affections: what the heart is most set upon most engages our thoughts — as gold does the covetous. And the one who conforms to the requirements of Psalm 1:1, 2, will certainly experience the blessings of 1:3.

There is the less need for us to dwell upon other passages, for they speak for themselves. "The young lions do lack and suffer hunger, but they that seek the Lord shall not want any good thing" (Psa. 34:10). That is, those who put Him first (Matt. 6:33), who seek Him wholeheartedly (Jer. 29:13), who diligently inquire after His will and earnestly endeavour to please and glorify Him in all things, shall not lack any good — which is assured them as an encouragement for obedience. "No good thing will He withhold from them that walk uprightly" (Psa. 84:11). As the Puritan, T. Brooks, pointed out, "Now this choice, this large promise, is made over only to the upright, and therefore as you would have any share in it maintain your uprightness." In his explanation of "them that walk uprightly," J. Gill included "Who have their conversation according to the Gospel of Christ, and walk in the sincerity of their hearts." "The fear of the Lord is the beginning of wisdom: a good understanding [see margin] have all they that do His commandments" (61:10). Upon which Gill said "Some understand it 'good success' or 'prosperity,'" and added, "such usually have prosperity in soul and *body*, in things *temporal* and spiritual," with which we fully concur.

"Let not mercy and truth forsake thee: bind them about thy neck, write them upon the table of thine heart. *So* shalt thou find favour and good success in the sight of God and man" (Prov. 3:3, 4). Was it not so with Joseph in Egypt (Gen. 39)? Was it not so with David in Saul's household (1 Sam. 18)? Was it not so with Daniel and his fellows in Babylon? "For God giveth to a man that is *good* in His sight, wisdom, and knowledge, and joy" (Eccles. 2:26): the phrase "a man that is good in His sight" is rendered who "pleaseth God" in Ecclesiastes 7:26. The passages which teach that God deals with men in this life according to their conduct are too many to cite, and the marvel is that the minds of so few professing Christians of this age are really affected by them. Take that well-known word, which has been illustrated all through history, "I will bless them that bless thee [Abram], and curse him that curseth thee" (Gen. 12:3), which so far from being exceptional, only exemplifies the principle we are seeking to demonstrate. Take again, "Blessed is he that considereth the poor, the Lord will deliver him in time of trouble; the Lord will preserve him and keep him alive: he shall be blessed upon the earth" (Psa. 42:1, 2).

Consider now some concrete cases. "And the Angel of the Lord called unto Abram out of heaven the second time and said, By Myself have I sworn saith the

Lord, for *because* thou hast done this thing and hast not withheld thy son, thine only son, that in blessing I will bless thee . . . and in thy seed shall all the nations of the earth be blessed, *because* thou hast obeyed My voice" (Gen. 22:15-18). What could possibly be plainer? So again God said to Isaac, "I will make thy seed to multiply as the stars of heaven and will give unto thy seed all these countries . . . *because* that Abram obeyed My voice, and kept My charge, My commandments" etc. (Gen. 26:4,5). "My servant Caleb *because* he had another spirit with him and followed Me fully, *him* will I bring into the land" (Num. 14:24). "Wherefore say, Behold I give unto him [Phinehas] My covenant of peace, and he shall have it, and his seed after him, even the covenant of an everlasting priesthood, *because* he was zealous for his God and made an atonement for the children of Israel" (Num. 25:12,13). "Hebron therefore become the inheritance of Caleb. . . .*because* he wholly followed the Lord God" (Joshua 14:14).

Said David, "The Lord rewarded me according to my righteousness, according to the cleanness of my hands hath He recompensed me" (2 Sam. 22:21). It seems strange that any one possessed of a spiritual mind should be perplexed by these words, for if they be understood according to their original and obvious meaning, there is nothing in them to occasion any difficulty. Let them be read in the light of their context, and they are clear and simple. David was alluding to God's delivering of him from Goliath and Saul, and from others of his foes: what had been his conduct toward them? Had he committed any serious crimes such as warranted their hostility? Had he grievously wronged any of them? Had they justly or unjustly sought his life? Read the record of David's history, and it will be found that it contains not a hint that he coveted the throne or hated Saul. As a fact, he was entirely innocent of any evil designs against any of them who so sorely persecuted him. This is plain from one of his prayers to God, "Let not those who are mine enemies *wrongfully* rejoice over me, neither let them wink with the eye that hated me without a cause" (Psa. 35:19).

It was because David had neither given his enemies just reason for their persecution and because so far from retaliating, he had borne them no malice, that he now enjoyed the testimony of a good conscience. His character had been grievously aspersed and many hideous things laid to his charge, but his conduct had been upright and conscientious to an uncommon degree. " In all his persecutions by Saul, he would not injure him or his party; nay, he employed every opportunity to serve the cause of Israel, though rewarded by envy, treachery and ingratitude" (Thos. Scott). When we are maligned and opposed by men, it is an inestimable consolation to have the assurance of our own heart unto our innocency and integrity, and therefore we should spare no pains when passing through a season of such trial in exercising ourselves "to have always a conscience void of offence, toward God and man" (Acts 24:14). David, then, was not here giving vent to the boasting of a pharasaical spirit, but was avowing his innocency before the bar of *human* equity. One is not guilty of pride in knowing himself to be innocent, nor is he so when realizing that God is rewarding him in providence because of his integrity; for each is an evident matter of fact.

In saying "The Lord rewarded me according to my righteousness" David enunciated one of the principles operative in the Divine government of this world. "Albeit that the dispensations of Divine grace are to the fullest degree sovereign and irrespective of human merit, yet in the dealings of Providence there is often discernible a rule of justice by which the injured are at length avenged and the righteous ultimately delivered" (C. H. Spurgeon). That statement evinces an intelligent grasp of the viewpoint from which David was writing, namely the governmental ways of God in time, and *not* the ground upon which He saves eternally. Those declarations of the Psalmist had nothing whatever to do with his justification in the high court of heaven, but concerned the guiltlessness of his conduct toward his enemies on earth, because of which God delivered him from them. It would indeed be most reprehensible for us to transfer such thoughts as are expressed in 2 Samuel 22:20-28, from the realm of providential government into the spiritual and everlasting kingdom, for *there* grace reigns not only supreme, but alone, in the distribution of Divine favours. On the other hand, a godly man with clear conscience must not deny his own consciousness and hypocritically make himself out to be worse than he is.

There are those who would dismiss by a wave of the hand what has been adduced above by saying, All that is Old Testament teaching, what occurred under the Dispensation of Law. But such an objection is utterly pointless, for the principles of the Divine government are *the same* in every era, and therefore the teaching of the New Testament on this subject is identical with that of the Old. For example: "Blessed are the merciful for they shall obtain mercy" (Matt. 5:7). That has nothing whatever to do with "salvation by works," for in those verses Christ is describing the character of His true disciples. Here He tells us they are "merciful," and in consequence "shall obtain mercy." It is not that God requires the unregenerate to be merciful in order to entitle them unto His saving mercy, but rather that the unregenerate *are* merciful, and according as they act in their true character, so will God order His governmental ways and paternal discipline toward them — "with what measure ye mete, it shall be measured to you again" (Matt. 7:2). On the one hand, "with the merciful, Thou wilt show Thyself merciful" (Psa. 18:25); on the other, "But if ye forgive not men their trespasses, neither will your Father forgive your trespasses" (Matt. 6:15).

That both Christ and the Father act toward Christians in keeping with their conduct is clear from John 14:21, 23 — such "manifestations" are withheld from those who fail to walk obediently. "For God is not unrighteous to forget your work and labour of love which ye have showed toward His name, in that ye have ministered to the saints, and do minister" (Heb. 6:10), which clearly implies that He would be unrighteous if He did not reward their benevolence. "For he that will love life and see good days, let him refrain his tongue from evil and his lips that they speak no guile. Let him eschew evil and do good; let him seek peace, and ensue it" (1 Peter 3:10, 11). "We have here an excellent prescription for a comfortable, happy life in this querulous, ill-natured world" M. Henry). To those who follow that prescription, Gill said, "such shall inherit the blessing, both *here* and hereafter." "Whatsoever we ask, we receive of Him, *because* we keep His commandments and do those things that are pleasing in His sight" (1 John 3:22)! *"Because* thou hast kept the Word of My patience, I also will keep thee from the hour of temptation which shall come upon all the world to try them that dwell upon the earth" (Rev. 3:10).

MISSING GOD'S BEST

Having shown at some length that the Old and New Testament alike teach there *is* such a thing as entering into any enjoying God's best — that if we meet His just requirements He will make our way prosperous — we must turn now to the darker side of the subject, and face the fact that it is sadly possible to *miss* God's best and bring down upon ourselves adversity. God has not only promised "no good thing will He withhold from them that walk uprightly" (Psa. 84:11), but He has also plainly informed us "Your iniquities have turned away these things, and your sins have withholden good things from you" (Jer. 5:25). Upon which John Gill said, "these mercies were kept back from them in order to humble them, and to bring them to a sense of their sins, and an acknowledgement of them." Adversities do not come upon us at haphazard, but from the hand of God; nor does He appoint them arbitrarily, but righteously. God will no more wink at the sins of His people than He will at those of the worldlings: were He to do so, He would not maintain the honour of His house. As Manton also pointed out on Jeremiah 5:25, "If there be any restraint of God's blessing it is because of man's sin."

"The way of transgressors is hard" (Prov. 13:15): while no doubt the primary reference there is unto the wicked, yet the principle expressed applies unmistakably to the redeemed as well. If, on the one hand, in keeping God's commandments there is "great reward," on the other hand, the breaking of them involves great loss. If it be true that Wisdom's ways are ways of pleasantness and all her paths are peace (Prov. 3:17), certain it is that if we turn from her ways, we shall be made to smart for it. Alas, how often we stand in our own light and choke the current of God's favours. It is not only an "evil thing" but a "bitter" one to forsake the Lord our God (Jer. 2:19). That is why sin is so often termed "folly," for it is not only a crime against God, but madness toward ourselves. Many are the mischiefs caused by our sinning, the chief of which is that we obstruct the flow of God's blessings. Sin costs us dear, for it not only immediately takes from us, but it prevents our future receiving of Divine bounties. In other words, wilful sinning prevents our receiving God's best for us.

"Believe in the Lord your God, *so* shall ye be established; believe His prophets, *so* shall ye prosper" (2 Chron. 20:20) states the principle clearly enough. Trust in the Lord with all your heart, and your souls shall be settled in peace and joy; receive with submission every discovery of His will through His Word and servants, and His providential smile shall be your portion. But, conversely, lean unto your own understanding and suffer unbelief to prevail, and assurance and tranquility of soul will wane and vanish; let self-will and self-pleasing dominate, and His providences will frown upon you. The connection between conduct and its consequences cannot be broken. Walk in the way of faith and holiness and God is pleased, and will evidence His pleasure toward us; enter the paths of unrighteousness and God is provoked, and will visit His displeasure upon us. When Israel's land was laid waste and their cities were burned, they were told "Hast thou not procured this unto thyself, in that thou hast forsaken the Lord thy God, when He led thee by the way?" (Jer. 2:17). Upon which M. Henry said, "Whatever trouble we are in at any time, we may thank ourselves for it, for we bring it upon our own hands by our forsaking of God." "The curse causeless shall not come" (Prov. 26:2).

Missing God's best is true of the *unsaved*. As long as unbelievers are left in this world, opportunity is given them of escaping from the wrath to come. Therefore they are exhorted – in the Scriptures, if not from the pulpit – "Seek ye the Lord while He may be found, call ye upon Him while He is near" (Isa. 55:6). For the same reason there is a *door* represented as being *open* to them, which the Master of the house will one day rise up and shut to (Luke 13:24, 25). Nothing could more clearly express the danger of delay than the language used in such passages. Nor is there anything in them which at all clashes with the Divine decrees. As one has pointed out, "All allow that men have opportunity in *natural* things to do what they do not, and to obtain what they obtain not; and if that be consistent with a universal providence which performeth all things that are appointed for us (Job. 23:14), why cannot the other consist with the purpose of Him who does nothing without a plan, but worketh all things after the counsel of His own will."

Slothfulness is no excuse in those who refuse to improve their lot; nor is intemperance any extenuation for a man's bringing upon himself physical, financial, and moral disaster. Still less does either prejudice or indolence release any from his accountability to accept the free offer of the Gospel. "Wherefore is there a price in the hand of a fool to get wisdom, seeing he hath no heart to it?" (Prov. 17:16). The "price in his hand" signifies the means and opportunity. "Wisdom" may be understood both naturally and spiritually. The "fool" is the one who fails to obtain what he might well and should procure. The reason he does not is simply that he lacks "a heart" or desire and determination. As M. Henry said, "He has set his heart upon other things, so that he has no heart to do his duty, or to the great concerns of his soul." Such fools the world is full of: they prefer sin to holiness, this world rather than heaven. "He who in his bargains exchanges precious things for trifles is a fool. Thus do men sell their time which is their money given for eternity, and they sell it for things unsatisfying, they sell themselves for naught" (Thomas Goodwin); and thereby they miss God's best.

"Wherefore is there a price in the hand of a fool to get wisdom, seeing he hath no heart to it?" (Prov. 17:16). After interpreting those words first as natural wisdom and knowledge, and "the price" as the worldly substance which a foolish man spends on riotous living, instead of purchasing useful books for the improvement of his mind, none other than John Gill said upon its higher application: "or spiritual wisdom and knowledge: the means of which are reading the Word, frequent opportunities for attending on a Gospel ministry . . . conversation with Gospel ministers and other Christians; but instead of making use of these he neglects, slights and despises them. And it is asked, with some degree of indignation and astonishment, why or to what purpose a fool is favoured with such means? *seeing* he hath no heart to it? to wisdom: he does not desire it, nor to make use of the price or means in order to obtain it; all is lost upon him, and it is hard to account for why he should have this price when he makes such an ill use of it." But Gill created his own difficulty: God provides the non-elect with spiritual means and opportunities to enforce their responsibility, so that their blood shall be upon their own heads, that the blame is *theirs* for missing His best.

But it is the Christian's doing so that we have chiefly in mind. Sad indeed is it to behold so many of them living more under the frown of God than His smile, and sadder still that so few of them have been taught *why* it is so with them, and *how* to recover themselves. The New Testament makes it clear that many of the primitive saints "ran well" for a time, and then something hindered them. Observation shows that the majority of believers "follow the Lord fully" (Num. 14:24) at the *outset* but soon "leave their first love." At the beginning, they respond readily to the promptings of the Spirit and adjust their lives to the requirements of the Word, until some demand is made upon them, some self-denying duty is met with, and they balk. Then the Holy Spirit is grieved, His enabling power is withheld, their peace and joy wane, and a spiritual decline sets in. Unless they put right with God what is wrong — repent of and contritely confess their sad failure — the rod of chastisement falls upon them; but instead of being "exercised thereby" (Heb. 12:11) some fatalistically accept it as "their appointed lot," and are nothing bettered thereby.

Now the Lord has plainly warned His people that if they meet not His just requirements, so far from enjoying His best, adversity will be their portion. "Take good heed therefore unto yourselves, that ye love the Lord your God. *Else* if ye do in any wise go back, and cleave unto the remnant of these nations, even these that remain among you, and shall make marriages with them, and go in unto them and they to you: Know for a certainty that the Lord your God will no more drive out any of these nations from before you; but they shall be snares and traps unto you, and scourges in your sides, and thorns in your eyes, until ye perish from off this good land which the Lord your God hath given you" (Joshua 23:11-13). The Jews held Canaan by the tenure of their obedience, and so do those who belong to "the Israel of God" (Gal. 6:15) now possess and enjoy their spiritual Canaan in proportion to their obedience. But as God has forewarned, "If His children forsake My Law, and walk not in My judgments; if they break My statutes and keep not My commandments; then will I visit their transgression with the rod and their iniquity with stripes. Nevertheless my lovingkindness will I not utterly take from him, nor suffer My faithfulness to fail" (Psa. 89:30-33).

That passage makes it unmistakably clear that while the chastenings from our Father proceed from both His faithfulness and holy love, yet they are also marks of His displeasure; and that while they are designed for our good — the recovery of us from our backsliding — yet they have been provoked by our own waywardness. The Father's rod is not wielded by an arbitrary sovereignty, but by righteousness. It is expressly declared, "For He *doth not afflict willingly* nor grieve the children of men" (Lam. 3:33), but only as we give Him occasion to do so. That important statement has not received the attention it deserves, especially by those who have so focused their thoughts upon God's eternal decrees as to quite lose sight of His governmental ways. Hence the tragic thing is that when chastisement becomes *their* portion, they know of nothing better than to "bow to God's sovereign will," which is very little different in principle from the world's policy of "seeking to make the best of a bad job," or "we must grit our teeth and endure it." Such a fatalistic and supine attitude ill becomes a regenerate soul; instead, he is required to be "exercised thereby."

Only too often such "bowing to the will of God" is so far from being a mark of spirituality, it rather evinces a sluggish conscience. God bids His people "*hear* ye the rod" (Mich. 6:9). It has a message for the heart, but we profit nothing unless we ascertain what the rod is saying to us — why it is God is now smiting us! In order to discover its message, we need to humbly ask the Lord *"show me wherefore Thou contendest with me"* (Job 10:2); "cause me to understand wherein I have erred" (Job. 6:24); reveal to me wherein I have displeased Thee, that I may contritely acknowledge my offence and be more on my guard against a repetition of it. The holiness of God will not tolerate sin in the saints, and when they go on in the same unrepentingly, then He declares, "Therefore, behold, I will hedge up thy way with thorns" (Hos. 3:6). Note well *"thy* way," not "My way." God sets the briars of trials and the sharp thorns of afflictions in the path of His disobedient children. If that suffices not to bring them to their senses, then he adds "and make a wall that she shall not find her paths" — His providences block the realization of their carnal and covetous desires.

"But My people would not hearken to My voice, and Israel would have none of Me. So I gave them up unto their own heart's lusts: they walked in their own counsels. Oh that My people had hearkened unto Me, Israel had walked in My ways! I *should* soon have subdued their enemies and turned My hand against their adversaries . . . He *should* have fed them also with the finest of the wheat, and with honey out of the rock should I have satisfied thee" (Psa. 81:11-16). When we meet with a passage like this our first duty is to receive it with meekness, and not to inquire, How is it to be harmonized with the invincibility of the Divine decrees? Our second duty is to prayerfully endeavour to understand its sense, and not to explain away its terms. We must not draw inferences from it which contradict other declarations of Holy Writ, either concerning the accomplishments of God's purpose or His dealing with us according to our conduct. Instead of reasoning about their teaching, we need to turn these verses into earnest petition begging God to preserve us from such sinful folly as marked Israel on this occasion.

There is nothing in those verses which should occasion any difficulty for the Calvinist, for they treat not of the eternal foreordinations of God, but of His governmental ways with men in this life. For the same reason there is nothing in them which in any wise supports the Arminian delusion that, having created men free moral agents, God is unable to do for them and with them what He desires without reducing them to mere machines. We should then, proceed on that which is obvious in them, and not confuse ourselves by reading in them anything obscure. The key to them is found in verses 11, 12: Israel walked contrary to God's will — not His decretive, but His preceptive. They acted not according to the Divine commandments, but, in their self-will and self-pleasing, determined to have their own way; and in consequence they forfeited God's best for them. Instead of His subduing their enemies, He allowed the heathen to vanquish them. Instead of providing abundant harvests, He sent them famines (2 Sam. 21:1). Instead of giving them pastors after His own heart, He suffered them to be deceived by false prophets (cf. 2 Thess. 2:10, 11).

"Oh that thou hadst hearkened to My commandments! then had thy peace been as a river, and thy righteousness as the waves of the sea" (Isa. 48:18). On which even Gill said, "their prosperity, temporal and spiritual, had been abundant, and would always have continued, have been increasing and everflowing." Failure to walk in the paths of God's precepts deprives us of many a blessing. In his review of *The Life and Letters of the late James Bourne* *(Gospel Standard,* October 1861), Mr. Philpot said, "There is deep truth in the following extract" — a sentence or two of which we here quote: "If I pay no reverence to such a word as this, 'Be not overcome of evil, but overcome evil with good' (Rom. 12:21), I shall fall into bondage, and find my prayer shut out. It will prove a hindrance to my approaches to God, for 'If I regard iniquity in my heart the Lord will not hear me' (Psa. 66:18)...If you attend not to the word of *exhortation*, you will find no communion with His people, no blessing of God upon the work of your hands."

After describing the sore judgments of God which were about to fall upon the wayward children of Israel, His faithful servant told them plainly, "Thy way and thy doings have procured these things unto thee: this is thy wickedness, because it is bitter, because it reacheth unto thy heart" (Jer. 4:18). Upon which Gill said "those calamities coming upon them, they had none to blame but themselves; it was their *own* sinful ways and works whereby that this ruin and destruction come on them." Consider also this passage: "Ye looked for much and lo, it came to little: and when ye brought it home, I did blow upon it. *Why?* saith the Lord of host" (Hag. 1:9). This searching question was put for their sakes, "that they might be made sensible of it, and in order to introduce what follows: 'because of mine house that is waste': which they suffered to lie waste, and did not concern themselves about the rebuilding of it; this the Lord resented, and for this reason blasted all their labours; and 'ye run every man unto his own house'" ' (Gill). How many a Christian today might trace God's "blowing upon" *his* temporal affairs unto his putting his carnal interests before the Lord's!

Consider now some individual examples. Do not the closing incidents recorded in the life of Lot make plain demonstration that *he* "missed God's best"? Witness his being forcibly conducted out of Sodom by the angels, where all his earthly possessions, his sons, and his sons-in-law perished; and when his wife was turned into a pillar of salt for her defiance. Behold his intemperance in the cave, then unwittingly commiting incest with his own daughters — the last thing chronicled of him! But "was there not a cause"? Go back and mark him separating from godly Abraham, coveting the plain of Jordan, pitching his tent "toward Sodom" (Gen. 13:12). Though "the men of Sodom were wicked and sinners before the Lord exceedingly," yet Lot settled in their midst, and even "sat in the gate of Sodom" (Gen. 19:1), i.e. held office there! Is it not equally evident that *Jacob* too missed God's best? Hear his own sad confession near the close of his career: "few and evil have the days of my life been" (Gen. 47:9). And is the explanation far to seek? Read his history, and it should at once be apparent that he was made to reap exactly as he had sown.

The chequered life of David supplies us with more than one or two illustrations of the same principle. Few men have experienced such sore social and domestic trials as he did. Not only was David caused much trouble by political traitors in his kingdom, but, what was far more painful, the members of his own family brought down heavy sorrows upon him. The second book of Samuel records one calamity after another. His favourite wife turned against him (6:20-22), his daughter Tamar was raped by her half brother (13:14), and his son Ammon was murdered (13:28, 29). His favourite son, Absalom, sought to wrest the kingdom from him, and then met with an ingominious end (18:14). Before David's death, yet another of his sons sought to obtain the throne (1 Kings 1:5), and he too was murdered (1 Kings 2:24,25). Since the Lord afflicts not willingly, but only as our sins give occasion, it behoves us to attend closely to what led up to and brought upon David those great afflictions. Nor have we far to seek. Read 2 Samuel 3:2-5, and note his *six wives*: he gave way to the lusts of flesh, and of the flesh he "reaped corruption"!

Painful though it be for us to dwell upon the failings and falls of the sweet Psalmist of Israel, especially since in so many respects he puts both writer and reader to shame, yet it must be remembered that "whatsoever things were written aforetime were written for *our learning*" (Rom. 15:4) — that we might heed such warnings, and be preserved from similar backslidings. His grievous offence against Uriah and Bathsheba is prefaced by the fact that he was indulging in slothful ease, instead of performing his duty (2 Sam. 11:1, 2) — observe well the ominous "But" at the close of verse 1! Though David sincerely and bitterly repented of those sins and obtained the Lord's forgiveness, yet by them he missed His best, and for the rest of his days lived under more or less *adverse* providences and the "sword" never departed from his house (2 Sam. 12:10). Nothing could more plainly evince that a holy God takes notice of our actions and deals with us accordingly, or make it manifest that it is our own folly which brings down the rod of God upon us. We read the historical portions of Scripture to little purpose or profit unless their practical lessons are taken to heart by us. Our consciences require to be searched by these narratives far more than our minds be informed by them!

Let us now point out that the same principle holds good in connection with the Divine government under the new covenant as obtained under the old. "And He did not many mighty works there *because of* their unbelief" (Matt. 13:58). What place has such a statement as that in the theology of hyper-Calvinists? None whatever. Yet it should have, otherwise why has it been placed upon record if it has no analogy today? As Matt. Henry rightly insisted, "Unbelief is the great obstacle to Christ's favour . . . . The Gospel is 'the power of God unto salvation,' but then it is 'to every one that believeth' (Rom. 1:16). So that if mighty works be not wrought in us it is not for want of power or grace in Christ, but want of faith in us." That was putting the emphasis where it must be placed if human responsibility is to be enforced. It was nothing but hardness of heart which precluded them from sharing the benefits of Christ's benevolence. When the father whose son was possessed by the demon that the disciples had failed to expel, said unto the great Physician, "If Thou canst do any thing, have compassion on us, and help us," He at once turned the "if" back again upon him, saying, "If thou canst believe, all things are possible to him that believeth" (Mark 9:22-23).

That we are the losers by our folly and that we bring trouble down upon ourselves by unbelief is illustrated in the case of the father of John the Baptist. When the angel of the Lord appeared unto him during the discharge of his priestly office in the temple, and announced that his prayer was answered and his wife would bear a son, instead of expressing gratitude at the good news and bursting forth in thanksgiving unto God, Zacharias voiced his doubts. saying, "Whereby shall I know this? for I am an old man, and my wife well stricken in years" Whereupon the angel declared, "Behold thou shalt be dumb, and not able to speak until the day that these things shall be performed, *because* thou believest not my words" (Luke 1:20), upon which Gill said, "He was stricken with deafness because he hearkened not to the angel's words, and dumbness because from the unbelief of his heart he objected to them. We learn from hence, what an evil unbelief is, and how much resented by God, and how much it becomes us to heed that it prevails not in us." To which he might well have added: and how God manifests His resentment against such conduct by sending adverse providences upon us!

Should it be said that the above incident occurred before the day of Pentecost — a pointless objection — then let us call attention to the fact that at a very early date *after* the establishment of Christianity God, in an extraordinary manner, visited with temporal judgments those who displeased and provoked Him. A clear case in point is the visible manner in which He dealt with Ananias and Sapphira (Acts 5). So too when Herod gratefully accepted the idolatrous adulations of the populace, instead of rebuking their sinful flattery, we are told, 'And immediately the angel of the Lord smote him, *because* he gave not God the glory; and he was eaten with worms" (Acts 12:23). God *does* suit His governmental ways according to the conduct of men, be they unbelievers. Not always so plainly or so promptly as in the examples just adduced, yet with sufficient clearness and frequency that all impartial and discerning observers may perceive that nothing happens by chance or mere accident, but is traceable to an antecedent cause or occasion; that His providences are regulated by righteousness.

"For I verily, as absent in body, but present in spirit, have judged already, as though I were present, concerning him that hath so done this deed, in the name of our Lord Jesus Christ, to deliver such a one unto Satan for the destruction of the flesh, that the spirit may be saved in the day of the Lord Jesus" (1 Cor. 5:3-5). A member of the Corinthian assembly had committed a grave offence, which was known publicly. For the same, he was dealt with drastically: something more than a bare act of ex-communication or being "disfellowshipped" being meant in the above verses. The guilty one was committed unto Satan for him to severly afflict his body — which is evidently meant by "the flesh" being here contrasted with "the spirit." That Satan has the power of afflicting the body we know from Job 2:7; Luke 13:16, etc. And that the apostles, in the early days of Christianity, were endowed with the authority to deliver erring ones unto Satan to be disciplined by him, is evident from 2 Corinthians 10:8; 13:10; 1 Timothy 1:20. Thus we see how a Christian was here visited with some painful disease because of his sins.

It is sadly possible for Christians to miss God's best through failure in their *home life*. This is evident from 1 Peter 3:7, "Likewise, ye husbands, dwell with them according to knowledge, giving honour unto the wife as unto the weaker vessel, and as heirs together of the grace of life; *that* your prayers be *not hindered.*" Incidentally that verse inculcates family worship, the husband and wife praying together. Further, it teaches that their treatment of one another will have a close bearing upon their joint supplications, for if domestic harmony does not obtain, what unity of spirit can there be when they come together before the throne of grace? By necessary implication that also shows how essential it is that they be "equally yoked together," for what fellowship hath righteousness with unrighteousness? and what communion hath light with darkness? What joint act of worship is possible between a child of God and a child of the Devil, between a regenerate soul and a worldling? Yet even where both the husband and the wife be true Christians, they are required to regulate their individual conduct by the precepts which God has given unto each of them: the wife that she be "in subjection to" her husband and diligent in cultivating "a meek and quiet spirit" (verses 1-6): the husband that he heeds the injunctions here given; otherwise their petitions will be "hindered," and God's best forfeited.

First, the husband is to act according to his knowledge that his wife is "the weaker vessel," which is not said in disparagement of her sex. As one has pointed out, "It is no insult to the vine to say that it is weaker than the tree to which it clings, or to the rose to say it is weaker than the bush that bears it. The strongest things are not always therefore the best — either the most beautiful or the most useful." Second, as such he is to "give honour to her": that is, his superior strength is to be engaged for her defence and welfare, rendering all possible assistance in lightening her burdens. Her very weakness is to serve as a constant appeal for a patient tenderness and forbearance toward her infirmities. Furthermore, he is ever to act in accordance with her spiritual equality, that they are "heirs together of the grace of life." Not only should the love which he has for her make him diligent in promoting her well-being, but the grace of which he has been made a partaker should operate in seeking the good of her soul and furthering her spiritual interests: discussing together the things of God, reading edifying literature to her when she is relaxing, pouring out together their thanksgivings unto God and making known their requests at the family altar.

Then it is, when those Divine requirements are met by both wife and husband, that they may plead that promise, "If two of you *shall agree* on earth as touching any thing that they shall ask, it shall be done for them of My Father which is in heaven" (Matt. 18:19). That agreement is far more than verbal or even mental: it is a spiritual one. The Greek word is *sumphoneo*, and literally signifies "to sound together." It is a musical term, as when two different notes or instruments make a harmonious sound. Thus, there must be oneness of heart, unity of spirit, concord of soul, in order for two Christians to "agree" before the throne of grace, for their joint petitions to be harmonious and melodious unto the Lord. It is music in the ear of their Father when the spiritual chords of a Christian husband and a Christian wife vibrate in unison at the family altar. But that can only obtain as they singly and mutually conduct themselves as "heirs together of the grace of life," their home life being ordered by the Word of God, everything in it done for His glory: the wife acting toward her husband as the Church is required to do as the Lamb's Wife, the husband treating her as Christ loves and cherishes His Church.

Contrariwise, if the wife rebels against the position which God has assigned her and refuses to own her husband as her head and lord, yielding obedience to him in everything which is not contrary to the Divine statutes, then friction and strife will soon obtain, for a godly husband must not yield to the compromising plea of "peace at any price." Equally so, if the husband takes unlawful advantage of his headship and be tyrannical, then, though the wife bear it meekly, her spirit is crushed, and love is chilled. If he treat her more like a servant or slave than a wife, the Spirit will be grieved, and he will be made to smart. If he be selfishly forgetful of her infirmities, especially those involved in childbearing, if he be not increasingly diligent in seeking to lighten her load and brighten her lot as the family grows, if he exercises little concern and care for her health and comfort, then she will feel and grieve over such callousness, and harmony of spirit will be gone. In such a case, their prayers will be "hindered," or, as the Greek word signifies, "cut off" — the very opposite of "agree" in Matthew 18:19! By domestic discord the heart is discomposed for supplication, and thus God's best is missed.

From the second and third chapters of the Revelation we learn that the Lord treats with local churches on the same principles as He does with individuals: that they too enter into or miss His best according to their own wisdom or folly. Thus, to the pastor of the Ephesian assembly, He declared, "I have against thee, because thou hast left thy first love. Remember therefore from whence thou art fallen, and repent, and do the first works; *or else* I will come unto thee quickly, and will remove thy candlestick out of his place, except thou repent" (2:4, 5) — how many such a "candlestick" *has* thus been removed! To the careless and compromising ones at Pergamos, who then suffered in their midst those who held doctrine which He hated, the Lord solemnly threatened, "Repent or else I will come unto thee quickly, and will fight *against* thee with the sword of My mouth" (2:14, 15) — those churches which are slack in maintaining holy discipline invite Divine judgment. While to the boastful and worldly Laodiceans the Lord declared, "I will spue thee out of My mouth" (3:16) — I will no longer own thee as My witness.

Writing on the need of members of a local church having "the same care of one another" (1 Cor. 12:25) and pointing out how that James 2:1-4, supplies an example of a company of saints where the opposite practice obtained, one wrote: "Instead of having the same care, when we make a difference between him 'with a gold ring and goodly apparel' and him or her with vile or poor clothing, we are being 'partial' . . . Do not be deceived with the thought that God does not behold such partiality: He will not prosper that church, but the members of the whole body will be made to suffer from this lack of the 'same care for one another'." And we would point out that this brief quotation is not taken from any Arminian publication, but from a recent issue of a magazine by the most hyper-Calvinist body we know of in the U.S.A. What we would particularly direct attention to in it is that when such a carnal church is "made to suffer" because of the pride and selfishness of some of its officers or members, then it has *missed* God's best. How many such churches are there in Christendom today!

"For this cause many are weak and sickly among you, and many sleep" (1 Cor. 11:30). Here is a clear case in point where many Christians missed God's best, and brought down upon themselves His temporal judgments because of their own misconduct. "For this cause" refers to their having eaten of the Lord's supper "unworthily" or unbecomingly — see verses 20 and 21. When numerous cases of sickness and death occur in a Christian assembly, they are not to be regarded as a matter of course, but made the subject of a searching examination before God and a humbling inquiring of Him. God was not dealing with these Corinthian saints in mere sovereignty, but in governmental righteousness, disciplining them for a grave offence. He was manifesting His displeasure at them because of their sins, afflicting them with bodily sickness — which in many instances ended fatally — on account of their irreverence and intemperance, as the "For this cause" unmistakably shows. This too has been recorded for our instruction, warning us to avoid sin in every form, and signifying that the commission of it will expose us to the Divine displeasure even though we be God's dear children. Here, too, we are shown that our entering into or missing of God's best has a real influence upon the health of our bodies!

That same passage goes on to inform us how we *may avert* such disciplinary affliction! "For if we would judge ourselves we should not be judged" (1 Cor. 11:31). There is a Divine judgment to which the saints are amenable, a judgment pertaining to this life, which is exercised by Christ as the Judge of His people (1 Peter 4:17). To Him each local church is accountable; unto Him each individual believer is responsible for his thoughts, words and deeds. As such He walks "in the midst of the seven golden candlesticks" (Rev. 2:1). Nothing escapes His notice, for "His eyes are as a flame of fire" and before Him all things are naked and opened (2:18). Not that He is strict to impute every iniquity, or rigorous to punish, for who then could stand before Him? The Lord is in no haste to correct His redeemed, but is slow to anger and loth to chasten. Nevertheless He is holy, and will maintain the honour of His own house, and therefore does He call upon His erring ones to repent under threat of judgment if they fail to do so. Not that He ever imposes any *penal* inflictions for their sins, for He personally suffered and atoned for *them*; but out of the love He bears them He makes known how they may avoid His governmental corrections.

"If we would judge ourselves, we should not be judged." There are some of the Lord's people who, when they be overtaken in a fault, expect immediate chastisement at His hands, and through fear of it their knees are feeble and their hands hang down. But that is going to the opposite extreme from careless indifference: both of which are condemned by the above verse. It is a law of Christ's judgment that "if we would judge ourselves, we should not be judged." That is, if we make conscience of having offended, and go directly to the Judge, unsparingly condemning ourselves and contritely confessing the fault to Him, He will pardon and *pass it by*. Though they be far from parallel, yet we may illustrate by the case of Nineveh under the preaching of Jonah. When the prophet announced "yet forty days and Nineveh shall be overthrown" (Jonah 3:4), more was intended than was expressed. He was not there proclaiming God's inexorable fiat, but was sounding an alarum to operate as a means of moral awakening. That "forty days" opened a door of hope for them, and was tantamount to saying, Upon genuine repentance and true reformation of conduct, a reprieve will be granted. That is no mere inference of ours, but a fact clearly attested in the immediate sequel.

"So the people of Nineveh *believed God*, and proclaimed a fast, and put on sackcloth" (verse 5); while the king published a decree to his subjects: "Cry mightily unto God: yea, let them turn every one from his evil way, and from the violence that is in their hands. Who can tell if God will turn and repent, and turn away from His fierce anger, that we perish not?" And we are told, "And God saw their works, that they turned from their evil way; and God repented of the evil that He had said He would do unto them; and He did it not" (verses 5-10). God's "repenting" here means that He altered in His *bearing* toward them because their conduct had changed for the better, thereby averting the judgment with which He had threatened them. Now if God dealt thus with a heathen people upon their repentance and reformation, how much more will Christ turn away the rod of chastisement from His redeemed when they truly repent of their sins and humble themselves before Him! For *them* there is no mere "who can tell if God will turn and repent," but the definite and blessed assurance that "If we confess our sins, He is faithful and just to forgive us our sins and to cleanse us from all unrighteousness" (1 John 1:9).

"For if we would judge ourselves, we should not be judged." O what tenderness and Divine longsufferance breathe in those words! That even when we have erred, yea, sinned grievously, a way is opened for us whereby we may escape the rod. Ah, but what Divine wisdom and righteousness are also evinced by them! "If we would *judge* ourselves" we should escape the disciplinary consequences of our sins. And why so? Because the rod is no longer needed by us. Why not? Because in such a case the desired effect has been wrought in us without the use of it! What is God's design *in* chastisement? To bring the refractory one to his senses, to make him realize he has erred and displeased the Lord, to cause him to right what is wrong by repentance, confession, and reformation. When *those* fruits are borne, then we *have* "heard the rod" (Micah 6:9) and it has accomplished its intended work. Very well then, if we truly, unsparingly, and contritely "judge" ourselves before God for our sins, then the rod is not required. Having condemned himself, turned back into the way of holiness, sought and obtained cleansing from all unrighteousness, he is brought to the very point — only more quickly and easily! — to which chastening would bring him!

"For if we *would* judge ourselves": those very words seem to imply there is both a slowness and a reluctance in the saints so to do — a thought which is confirmed in the next verse. Alas, many of those who have left their first love are in such a backslidden and sickly case spiritually that they are incapable of judging themselves. Their conscience has become so dull through the frequent excusing of what they deemed trifling things, their walk is so careless, that they offend their Judge and are virtually unaware of doing so. "Strangers have devoured his strength, and he knoweth it not; yea, grey hairs [the mark of decline and decay] are here and there upon him, yet he knoweth not" (Hos. 7:9). Since, then, they are *not* exercised over their sins, the rod must awaken them; for their holy Lord will not tolerate unconfessed sins in His own. But others, who have not deteriorated to such a sad degree, are conscious of their faults, yet nevertheless do not judge themselves for the same. Why? What causes such reluctance to humble themselves before God? What, but accursed pride! In such case, His mighty hand will bring them down, and hence it follows:

"For when we *are* judged, we are *chastened* of the Lord, that we should not be condemned with the world" (verse 32). Such was the case with the Corinthians. They sinned again and again in different ways, and were unexercised. They were "carnal," and among them were envying and strife, yet they judged not themselves. The Lord gave them space for repentance, but they repented not, until, in the profanation of His holy supper, He was obliged to act, visiting them with bodily sickness and death. Thus, from the words, "when we are judged, we are chastened of the Lord," the conclusion is unescapable: we have failed *to condemn* ourselves. As it is a rule of Christ's kingdom that when His people own their offences and turn from the same, He spares the rod; so it is equally a rule in His kingdom that when they sin and confess it not, but continue in the same, then He chastens them. And there is infinite mercy in that, for it is *that* they "should not be condemned with the world." His own wayward children are chastised here in this world, but the ungodly will bear the full punishment of their sins for ever and ever in Hell! Sin *must be* "condemned": either by us, or by the righteous Judge — here, or hereafter. How much better to judge ourselves and thereby escape His judgment!

RECOVERY OF GOD'S BEST

We have considered various cases, both of individuals and corporate companies, who *missed* God's best, and saw how ill it fared with them. We pointed out how that if we judge ourselves for our sins we shall *escape* God's chastening rod. We now turn to the question, Is it possible for a Christian who has missed God's best to be *recovered* to full communion with Him and restored to His providential smile? Possible, yes; easy, no. Before we show how that possibility may be realized, let us solemnly ponder what brought that poor soul into such a sorry plight — a plight into which both writer and reader will certainly fall unless we are ever on our prayerful guard. The grand but simple secret of a healthy and prosperous spiritual life is to *continue* as we began (Col. 2:6): by daily trusting in the sufficiency of Christ's blood and yielding ourselves to His lordship, seeking to please and honour Him in all things. As the believer walks with Christ in the path of obedience, following the example which He has left him, peace will possess his soul and joy will fill his heart, and the smile of God will be upon him. But unless he, by grace, fulfil those conditions, such will not be his happy portion.

If the believer slackens in maintaining daily fellowship with Christ and drawing from His fullness, if he fails to feed regularly on the Word and becomes less frequent in his approaches to the throne of grace, then the pulse of his spiritual life will beat more feebly and irregularly. Unless he meditates oft on the love of God and keeps fresh before his heart the humiliation and sufferings of Christ on his behalf, his affections will soon cool, his relish for spiritual things will wane, and obedience will neither be so easy nor so pleasant. If such a spiritual decline be neglected or excused, it will not be long ere indwelling sin gains the upper hand over his graces, and his heart will more and more glide imperceptibly into carnality and worldliness. Worldly pleasures, which previously repelled and were perceived to be vanities, will begin to attract. Worldly pursuits, which had been only a means, will become his end, absorbing more and more of his attention and having a higher value in his eyes. Or worldly cares, which he had cast upon the Lord, will now oppress and weigh him down. And unless there be a humbling of himself before God (and His providence hinder), he will soon be found in the ways of open transgression. Backsliding begins in the *heart*!

The case of a backslider is much more serious than that of one who has been "overtaken in a fault" (Gal. 6:1). For with him it is not a matter of a sudden suprisal and a single stumble, but rather of a steady deterioration and definite departure from the Lord. Nor is it, in its early stages, manifested openly, and hence his brethren may be quite unaware of it. A secret canker of unwatchfulness and coldness has infected him: he has yielded to a spirit of laxity and self-indulgence. When first aware of his decline, instead of being alarmed, he ignored it; instead of weeping over it before God, he went on in his carnality, until his graces became inoperative and all power to resist the devil was gone. With such the Holy Spirit is grieved and His quickening influences are withdrawn and His comforts are withheld. There are indeed degrees of backsliding: with some it is partial, with others total; yet while one remains in that case, it is impossible for the saint to determine which; nor is there anything in Scripture which gives a warrantable sense of security unto such a one, or which countenances any man to be easy in his sins; but very much the contrary.

Inexpressibly sad is the case of one who continues for a season in a backslidden state. He has displeased God, dishonoured Christ, in many instances has become a stumbling-block to fellow Christians, especially to younger ones. He has made himself miserable. He has sinned and repented not; departed from God, and confessed it not. Formerly he walked in happy fellowship with God, the light of His countenance shone upon him, and that peace which passeth all understanding possessed his soul. But now the joy of salvation is no more his portion. He has lost his relish for the Word and prayer has become a burden. He is out of touch with God, for his iniquities have separated him from Him (Isa. 59:2), and he can find no rest unto his soul. He has been spoilt for the world and cannot now find even that measure of satisfaction in carnal things which the ungodly do. Wretched indeed is his plight. "The backslider in heart shall be filled with his *own* ways" (Prov. 14:14): it cannot be otherwise, for he no longer has any delight in the ways of God. His own backslidings reprove him, so that he is made to know and see what "an evil and bitter thing it is to depart from the Lord his God" (Jer. 2:19), and thereby miss His best.

Yet, pitiful though his case be, it is not hopeless, for the call goes forth "Turn, O backsliding children, saith the Lord" (Jer 3:14). Nevertheless, response thereto is not the simple matter that lookers-on might suppose. It is very much easier to depart from God than to return unto Him. Not that His terms of recovery are rigorous, but because the soul is straitened. It is difficult for the backslider to perceive the nature and seriousness of his condition, for sin has a blinding and hardening effect, and the more he falls under the power of it, the less does he discern the state he is in. Even when his eyes begin to be opened again, there is an absence of real desire for recovery, for sin has a paralysing influence, so that its victims are "at ease in Zion." Even David was insensible of his awful plight when Nathan first approached him, and it was not until the prophet pointedly declared "Thou art the man" that Satan's spell over him was broken. It is therefore much to be thankful for when such are awakened from their slumber and made to hear that word "Return, ye backsliding children, and I will heal your backslidings" (Jer. 3:22).

But even then the soul is reluctant to meet God's terms. If nothing more were required than a lip acknowledgment of his offences and a return to outward duties, no great difficulty would be experienced; but to really fulfil the Divine conditions for restoration is a very different matter. As John Owen affirmed,

"Recovery from backsliding is the hardest task in the Christian religion; one which few make either comfortable or honourable work of." There has to be an asking, a seeking, a knocking, if the door of deliverance is to be opened to him. As John Brine (whose works were favourably reviewed in the *Gospel Standard*) wrote to God's people two hundred years ago, "Much labour and diligence are required unto this. It is not complaining of the sickly condition of our souls which will effect this cure: confession of our follies that have brought diseases upon us, though repeated ever so often, will avail nothing toward the removal of them. If we intend the recovery of our former health and vigour, we must *act* as well as complain and groan." Let us now endeavour to point out how God requires such a one *to* "act."

"He that covereth his sins shall not prosper; but whoso confesseth and forsaketh them shall heve mercy" (Prov. 28:13) epitomizes both sides of the case. Sin is a disease of the soul, and (like a bodily one) by concealing it, we make it increase and become desperate. As the Puritan, Joseph Caryl, pointed out, "Sin increases two ways in the concealment of it. First, in its *guilt*. The obligation to punishment takes stronger hold upon the soul, and every man is bound the faster with the chains of darkness by how much more he labours to keep his sins in the dark. The longer a sin remains on the conscience unpardoned, the more does the guilt of it increase. Second, in the filth and *contagion* of it, in the strength and power of it. It grows more master, and masterly, and at last raves and rages, commands and carries all before it." To "cover" our sins is a refusal to bring them out into the light by an honest confession of the same unto God; in the case of our fellows, refusing to acknowledge our offences unto those we have wronged. This reprehensible hiding of sin is an adding of sin unto sin, and is a certain preventative of prosperity, and if persisted in will cover the perpetrator with shame and confusion for ever.

To "cover" sin is to hide it within our own bosoms, instead of openly acknowledging it. Thus it was with Achan even when the tribes were solemnly arraigned before Joshua and Eleazar, the high priest: he solemnly maintained silence until his crime was publicly exposed. Some seek to conceal their sins by framing excuses and attempting a self-extenuation: they seek to throw the blame upon their circumstances, their fellows, or Satan — upon anything or anyone except *themselves*! Others proceed to a still worse device, and seek to cloak their sin by a lie, denying their guilt. As did Cain, for when God made inquisition for blood and inquired of him "Where is Abel thy brother?" he answered "I know not." So too Gehazi blankly denied his wrong when charged by Elisha (2 Kings 5:25). In like manner acted Ananias and Sapphira. Three things induce men to make coverings for their sins. First, *pride*. Man has such high thoughts of himself that when guilty of the basest things, he is too self-opinionated to own them. Second, *unbelief*. Those who have not faith to believe that *God* can and will cover confessed sins, vainly attempt to do so themselves. Third, *shame and fear* cause many to hide their sins. Sin is such a hideous monster they will not own it as *theirs*.

"But whoso confesseth and forsaketh them shall have mercy." Confession of sin is an indispensable part of repentance, and without repentance there can be no remission (Acts 3:19). "I acknowledged my sin unto Thee, and mine iniquity have I not hid. I said I will confess my transgressions unto the Lord, and Thou forgavest the iniquity of my sin" (Psa. 32:5) — the pardon was upon his confession. Those who are so convicted of their sins as to be humbled and sorrowed by a sight and sense of the same, will not hide them out of sight. Nor will their confession be merely a formal one of the lips, but rather the sobbings of a contrite heart. And instead of generalizing, there will be a particularizing; instead of seeking to excuse or gloss over the offence, it will be painted in its true colours and its aggravations frankly owned. There will be an acknowledgment of the fact and of the fault: an unsparing self-condemnation. The language of David in the opening verses of Psalm 51 will be found most suited to his case. The sin or sins will be confessed sincerely, contritely, fully, with a self-abasement and self-loathing. The cry will be made "O Lord, pardon mine iniquity for it is *great*" (Psa. 25:11).

"And forsake them." To "forsake" our sins is a voluntary and deliberate act. It signifies to hate and abandon them in our affections, to repudiate them by our wills, to refuse to dwell upon them in our minds and imaginations with any pleasure or satisfaction. It necessarily implies that we renounce them, and are resolved by God's grace to make the utmost endeavour to avoid any repetition of the same. "We must keep at a distance from those persons and snares which have drawn us into instances of folly, which have occasioned that disorder which is the matter of our complaint. Without this we may multiply acknowledgments and expressions of concern for our past miscarriages to no purpose at all. It is very great folly to think of regaining our former strength so long as we embrace and dally with those objects through whose evil influence we have fallen into a spiritual decline. It is not our bewailing the pernicious effects of sin that will prevent its baleful influence upon us for time to come, except we are determined to *forsake* that to which is owing our melancholy disease" (John Brine). There must be a complete break from all that poisons the soul.

But suppose the saint *does not* promptly thus confess and forsake his sins, then what? Why, in such a case, he will "not prosper": there will be no further growth in grace, nor will the providential smile of God be upon him. The Holy Spirit is grieved, and will suspend His gracious operations within his soul, and henceforth his "way" will be made "hard." Such was the experience of David: "When I kept silence, my bones [a figure of the supports of the soul] waxed old through my roaring all the day long. For day and night Thy hand was heavy upon me: my moisture [or vigour or freshness] is turned into the drought of summer" (Psa. 32:3, 4). Sin is a pestilential thing which saps our spiritual vitality. Though David was silent as to confession, he was not so as to sorrow. God's hand smote him so that he was made to groan under His chastening rod. Nor did he obtain any relief until he humbled himself before God by confessing and forsaking his sins. Not that there is anything meritorious in such acts which entitles their performer to mercy, but that this is the holy order which God has established. He will not connive at our sins, but withholds His mercy until we take sides with Him in the hatred of them.

"If My people which are called by My name shall humble themselves, and pray, and seek My face, and turn from their wicked ways; then will I hear from heaven, and will forgive their sin and will heal their land" (2 Chron. 7:24). This passage shows us, first, that God sends temporal judgments upon His people because of their sins. Second, it makes known what they are to do when His rod is upon them. Third, it contains a precious promise for faith to lay hold of. Let us carefully note what was required from them. First, "If My people shall humble themselves," which is similar to the "judge ourselves" in 1 Corinthians 11:31, but here when chastisement is upon them. Leviticus 26:41, casts light upon it: "if . . . they *accept* the punishment of their iniquity," which is the opposite of asking, What have I done to occasion this? "After all that is come upon us for our evil deeds and for our great trespass, seeing that Thou our God hast punished us *less* than our iniquities *deserve*" (Ezra 9:13) illustrates. David "humbled" himself when he owned, "I know, O Lord, that Thy judgments are right and that Thou in faithfulness hast afflicted me" (Psa. 119:75). He took sides with God against himself, and acknowledge his unrighteousness.

Until the stricken one has humbled himself it is vain to think of proceeding farther, for pride and impenitence bar any approaches unto the Holy One. But "if" we *have* duly "humbled" ourselves, second, "and pray." Only as we take our place in the dust before Him can we truly do so. And for what will such a one make request? Surely for a deeper sense of God's holiness and of his own vileness: for a broken and contrite heart. Accompanying his "humbling" and as an expression thereof, there will be the penitent confession, and that will be followed by a begging for faith in God's mercy and a hope of cleansing and restoration. Third, "and seek My face," which goes farther than "and pray": expressing diligence, definiteness, and fervour. The omniscient One cannot be imposed upon by mere lip-service, but requires the heart. There has to be a face-to-face meeting with the One we have displeased: He will not gloss over our sins; nor must we. Hosea 14:2, 3, should be made use of, for the Lord has there made known the very words which we may appropriately use on such occasions. Fourth, "and turn from their wicked ways" (which had brought judgment upon them) has the same force as "forsake" our sins in Proverbs 28:13.

"Then will I hear from heaven, and will forgive their sin, and will heal their land." Here is the gracious promise. But mark well its opening "Then": only when we have fully met its conditions. We have no warrant to look for its fulfilment until its qualifying terms are observed by us. Note, too, its blessed scope: a hearing from God is obtained, His forgiveness is assured, and His healing is available for faith to claim. Say, Lord I have by Thy grace, and to the best of my poor ability humbled myself, sought Thy face, and renounced my wicked ways; now do as Thou hast said: *"heal* my land" — whether it be my body, my loved one, or my estate. Remove Thy rod, and let Thy providential smile come upon me again. Make a believing use of and plead before God the promises of Hosea 14:4-8! "According unto your faith be it unto you" (Matt. 9:29) is most pertinent at this point. God is pledged to honour faith, and never does He fail those who trust Him fully; no, not when they count upon Him to work a miracle for them, as this writer can humbly but thankfully testify. How many Christians live below their privileges!

"Jehovah-rophi" ("the Lord that healeth thee": Ex. 15:26) is as truly one of the Divine titles as "Jehovah-tsidkneu" ("the Lord our righteousness": Jer. 23:5), yet how very few of His own people count upon Him as such; but instead, act like worldlings in such a crisis and put their confidence in human physicians. Is it possible for one who through long-continued self-indulgence has missed God's best and brought down upon himself and family temporal adversity, to be fully recovered and restored to His favour? Who can doubt it in the light of this precious, but little-known promise, "I will restore to you the years the locusts hath eaten" (Joel 2:25)! Is not the One with whom we have to do "the God of *all* grace" (1 Peter 5:10); then who is justified in placing any limitation thereon! Yet, let it not be overlooked that Divine grace ever works "through righteousness" (Rom. 5:21) and never at the expense of it, as it would if God were to make light of sin and condone our transgressions. And let it also be carefully borne in mind that the Divine promises are addressed *to faith*, and must be personally appropriated by us in childlike confidence if we are to enjoy the good of them. "All things are possible to him that believeth" (Mark 9:23).

Let the reader turn to the prophet Joel and ponder the whole of chapter 1 and the first eleven verses of 2. Israel had sinned grievously and repeatedly, and the Lord had smitten them severely. But at 2:12, we read, "Therefore [in view of these chastisements, particularly the plague of locusts] also now, saith the Lord, turn ye to Me with all your heart, and with fasting, and with weeping, and with mourning. And rend your heart and not your garments, and turn unto the Lord your God: for He is gracious and merciful, slow to anger, and of great kindness, and repenteth Himself of the evil." Then, because in this instance the whole nation was involved, the Lord gave orders for them to "Sanctify a fast" and to "call a solemn assembly," bidding "the ministers of the Lord weep before the porch and the altar, and let them say, Spare Thy people, O Lord, and give not Thine heritage to reproach"; assuring them *"Then* will the Lord be jealous for His land, and pity His people," promising "I will send you corn and wine and oil, and ye shall be satisfied therewith . . . I will *remove* the northern army [His scourge] . . . Fear not. O land, be glad and rejoice for the Lord will do great things" (2:15, 21).

Then follow those blessed words, "Be glad then, ye children of Zion, and rejoice in the Lord your God . . . I will *restore* to you the years that the locusts hath eaten." Upon their compliance with those aforementioned requirments of God, that promise was left for faith to lay hold of and for hope to count upon. And think you, my reader, that the promise was placed on record only for the benefit of those who lived thousands of years ago? Surely, we have good reason to say, as the apostle did in another connection, "It was not written for his sake alone . . . but *for us also"* (Rom. 4:23,24). Yes, nevertheless, it avails us nothing unless faith lays hold of and makes it our own. Once more we quote that declaration "according to *your faith* be it unto you," reverently reminding the Calvinistic reader that those are not the words of James Arminius, but of God the Son. If ever there is one time more than another when we have need to cry "Lord, increase our faith" it is when we are pleading 1 John 1:9, and more especially when looking to God for a full restoration to His best and counting upon His fulfilling Joel 2:25, unto us.

OBJECTIONS

Many other passages might be quoted, both from Old and New Testaments, which illustrate the principle and fact which we have demonstrated, wherein we have shown that if we conduct ourselves contrary to the revealed will of God we shall certainly suffer for it both in soul and in body, that if we follow a course of self-pleasing we shall deprive ourselves of those spiritual and temporal blessings which the Word of God promises to those whose lives are ordered by its precepts. The teaching of Holy Writ is too clear to admit of any doubt that it makes a very real and marked difference whether a Christian's ways please or displease the righteous Ruler of this world: the difference of whether God be for him or against him — not in the absolute sense, but in His governmental and providential dealings. Sufficient should have been adduced to convince any candid mind that God acts towards His saints today on precisely the same basis as He did with them under the old economy, that His ways with them are regulated by the same principles now as then. This supplies a solution to many a problem and explains not a little in God's dealings with us — as it furnishes the key to Jacob's chequered life, and shows why the chastening rod of God fell so heavily upon David and his family.

Nevertheless much of what has been presented is no doubt new and strange to many, if not to most of our readers. Alas, that it should be so, for what can be of greater practical importance than for the Christian to be instructed in how to please God and have His providential smile upon his life? What is more needed today than to warn him against the contrary, specifying what will forfeit the same; and to make known the way of recovery to one who *has* missed God's best? How very much better for preachers to devote themselves unto *such* subjects, rather than culling sensational items from the newspapers or the radio to "illustrate" their vain speculations upon Prophecy. So too, how much more profitable than for them to deliver abstract disquisitions upon what are termed "the doctrines of grace," or uttering contentious declamations against those who repudiate the same. The *practical* side of the Truth is sadly neglected today, and in consequence not only are many of God's dear children living far below their privileges, but they have never been taught what those privileges are, nor what is required in order for them to enjoy the same in this life.

Since the ground we have been covering is so unfamiliar to many, we felt it would not be satisfactory for us to end here. Though what we have advanced is so clearly and fully based upon and confirmed by the teaching of God's Word, yet probably various questions have arisen in the minds of different readers to which they would welcome an answer, difficulties raised in their thoughts which they would like to have removed. It is only right that we should squarely face the principal objections which are likely to be made against what we have said. Yet, let it be pointed out, first, that no objection brought against anything which is clearly established from the Word can possibly invalidate it, for Scripture never contradicts itself. And second, that our inability to furnish a satisfactory solution is no proof that our teaching is erroneous — a child can ask questions which no adult can answer. In all the ways and works of God there is, to us, an element of *mystery*: necessarily so, for the finite cannot comprehend the infinite. The wisest among God's saints and servants now see through a glass darkly and know but "in part," and therefore it is their wisdom to pray daily "that which I see not, teach Thou me" (Job 34:32).

Yet, while acknowledging that there *is* an element of mystery, profound and impenetrable, that is far from saying that God has left His people in darkness, or that they have neither the capacity nor the means of knowing scarcely anything about the principles which regulate the Most High in His dealings with the children of men. If, on the one hand, it be true that His judgments "are a great deep" (Psa. 36:6), that "Thy way is in the sea, and Thy path in the great waters, and Thy footsteps are not known" (Psa. 77:19) to carnal reason; on the other hand, we are told "He discovereth deep things out of darkness" (Job 12:22) and "He *revealeth* the deep and secret things" (Dan. 2:22). While it be true that God's judgments are unsearchable and His ways "past finding out" (Rom. 11:33) by human wisdom; yet it is also true, blessedly true, that "in Thy light shall we see light" (Psa. 36:9) that "He *made known* His ways unto Moses" (Psa. 103:7). In His Word the Lord has been pleased to make known unto us not a little, and it is our privilege and duty to thankfully receive *all* the light which God has therein vouchsafed us; to attempt to go beyond it, to enter into speculation, is not only useless, but impious.

1. How is it possible for any person to "*miss* God's best," since He has foreordained everything that comes to pass (Rom. 11:36), and therefore has eternally appointed the precise lot and portion of each individual? That, we think, is a fair and frank way of stating the principal objection which Calvinists are likely to make. Our first reply is, Such an objection is quite beside the point, for in these articles we are not discussing any aspect of God's sovereignty, but rather are treating of that which concerns human responsibility. If the rejoinder be made, But human responsibility must not be allowed to crowd out the essential and basic fact of God's sovereignty, that is readily granted; nor, on the other hand, must our adherence to God's sovereignty be suffered to neutralize or render nugatory the important truth of man's responsibility. One part of the Truth must never be used to nullify another part of it: both Romans 11:36, and Galatians 6:7, must be given their due places. When we attempt to *philosophize* about God's sovereignty and human accountability we are out of our depth. They are to be received by faith, and not reasoned about. Each of them is plainly taught and enforced in the Scriptures, and both must be held fast by us, whether or no *we* perceive their "consistency."

Nothing is easier than to raise difficulties and objections. If some of the "hypers" prefer reasoning to the actings of faith, let us meet them on their own ground for a moment and give them some questions to exercise their minds upon. "Then said David, Will the men of Keilah deliver me and my men into the hand of Saul?" (1 Sam. 23:12). It is unmistakably evident from the sequel that God had ordained David should escape; yet He answered, "They *will* deliver thee up." Query: How could they, since God had decreed otherwise! "Thou shouldest have smitten five or six times, *then* hadst thou smitten Syria till thou hadst consumed it; whereas thou shalt smite Syria but thrice" (2 Kings 13:9). Query: what possible difference to the issue could be made by the number of times the king smote upon the ground? If God had predestinated that Syria should be "consumed," could any failure in the faith of Joash prevent or even modify it? On the other hand, do not those words of Elisha plainly signify that the extent to which Israel would vanquish Syria turned upon the measure of the king's apporpriation of the promise "for thou shalt smite the Syrians in Aphec till thou hast consumed them"? Which horn of the dilemma does the reasoner prefer?

Again, when the wicked Haman induced Ahasueras to seal the decree written in his name, that all the Jews scatterd abroad throughout his kingdom should be slain on a certain day, Mordecai was grief-stricken by the terrible news. Esther sent one of the royal chamberlains to ascertain the cause of his sorrow. Whereupon her uncle handed the messenger a copy of the decree to show unto Esther, with the charge that "she should go in unto the king to make supplications unto him" (4:8). Esther sent back the messenger to Mordecai to say, "Whosoever, whether man or woman, shall go unto the king in the inner court who is not called, there is one law of his to put him to death, except such to whom the king shall hold out the golden sceptre, that he may live: but I have not been called to come in unto the king these thirty days." To which Mordecai replied, "If thou holdest thy peace at this time, then shall there enlargement and deliverance arise to the Jews from another place; but thou and thy father's house shall be destroyed" (verse 14). Query: if God had eternally purposed that the Jews should be delivered through the intervention of Esther, how could it possibly come "from *another* place" and she and her family be destroyed!

If our minds be dominated by our outlook upon life narrowed down to a consideration of the inexorableness of the Divine determinations, then a spirit of irresponsibility will necessarily ensue. It is with the revealed and not with the secret will of God we need to be concerned. "The secret things belong unto the Lord our God: but those things which are revealed [in His Word] belong unto us and to our children for ever, that we may *do* all the words of this Law" (Deut. 29:29). It is the Divine precepts and promises which are to engage our attention. "According unto your faith be it unto you" (Matt. 9:29) said Christ, *not* "according unto the Divine decrees." Are we intimating that faith can set aside the Divine decrees or obtain something superior to them? Certainly not: instead, we are pointing out *where* the great Teacher placed *His* emphasis. We must not resolve all of God's dealings with us into bare sovereignty: to do so is to lose sight of His righteousness. The unbalanced teaching of hyper-Calvinism has produced a most dangerous lethargy — unperceived by them, but apparent to "lookers on." Those who dwell unduly upon the Divine decrees are in peril of lapsing into the paralysis of fatalism. There were times when even Mr. Philpot felt that, as the following quotations from his writings will show:

"However sovereign the dispensations of God are, no one who fears His great name should so shelter himself under Divine sovereignty as to remove all blame from himself. When the Lord asks 'hast thou not procured this to thyself?' the soul must needs reply, Yea, Lord, I surely have. This is a narrow line, but one which everyone's experience, where the conscience is tender, will surely ratify. Though we can do nothing to comfort our own souls, to speak peace to our own conscience, to bring the love of God into our hearts, to apply the balm of Gilead to bleeding wounds, and summon the great Physician to our bedside, we *may* do many things to *repel* this moment what we would seem to invite the next . . . We cannot make ourselves fruitful in every good word and work, but we may by disobedience and self-indulgence bring leanness into our souls, barrenness into our frames, deadness into our hearts, and in the end much guilt upon our consciences" (Sermon on Jer. 8:22). The same writer when exposing the error of nonchastisement said, "It nullifies the eternal distinction between good and evil, and makes it a matter of little real moment whether a believer walk in obedience or disobedience." Then let those who have succeeded him devote more of their endeavours into pressing God's precepts upon His people, and stressing the necessity, importance, and value of an obedient walk; and in faithfully showing the serious losses incurred by disobedience.

2. To affirm that our having God's blessing upon us is the consequence of the Christian's pleasing of Him, may appear unto some as derogatory unto Christ, as militating against His merits. They will ask, Does not the believer owe every blessing to the *alone* worthiness of his Surety? Answer: that is to confound things which differ. We must distinguish between God's sovereign will as the originating cause, the work of Christ as the meritorious cause, the operation and application of the Spirit as the efficient cause, and the repentance, faith and obedience of the Christian as the instrumental cause. Keep each of those in its order and place and there will be no confusion. If that be too abstruse, let us put it this way. Is not Christ most glorified by them when His redeemed follow the example which He has left them and walk as He also walked (1 John 2:6)? If so, will not the governmental smile of God be upon such? Conversely, would God be honouring His beloved Son if His providences were favourable unto those who act in self-will, rather than in subjection to their Master? Further, if God's *present* rewarding of our obedience impugn the merits of Christ, then equally so will the *future* rewarding He has promised, for neither time nor place can make any difference in the essential nature of things.

It is so easy for us to mar the fair proportions of Truth and destroy its perfect symmetry. In our zeal, there is ever the tendency to take one aspect of Truth and press it so far as to cancel out another. Not only so in causing God's sovereignty to oust human responsibility, but to make the merits of Christ bar God from exercising His perfections in the present government of this world. Some have gone so far as to blankly deny that God ever uses the rod upon His children, arguing that Christ bore and took away all their sins, and therefore God could not chasten them for their transgressions without sullying the sufficiency of His Son's atonement, thereby repudiating Psalm 89:30-32; Hebrews 12:5-11. Here too we must distinguish between things that differ. It is important for us to see that while the penal and eternal consequences of the believer's sins have been remitted by God, because atoned for by Christ, yet the disciplinary and temporal effects thereof are not cancelled — otherwise he would never be sick or die. God never chastens His people penally or vindictively, but in love, in righteousness, in mercy, according to the principles of His government: rewarding them for their obedience, chastening for their disobedience, and thereby and therein Christ is honoured and not dishonoured.

3. Since all God's actings unto His people proceed from His uncaused, amazing, and super-abounding *grace*, how can it be maintained that He regulates His dealings with them according to *their conduct*? Easily, for there is nothing incompatible between the two things: they are complementary and not contradictory. As all the perfections of God are not to be swallowed up in His sovereignty, neither are they all to be merged into His grace. God is holy as well as benignant, and His favours are never bestowed in disregard of His purity.

Divine grace never sets aside the requirements of Divine righteousness. When one has been truly saved by grace, he is taught to deny ungodliness and worldly lusts, and if he fails to do so, then the rod of God falls upon him. David was as truly saved by grace through faith, apart from any good works, as was the apostle Paul; but he was also required to be "holy in all manner of conversation" as are the New Testament saints; and when he failed to be so, severe chastening was his portion. And it was *grace*, though holy and righteous grace, which dealt thus with him, that he "should not be condemned with the world" (1 Cor. 11:32).

The Christian needs to be viewed not only as one of God's elect — one of His high favourites, and not only as a member of the Father's family, and as such amenable to His paternal discipline, but also as a human being, a moral agent, a subject of God's government, and therefore is he dealt with accordingly by the Ruler of this world. As such, God has appointed an inseparable connection between conduct and the consequences it entails, and therefore is He pleased to manifest, by His providences, His approbation or His disapprobation of our conduct. It is not that the one who walks in the paths of righteousness thereby brings God into his debt, but that He condescends to act toward us according to the principle of gracious reciprocity. No creature can possibly merit aught good at the hands of God, for if he rendered perfect and perpetual obedience, he has merely performed his duty, and hath profited God — essentially considered — nothing whatever. Moreover, the recompense itself is a free gift, an act of pure grace, for God is under no compulsion or obligation to bestow it.

4. When pointing out in connection with "He did not many mighty works there *because* of their unbelief" (Matt. 13:28) that "Unbelief is the great obstacle to Christ's favours" (Matthew Henry), that *they* closed the door upon His deeds of mercy, it may be thought by some that we are approving the horrible impiety that the creature has the power to thwart the Creator. And when we emphatically deny any such idea, objectors are likely to ask, But how can you escape such a consequence? Easily: faith is God's own prescribed ordinance, and therefore He is in no wise checkmated when He refuses to act contrary to His own appointed way. Obviously, He is by no means obliged to set a premium on unbelief or countenance contempt of His means. Mark 6 expresses it more strongly: "He *could* there do no mighty works," etc. (verse 5). When it is said God "cannot lie" and "cannot be tempted with evil." so far from signifying any limitation of His power, the perfection of His holiness is intimated. So with Christ. Among a people who were "offended in Him" because they regarded Him as "the carpenter," no *moral end* had been furthered by His dazzling their eyes with prodigies of His might, and therefore He cast not His pearls before swine.

5. Another class of readers, viz. those who have imbibed the poison of "Dispensationalism." will complain that our teaching in these articles is legalistic, confounding the old and new covenants, that God's dealings with Jacob, David, and the nation of Israel furnish no parallel with His conduct toward us in this era. But that is a serious mistake. There is far more of essential oneness between the administration of those two economies than there was incidental divergencies, as Calvin long ago demonstrated in his *Institutes* — see his chapters upon "The Similarity of the Old and New Testaments" and "The Difference of the two Testaments." The principal difference between the Mosaic

and Christian dispensations was neither in "the way of salvation," the spiritual portion of God's children, nor the principles of His government; but rather that spiritual things were presented to their view largely under types and shadows, whereas we have the substance itself openly set before us. Beneath all the trivial contrasts there is a fundamental unity between them, and it betrays a very superficial mind which delights in magnifying those contrasts, while ignoring or denying their basic oneness. But, as we have shown, the New Testament teaching on our present subject is identical with that of the Old, "Knowing that whatsoever good thing any man doeth, the same shall he *receive* of the Lord" (Eph. 6:8) is both an echo and summary of the Law and the Prophets.

The underlying unity of the two Testaments is plainly intimated in that Divine declaration "whatsoever was written aforetime was written for our learning" (Rom. 15:4). But what could *we* "learn" from God's dealings with His people of old if He be now acting according to radically different principles? Nothing at all. Nay, in such a case it would follow that the less we read the Old Testament the better for us, for we should only be confused. The fact is that the principles of God's government are like Himself — immutable, the same in every age. "Righteousness and judgment" (Psa. 97:2) are just as truly the "habitation of His throne" today as when He cast out of heaven the apostate angels, and as when He destroyed the antediluvians — which was long before Moses! That God now deals with Christians on precisely the same basis as He did with the children of Israel, is unequivocally established by 1 Corinthians 10:6, where, after describing the privileges they had enjoyed and God's overthrowing them in the wilderness because of their unbelief, we are told "Now these things were *our* examples, to the intent we should not lust after evil things, as they also lusted": that is, they are real and solemn warnings for us to take to heart, specimens of those judgments which will befall *us* if we emulate their sinful conduct.

Nay, Scripture requires us to go yet farther. So far from the higher blessings of this Christian era lessening our responsibility, they much increase the same. The greater our privileges, the greater our obligations. "For unto whomsoever much is given, of him shall be much required" (Luke 12:48), as the one who received five talents was required to yield more than those who received but one or two. "He that despised Moses' law died without mercy under two or three witnesses, of how much *sorer* punishment, suppose ye, shall he be thought worthy, who hath trodden under foot the Son of God!" (Heb. 10:28, 29) The principle of that verse clearly signifies that the more light we have been favoured with the deeper are our obligations, and the greater the guilt incurred when those obligations are not met. "But there is forgiveness with Thee, that Thou mayest be feared" (Psa. 130:4). Yes, "feared" and not trifled with, by giving free rein to our lusts. A true apprehension of Divine mercy will not embolden unto sin, but will deepen our hatred of it, and make us more diligent in striving against it. Those who "know the grace of God in truth" (Col. 1:6) — in contrast with the ones who have merely a theoretical knowledge of it — so far from being careless of their ways and indifferent to the consequences, will be most diligent in endeavouring to please and glorify Him who has been so good to them.

6. Some are likely to complain that our teaching is too idealistic and impracticable, that we have presented an unattainable standard, arguing that in our present condition it is impossible to enjoy God's best if that be dependent

upon our daily life being well-pleasing unto Him. We shall be reminded that only one Perfect Man has trod this earth, and that while the flesh indwells the Christian, failures and falls are inevitable. Nor should we be surprised at fault being found with that which rebukes the low level of Christian experience in this decadent age: those that are at ease in Zion do not welcome anything which searches the conscience and is calculated to arouse them from their deplorable apathy. But the One with whom each of us has to do declares, "Be ye holy, for I am holy" (1 Peter 1:16), and therefore does He bid us "Awake to righteousness, and sin not" (1 Cor. 15:34), "Put ye on the Lord Jesus Christ, and make not provision for the flesh unto the lusts thereof" (Rom. 13:14), "He that saith he abideth in Him, ought himself also so to walk, even as He walked" (1 John 2:6).

But we have not said that our enjoyment of God's smile *is* dependent upon our actually measuring up to that standard, though nothing short of it must be our constant aim and earnest endeavour. There is a great difference between a relative falling short of that standard and a life of defeat, between daily trespasses and being the slave of some dominant lust. Had we said that one must lead a *sinless* life in order to enter into God's best, the above complaint had been pertinent. But we have not. If the heart be true to God, if it be our sincere desire and diligent effort to please the Lord in all things, then His approbation and blessing will certainly be upon us. And if such really be our intention and striving, then it will necessarily follow that we shall mourn over our conscious failures in missing that mark and will promptly and contritely confess the same — it is by *that* we may test and prove the genuineness of our sincerity. It is not the sins of a Christian, but his *unconfessed* sins, which choke the channel of blessing and cause so many to miss God's best.

What has just been stated is clearly established by "he that covereth his sins shall not prosper" (Prov. 28:13). It is always an inexcusable and grievous thing for a saint to commit any sin, yet it is far worse to refuse to acknowledge the same: that is to "add sin to sin" (Isa. 30:1); yea, it evinces a spirit of defiance. So far from such a one prospering, he closes the door against God's favours (Jer. 5:24). As the hiding of a disease prevents any cure, so to stifle convictions, seek to banish them from the mind, and then try and persuade ourselves that all is well, only makes bad matters worse. None but the penitent confessor can be pardoned (Psa. 32:5; 1 John 1:9). In the great majority of cases the chief reason why believers miss God's best is because they fail to keep short accounts with Him. They do not make conscience of what the world regards as innocent blemishes and which empty professors excuse as "trifling faults." And the result is that the conscience becomes comatose, laxity is encouraged, the Holy Spirit is grieved, Satan gains increasing power over him, and his unrepented sins hide God's face from him (Isa. 59:2).

7. It may be inquired, How do you harmonize your teaching that God's frown is upon His people while they follow a course of self-will and self-gratification, when it is written "He hath not dealt with us after our sins, nor rewarded us according to our iniquities" (Psa. 103:10)? Answer: there is nothing *to* harmonize, for the two things in no wise conflict. That Scripture is not speaking of God's present governmental dealings, but of what took place at conversion, when the penal consequences of all our sins were remitted. That is clear from what immediately follows, for after extolling the exalted character of God's

mercy, the Psalmist declared "As far as the east is from the west, so far *hath* He removed our transgressions from us" (verses 11, 12). God hath not dealt with the one who savingly believes the Gospel "after his sins," because He laid them upon his Surety and dealt with Him accordingly; and being infinitely just, the Divine Judge will not exact payment twice. Therefore, instead of rewarding him according to his iniquities he recompenses him according to the merits of his Redeemer.

If that were *not* the meaning of Psalm 103:10, we should make the Scriptures contradict themselves — an evil against which we need ever to be upon our guard. Psalm 89:30-32, shows that God *does* deal with His disobedient children according to their sins — in a disciplinary way, in this life — expressly declaring that "then will I visit their transgression with the rod, and their iniquity with stripes." And yet there is a very real and blessed sense in which the principle of the former passage applies here too. For, first, God is not severe and rigorous in marking every offence: if our love be warm and the general course of our conduct pleases Him, He passes by our nonwilful sins. And, second, God does not chasten immediately when we offend Him, but graciously grants us space for repentance, that the rod may be withheld. Third, He does not chasten us fully, according to our deserts, but tempers His righteousness with mercy. Even when plying the rod upon us "His compassions fail not," and therefore "we are not consumed" (Lam. 3:22). God dealt so with His people under the *old* economy: Ezra 9:13; Psalm 130:3!

8. Notwithstanding what has just been pointed out, the objection is likely to be made. Such teaching as yours is calculated to afford very "cold consolation" to some of God's afflicted people; you are acting only as a "Job's conforter" to them. Nor is such a demur to be wondered at in a day when the clamant cry of an apostate Christendom is "speak unto us smooth things, prophesy deceits" (Isa. 30:10). Though that be the language of the unregenerate, yet when Christians are in more or less of a backslidden condition, only too often that becomes the desire of their hearts also; and when the rod of God be upon them they crave pity and sympathy rather than love's faithfulness. What such souls most need is *help*, real help and not maudlin sentimentality. To give soothing syrup to one needing a bitter purgative is not an act of kindness. The chastened one requires to be reminded that God "does not afflict willingly," then urged to "search and try his ways and turn again to the Lord" (Lam. 3:40), and assured that upon true confession he will be forgiven.

9. But it may be objected, Did not David deeply repent of, contritely confess, and sincerely forsake his sins in the matter of Bathsheba and Uriah, yet God's rod was not removed from him and his family! That is, admittedly a more difficult question to answer. Nor should we look to the absolute sovereignty of God for its solution, for rather would that be cutting the knot instead of endeavouring to untie it. It should be evident to all that David's was no ordinary case, and that his sins were such as the Mosaic law called for capital punishment. Moreover, his iniquities were greatly aggravated by virtue of the position which he occupied: as a prophet, the sweet Psalmist of Israel, their king. Crimes committed by those in high civic or ministerial office are far more heinous and involve graver consequences than do those same crimes when committed by private persons. Therefore, though the Lord "forgave the iniquity of his sin"

(Psa. 32:5), yet He declared "the sword shall never depart from thine house (2 Sam. 12:10). The guilt and penal effects were remitted, but the governmental consequences remained.

"Howbeit, because by this deed thou hast given great occasion to the enemies of the Lord to blaspheme, the child also born unto thee shall surely die" (2 Sam. 12:14). And though he "besought God for the child, and fasted, and lay all night upon the earth," it was in vain; the sin of the father was visited upon the son, to show that God was "no respecter of persons" even where a monarch, and one beloved by Himself, was involved. And "the sword" never did depart from his house, for one after another of his sons met with a violent end. Such transgressions of Israel's king received no ordinary chastisements from God, to show that He would not countenance such actions, but vindicate His honour by manifesting His abhorrence of them. Thus, the governmental consequences of David's sins not being remitted upon his repentant confession is to be accounted for on the ground of his *public* character. Another example or illustration of the same principle is found in the case of Moses and Aaron, who because of their unbelief at Meribah, being Israel's leaders, were debarred from entering Canaan (Num. 20:12, 24).

10. As our readers have pondered the foregoing articles, it is probable that not a few have reverted in their minds to the experiences of *Job*, and wondered how it is possible to square with *them* the substance of what we have been writing. Obviously it is quite outside our present scope to enter upon anything like a full discussion of the book which describes the severe trials of that holy patriarch. Four brief statements must here suffice. First, that book presents to our notice something which is extraordinary and quite unique, as well as profoundly mysterious, namely, the position which Satan there occupies and his challenge of the Lord (Job 1:6-12). Second, it is therefore unwarrantable for us to appeal to the experiences of Job in *this* connection, for his case was entirely unprecedented. That which was there involved was not any controversy which God had with Job, but rather His contest with *Satan* in evidencing him to be a liar, disproving his charge that Job served God only for the benefit which he derived from Him for the same.

Satan's attack was not upon the patriarch, but was aimed at the Lord Himself, being tantamount to saying, Thou art incapable of winning the confidence and love of man by what Thou art in Thyself: deal roughly and adversely with him, and Thou wilt find that so far from him delighting in Thee and remaining loyal to Thee, he "will curse Thee to Thy face." Thus the excellency of the Divine character was thereby impugned and His honour challenged. The Lord condescended to accept Satan's challenge, and in the sequal demonstrate the emptiness of it by delivering His servant Job into His enemy's hand and permitting him to afflict him severely in his estate, his family, and in his own person. The central theme and purpose of the book of Job is not only missed, but utterly perverted, if we regard its contents as a description of God's chastening of Job for his sins (or "self-righteousness"), rather than a vindicating of His own honour and giving the lie to Satan's accusation by the making of Job's love and faith evident. So far from his cursing God, Job said, "Blessed be the name of the Lord," and after Satan had done his worst, "though He slay me, yet will I trust in Him."

Third, before Satan was allowed to lay a finger on Him, the Lord expressly declared of Job "There is none like him in the earth: a perfect [sincere] and an upright man, one that feareth God and escheweth evil" (1:8). Thus, at the outset, all ground for uncertainty of Job's moral condition is removed. The very fact that the first verse of the book contains such an affirmation renders it quite excuseless for anyone to conclude that in what follows we see the Lord dealing with Job on the ground that he had done something which displeased Him. Instead, no other saint in all the Scriptures is more highly commended by the Holy Spirit. Fourth, it should be carefully borne in mind that the book closes by informing us that "the Lord gave Job twice as much as he had before," that "The Lord blessed the latter end of Job more than his beginning" (42:10, 16). Thus, so far from conflicting with or contradicting our thesis that the righteous prosper, that the providential smile of God rests upon those whose ways please Him, the case of Job is a striking proof of the same!

11. The sufferings of our blessed Lord prior to the cross may present a difficulty unto a few in this connection. *There* was One who "set the Lord always before Him" (Psa. 16:8) and who could aver "I do always those things that please Him" (John 8:29). How then are we to account for the fact that He was "The Man of sorrows and acquainted with grief," that from the hour of His birth into this world unto His death, trial and tribulation, suffering and adversity, was His portion? Surely that should not occasion a problem or call for much elucidation. *All* of Christ's sufferings were due *to sin:* not His own, but his Church's. God would not allow an innocent person to suffer, much less His beloved Son to be unrighteously afflicted at the hands of the wicked. We never view aright the ill-treatment and indignities Christ experienced, both before and throughout His ministerial life, until we recognize that from Bethlehem to Calvary He was the vicarious Victim of His people, bearing their sins and suffering the due reward of their iniquities. He was "made under the Law" (Gal. 4:4), and as the Surety of transgressors was therefore born under its curse. At the moment of His birth the sword of Divine justice was unsheathed and returned not to its scabbard.

12. Others may ask, What about the severe and protracted sufferings of the apostle Paul (2 Cor. 11:23-27). They were neither extraordinary, like Job's, nor vicarious like Christ's! True, and that leads us to make this important observation: let none conclude from these articles that *all* suffering is to be regarded as *retributive*. That would be just as real a mistake as the one made by those who go to another extreme and suppose that all the suffering of saints is remedial, designed for purification and the development of their graces—which has provided a welcome sop for many an uneasy conscience! The subject of suffering is a much wider one than what has been dealt with in these articles, wherein but a single phase—the retributive—has been dealt with. It would take us too far afield to enter upon a systematic discussion of the whole problem of human sufferings, yet it is necessary for us to point out several important distinctions. Some suffering is to be attributed to the sovereignty of God (John 9:2, 3), yet we believe such cases are few in number.

Some suffering is due to heredity (Ex. 20:5): the whole of Achan's family were stoned to death for their father's sin (Josh. 7:24, 25), and the leprosy of

Naaman was judicially inflicted upon Gehazi and his children (2 Kings 5:7). Much suffering is retributive, a personal reaping of what we have sown. Some is remedial or educative (2 Cor. 4:16,17; James 1:2,3), fitting for closer communion with God, and increased fruitfulness. Other suffering is for righteousness' sake, for the Gospel's sake, and Christ's sake (Matt. 5:10, 11), which was what the apostle experienced, and which the whole "noble army of martyrs" endured at the hands of pagan Rome, when Christians were cast to the lions, and equally at the hands of Papal Rome, when countless thousands were vilely tortured and burned at the stake, and which would be repeated today if the pope and his cardinals had the power, for "*semper idem*" (always the same) is one of their proud boasts. We must distinguish sharply then between "tribulation" or persecution (John 16:33; 2 Tim. 3:12) for righteousness' sake, and Divine chastisement because of our sins.

There is no valid reason why the Christian should be confused in his mind by the above distinctions: nor will he be if he notes carefully the Scripture references given to them. Our purpose in drawing them was not only for the sake of giving completeness to these articles, and to supply preachers with a rough outline on the wider subject of "suffering," but chiefly in order to *point a warning*. It is entirely unwarrantable for us to conclude from the sight of an afflicted saint that he or she has missed God's best and is being chastised for his or her offences, though very often such is undoubtedly the case. But in our own personal experience, when God's providential smile be no longer upon us, and especially if the comforts of His Spirit be withdrawn from us, then it is always the wisest policy to assume that God is manifesting His displeasure at something in our lives, and therefore should we definitely, humbly and earnestly beg Him to convict us of wherein we have offended, and grant us grace to contritely confess and resolutely forsake the same.

The two forms of suffering most commonly experienced by the great majority of Christians are retributive—for their faults, and honorary—for the Truth's sake: though where there is much of the one there is rarely much of the other. Nor should there be any difficulty in identifying each of them, except that we must not mistake as the latter that coldness and estrangement of friends which is due to our own boorishness, for not a few pride themselves they are suffering for their faithfulness when in reality they are being rebuked and ostracised for their uncharitableness, or "as a busybody in other men's matters" (1 Peter 4:15). A close and humble walking with God, an uncompromising cleaving to the path of His commandments, is sure to stir up the enmity and evoke the opposition of the unregenerate, especially of empty professors, whose worldliness and carnality are condemned thereby. But whatever persecution and tribulation be encountered for *that* cause is a privilege and honour, for it is a having fellowship with Christ's sufferings (1 Pet. 4:13), and such should "rejoice that they are counted worthy to suffer shame for His name" (Acts 5:41). It is the *absence* of this type of suffering which evinces we are hiding our colours in order to avoid being unpopular.

CONCLUSION

Surely it is self-evident that the attitude of a holy God will be very different toward "a vessel wherein is no pleasure" (Hos. 8:8) and one who is "a vessel unto honour, sanctified and *meet* for the Master's use, prepared unto every good work" (2 Tim. 2:21). As we pointed out in an earlier article, an enjoyment of God's best will *not* exempt from the common tricks and vicissitudes of life but *will* encure having them sanctified and blest to him, as it will also deliver from those troubles and afflictions in which the follies of many Christians involve them. "Say ye to the righteous, that it shall be *well,* for they shall eat the fruit of their doings" (Isa. 3:10), on which the Puritan, Caryl, said, "They shall have good for the good they have done, or according to the good which they have done. If any object, But may it not be ill with men that do good and are good? Doth the Lord always reward to man according to his righteousness? I answer, first, It is well at present with most that do well. Look over the sons of men, and generally ye shall find that usually the better they are, the better they live. Second, I answer, It shall be well with all that do well in the issue, and for ever" (vol. 10, p. 439).

Finally, we again urge upon young Christians to form the habit of keeping short accounts with God, to promptly confess every known sin unto Him, even though it be the same sin over and over again. There is no verse in all the Bible which this writer has made more use of and pleaded so frequently as 1 John 1:9. Failure at this point is a certain forerunner of trouble. Only too often Christians, particularly in seasons of temporal prosperity, will not take the time and trouble to search their hearts and lives for those things which displease the Holy One. Hence it is that God so often has occasion to take his refractory children apart from the world, laying them upon beds of sickness, or bringing them into situations where they *will* "consider their ways" (Hag. 1:5). If they then refuse to do so, they shall "suffer loss" (1 Cor. 3:15) eternally. It is greatly to be feared that not a few who will, by grace, enter the everlasting kingdom of our Lord and Saviour Jesus Christ shall, through their own follies, fail to have "an *abundant* entrance" (2 Pet. 1:11) thereinto. O that neither writer nor reader may be among those saints who will be "*ashamed* before Him at His coming" (1 John 2:28). We shall not, if we put everything right between our souls and Him in the present!

SLEEPY SAINTS

What an anomaly! Drowsing on the verge of eternity! A Christian is one who, in contrast to the unregenerate, has been awakened from the sleep of death in trespasses and sins, made to realize the unspeakable awfulness of endless misery in hell and the ineffable joy of everlasting bliss in heaven, and thereby brought to recognize the seriousness and solemnity of life. A Christian is one who has been taught experientially the worthlessness of all mundane things and the preciousness of Divine things. He has turned his back on Vanity Fair and has started out on his journey to the Celestial City. He has been quickened into newness of life and supplied with the most powerful incentives to press toward the mark for the prize of the high calling of God in Christ Jesus. Nevertheless, it is sadly possible for him to suffer a relapse, for his zeal to abate, his graces to languish, for him to leave his first love, and become weary of well-doing. Yea, unless he be very much on his guard, drowsiness *will* steal over him, and he will fall asleep. Corruptions still indwell in him, and sin has a stupefying effect. He is yet in this evil world, and it exerts an enervating influence. Satan seeks to devour him, and unless resisted steadfastly will hypnotize him. Thus, the menace of this spiritual "sleeping sickness" is very real.

Slumbering saints! What an incongruity! Taking their ease while threatened by danger. Lazing instead of fighting the good fight of faith. Trifling away opportunities to glorify their Saviour, instead of redeeming the time: rusting, instead of wearing out in His service. We speak with wonderment and horror of Nero fiddling while Rome was burning, but far more startling and reprehensible is a careless Christian who has departed from God, bewitched by a world which is doomed to eternal destruction. Such a travesty and tragedy is far from being exceptional. Both observation and the teaching of Scripture prove it to be a common occurrence. Such passages as the following make it only too evident that the people of God *are* thus overcome. "It is high time to awake out of sleep, for now is our salvation nearer than when we believed" (Rom. 13:11). "Awake to righteousness, and sin not" (1 Cor. 15:34). "Awake thou that sleepest" (Eph. 5:14). Each of those clamant calls is made to the saints. So, too, is that exhortation addressed to them, "Ye are all the children of light, and the children of the day: we are not of the night nor of darkness. Therefore let us not sleep, as do others; but let us watch and be sober" (1 Thess. 5:5,6).

Our Lord gave warning of the same phenomenon in Matthew 25:1-13, which points some very searching lessons upon the subject now before us. We do not propose to give an exposition of those verses, still less waste time on canvassing the conflicting theorizings of men thereon. Instead of indulging in useless speculations upon what has been termed the "prophetic" applications of that passage, we intend to dwell upon what is of far more practical importance and profit to the Christian's walk. First, let it be duly noted that this parable of the Virgins was delivered by Christ not to a promiscuous multitude, but to His own disciples: it was *to them* that He said, "Watch, therefore, for ye know neither the day nor the hour wherein the Son of man cometh" (verse 13). Therein He exhorted His followers to maintain an attitude of the utmost alertness and diligence, to be on their guard against a sudden surprisal, to see to it that they were in a constant state of readiness to welcome and entertain Him at His appearing. In that thirteenth verse Christ clearly indicated the principal design of this parable, namely, to enforce the Christian duty of watchfulness, particularly against the tendency and danger of moral drowsiness and spiritual apathy in the performance of our duties.

Second, we would here earnestly warn the reader against placing any restrictions on the words of Holy Writ. In the light of the Analogy of Faith, that is the general tenor of Scripture, it is quite unwarrantable for us to *limit* the words "wherein the Son of man cometh" to His ultimate appearing at the end of this age or world. It is our duty to make use of the Concordance and carefully observe the different senses in which the "coming" of Christ is referred to in the Word, and distinguish between them. For example, the communications of grace to God's people in the administration of His Word and ordinances is spoken of thus, *"He* shall *come down* like rain upon the mown grass, as showers that water the earth" (Psa. 72:6, and cf. Deut. 32:2). Again, there was a *judicial* coming of the Lord in the destruction of Jerusalem, when He made good the threat, "What shall the Lord of the vineyard do? *He will come* and destroy the husbandmen, and will give the vineyard to others" (Mark 12:9)—He came not literally in Person, but instrumentally by the Romans! Then there is also a "coming" of

Christ to His people in the renewed manifestations of His love: "If a man love Me, he will keep My words; and My Father will love him, and We will *come* unto him" (John 14:23).

Christ has come to His people *vicariously:* as He declared unto the apostles, "I will not leave you comfortless: *I will come* to you" (John 14:18), where according to the preceding verses the principal reference is plainly to the public descent of the Holy Spirit on the day of Pentecost. Again, Christ often visits His people in the chariot of *His providence:* sometimes favourably, at others adversely, as in "Remember therefore from whence thou art fallen, and repent, and do the first works, or else *I will come* unto thee quickly, and will remove thy candlestick" (Rev. 2:5, and cf. verse 16). Again, He "comes" *instrumentally* by the ministry of the Gospel: "And that He might reconcile both unto God in one body by the Cross, having slain the enmity thereby, and *came* and preached peace to you which were afar off" (Eph. 2:16, 17, and cf. Luke 10:16). Again, He comes *spiritually* to those who yearn for and seek after fellowship with Him: "I will come in to him, and sup with him, and he with Me" (Rev. 3:20). Finally, He will come literally and visibly (Acts 1:11; Rev. 1:7). Thus it is a serious mistake to jumble together the communicative, judicial, manifestative, vicarious, providential, instrumental, and spiritual "comings" of Christ; as it also is to *restrict* to His second advent every verse where it speaks of His "coming" or appearing.

In like manner, it is equally wrong for us to limit our Lord's "Watch therefore, for ye know neither the day nor the hour wherein the Son of man cometh" to a "looking for that blessed hope and the glorious appearing of our great God and Saviour Jesus Christ." Most of the other seven things mentioned above are *not* to be excluded therefrom. We are to be on the *qui vive* (or alert) for His approaches to us in the means of grace, attentive to His appearings before us in providence, recognize Him in the ministry of the Gospel, and expectantly wait His visits of intimate fellowship. The Christians's continuance in this world is the period of both his "watching" and his "waiting" for removal therefrom; and since he knows not whether that will be by death or by his being caught up to meet the Lord in the air, he is to be prepared for either event—if he be so for the former, he will be for the latter. This call for him to "watch" signifies that he is to "keep his heart with all diligence" (Prov. 4:23), "Keep himself from idols" (1 John 5:21), "Keep himself in the love of God" (Jude 21). It bids us "Watch and pray, that ye enter not into temptation, knowing that [though] the spirit be willing, the flesh is weak" (Matt. 26:41). In a word, that exhortation requires us to attend to the interests of our souls with unremitting diligence and circumspection.

"Then shall the kingdom of heaven be likened unto ten virgins, which took their lamps and went forth to meet the Bridegroom" (Matt. 25:1). This is not said to be a similitude of the attitude of "the Bride" toward her Bridegroom, for the scope of it is wider, taking in the whole sphere of Christian profession. Hence in what follows the "Virgins" are divided into two groups—the regenerate and the unregenerate. Thus it would have been inaccurate to designate the whole of *them* "the Bride"! It is therefore a *discriminating* parable, like that of the wheat and tares, and that of the good and bad fish in Matthew 13. If it be asked, Why should Christ address such a parable unto the apostles, the answer is, Because there was a Judas among *them!* It is outside our present scope to consider the "foolish" virgins: suffice it to say that *externally* they differed not from the "wise" ones. They represent not the irreligious and immoral, but unsaved church members, those who have "escaped the pollutions of the world through the knowledge of the [not "their"!] Lord and Saviour Jesus Christ" (2 Peter 2:20), but who have never experienced a miracle of grace in their hearts. Though having lamps in their hands, they had no oil "in their vessels" (verses 3 and 4)—no grace in their souls! This calls for writer and reader to make honest and careful examination of themselves, to "give diligence to make his calling and election sure" (2 Peter 1:10).

"Then shall the kingdom of heaven be likened unto ten virgins." Many and varied are the figures used to describe the disciples of Christ. They are spoken of as salt, as lights, as sheep, as living stones, as kings and priests. When complete, and in its corporeal capacity, the Church is referred to as the Lamb's "Wife," but individually they are termed "the virgins, her companions" (Psa. 45:14, and cf. Song of Solomon 8:13; Rev. 1:9) They are called "virgins" for the purity of their faith: for none—no matter how pleasing is his personality or irreproachable his outward conduct—who is fundamentally unsound is to be regarded as a Christian. Thus the apostle, when expostulating with a local church for giving a hearing to false teachers, told them, "For I am jealous over you with godly jealousy: for I have [ministerially] espoused you to one Husband, that I may present you as a chaste virgin to Christ" (2 Cor. 11:2). Again; they are called "virgins" for the purity of their worship. God is a jealous God and will not brook any rival, and therefore we find, all through Scripture, that idolatry is expressed as harlotry, hence the vile and corrupt Papacy is designated "The mother of harlots" (Rev. 17:5). Once more: they are called "virgins" for the purity of their walk, refusing friendship and fellowship with the adulterous world, cleaving to Christ—"they are virgins: these are they which follow the Lamb whithersoever He goeth" (Rev. 14:4).

The saints are expressly bidden *to go forth* to meet the Bridegroom. "Go forth, O ye daughters of Jerusalem, and behold king Solomon with the crown wherewith his mother crowned him in the day of his espousals" (Song of Solomon 3:11)—an exceedingly interesting and blessed verse which we must not dwell upon. It is the antitypical Solomon, the prince of peace, who is here in view. His "mother" is the natural Israel, from whom according to the flesh He sprang—a figure of the spiritual Israel, in whose hearts He is "formed" (Gal. 4:19). The "day of his espousals" was when Israel entered into a solemn covenant with the Lord (Jer. 2:2, and see Exod. 24:3-8, for the historical reference), adumbrating our marital union with Christ, when we "gave our own selves to Him" (2 Cor. 8:5) and were "joined unto the Lord" (2 Cor 6:17), crowning Him the King of our hearts and lives. Here the "daughters of Jerusalem"—the same as the "virgins"—are bidden to "behold" their majestic and glorious King: to attentively consider the excellency of His person, to be engaged with His perfections, to admire and adore the One who is "Altogether Lovely." But in order thereto there must be active effort on their part. Not to the dilatory does Christ reveal Himself (Song of Solomon 3:1).

"Which took their lamps, and went forth to meet the Bridegroom." The taking of their lamps signifies making an open profession of their faith. They were not secret disciples, hiding their light under a bushel, but those who were unashamed to be known as the followers of Christ. Luke 12:35, serves to explain this force of the figure: "Let your loins be girded about, and your *lamps* [more literally] burning, and ye yourselves like unto men that wait for their Lord." Of His forerunner Christ said, "He was a burning and shining lamp" (John 5:35). But other thoughts are suggested and things implied by these virgins taking their lamps. It tells us they availed themselves of suitable means, making provision against the darkness which they would encounter. The principal means for the Christian is the Word, which is "a lamp [same Greek word as in Luke 12:35, and John 5:35] that shineth in a dark place" (2 Peter 1:19). It also shows they had no intention of going to sleep, but purposed to remain vigilant; which renders more searching what follows. It also intimates they were sensible of the difficulty of their task. Only one who, after a full day's work, has sat out the night by a sick bed knows how hard it is to keep alert throughout the long hours of darkness.

It needs to be clearly realized by the believer that the Word is supplied him not only as "bread" to feed upon, a "sword" for him to employ in repulsing the attacks of his enemies, but also as an illuminator: "Thy Word is a lamp unto my feet" (119:105), revealing those paths in which I must walk if I would meet with the eternal Lover of my soul. "And went forth to meet the Bridegroom." *That* must ever be our object in the use of means and attendance upon the administration of the Divine ordinances. That going forth to meet the Lord is to be understood as expressing both external and internal action. Externally, it signifies separation from the world, especially its pleasures, for Christ will not be met with while we waste our time engaging in them. "Be not unequally yoked together with unbelievers ... come out from among them" (2 Cor. 6:14-17) must be heeded if we would "meet the Bridegroom." More particularly, their going forth denoted a turning of their backs upon the apostate ecclesiastical system: Christ had informed His disciples that he had abandoned a Judaism which had rejected Him (Matt. 23:37, 38), so if they would meet with Him, they too must "go forth unto Him outside the camp" (Heb. 13:15). The same is true now.

If the Christian would meet with and have blessed fellowship with Christ, he must not only walk in separation from all intimacy with the profane world, but turn his back on every section of the religious world which gives not Christ the pre-eminence. That calls for the denying of self and "bearing His reproach." Our readiness so to do will depend upon how highly we esteem Him. *Internally*, it signified the activity of their affections. It imports their delight in Him, that He was the Object of their desires and expectations. It connotes the exercise of their graces upon Christ, an outgoing of the whole soul after Him; *such* a going out after Him as David had: "One thing [supremely] have I desired of the Lord, that will I seek after: that I may dwell in the house of the Lord [the place of communion] all the days of my life, to behold the beauty of the Lord" (Psa. 27:4). There can be no soul-satisfying beholding of His excellency unless there be deep longing for and earnest seeking after Him, which is what is purported by the "went forth to *meet* the Bridegroom!"

"Went forth to meet the Bridegroom" denotes a craving for fellowship with and a definite seeking after Him, and where *they* be absent it is vain to think we are among those who "love His appearing." Those words refer to the exercise of the believer's graces, so that he can say "My soul followeth hard after Thee" (Psa. 63:8). Of *faith*, acted upon its Object, viewing Him as His person and perfections are portrayed in the Word. Of *hope*, expecting to meet with Him, for Him to "manifest Himself unto us" (John 14:21), as well as being for ever with Him. Of *love*, which desires its Beloved and cannot be content away from Him. It is for the affections to be set upon things above where Christ sitteth on the right hand of God, resulting in a stranger and pilgrim character on earth. It is a going out of self, absorbed with the One who loves us and gave Himself for us. Only so can He be experientially encountered, beheld with delight, fellowshipped. That "went forth to meet the Bridegroom" is *such* a going forth of the affections and exercise of our graces upon Him as made Paul to say, "But what things *were* gain to me, those I counted loss for Christ: yea doubtless, I count all things but loss for the excellency of the knowledge of Christ Jesus my Lord" (Phil. 3:8, 9).

"While the Bridegroom tarried, they all slumbered and slept" (Matt. 25:6). How pathetic! How searching and solemn! The season of *His* tarrying was the time of *their* failing. They did not continue as they began. Their graces were not kept in healthy exercise. They ceased to attend unto the great business assigned them. They grew weary of well-doing. Instead of occupying our heads with the "prophetic" fulfilment of the verse, we need to bare our hearts and suffer them to be searched by it. Instead of saying, Those words now accurately describe the present condition of Christendom as a whole, we need to inquire how far they pertain to each of us individually. Far more to the point is it to ask myself, *Am I a slumbering and sleeping Christian?* Nor is that question to be answered hurriedly. If on the one hand I need to beware of thinking more highly of myself than I ought, or pretend all is well with me when such is not the case; on the other, God does not require me to act the part of a hypocrite, and in order to acquire a reputation for humility claim to be worse than I am. Peter was not uttering a presumptuous boast when he said unto Christ "Thou knowest that I love Thee." But Judas was an impostor when he greeted Him with a kiss.

But before we can truthfully answer the question, Am I spiritually asleep? we must first ascertain what are the marks of one who *is* so. Let us then, in order to assist the honest inquirer, describe some of the *characteristics* of sleep. And since we are not making any effort to impress the learned, we will be as simple as possible. The things which characterize the body when it is asleep will help us to determine when the soul is so. When the body is asleep it is in a state of inactivity, all its members being in repose. It is also a state of unconsciousness, when the normal exercises of the mind are suspended. It is therefore a state of insensibility to danger, of complete helplessness. Spiritual sleep is that condition wherein the faculties of the believer's soul are inoperative and when his graces no longer perform their several offices. When the mind ceases to engage itself with Divine things, and the graces be not kept in healthy exercise, a state of slothfulness and inertia ensures. When the grand truths of Scripture regarding God and Christ, sin and grace, heaven and hell, exert not a lively and effectual influence upon us, we quickly become drowsy and neglectful.

A slumbering faith is an inactive one. It is not exercised upon its appointed Objects nor performing its assigned tasks. It is neither drawing upon that fullness of grace which is available in Christ for His people, nor is it acting on the precepts and promises of the Word. Though there still be a mental assent to the Truth, yet the heart is no longer suitably affected by that which concerns practical godliness. Where such be the case a Christian will be governed more by tradition, sentiment, and fancy, rather than by gratitude, the fear of the Lord, and care to please Him. So too when his hope becomes sluggish, he soon lapses into a spiritual torpor. Hope is a desirous and earnest expectation of blessedness to come. It looks away from self and this present scene and is enthralled by "the things which God hath prepared for them that love Him." As it eyes the goal and the prize, it is enabled to run with patience the race set before us. But when hope slumbers he becomes absorbed with the objects of time and sense, and allured and stupefied with present and perishing things. Likewise when love to God be not vigorous, there is no living to His glory; self-love and self-pity actuating us. When the love of Christ ceases to constrain us to self-denial and a following the example He has left us, the soul has gone to sleep.

Where those cardinal graces be not in healthy exercise, the Christian loses his relish for the means of grace, and if he attempts to use them it is but perfunctorily. The Bible is read more from habit or to satisfy conscience than with eager delight, and then no impression is left on the heart, nor is there any sweet meditation thereon afterwards. Prayer is performed mechanically, without any conscious approach unto God or communing with Him. So in attending public worship and the hearing of the Word: the duty is performed formally and without profit. When the body sleeps it *neither eats nor drinks:* so it is with the soul. Faith is the hand which receives, hope the saliva which aids digestion, love the masticator and assimilator of what is partaken. But when they cease to function the soul is starved, and it becomes weak and languid. The more undernourished be the body the less strength and ability has it for its tasks. In like manner, a neglected soul is unfit for holy duties, and the most sacred exercises become burdensome. Thus, when a saint finds his use of the means of grace wearisome and the discharge of spiritual privileges irksome, he may know that his soul is slumbering Godwards.

In the parable itself four *causes* of spiritual sleep are indicated. 1. *Failure to remain watchful.* In its wider sense "watching" signifies an earnest taking heed unto ourselves and our ways, realizing how prone we are to "turn again to folly" (Psa. 85:8). So long as the saint be left in this world, he is in constant danger of bringing reproach upon the holy Name he bears, and becoming a stumbling-block to his brethren. Watchfulness (the opposite of carelessness) is exercising a diligent concern and care for our souls, avoiding all occasions to sin, resisting temptation (Matt. 26:41). It is to "stand fast in the faith, quit you like men" (1 Cor. 16:13)—be regular in our duties. When we be lax in serving the Lord, in mortifying our lusts, and less fervent and frequent in prayer, then slumber has begun to steal over us. Ultimately, it respects "looking for that blessed hope," which is a very different thing from awaiting the fulfilment of prophecy or the accomplishing of an item in God's "dispensational programme." It is far more than expecting an important event, namely, the second advent of Christ Himself, and that implies delight in Him, yearning after Him, practical readiness for His appearing: Luke 12:35, 36.

2. *The Bridegroom's delay* resulted in lack of perseverance on their part. Since we know not how soon or how long deferred will be our call to depart from this

world, we need to be unremitting in duty, in a state of constant readiness. Not only a desirous expectation but a "patient waiting for Christ" (2 Thess. 3:5) is required of us. "Blessed are those servants whom the Lord when He cometh shall find watching . . . If he shall come in the second watch, or come in the third watch, and find them so, blessed are those servants. And this know, that if the good man of the house had known what hour the thief would come, he would have watched and not have suffered his house to be broken through" (Luke 12:37, 38). It was because Moses tarried so long in the mount that Israel grew weary of waiting and gave way to their lusts—a warning to us not to relax our vigilance. How long had the Old Testament saints to wait for His first advent! "Behold the husbandman waiteth for the precious fruit of the earth and hath long patience for it . . . be ye also patient: stablish your hearts" (James 5:7, 8), exercising faith and hope. See Luke 21:36.

3. *Intimacy with graceless professors.* The wise virgins failed because they were in too close contact and fellowship with the foolish ones. That is confirmed by the Divine warning "Be not deceived: evil companionships [the verbal form of that Greek word is rendered "communed with" in Acts 24:26] corrupt good manners," which is immediately followed by "Awake to righteousness, and sin not" (1 Cor. 15:33,34), showing us that intimacy with the Christless produces lethargy. "We are more susceptible of evil than good: we catch a disease from one another, but we do not get health from one another. The conversations of the wicked have more power to corrupt than the good to excite virtue. A man that would keep himself awake unto God, and mind the saving of his soul, must shake off evil company" (Manton). See Psalm 119:115. It is not the openly profane, but the loose and careless professor who is the greatest menace to the Christian. Hence "having a form of godliness but denying [inaction] the power thereof, from such *turn away*" (2 Tim. 3:5).

4. *Inattention to the initial danger:* they "slumbered" (a lighter form) before they slept! How that shows the need for taking solemn and earnest heed to the beginnings of spiritual decline! If we yield to a spirit of languor we shall soon lapse into a sound sleep. One degree of slackness and carelessness leads to another: "Slothfulness casteth into a deep sleep" (Prov. 19:15), Once our zeal abates and our love cools, we become remiss and heedless. If we do not fight against a cold formality when engaged in sacred exercises, we shall ultimately cease them entirely. All backsliding begins in the heart! Sin stupefies before it hardens. If we cease to heed the gentle strivings of the Spirit, conscience will become calloused. "David, when he fell into adultery and blood, he was like one in a swoon . . . We have need to stand always upon our watch. Great mischiefs would not ensue if we took notice of the beginnings of those distempers which afterwards settle upon us" (Manton).

Other causes of spiritual sleepiness which are not directly indicated in this parable are specified in or may be deduced from other passages. For example: "Turn away mine eyes from beholding vanity; quicken Thou me in Thy way" (Psalm 119:37). The apposition of those two petitions clearly connotes that an undue occupation with worldly things has a deadening effect upon the heart. Nothing has a more enervating influence on the affections of a believer than for him to allow himself an inordinate liberty in carnal vanities. Again, "Take heed to yourselves, lest at any time your hearts be overcharged with surfeiting and drunkenness, and cares of this life; and so that day come upon you unawares . . . Watch ye therefore, and pray always" (Luke 21:34-36). Gluttony not only dulls the senses of the body but renders the mind sluggish too, and thereby the whole man is unfitted for the discharge of spiritual duties, which call for the engaging and putting forth of "all that is within us" (Psalm 103:1); equally so do carking cares which engross the attention and stupefy the understanding and render the affections torpid. Yet more searching is it to observe that "be sober" *precedes* "be vigilant" in 1 Peter 5:8. Sobriety is freedom from excesses, particularly a sparing use made of the lawful comforts of this life. Any form of intemperance breeds inertia. If, then, we are able to keep wide awake, we must be "temperate in *all* things" (1 Cor. 9:25).

The *consequences* of spiritual sloth are inevitable and obvious. Space allows us to do little more than name some of the chief ones. (1) Grace becomes inoperative. When faith be not exercised upon Christ, it nods and ceases to produce good works. When hope languishes and becomes inactive, the heart is no longer lifted above the things of time and sense by a desirous expectation of good things to come. Then love declines and is no longer engaged in pleasing and glorifying God. Zeal slumbers and instead of fervour there is heartless formality in the use of means and performance of duties. (2) We are deprived of spiritual discernment, and no longer able to experientially perceive the vanity of earthly things and value of heavenly, and the need of pressing forward unto them. (3) A drowsy inattention to God's providences. Eyes closed in sleep take no notice of His dealings with us, weigh not the things which befall us. Mercies are received as a matter of course, and signs of God's displeasure are disregarded (Isa. 42:25).

(4) Unconcernedness in the commission of sin, so that we cease mortifying our lusts and resisting the Devil. Spiritual stupidity makes us insensible to our danger. It was while David was taking his ease that he yielded to the Devil (2 Sam. 11:1, 2). (5) The Holy Spirit is grieved and His gracious operations are suspended and His comforts withheld. (6) So far from us overcoming the world, when our spiritual senses be dulled, we are absorbed with its attractions or weighted down by its cares. (7) We are robbed by our enemies (Luke 12:39)—of God's providential smile, of our peace and joy. (8) Fruitlessness: see Proverbs 24:30, 31. (9) Carnal complacency: peace and joy being derived from pleasant circumstances and earthly possessions, rather than Christ and our heritage in Him. (10) Spiritual poverty: see Proverbs 24:33, 34. (11) Indifference to the cause and interests of Christ: it was while men slept Satan sowed his tares, and abuses creep into the church. (12) A practical unpreparedness for Christ's coming: Luke 21:36; Rev. 16:15.

Let us now point out some of the *correctives.* 1. Spiritual sleepiness is best prevented by our faith being engaged with the person and perfections of Christ; it is not monastic retirement, nor the relinquishment of our lawful connection with the world, but the fixing of our minds and affections upon the transcendant excellency of the Saviour, which will most effectually preserve us from being hypnotized by the baits of Satan. A believing and adoring view of Him who is "Fairer than the children of men" will dim the lustre of the most attractive objects in this world. When the One who is "altogether lovely" is beheld by anointed eyes the flowery paths of this scene become a dreary wilderness, and the soul is quickened to press forward unto Him, until it sees the

King in his beauty face to face. 2. Especially will a keeping fresh in our hearts the unspeakable sufferings of the Saviour draw us away from threatened rivals, and inspire grateful obedience to Him. "For the love of Christ [particularly His dying love] constraineth us" (2 Cor. 5:14). 3. By praying daily for God to quicken and revive us. 4. By being doubly on our guard when things are going smoothly and easily. 5. By maintaining a lively expectation of Christ's appearing (Heb. 9:28). 6. By attending to such exhortations as Hebrews 12:2, 3, allowing no abatement of our vigour. 7. By putting on the whole armour of God (Eph. 6:13-18).

CHRISTIAN EMPLOYEES

How intensely practical is the Bible! It not only reveals to us the way to Heaven, but it is also full of instruction concerning how we are to live here upon earth. God has given His Word unto us to be a lamp unto our feet and a light unto our path: that is, for the regulating of our *daily walk*. It makes known how God requires us to conduct ourselves in all the varied relations of life. Some of us are single, others married; some are children, others parents; some are masters, others servants. Scripture supplies definite precepts and rules, motives and encouragements for each alike. It not only teaches us how we are to behave in the church and in the home, but equally so in the workshop and in the kitchen, supplying necessary exhortations to both employers and employees—clear proof God has not designed that all men should be equal, and sure index that neither "Socialism" nor "Communism" will ever universally prevail. Since a considerable portion of most of our lives be spent in service, it is both for our good and God's glory that we heed those exhortations.

A secular writer recently pointed out that "work has increasingly come to be regarded as a distasteful means to the achievement of leisure, instead of leisure as a recuperative measure to refit us for work." That is a very mild way of saying that the present generation is pleasure mad and hates any kind of real work. Various explanations have been advanced to account for this: such as the ousting of craftsmanship by machinery, the fear of unemployment discouraging zeal, the doles, allowances and reliefs which are available for those who don't and won't work. Though each of those has been a contributing factor, yet there is a more fundamental and solemn cause of this social disease, namely, the loss of those moral convictions which formerly marked a large proportion of church-goers, who made conscience of serving the Lord while engaged in secular activities, and who were actuated by the principles of honesty and integrity, fidelity and loyalty.

Nowhere has the hollowness of professing Christians been more apparent, during the last two or three generations, than at this point. Nowhere has more reproach been brought upon the cause of Christ than by the majority of those employees who bore His name. Whether it be in the factory, the mine, the office, or in the fields, one who claims to be a follower of the Lord.

Jesus should stand out unmistakably from his fellow employees who make no profession. His punctuality, his truthfulness, his conscientiousness, the quality of his work, his devotion to his employer's interests, ought to be so apparent that there is no need for him to let others know by his *lips* that he is a disciple of

Christ. There should be such a marked absence of that slackness, carelessness, selfishness, greed and insolence which mark the majority of the ungodly, that all may see he is motivated and regulated by higher principles than they are. But, if his conduct belies his profession, then his companions are confirmed in their opinion that "there is nothing in religion but talk."

Nor does the whole of the blame rest upon them: *the pulpit* is far from being guiltless in this matter. The Lord has expressly bidden His servants to preach thereon, as being a subject of great importance and an essential part of that doctrine which is according to godliness. "Let as many servants as are under the yoke count their own masters worthy of all honour, that the name of God and His doctrine be not blasphemed. And they that have believing masters, let them not despise them because they are brethren, but rather do them service, because they are believing and beloved, partakers of the benefit: *these things teach* and exhort" (1 Tim. 6:1, 2). But where is the minister today who does so? Alas, how many have despised and neglected such practical yet unpopular teaching! Desirous of being regarded as "deep," they have turned aside unto doctrinal disputes or prophetical speculations which profit no one. God says "If any man teach otherwise . . . he is a fool, knowing nothing" (1 Tim. 6:3. 4)!

Once again is the pastor Divinely ordered, "But speak thou the things which become sound doctrine: that the aged men be sober . . . the aged women likewise . . . young men likewise exhort to be sober-minded . . . Servants to be obedient unto their own masters, to please them well in all things; not answering again, not purloining, but showing all good fidelity; that they may adorn the doctrine of God our Saviour in all things" (Titus 2:1-9). Are you, fellow minister, speaking upon *these* things? Are you warning servants that all needless absenteeism is a sin? Are you informing those of your church members who are employees that God requires them to make it their constant endeavour to give full satisfaction unto their masters in every part of their conduct: that they are to be respectful and not saucy, industrious and not indolent, submissive and not challenging the orders they receive? Do you teach them that their conduct either *adorns* or *disgraces* the doctrine they profess? If not, you are sadly failing in carrying out your commission.

In view of the almost total silence of the pulpit thereon, it is striking to see how frequently the New Testament epistles inculcate and enlarge upon the duties of employees. In Ephesians 6 we find the apostle exhorting, "Servants be obedient to them that are your masters according to the flesh, with fear and trembling, in singleness of heart, as unto Christ. Not with eye-service, as men-pleasers, but as the servants of Christ, doing the will of God from the heart. With good will doing service, as to the Lord, and not to men" (verses 5-7). Christian servants are required to comply with the calls and commands of their employers: to do so with respectful deference to their persons and authority, to be fearful of displeasing them. They are to be as diligent in their work and to discharge their duties with the same conscientious solicitude when their master is *absent* as when his eye is upon them. They are to perform their tasks "with good will," not sullenly and reluctantly, but thankful for an honest means of livelihood. And all of this as "the servants of Christ," careful not to dishonour Him by any improper behaviour, but seeking to glorify Him: working from such motives as will sanctify our labours and make them a "spiritual sacrifice" unto God.

In Colossians 3 the apostle also exhorted, "Servants, obey in all things your masters according to the flesh, not with eye-service, as men-pleasers, but in singleness of heart, fearing God. And whatsoever ye do, do it heartily, as to the Lord, and not unto men" (verses 22, 23). Every lawful command he must obey, however distasteful, difficult or irksome. He is to be faithful in every trust committed to him. Whatsoever his hand findeth to do, he must do it with his might, putting his very best into it. He is to do it readily and cheerfully, taking pleasure in his work. All is to be done "as to the Lord," which will transform the secular into the sacred. Then it is added, "Knowing that of the Lord ye shall receive the inheritance: for ye serve the Lord Christ" (verse 24)—what encouragement to fidelity is that! "But he that doeth wrong, shall receive the wrong which he hath done" (verse 25) is a solemn warning to deter from failure in duty, for "either in this world or the other, God will avenge all such injury" (J. Gill).

"Servants be subject to your masters with all fear: not only to the good and gentle, but also to the froward. For this is thankworthy, if a man for conscience endure grief, suffering wrongfully" (1 Peter 2:18, 19). This repeated insistence of the apostles for employees discharging their duties properly, indicates not only how much the glory of God is involved therein, but also that an *unwillingness* on their part makes such repetition necessary—evidenced by those who take two or three days' extra holiday by running off to religious meetings, thereby putting their masters to inconvenience. Holiness is most visible in our daily conduct: performing our tasks in such a spirit and with such efficiency as will commend the Gospel unto those we serve. Let it be borne in mind that these instructions apply to *all* servants, male and female, in every station and condition. Let each reader of these pages who is an employee ask himself or herself, How far am I really making a genuine, prayerful and diligent endeavour to comply with God's requirements in the performance of my duties? Let no "rules of unions" nor "regulations of shop stewards" be allowed to set aside or modify these Divine commandments.

It is to be pointed out that the above precepts are enforced and exemplified in the Scriptures by many notable examples. See how the Spirit delighted to take notice of the devotion of Eliezer, even praying that the Lord God would "send me good speed this day, and show kindness unto my master Abraham" (Gen. 24:12), and note how faithfully he acquitted himself and how well he spake of his master. Jacob could say, "ye know that with all my power I have served" (Gen. 31:6): can *you* aver the same? Though a heathen "his master saw that the Lord was with him, and that the Lord made all that he did to prosper in his hand. And Joseph found grace in his sight" (Gen. 39:3, 4): what a testimony was that! Scripture also chronicles the unfaithfulness of Elisha's servant and the fearful judgment which came upon him (2 Kings 5:20-27). Finally, let all domestics and employees remember that the *servant place* has been honoured and adorned for ever by the willing and perfect obedience of the incarnate Son of God!

"Whatsoever thy hand findeth to do, do with thy might" (Ecc. 9:10)—put your very best into it.

THE WORK OF THE LORD

Our present design is twofold: to censure a misuse, and to explain the meaning of the following verse: "Therefore, my beloved brethren, be ye steadfast, unmoveable, always abounding in the work of the Lord; forasmuch as ye know that your labour is not in vain in the Lord" (1 Cor. 15:58). In the heedless hurry of this slipshod age not a few have taken those words as though they read, "Work *for* the Lord," and have used them as a slogan for what is now styled "Christian service," most of which is quite unscriptural—the energy of the flesh finding an outlet in certain forms of religious activities. In this day of pride and presumption it has been quite general to speak of engaging in work for the Lord, and to entertain the idea that He is beholden to such people for the same, that were their labours to cease, His cause would not prosper. To such an extent has this conceit been fostered that it is now a common thing to hear and read of our being "co-workers with God" and "co-operators" with Him. It is but another manifestation of the self-complacent and egotistical spirit of Laodicea (Rev. 3:17), and which has become so rife.

But it is likely to be asked, Does not Scripture itself speak of the saints, or at least ministers of the Gospel, being "co-workers with God"? The emphatic answer is No, certainly not. Two passages have been appealed to in support of this carnal and blatant notion, but neither of them when rightly rendered teach any such thing. The first is 1 Corinthians 3:9, which in the Authorized Version is strangely translated "For we are labourers together with God." Literally the Greek reads, "For God's we are: fellow-workers; God's husbandry, God's building, ye are." The apostle had just rebuked the Corinthians (3:1-3), particularly for exalting some of the servants of God above others (verse 4). He reminded them, first, that the apostles were but ministers or "servants," mere instruments who were nothings unless God blessed their labours and "gave the increase" (verses 6, 7). Then, he pointed out that one instrument ought not to be esteemed above another, for "he that planteth" and "he that watereth are one" (verse 8) and shall each "receive his own reward." While in verse 9 he sums up by saying those instruments are "God's"—of His appointing and equipping; "fellow-workers," partners in the Gospel field.

The second passage appealed to lends still less colour to the conceit we are here rebutting: "We then as workers together with Him beseech you" (2 Cor. 6:1), for the words "with Him" are in italics, which means they are not contained in the original, but have been supplied by the translators. This verse simply means that the instruments God employed in the ministry of the Gospel were joint-labourers in beseeching sinners not to receive His grace in vain. There is no thought whatever of "co-operating" with God. Why should there be? What assistance does the Almighty need! Nor does He ever voluntarily *receive* any (Job 22:2, 3; Luke 17:10). What an absurdity to suppose the finite could be of any help to the Infinite! At most, we can but concur with His appointments, and humbly present ourselves before Him as empty vessels to be filled by Him. It is wondrous condescension on His part if He designs to employ us as His agents; the honour is ours, we confer no favour on Him. The Lord is the sole Operator; His servants the channels through which He often—though by no means always—operates. Ministers are not co-ordinates with God, but subordinates to Him.

There is something particularly repulsive to a spiritual mind in the concept of worms of the earth "co-operating" with the Most High, for it is a virtual deifying of the creature, a placing of him on a par with the Creator. Surely it is enough simply to point out that fact for all humble and Spirit-taught souls to reject with abhorrence such a grotesque fiction. Different far was the spirit which possessed the chief of the apostles. Said he "I laboured more abundantly than they all: *yet not I*, but the grace of God which was with me" (1 Cor. 15:10). When the Twelve responded to their Master's commission we are told that "they went forth and preached everywhere, *the Lord* working with them" (Mark 16:20)—otherwise their labours had yielded naught. Paul placed the honour where it rightfully belonged when he declared "I will not dare to speak of those things which *Christ* hath not wrought by me" (Romans 15:18). How different was that from regarding himself as a "co-operator" with Him! It is just such creature boasting which has driven the Lord outside the churches.

In view of what has been pointed out above, it is scarcely surprising that those possessed of more zeal than knowledge should eagerly lay hold of a clause in 1 Corinthians 15:58, and adopt it as their motto. Such activities as holding Gospel services in the streets, engaging in what is called "personal work," taking part in meetings where young people are led to believe they are "giving their testimony for Christ," and other enterprises for which there is no warrant whatever in the Epistles (where church members are more directly instructed and exhorted), are termed "working for the Lord" or "serving Christ." Very different indeed is the task which *He* has assigned His followers: a task far more difficult to perform, and one which is much less palatable to the flesh. Namely to keep their hearts with all diligence: mortifying their lusts, and developing their graces (Col. 3:5, 12), to cleanse themselves from all filthiness of the flesh and spirit and perfect holiness in the fear of God (2 Cor. 7:1), to witness for Christ by their *lives*, "showing forth His praises" (1 Peter 2:9).

There is therefore a real need for the inquiry, Exactly what is meant by "the work of the Lord" in 1 Corinthians 15:58? It should at once be apparent that we do not have to go outside the verse itself for proof that the popular understanding which now obtains of it is thoroughly unwarrantable. First, it is not one which specially concerns ministers of the Gospel nor "Christian workers," but instead, pertains to *all* the saints, for it is addressed to the "beloved brethren" at large. Second, the work of the Lord which it enjoins calls for us to be "steadfast and immoveable," which are scarcely the qualities to be associated with what the churches term "Christian service"—had *that* been in view such adjectives as "zealous and untiring" had been far more pertinent. Third, the duty here exhorted unto is one which allows of no intermission, as the "always abounding in" expressly states—even the most enthusiastic "personal workers" would scarcely affirm that! Finally, the "knowing [not praying or hoping] that your labour is *not in vain* in the Lord" makes it clear that the well-meant but misguided efforts of the religious world today are not in view.

Grammatically "the work of the Lord" may import either that work which He *performs*, or that which He *requires* from His people. The fact that it is one unto which He calls *them,* obliges us to understand it in the second sense. When Christ was asked "What shall we do, that we might work the works of God?" (John 6:28) it should be obvious that they meant, What are those works which God requires of us? Our Lord answered: "This is the work of God: that ye believe on Him whom He hath sent": *that* is what He has commanded (1 John 3:23) and that is what will be acceptable unto Him. The same inquiry should proceed from the Christian: What is the all-inclusive work which God has assigned us? The summarized answer is given in 1 Corinthians 15:58: the "work of the Lord," in which the saints are to be always abounding, is a general designation of the whole of Christian duty. As "the way of the Lord" (Genesis 18:19) signifies the path of conduct which He has marked out for us, so "the work of the Lord" connotes that task He has prescribed us.

As is generally the case with erroneous interpretations, our moderns have taken this verse out of its setting and ignored its controlling context, paying no attention to its opening "Therefore." 1 Corinthians 15 is the great resurrection chapter, and may be outlined thus. First, the resurrection of Christ Himself (verses 1-11). Second, His rising from the dead secures the "resurrection of life" to all His people (verses 20-28). Third, the nature of their resurrection bodies (verses 42-54). In between those divisions, denials of the resurrection are refuted and objections thereto answered. Further indication is this that to terminate the chapter with an injunction to engage in what is termed "Christian service" would be totally foreign to what precedes. Instead, the apostle closes his teaching on resurrection with a triumphant thanksgiving (verses 55-57) and an ethical inference drawn from the same. Therein is illustrated a fundamental characteristic of the Scriptures: that doctrinal declaration and moral exhortation are never to be severed, the former being the ground upon which the latter is based: first a statement of the Christian's privileges, and then pointing out the corresponding obligation.

In the context the Holy Spirit has set before us something of the glorious future awaiting the redeemed of Christ: in verses 55-58 He makes practical application of the whole to the immediate present. Doctrine and duty are never to be divorced. Neither in the promise nor the precept is "the life that now is" separated from "that which is to come." All Truth is designed to have a sanctifying effect upon our daily walk. Something more than a mere head belief of the contents of Scripture is required of us, namely an incorporating of them in the character and conduct. Truth so blessed as that set forth in verses 42-54 should fill the hearts of believers with joy (verses 55-57), and move them to the utmost diligence and endeavour to please and glorify the Lord (verse 58). The "But thanks be to God, which giveth us the victory through our Lord Jesus Christ" (verse 57) is the language of *faith,* for faith gives a present subsistence to things which are yet future. The final verse announces the transforming effect which such a revelation and a hope so elevating should have upon us; or, stating it in other words, this injunction makes known the corresponding obligation which such a prospect entails. What that transforming effect should be, what that obligation consists of, we shall now seek to state.

"Therefore, my beloved brethren, be ye steadfast, unmoveable, always abounding in the work of the Lord, forasmuch as ye know that your labour is not in vain in the Lord." An analysis of this verse shows that it consists of two things: an exhortation and motives to enforce the same. The exhortation includes a threefold task: to be "steadfast" in the faith, in our convictions of the Truth; to be "unmoveable" in our affections, in our expectations of the things promised; to be "always abounding in the work of the Lord," in doing His will, in performing those good works which He has foreordained we should walk in. The "work of the Lord" may be regarded first as a general expression, comprehending all that He requires from us in the way of duty: in the exercise of every grace and the practice of every virtue. "Always abounding in the work of the Lord" signifies ever engaged in obeying His Word, seeking His glory, aiming at the advance of His kingdom. More specifically, it imports that lifelong task which He has set before us, and which may be summed up in two words—mortification and sanctification: the denying of self and putting to death of our lusts; the developing of our graces and bringing forth the fruits of holiness.

Strictly speaking, it is "the work of the Lord" to which we are here called, and the steadfastness and immovability are prerequisites to our "always abounding" therein. But we shall consider them as separate duties. First, "be ye steadfast" in the faith and profession of the Gospel, and not "tossed to and fro and carried about with every wind of doctrine" (Eph. 4:14). Be firmly fixed in your convictions: having bought the Truth, sell it not. "Prove all things, hold fast that which is good." That by no means precludes further progress of attainment, for we are to press forward unto those things which are still before; yet in order thereto there must be stability and resolution, a "holding fast the faithful Word" (Titus 1:9), an eschewing of all false doctrine.

Second, "unmoveable," which is a word implying testing and opposition. Suffer not the allurements of the world nor the baits of Satan to unsettle you. Be not shaken by the trials of this life. Be patient and persevering whatever your lot. Seek grace to say of all troubles and afflictions, what Paul said of bonds and imprisonments—"none of these things move me." And why should they? None of them impugn God's faithfulness. Moreover, they work for us "a far more exceeding and eternal weight of glory while we look not at the things which are seen." Then be unwavering in your expectations and "be not moved away from the hope of the Gospel," no matter what opposition you encounter. Notwithstanding your discouraging failures, the backslidings of fellow Christians, the hypocrisy of graceless professors, "hold fast the confidence and rejoicing of the hope firm unto the end" (Heb. 3:6).

Third, "always abounding in the work of the Lord": constantly occupied in doing those good works which honour God. More specifically: "Whether therefore ye eat or drink, or whatsoever ye do, do all to the glory of God" (1 Cor. 10:31). "Giving all diligence, add to your faith, virtue, and to virtue, knowledge; and to knowledge, temperance; and to temperance, patience; and to patience, brotherly kindness; and to brotherly kindness, love; for if these things be in you, and abound, they make you that ye shall neither be barren nor unfruitful in the knowledge of our Lord Jesus Christ . . . for if ye do these things ye shall never fall: for so an entrance shall be ministered unto you abundantly into the everlasting kingdom of our Lord and Saviour Jesus Christ" (2 Peter 1:5-11). *That* is "the work of the Lord," that the task assigned us. Then let not the difficulty of such duties nor the imperfections of your performances dishearten you; suffer not the hatred of your enemies nor the severity of their opposition to deter you. "Let us not be weary in well doing, for in due season we shall reap, if we faint not" (Gal. 6:9).

"Therefore, my beloved brethren, be ye steadfast, unmovable, always abounding in the work of the Lord, forasmuch as ye know that your labour is not in vain in the Lord" (1 Cor. 15:58). In the previous portion of this article we did little more than give a topical treatment of this verse: let us now furnish a contextual exposition of it. In verses 55 and 56 the apostle asked, "O death, where is thy sting? O grave, where is thy victory?" to which he replied, "The sting of death is sin, and the strength of sin is the law." Then he exultantly cried: "But thanks be to God, which giveth us the victory through our Lord Jesus Christ" (verse 57). The tense of the verb should be closely observed: it is not "hath given" nor "will give," but "giveth us the victory." It is also to be carefully noted that the "victory" here referred to is one over death and the grave viewed in connection with sin and the Law, and that it is shared by all saints and is not some peculiar experience which only a few fully consecrated souls enter into. Obviously, that victory will only be fully and historically realized on the resurrection morning; yet even now it is apprehended by faith and enjoyed by hope, and, in proportion as it really *is* so, will the believer know practically something of "the power of Christ's resurrection."

"Thanks be to God, which giveth us the victory through our Lord Jesus Christ" is the language of joyful *faith*, in response to the revelation given in the previous fifty-six verses. Christ's triumph over death as the wages of sin and the penalty of the Law ensures the resurrection of all His sleeping saints, for it was as their federal Head (verses 20-22) that He suffered for their sins and bore the Law's curse, as it was that as "the last Adam" (verse 45) He was victorious over the tomb. As faith lays hold of that blessed truth and its possessor appropriates a personal interest therein, he realizes that he *himself* has (judicially) passed from death to life, that sin cannot slay nor the Law curse him, that he is justified by God "from all things" (Acts 13:39). Such a realization cannot but move him to exclaim "Thanks be to God." By virtue of his union with Christ, for him death's sting has been extracted, and therefore it has been robbed of all terror. It is sin which gives power and horror to death, but since Christ has made full atonement for the believer's sin and obtained remission for him, death can no more harm him than could a wasp whose venomous sting had been removed—though it might still buzz and hiss and attempt to disturb him.

"The strength of sin is the Law": its power to condemn was supplied by the transgressing of it. But since Christ was made a curse for us we are released therefrom. The entire threatening and penalty of the Law was executed upon the Surety, and therefore those in whose stead He bore it are exempted from the same. But more: because in Eden sin violated the holy commandment of the Lawgiver, the Law received a *commanding power* over the sinner, making sin to rage and reign in him, compelling him to serve it as a slave. That was but just. Since man preferred the exercise of self-will to submission to the authority of his Maker, the Law was given both a condemning and commanding power over him. In other words, the enthralling power or strength which sin exerts over its subjects is an intrinsic part of the Law's curse. The Law commands holiness, but by reason of man's depravity its very precepts exasperate his corruptions—as the sun shining on a dung-heap stirs up its filthy vapours. God punishes sin with sin: since the commission of sin was man's choice, the strength of sin shall be his doom. But Christ has not only delivered His people from the penalty of sin, but from its reigning power too, so that His promise is "Sin shall not have dominion over you" (Romans 6:14).

"Therefore, my beloved brethren, be ye steadfast, unmovable, always abounding in the work of the Lord": let *that* be your response to mercies so great. Manifestly, the apostle is here drawing a conclusion from all that precedes, particularly from what is said in verses 56 and 57. Divine grace, through the death and resurrection of Christ, has *judicially* delivered the believer from both the guilt and dominion of sin, and from the whole curse of the Law. How then shall he answer to such blessings? Why, by seeing to it that those mercies are now made good by him in a *practical* way. And how is he to set about the same? First, by complying with Romans 6:11: "Likewise, reckon ye also yourselves to have died indeed unto sin, but alive unto God through Jesus Christ our Lord"; which in the light of the previous verse signifies: By the exercise of faith in what the Word declares, regard yourselves as having legally passed from death to life in the person of your Surety. Second, by heeding Romans 6:12: "Let not sin therefore reign in your mortal body, that ye should obey it in the lusts thereof"; which means: Suffer not indwelling sin to lord it over you. Since you be absolved from all you did in the past, yield obedience to God and not to your corruptions.

We cannot rightly interpret 1 Corinthians 15:58, unless its connection with verses 56 and 57 be duly noted. Its opening "Therefore" is as logical and necessary as the one in Romans 6:12, and what follows that passage enables us to understand our present one. "Neither yield ye your members as instruments of unrighteousness unto sin; but yield yourselves unto God as those that are alive from the dead, and your members as instruments of righteousness unto God": that is, conduct yourselves *practically* in harmony with what is true of you (in Christ) *legally*. Another parallel passage is, "Forasmuch as Christ hath suffered for us in the flesh, arm yourselves likewise with the same mind" (1 Peter 4:1), where the doctrinal fact is first stated, and then the practical duty enjoined. Legally, "victory" is ours *now*, as our justification by God demonstrates. Experientially, we have been freed from the dominion of sin, and are delivered, in measure, from its enticing power, for there is now that in us which hates and opposes it. At death, sin is completely eradicated from the soul; and at resurrection its last trace will have disappeared from the body. From his exposition of the grand truth of resurrection the apostle made practical application, exhorting the saints to walk in newness of life.

In view of our participation in Christ's victory, we are here informed of the particular duty which is incumbent upon us, namely to strive against sin, resist temptation, overcome Satan by the blood of the Lamb, and bring forth the fruits of holiness to Him. But, in order thereto, we must be "steadfast" in the conviction of our oneness with Christ in His death and resurrection, and "unmovable" in our love and gratitude to Him. The Greek for *"always abounding in* the work of the Lord" conveys the idea of quality more than quantity, progressive improvement rather than multiplicity of works—"continually making advance in true piety" (Matt. Henry). *Excel in it* is the thought: rest not satisfied with present progress and attainments, but each fresh day endeavour to perform your duty better than on the previous one. This lifelong task of mortification and sanctification is called "the work of the Lord" because it is the one which He has assigned us, because it can be performed only in His strength, and because it is that which is peculiarly well pleasing in His sight.

That duty can only be discharged in a right spirit as faith apprehends the Christian's union with Christ, and then thankfully acts accordingly. There cannot be any Gospel holiness without such a realization. There can be no evangelical obedience until the heart is really assured that Christ has removed death's "sting" for us and has taken away from the Law the "strength of sin." Only then can the believer serve God in "newness of spirit": that is, in loving gratitude, and not from dread or to earn something. Only then will he truly realize that as in the Lord he has "righteousness" for his justification, so in Him he has "strength" (Isaiah 45:22) for his walk and warfare. Thus the opening "Therefore" of our verse not only draws a conclusion which states the obligation entailed by the inestimable blessings enumerated in the context, but also supplies a power *motive* for the performance of that obligation—a performance which is to be regarded as a great privilege. Since "Christ died for our sins" (verse 3), since He be "risen from the dead, and become the first fruits of them that slept" (verse 20), since *we* shall be "raised in glory" and "bear the image of the heavenly," let our gratitude be expressed in a life of practical holiness.

A second motive to inspire the performance of this duty is contained in the closing clause of our verse: "forasmuch as ye know that your labour is not in vain in the Lord." He will be no man's Debtor: every sincere effort of gratitude—however faulty its execution—is valued by Him and shall be recompensed. "God is not unrighteous to forget your work and labour of love which ye have showed toward His name" (Heb. 6:10). The Christian should be fully assured that a genuine endeavour to do God's will and promote His glory will receive His smile, produce peace of conscience and joy of heart here, and His "well done" hereafter. "In the keeping of His commandments there is great reward." This was the motive which animated Moses in his great renunciation (Heb. 11:24-26): "he had respect unto the recompense of the reward."

"Forasmuch as ye know that your labour is not in vain in the Lord." "Labour" is a stronger word than "work," signifying effort to the point of fatigue. "In the Lord" means in union with and dependence upon Him. Such labour shall not be strength spent for naught. Yet *that* is exactly what it appears to be to the Christian. To him it seems his efforts to mortify his lusts and develop his graces are utterly futile. He feels that his best endeavours to resist sin and bring forth the fruits of holiness are a total failure. That is because he judges by sight and sense! God, who looks at the heart and accepts the sincere will for the deed, reckons otherwise. "Ye know that your labour is not in vain in the Lord": such an assurance is ours in exact proportion to the measure of faith. The more confident our hope of reward, the more determined will be our efforts to mortify sin and practice holiness — the *only* "labour" *God* has assured us "is *not* in vain"!

EVANGELICAL OBEDIENCE

No matter how cautiously one may deal with obedience, if he is to be of any service to the real people of God, his efforts are sure to be put to a wrong and evil use by hypocrites, for they will "wrest it, as they do also the other Scriptures, unto their own destruction" (2 Peter 3:16). Such is the perversity of human nature. When a discriminating sermon is preached, the particular design of which is to draw a clear line of demarcation between genuine and nominal Christians, and "take forth the precious from the vile" (Jer. 15:19), the graceless professor will *refuse* to make application of the same and examine his own heart and life in the light thereof; whereas the possessor of Divine life is only too apt to draw a wrong deduction and deem himself to be numbered among the spiritually dead. Contrariwise, if the message be one of comfort to God's little ones, while too many of them are afraid to receive it, others who are not entitled will misappropriate it unto themselves. But let not a realization of these things prevent the minister of the Gospel from discharging his duty, and while being careful not to cast the children's bread unto the dogs, yet the presence of such is not to deter him from setting before the children their legitimate portion.

Before developing our theme, we will define our terms. "Evangelical obedience" is obviously the opposite of *legal*, and that is of two sorts. First, the flawless and constant conformity unto His revealed will which God required from Adam and which He still demands from all who are under the Covenant of Works; for though man has lost his power to perform, God has not relinquished His right to insist upon what is His just due. Second, the obedience of unregenerate formalists, which is unacceptable unto God, not only because it is full of defects, but because it issues from a natural principle, is not done in faith, and is rendered in a mercenary spirit, and therefore consists of "dead works." Evangelical is also to be distinguished from *imputed* obedience. It is blessedly true that when they believe on the Lord Jesus Christ, God reckons to the account of all the subjects of the Covenant of Grace the perfect obedience of their Surety, so that He pronounces them justified, or possessed of that righteousness which the Law requires. Yet *that* is not the only obedience which characterizes the redeemed. They now *personally* regulate their lives by God's commands and walk in the way of His precepts; and though their performances have many blemishes in them (as they are well aware), yet God is pleased for Christ's sake to accept the same.

It should need no long and laborious argument to demonstrate that God must require obedience, full and hearty obedience, from every rational agent, for only thus does He enforce His moral government over the same. The one who is indebted to God for his being and sustenance is obviously under binding obligations to love Him with all his heart, serve Him with all might, and seek to glorify Him in all that he does. For God to issue commands is for Him to impose His authority on the one He has made; for him to comply is but to acknowledge his creaturehood and render that submission which becomes such. It is as the Lawgiver that God maintains His sovereignty, and it is by our obedience that we acknowledge the same. Accordingly we find that upon the day of his creation Adam was placed under law, and his continued prosperity was made dependent upon his conformity thereto. In like manner, when the Lord took the nation of

Israel into covenant relationship with Himself, He personally made known His laws unto them and the sanctions attached thereto.

There are no exceptions to what has just been pointed out. The inhabitants of heaven, equally with those of earth, are required to be in subjection to their Maker. Of the angels it is said they "do His commandments, hearkening unto the voice of His word" (Psalm 103:20). When His own Son became incarnate and assumed creature form, He too entered the place of obedience and became subservient to God's will. Thus it is with His redeemed. So far from the subjects of the Covenant of Grace being released from submission to the Divine Law, they are under additional obligations to render a joyful and unqualified obedience to it. "Thou hast commanded us to keep Thy precepts diligently" (119:4). Upon which Manton said, "Unless you mean to renounce the sovereign majesty of God, and put Him besides the throne, and break out into open rebellion against Him, you must do what He has commanded. 'Charge them that be rich' (1 Tim. 1:9)—not only *advise*, but *charge* them!" Christ is Lord as well as Saviour, and we value Him not as the latter unless we honour Him as the former (John 13:13).

Not only does God require obedience, but an obedience which issues from, is animated by, and is an expression of, *love*. At the very heart of the Divine Decalogue are the words "showing mercy unto thousands of them that love Me and keep My commandments" (Exodus 20:6). While there must be respect for His authority, unless there is also a sense of God's goodness, and an outgoing of the affections unto Him because of His excellency, there can be no hearty and acceptable obedience. The severest self-denials and the most lavish gifts are of no value in God's esteem unless they are prompted by love. The inseparability of love and obedience was made plain by Christ when He said, "If ye love Me, keep My commandments" (John 14:15). "He that hath My commandments and keepeth them, he it is that loveth Me" (John 14:27). "If a man love Me, he will keep My words" (John 14:27). Likewise taught His apostles: "This is the love of God: that we keep His commandments" (1 John 5:3). "Love is the fulfilling [not a substitute for, still less the abnegation] of the Law" (Romans 13:10), for it inspires its performance.

To proceed one step farther: God has graciously promised to work obedience in His people. "I will put My spirit within you, and cause you to walk in My statutes, and ye shall keep My judgments and do them" (Ezek. 36:27)—He would not only point out the way, but move them to go therein; not force by external violence, but induce by an inward principle. "They shall all have one Shepherd: they shall also walk in My judgments and observe My statutes" (Ezek. 37:24). Christ makes them willing in the day of His power that He should rule over them, and then directs them by the sceptre of His righteousness. Under the new covenant God has engaged Himself to create in His people, by regenerating grace, a disposition which will find the spirituality and holiness of His requirements congenial unto it. "I will put My laws into their minds and write them in their hearts" (Heb. 8:10): I will bestow upon them a new nature which will incite unto obedience and cause them to delight in My Law after the inward man. Herein lies a part of their essential conformity unto Christ: "I delight to do Thy will, O My God; yea, Thy Law is within My heart" (Psalm 40:8).

In accordance with those promises, we find that in the ministry of Christ two things were outstandingly prominent: His enforcement of the claims of God's righteousness and His proclamation of Divine grace unto those who felt their deep need. Matthew 5:17-20; 19:16-21; 22:36-40, exemplify the former; Matthew 11:4-6, 28-30; 15:30, 31; Luke 23:42, 43; John 4:10, illustrate the latter. The Son of God came not to this earth in order to open a door unto self-pleasing and loose living, but rather to maintain God's holiness and make it possible for fallen creatures to live a holy life. Christ came here not only as a Saviour, but as a Lawgiver (Deut. 18:18, 19), "to be Ruler in Israel" (Micah 5:2), and therefore is He "the author of eternal salvation unto all them that *obey* Him" (Heb. 5:9). His mission had for its design not to lessen God's authority or man's responsibility, but to put His people into a greater capacity for serving God. Hence we find Him saying to His disciples, "Ye are My friends, if ye do whatsoever I command you" (John 15:14); and when commissioning His servants, He bade them teach believers "to observe all things whatsoever I commanded you" (Matt. 28:20).

Love to God and our neighbour is indeed the great duty enjoined by Law (Deut. 6:5; Lev. 10:18) and Gospel alike (Gal. 5:13, 14), yet is it a love which manifests itself by a hearty obedience (2 John 6). Though Christ delivers from the curse of the Law, yet not from its precepts: "That we, being delivered out of the hand of our [spiritual] enemies, might serve Him without fear, in holiness and righteousness before Him, all the days of our life" (Luke 1:74, 75). Every privilege of the Gospel entails an added obligation upon its recipient. As creatures it is our bounden duty to be in entire subjection to our Creator; as new creatures in Christ it doubly behoves us to serve God cheerfully. It is a great mistake to suppose that grace sets aside the claims of righteousness, or that the Law of God demands less from the saved than it does from the unsaved. Nowhere are the high demands of God set forth more fully and forcibly than in the epistles addressed to the saints. Take these as samples: "As He which hath called you is holy, so be ye holy in all manner of conversation" (1 Peter 1:15); "That ye might walk worthy of the Lord unto all pleasing, being fruitful in every good work" (Col. 1:10).

But right here a formidable difficulty presents itself. On the one hand the renewed soul clearly perceives the necessity and propriety of such a standard being set before him, and cordially acquiesces therein; yet on the other hand he has to acknowledge "to will is present with me, but how to perform that which is good I find not" (Romans 7:18). Though it is his deepest longing to measure up fully to the Divine standard, yet he is incapable of doing so; and though he cries earnestly unto God for enabling grace and unquestionably receives no little assistance from Him, yet at the close of this life his desire remains far from being realized. Now the healthy Christian is deeply exercised over this, and instead of excusing his failures cries, "O that my ways *were* directed to keep Thy statutes" (Psalm 119:5). But that is only half of the problem, and the least difficult half at that. The other half is, How is it possible for a holy God to accept and approve of imperfect obedience from His children? That He will not lower His standard to the level of their infirmities is clear from the passages quoted above; yet that He *does* both graciously receive and reward their faulty performances is equally plain from other verses.

In what has just been stated we discover one of the fundamental differences between the Covenants of Works and Grace. Under the former a rigorous and inflexible demand was made for perfect and perpetual conformity to God's Law, and no allowance or relief was afforded for the slightest infraction of it. A single default, the least failure, was reckoned guilty of breaking all the commandments (James 2:10), for not only are they, like so many links in the same chain, a strict unit, but the authority of the Lawgiver behind them was flouted. Nor was any provision made for the recovery of such a one. The constitution under which the first man, and the whole human race in him, was placed was without any mediator or sacrifice, and no matter how deep his remorse, or what resolutions of amendment he made, the transgressor lay under the inexorable sentence: "The soul that sinneth it shall die," for God will by no means clear the guilty. Moreover, under the first covenant, God provided no special grace to enable its subjects to meet His requirements. He made man in His own image, and pronounced him "very good," and then left him to his native and created strength. Finally, under that covenant man was required to yield obedience in order to his justification, for upon his compliance he was entitled unto a reward.

Now under the Covenant of Grace everything is the very opposite of that which obtained under the Covenant of Works. Complete subordination to the Divine will is indeed required of us, yet not in order to our justification before and acceptance with God. Instead, the moment we believe on the Lord Jesus and place our whole dependence on the sufficiency of His sacrifice, His perfect obedience is reckoned to our account, and God pronounces us righteous in the high court of heaven and entitled to the reward of His Law. Consequently our subsequent obedience is rendered neither under threat of damnation nor from a mercenary spirit, but out of gratitude for our deliverance from the wrath to come and because of our acceptance in the Beloved. Nor are we left to our own strength, or rather weakness. God does not barely command us, and then leave us to ourselves, but works in us both to will and to do His good pleasure. He communicates to us His blessed Spirit and makes available that fullness of grace and truth which there is in Christ our Head, for He is not only a Head of authority, but also of efficacious influence: "From whom the whole Body [Church] fitly joined together and compacted by that which every joint supplieth, according to the effectual working in the measure of every part" (Eph. 4:16).

What is yet more to the point in connection with our immediate subject, under the New Covenant provision *has been made* for the failures of its subjects. God does not reject their obedience because it is faulty, but graciously accepts the same when it is prompted by submission to His authority, is performed by faith, is urged by love, and is done with sincerity of purpose and endeavour. Sin has disabled from an exact keeping of God's commandments, but He approves of what issues from an upright heart and which unfeignedly seeks to please Him. We are bidden to "have grace whereby we may serve God acceptably [not flawlessly!] with reverence and godly fear" (Heb. 12:29). While God still justly requires from us a perfect and perpetual obedience, nevertheless He is graciously pleased to receive and own genuine efforts to conform to His will. He does so because of the merits of Christ and His continued mediation on our behalf. Having accepted our persons He also accepts our love-offerings—note the order in Genesis 4:4. We present spiritual sacrifices unto Him, and they are "acceptable to God *by Jesus Christ*" (1 Peter 2:5).

That we are here propounding no new and dangerous error will be seen from the following quotations. "Notwithstanding, the persons of believers being accepted through Christ, their good works are also accepted in Him: not as though they were in this life wholly unblameable and unreproveable in God's sight, but that He, looking upon them in His Son, is pleased to accept and reward that which is sincere, though accompanied with many weaknesses and imperfections" (Westminster Confession). "I call it Gospel obedience, not that it differs in *substance* from that required by the Law, which enjoins us to love the Lord our God with all our hearts, but that it moves upon *principles*, and is carried on unto *ends*, revealed only in the Gospel" (John Owen). According to the modification of the new covenant, "God, out of His love and mercy in Christ Jesus, accepts of such a measure of love and obedience as answereth to the measure of sanctification received" (Manton).

Though the above quotations are far from being Divinely inspired, and therefore are without any binding authority upon the children of God, nevertheless, they are from men who were deeply taught and much used by the Holy Spirit, and so are deserving of our serious and prayerful attention. While the Christian is forbidden to call any man "father," that is far from signifying that he should despise such teachers. There is no Antinomian laxity in the above citations, but a holy balance such as is scarcely ever found in the ministry of our day.

We have pointed out that God justly requires a perfect obedience from all rational creatures, and that under no circumstances will He lower His demand. Every regenerate soul concurs with God's holy claim, and deeply laments his inability to meet that claim. We also affirmed that under the moderation of the New Covenant constitution God is graciously pleased to accept and approve of an obedience from His people which, though sincerely desiring and endeavouring to measure up to His perfect standard, is, through their remaining corruptions and infirmities, a very defective one; and that He does so without any reflection upon His honour. We followed that brief averment by giving excerpts from some of the Puritans—the number of which might easily be multiplied—not for the purpose of buttressing our own teaching, but in order that it might be seen that we are not advancing here any dangerous or strange doctrine. Nevertheless, the majority of our readers will require something from an infinitely higher authority than that on which to rest their faith, and to it we now turn.

In Genesis 26:5, we find the Lord declaring: "Abraham obeyed My voice, and kept My charge—My commandments, My statutes, and My laws." Yet he did not do so perfectly, for he was a man "subject to like passions as we are"; nevertheless God owned his obedience, and, as the context there shows, rewarded him for the same. Sincere obedience, though it be not sinless, is acceptable unto God; if it were not, then it would be impossible for any of His children to perform a single act in this life which was pleasing in His sight. Not only so, but many statements made in the Scriptures concerning saints would be quite unintelligible to us—statements which *oblige us* to believe that God receives the hearty yet imperfect endeavours of His people; yea, that He attributes unto the same a far higher quality than they do. Thus, He said of Job "that man was perfect and upright, and one that feared God and eschewed evil"

120

(1:1): yet as we read all that is recorded of him it soon becomes apparent that he, like ourselves, was "compassed with infirmity."

When the Lord declared concerning David His servant that "he *kept* My commandments and My statutes" (1 Kings 11:34), He was speaking relatively and not absolutely. "The Lord delights in the way of a good man" (Psalm 37:23), notwithstanding that he often stumbles, yea, falls, in the same. There are but two classes of people in the sight of God: "the children of disobedience" (Eph. 2:2) and "obedient children" (1 Peter 1:14), yet many a regenerate soul is fearful of classifying himself with the latter. But he ought not—his scruples are due to an insufficiently enlightened conscience. When the Lord Jesus said to the Father of those whom He had given Him, "they have *kept* Thy Word" (John 17:8), surely it is obvious that He was not affirming that their obedience was perfect. "Evangelical keeping is filial and sincere obedience. Those imperfections Christ pardoneth, when He looketh back and seeth many errors and defects in the life, as long as we bewail sin, seek remission, strive to attain perfection. All the commandments are accounted kept when that which is not done is pardoned" (Manton). When the heart beats true to Him, Christ makes full allowance for our frailties.

With the Word of God in his hands there is no excuse for anyone who has, by Divine grace, been brought to hate sin and love God to stumble over the point we are now treating of. David had many failings and some of a gross and grievous nature, yet he hesitated not to say unto God himself: "I have *kept* Thy precepts" (Psalm 119:56). In *what sense* had he done so? Inwardly: in spirit, in holy resolution and earnest endeavour; outwardly too in the general current of his life; and wherein he failed, he deeply repented and obtained forgiveness from God. Christ will yet say to each one who has improved the talents entrusted to him, "Well done, good and faithful servant" (Matt. 25:21), yet that is far from implying that therein he was without fault or failure. When Paul prayed for the Hebrew saints that God would make them "perfect in every good work to do His will, working in you that which is wellpleasing in His sight," he was making request for those indwelt by sin, as his added "acceptable *through* Jesus Christ" (Heb. 13:21) necessarily implied. "Whatsoever we ask we receive of Him, because we keep His commandments" (1 John 3:22) would have no comfort for us if God accepted only sinless obedience.

"Man looketh on the outward appearance, but the Lord looketh on the heart" (1 Samuel 16:7). Those words are capable of more than one legitimate application, but they are peculiarly pertinent here. True, God is very far from being indifferent to the *substance* of our obedience, yet the spirit in which it is performed is what He notices first. Duties are not distinguished by their external form, but by their internal frame—one may perform the same duty from fear or compulsion which another does freely and out of love. "Waters may have the same appearance, yet one be sweet and the other brackish. Two apples may have the same colour, yet one may be a crab and the other of a delightful relish. We must look to the Rule that the matter of our actions are suited to it; otherwise we may commit gross wickedness, as those did who thought that they did God service by killing His righteous servants (John 16:2). We must look also to the face of our hearts, otherwise we may be guilty of gross hypocrisy" (S. Charnock). The Pharisees kept the sabbath with great strictness, yet their outward conformity unto that Divine Law was far from being acceptable in God's sight.

"The Lord weigheth the spirits" (Prov. 16:2). That has a meaning which should make each of us tremble; yet it should also be of great comfort to the regenerate, and evoke thanksgiving. If on the one hand the omniscient One cannot be imposed upon by the most pious appearance and utterances of the hypocrite, yet on the other He knows those "who *desire* to fear His name" (Neh. 1:11), even though some of their actions proceed from a contrary principle. All the intentions and motives of our hearts are naked and open before the eyes of Him with whom we have to do, and full consideration is given thereto as God estimates our performances. Was not this very truth both the comfort and confidence of erring Peter when he declared to his Master: "Lord, Thou knowest all things: Thou knowest that [contrary to appearances] I [really and truly] love Thee" (John 21:17). "If Thou, Lord, shouldest mark iniquities [the shortcomings of Thy full and righteous demands] . . . who shall stand?" (Psalm 130:3). Not one of His people. But, as the next verse goes on to assure us, "there is forgiveness with Thee that Thou mayest be feared"—yes, held in awe, and not trifled with. Blessed balance of truth!

"For if there be first a *willing mind*, it is accepted according to that a man hath, and not according to that he hath not" (2 Cor. 8:12): upon which Matthew Henry's commentary says: "The willing mind is accepted when accompanied with sincere endeavours. When men purpose that which is good and endeavour according to their ability to perform also, God will accept of what they have or can do, and not reject them for what they have not and what is not in their power to do; and this is true as to other things besides the work of charity." Yet it was prudently added: "But let us note here, that this Scripture will not justify those who think good meanings are enough, or that good purposes and the profession of a willing mind are sufficient to save them. It is accepted indeed, where there is a performance as far as we are able." A readiness of disposition is what God regards, and that disposition is judged by Him according to the resources which are at its command. Our Father estimates what we render unto Him by the purity of our intentions. Little is regarded as much when love prompts it. If the heart be really in it, the offering is well pleasing to Him whether it be but "two young pigeons" (Luke 2:24) or tens of thousands of oxen and sheep (1 Kings 8:63).

"The Covenant of Grace insists not so much upon the measure and degree of our obedience, as on the quality and nature of every degree—that it be sincere and upright" (Ezek. Hopkins). In contrast with legal obedience, evangelical consists of honest aims and genuine efforts, striving to live holily and to walk closely with God, according to the rules He has prescribed in His Word, and, according to the gracious condescension, yet equity, of the Gospel, is received and rewarded by God for Christ's sake. That holy purposes and sincere resolutions *are* accepted by God, though they be not really accomplished, is clear from what is recorded of Abraham, namely that "he offered up his son" (James 2:21), for he never actually "offered up" Isaac, except in intention and willingness. Upon which Manton said: "God counteth that to be done which is about to be done, and taketh notice of what is in the heart, though it be not brought to practice and realization. Yet not idle purposes when men hope to do tomorrow what should and can be done today." "We make it our aim, whether at home [in the body] or absent, to be wellpleasing unto Him" (2 Cor. 5:9) must be our grand and constant endeavour.

Another example to the point is the case of David, who desired and planned to provide a more suitable dwelling-place for Jehovah in Israel's midst. As Solomon, at a later date, declared: "But the Lord said to David my father, Forasmuch as it was in thine heart to build a house for My name, thou didst well, in that it was in thine heart" (2 Chron. 6:8). God graciously accepted the will for the deed, and credited His servant with the same. So it is with evangelical obedience: that which is truly sincere and is prompted by love unto God, though very imperfect, he graciously accepts as perfect. When He appeared before Abraham, the father of all them that believe, He declared, "I am the Almighty [all-sufficient] God, walk before Me and be thou perfect" (Gen. 17:1), which in the margin is accurately and helpfully rendered "upright or sincere," for absolute perfection is in this life impossible. Legal obedience was approved by *justice*, evangelical obedience is acceptable unto *mercy*. The former was according to the unabated rigour of the Law, which owned nothing short of a conformity without defect or intermission, whereas the latter is received by God through Christ according to the milder dispensation of the Gospel (Gal. 3:8).

2 Chronicles 30 records a very striking instance where God accepted the will for the deed, and enforced not the full requirements of His Law. "A multitude of the people, even many of Ephraim and Manasseh, Issachar and Zebulon, had not cleansed themselves, yet did eat of the passover otherwise than it was written. But he prayed for them, saying, The good Lord pardon everyone that prepareth his heart to seek God, the Lord God of his fathers, though he be not cleansed according to the purification of the sanctuary." Hezekiah apprehended God's mercy better than do some of His people today! "And the Lord hearkened to Hezekiah, and healed the people" (verses 19, 20). Ah, but note well that the king had restricted his request unto those who had "prepared their hearts to seek"! Such uprightness was the very opposite of what we read of in Deuteronomy 29:19, 20: "And it come to pass, when he heareth the words of this curse, that he bless himself in his heart, saying, I shall have peace, though I walk in the imagination of mine heart, to add drunkenness to thirst: the Lord will not spare him, but the anger of the Lord and His jealousy shall smoke against that man."

Sincere obedience necessarily presupposes regeneration, for filial submission can proceed only from a real child of God. A spiritual life or "nature" is the principle of that obedience, for when we are renewed by God there is newness of conversation. That which is born of the Spirit is spirit (John 3:6)—disposed and fitted for spiritual things. Yet *after* renewal there still remains much ignorance in the understanding, impurity in the affections, perversity in the will, yet so as grace prevails over nature, holiness over sin, heavenliness over worldliness. "But the high places were not removed; nevertheless, Asa's heart was perfect [upright] with the Lord all his days" (1 Kings 15:14). Though God writes His Law on our hearts (Heb. 8:10), yet as Ezek. Hopkins pointed out, "This copy is eternally durable, yet it is but as a writing upon sinking and leaky paper, which in this life is very obscure and full of blots." It is also termed "the obedience of faith" (Romans 1:5), because without faith it is impossible to please God; yet how feeble our faith is! It is therefore an obedience which is performed in reliance upon Christ's mediation (Rev. 8:3, 4) and enablement (Phil. 4:13).

But now we must endeavour to furnish a more definite and detailed answer to the pressing question: How am I to determine whether *my* obedience is really sincere and acceptable to God? By testing it with these criteria: First, is it one which, in its negative character, has a universal antipathy for sin? "The fear of the Lord is to hate evil" (Prov. 8:13)—such is the purity of that nature communicated to God's child at the new birth. Though evil still cleaves to and indwells him, yet his heart loathes it. His hatred of evil is evidenced by dreading and resisting it, by forsaking it in his affections and denying self, by bitterly mourning when overcome by it and confessing the same unto God, by exercising the contrary graces and cultivating the love of holiness. Where there exists this fear of the Lord which abhors evil, it will make no reserve or exception, nor tolerate or "allow" any form or phase of it. Instead, it will aver with the Psalmist: "I hate *every* false way" (119:104, 128), because contrary to the God I love, and as polluting to my soul.

Second, is it one which diligently endeavours to regulate the inner man as well as the outer? God's requirement is: "My son, forget not My law, but let thine *heart* keep My commandments" (Prov. 3:1). It was at this point that the hypocritical Pharisees failed so completely, for, said Christ: "Ye are like unto whited sepulchres which indeed appear beautiful outward, but are within full of dead men's bones and all uncleanness" (Matt. 23:27). The Lord has bidden us "keep thy heart with all diligence" (Prov. 4:23), and that calls for the checking of sinful thoughts, the mortifying of evil imaginations, the resisting of pride, self-will and unbelief; the scrutinizing of our motives and aims, and making conscience of temptations and occasions to sin. Third, is it one which has the glory of God for its aim? The heart is very deceitful, and much of human religion is prompted by nothing higher than to be "seen of men" and gain a reputation for personal piety. How searching are those words: "he that speaketh of himself seeketh his own glory" (John 7:18)! True piety is modest and self-effacing, aiming only at honouring the Lord and pleasing Him.

Fourth, is it one which has an appropriation of the whole revealed will of God, enabling me to say, "I esteem *all* Thy precepts" (Psalm 119:128)?—for the wilful rejection of one is the virtual of all. Though we fail miserably in some, and keep none of them perfectly, yet do our hearts approve of every duty enjoined? Fifth, is there a genuine willingness and honest desire to render full obedience unto God? If so, we shall not voluntarily and allowedly fall short of the highest perfection, but have an equal regard unto every Divine statute, not dispensing with nor excusing ourselves from the most severe and difficult. Sixth, is there a firm resolution ("I have sworn, and I will perform it"—119:106), a genuine effort ("I have inclined my heart to perform Thy statutes alway"—119:112), a persevering industry ("reaching forth unto those things which are before" and "pressing toward the mark"—Phil. 3:12-14), an assiduous striving to please God in all things? Seventh, is it accompanied by a conscience which testifies that though only too often I transgress, yet I loathe myself for it, and honestly endeavour to conform to the whole of God's will? Such an obedience God accepts and accounts perfect, because the falls are due to the subtlety of Satan, the deceitfulness of sin and the weakness of the flesh, rather than to a deliberate defiance and determined obstinacy.

Nowhere else in Scripture are the character and conduct of a saint so clearly and fully delineated as in Psalm 119, and the conscientious Christian should frequently compare himself with it. All through that Psalm we find holy resolution and earnest endeavour side by side with conscious weakness and frailty but dependence upon God. "Thou hast commanded us to keep Thy precepts diligently" (4)—"O that my ways were directed to keep Thy statutes" (5)—"I will keep Thy statutes: O forsake me not utterly" (8)—"With my whole heart have I sought Thee: O let me not wander from Thy commandments" (10)—"I will run the way of Thy commandments, when Thou shalt enlarge my heart" (32)—"Consider how I love Thy precepts: quicken me, O Lord, according to Thy lovingkindness" (159)—"Let Thine hand help me; for I have chosen Thy precepts" (173). Thus there are both holy yearning and activity, yet constant looking to God for strength and enablement.

Thus will it be seen that sincere obedience consists not of a sinless conformity to God's will, but of genuine desires and proportionate efforts after it. It comprises two parts: the mortification of our corrupt affections and the vivification of our graces, so that we increase in strength and make further advances in true piety. So also has it two adjuncts or attendants: repentance for past sins, and the exercise of faith for present grace. Failures are reflected upon with hatred and shame, are confessed to God with sorrow and contrition, earnestly resolving and endeavouring to abstain from any further repetition of them. Faith looks to the merits of Christ, pleads the virtues of His blood, rests upon His intercession for us in heaven, lays hold of the promises, and counts upon God's acceptance of our imperfect obedience for His Son's sake, knowing that it deserves not His approbation, and is rewarded (Psalm 19:11) not as a matter of debt, but of pure grace. Then let none conclude that they have no grace because there are so many imperfections in their obedience: a child may be weak and sickly, yet a legitimate one! Renew your repentance daily, rely wholly on the mediation of Christ, and draw upon His fullness.

PRIVATE JUDGMENT

It is our present design to treat of the right, the necessity and the duty of each person freely to exercise his reason, conscience and will, especially in matters pertaining to his soul. Every man has the right to think for himself and express or aver his thoughts on political, moral and spiritual matters, without being subject to any civil or ecclesiastical penalty or inconvenience on that account. Conversely, no man is entitled to force his ideas upon others and demand that they subscribe thereto, still less to propagate them to the disturbing of the public peace. This is a truth which needs proclaiming and insisting upon today, not only because of the widespread apathy towards taking a firm stand for the same, but because the dearly bought liberties which have for so many years been enjoyed by those living in the English-speaking world are now in danger of being filched from them. On the one hand is the steady growth of what is termed "Totalitarianism," under which the minds and bodies of its subjects are little more than robots; and on the other hand is the rapidly increasing power and arrogance of Rome, in which the souls of its members are the slaves of a rigid and merciless tyranny.

In writing upon the freedom of the individual, it is our design to shun as far as possible anything which savours of *party* politics; yet, since the scope of our present theme requires us to say at least a few words on the right of *civil* liberty, we cannot entirely avoid that which pertains to human governments. But instead of airing our personal views, we shall treat only of those broad and general principles which are applicable to all nations and all ages, and restrict ourselves very largely to what the Holy Scriptures teach thereon. God has not left His people, or even men at large, without definite instruction concerning their civil and spiritual duties and privileges, and it behoves each of us to be informed and regulated thereby. Broadly speaking, the purpose of the State is to promote the welfare of the commonwealth, and to protect each individual in the enjoyment of his temporal rights; but it is entirely *outside* its province to prescribe the religion of its subjects. Rulers, be they civil or ecclesiastical, have only a delegated power, and are the agents and servants of the community, who entrust to them so much power as is necessary to the discharge of their office and duty.

No human government is perfect, and it may appear to us that a particular form of government is acting unwisely in its legislation and arbitrarily in its administration. The question therefore arises, How should a Christian citizen act under a particularly *offensive* one? First, the Word of God requires from him full submission and obedience to all those of its enactments which are not in themselves *sinful:* and that not because the government is one of his choice or because its policy meets with his approval, but because God Himself has ordered, "Let every soul be subject unto the higher powers. For there is no power but of God ... Whosoever therefore resisteth the power, resisteth the ordinance of God" (Romans 13:1, 2). Whatever be the particular *form* of government, it is of Divine ordering, and His providence has placed us under it. This is also evident from both the teaching and personal example of Christ, who bids us, "Render therefore unto Caesar the things which are Caesar's" (Matt. 22:21). But second, if the government should demand of me compliance with anything which is

125

126

contrary to the revealed will of God, then it is my bounden duty to *refuse* obedience; yet in such a case God requires me to submit meekly to any penalty imposed upon me for my declining to comply.

That a child of God *must* refuse to do the bidding of a government which it enjoins something contrary to the Divine will is clear from the cases of the three Hebrews (Daniel 3:18), and of Daniel in Babylon (5:10-13), who firmly declined to conform unto the king's idolatrous demands. It is equally evident from the case of the apostles, who, when they were commanded by the authorities "not to speak at all nor teach in the name of Jesus," answered "whether it be right in the sight of God to hearken unto you more than unto God, judge ye" (Acts 4:19, and cf. 5:29). Yet note well that, while insisting upon their spiritual rights, in neither case did any of them defend themselves or their cause by resorting to violence against the chief magistrate. Let it be steadily borne in mind that an incompetent or an unjust government is better than none, for the only other alternative is anarchy and a reign of terror, as history clearly and tragically testifies—witness the horrors perpetrated in Paris, when its streets literally ran with blood at the great French Revolution; and the awful carnage and sufferings which more recently obtained in Russia when the regime of the Czars was overthrown. "It is better, if the will of God be so, that ye suffer for well doing, than for evil doing" (1 Peter 3:17).

A further question needs considering at this point: *Who* is to be the judge of *which* decrees of a government are *sinful?* Obviously, in the last resort, the citizen himself. That is the scriptural and protestant doctrine of the right of private judgment: to test what the law of the land requires by the Divine Law. God's authoritative Word forbids me doing anything which He has prohibited or which is morally wrong. If any form of government insists upon being the absolute judge of its own case, then there is an end of personal independence and freedom. Every rational being lies under moral obligations to God—obligations which are immediate and inevitable. No government, and no human creature, can answer for him before God in a case of conscience or come between him and his guilt; and therefore it is the most monstrous injustice and iniquity that any power, save the Divine, should dictate to the conscience. It may be said that this is a dangerous doctrine, that it is likely to lead to disorder and insurrection. Not so where the *two* parts of it be maintained: the right to refuse *only* when something is demanded which God's Word forbids, and the duty of meekly submitting to the penalty thereof—the latter will check a misuse of the former.

Under no conceivable circumstances should any man relinquish the right to think and decide for himself. His reason, will and conscience are Divine gifts, and God holds him responsible for the right use of them, and will condemn him if he buries his talents in the earth. But as it is with so many other of His favours, this one is not valued at its true worth and soon may not be prized at all unless it be entirely removed and there be a return to the bondage of the "dark ages." A considerable majority of the present generation are largely if not wholly unaware—so ignorant as they of history—that for centuries, even in Britain, civil liberty and the right of private judgment upon spiritual things were denied the masses by both State and Church, politicians and prelates alike lording it over the people. Nor was their tyrannical dominion easily or quickly broken: only after much suffering and a protracted fight was full freedom secured. Alas, that such a dearly bought and hard-won privilege should now be regarded so lightly and be in real danger of being lost again. Nearly two hundred years ago Toplady pointed out, "Despotism has ever proved an insatiable gulf. Throw ever so much into it, it would still yearn for more." Significantly did he add, "Were liberty to perish from any part of the English-speaking world, the whole would soon be deluged by the black sea of arbitrary power."

But we must now turn to that part of our subject which more especially concerns the child of God and his *spiritual* interests. There are three basic truths which the battle of the Reformation recovered for Christendom: the sufficiency and supremacy of the Scriptures, the right of private judgment, and justification by faith without the deeds of the law. Each of those was flatly denied by the Papacy, which taught, and still insists, that human "traditions" are of equal authority with God's Word, that the Romish church alone is qualified to explain the Bible or interpret its contents, and that human merits are necessary in order to our acceptance with God. Having treated at some length, in recent articles, with the first, we are now considering the second. Rightly did Luther affirm that man is responsible to none but God for his religious views and beliefs, that no earthly power has any right to interfere in the sacred concerns of the soul—to be lord of his conscience or to have dominion over his faith. But while the Reformers contended vigorously for the right and privilege of each individual to read the Scriptures for himself, and, under the illumination and guidance of the Holy Spirit, to form his own opinions of what they teach, yet considerable *qualification* was made in the application and outworking of that principle in actual practice. So it was too in the century that followed, commonly termed "the Puritan period."

The early Reformers and many of the Puritans were for one uniform mode of worship and one form of temporal government, with which all *must* comply outwardly, whatever their individual convictions and sentiments. However desirable such a common regime might appear, to *demand* subjection thereunto was not only contrary to the very essence and spirit of Christianity, but also at direct variance with the right of private judgment. No man should ever be *compelled*, either by reward or punishment, to be a member of any Christian society, or to continue in or of it any longer than he considers it is his duty to do so. Any attempt to *enforce* uniformity is an attack upon the right of private judgment, and is to invade the office of Christ, who alone is the Head of His people. But alas, how few are fit to be entrusted with any measure of authority. When Anglicanism was supreme, at the close of the sixteenth century, anyone who failed to attend the parish church was subject to a fine! In the next century, when the Presbyterians held the reins, they proved to be equally intolerant to those who differed from them.

"Each party agreed too well in asserting the necessity for uniformity in public worship, and of using the sword of the magistrate for the support and defence of their principles, of which both made an ill use whenever they could grasp the power into their own hands. The *standard* of uniformity according to the Bishops was the Queen's supremacy and the laws of the land; according to the Puritans, the decrees of provincial and national synods, allowed and enforced by the civil magistrate; but neither party was for admitting that liberty of conscience which is every man's right, so far as is consistent with the peace of the civil government" (Daniel Niel's *History of the Puritans*, volume 2, page 92). Well did that faithful and impartial historian point out, "Christ is the sole lawgiver of His Church, and has appointed all things necessary to be observed in it to the end of the world; therefore, when He has indulged a liberty to His followers, it is as much their duty to maintain it, as to observe any other of His precepts." Differences of opinion, especially in "church government," soon led to further divisions and the formation of parties and sects, and in many instances Protestants were as dictatorial and tyrannical as the Papists had been, demanding unqualified submission to *their* articles of faith and forms of worship. Only after bitter persecution and much hardship did real religious liberty gradually emerge, and never yet has it fully and universally obtained in Protestantism.

No doubt it would be interesting to many of our readers were we to trace the gradual emergence of religious freedom from bondage in Germany, Switzerland, Holland, Britain and the U.S.A., and the various and often unexpected set-backs experienced; but even a bare outline of its history would be too lengthy a digression. Nor is it hardly necessary. Human nature is the same in all lands, and in all ages, and those possessing a workable knowledge of the same in themselves and their fellows can easily visualize with their minds the *nature* of those events. Most of us, if we are honest, must acknowledge that there is quite a bit of the pontiff in us, and therefore we should not be surprised to learn that there have been many popish men in most sections of Christendom, and that a spirit of intolerance and uncharitableness has often marred the characters of real Christians. It has been comparatively rare for those of prominence to insist that "Every species of positive penalty for differing modes of faith and worship is at once anti-Christian, and impolitic, irrational and unjust. While any religious denomination of men deport themselves as dutiful subjects of the State, and as harmless members of the community, they are entitled to civil protection and social esteem, whether they be Protestants, Papists, Jews, Mohammedans, or Pagans" (Toplady). *That* and nothing short of that, is a true Christian and Catholic spirit.

"Seek ye out of the book of the Lord, and read" (Isaiah 34:16), for in it alone is His will made known, the Divine way of salvation revealed, and a perfect rule and standard of conduct set before us. That Book is a Divine communication, an authoritative "Thus saith the Lord." It is addressed to the entire human race, and is binding on every member of it. By it each of us will be judged in the day to come. It is therefore both the duty and privilege of every person to read it for himself, that he familiarize himself with its contents, perceive their meaning, and conform his conduct to its requirements. It is to be read reverently, for it is the voice of the Most High which speaks therein. It is to be read impartially, setting aside personal prejudices and preconceived ideas, receiving it without doubting or question. It is to be read humbly, begging its Author to enlighten the understanding and teach His way. It is to be read constantly, daily, so that we may drink into its spirit and make it our counsellor. It is not only to be read, but also "seek ye out of the book": take the trouble to compare one part with another, and thereby obtain its full light on each particular subject and detail. By such pains it will be found that the Holy Scriptures are self-interpreting.

In a matter so momentous as my obtaining a correct understanding of God's will for me, and where the eternal interests of my soul are concerned, it deeply concerns me to obtain *first-hand* information of the same, and not to accept blindly what others say and do, or receive without question what any church teaches. I must rigidly examine and test by God's Word all that I hear and read. "Every one of us shall give account of himself to God" (Romans 14:12). Religion is an intensely personal thing which cannot be transacted by proxy. It consists of immediate dealings between the individual soul and its Maker. No one can repent for me, believe for me, love God for me, or render obedience to His precepts on my behalf. Those are personal acts which God holds me responsible to perform. Every man is responsible for his beliefs. Neither ignorance nor error is merely a misfortune, but something highly culpable, since the Truth is available unto us in our mother tongue. If some be deceived by false prophets, the blame rests wholly on themselves. Many complain that there is so much difference and contrariety among preachers, they scarcely know what to believe or what to do. Let them do as God has bidden: "seek ye out of the book of the Lord"!

God has given me that precious Book for the very purpose of making known to me what I am to believe and do, and if I read and search it with a sincere desire to understand its meaning and be regulated by its precepts, I shall not be left in the dark. If I so act, there will be an end to my perplexity because of the "confusion of tongues" in the religious world, for there are no contradictions, no contrarieties in God's Word. He holds me responsible to test everything preachers say: "To the law and to the testimony: if they speak not according to this word, it is because there is no light in them" (Isaiah 8:20). That Word is the sole standard of faith and practice, the "sure word of prophecy" to which we do well to give heed as unto a light shining in a dark place (2 Peter 1:19). Faith rests not upon the testimony of any man, nor is it subject to any man. It rests on the Word of God, and it is amenable to Him alone. "He that builds his faith upon preachers, though they preach nothing but the Truth, and he pretends to believe it, hath indeed no faith at all, but a wavering opinion, built upon a rotten foundation" (John Owen). Then "cease ye from man ... for wherein is *he* to be accounted of?" (Isaiah 2:22), and "Trust in the Lord with all thine heart, and lean not unto thine own understanding." (Prov. 3:5).

Each one of us is directly responsible to God for the use he makes and the compliance he renders to His Word. God holds every rational creature accountable to ascertain from His living oracles what is His revealed will and to conform thereunto. None can lawfully evade this duty by paying someone to do the work for him. Whatever help may be obtained from God's ministers, we are not dependent on them. To understand and interpret the Scriptures is not the prerogative of any ecclesiastical hierarchy. We have the Bible in our own mother tongue. The throne of grace is available, whither we may turn and humbly make request, "Teach me, O Lord ... Thy statutes ... Give me understanding ... Make me to go in the path of Thy commandments" (Psalm 119:33-35). We have the promise of Christ to rest upon: "If any man will do His will, he shall know of the doctrine" (John 7:17). Hence there is no valid excuse either for spiritual ignorance or for misconception of what God requires us to believe and do. Unto His children God has graciously imparted His Spirit that they may "*know* the things that are freely given to us of God" (1 Cor. 2:12). Yet it is only as God's Word is personally received into the heart that it "effectually worketh also in you that believe" (1 Thess. 2:13).

There is an urgent *need* for each person who values his soul and its eternal interests to spare no pains in making himself thoroughly familiar with God's holy Word and prayerfully endeavouring to understand its teaching, not only for the pressing reason stated above, but also because of the babel now obtaining in Christendom, and particularly in view of the numerous emissaries of Satan, who lie in wait at every corner, ready to seduce the unwary and the indolent. As pointed out in our last, the conflicting teaching which now abounds in the churches renders it all the more imperative that each of us should have strong and scripturally formed convictions of his own. Our Lord has expressly bidden us, "Beware of false prophets, which come to you in sheep's clothing, but inwardly they are ravening wolves" (Matt. 7:15). That solemn warning points a definite duty, and also implies our being qualified to discharge the same. That duty is to examine closely and test carefully by God's Word all that we read and hear from the pens and lips of preachers and teachers; and that, in turn, presupposes we are well acquainted with the Word, for how else can we determine whether an article or a sermon be scriptural or unscriptural?

There is nothing external by which perverters of the Truth may be identified. Not only are many of them men of irreproachable moral character and pleasing personality, but they appear to be deeply devoted unto Christ and His cause. Nor are they few in number, for we are told that "many false prophets are gone out into the world"—a statement which is prefaced by "Beloved, believe not every spirit, but *try* the spirits whether they are of God" (1 John 4:1): that is, diligently weigh their teaching in "the balances of the sanctuary." These seducers of souls profess to be real Christians, and are often to be met with even in the circles of the orthodox. Though at heart ravening wolves, they are disguised "in *sheep's* clothing"—pretending to have a great love for souls, they ensnare many. They feign to be the very opposite of what they are, for instead of being the servants of Christ they are the agents of Satan "transformed as the ministers of righteousness" (2 Cor. 11:15). Therein lies their "cunning craftiness, whereby they lie in wait to deceive" (Eph. 4:14) people by "good words and fair speeches," and thus delude the "hearts of the simple" (Romans 16:18).

Having shown the very real *need* there is for each person to form his own judgment of what God's Word teaches, we now turn to consider his God-given *right* to do so. This is plainly signified or clearly implied in many passages. "For the ear *trieth* words, as the mouth tasteth meat" (Job 34:2, 3). Upon which the Puritan, Joseph Caryl, very pertinently asked, "You will not swallow words until you have tried them. Why else have we ears to hear? Why are we trusted with reason to judge things with, or with rules to judge them by? There is no greater tyranny in the world than to command men to believe (with implicit faith) as others believe, or to impose our opinions and assertions upon those who hear them and not give them liberty to try them." Allow none to dictate to you, my reader, upon spiritual matters. He that is called in the Lord is "the Lord's free man," and hence it follows, "Ye are bought with a price: be not ye the servants of men" (1 Cor. 7:22, 23).

"Let every man be fully persuaded in his own mind" (Romans 14:5). In order to ascertain the precise scope of those words we must examine the setting in which they occur. They were first addressed to the saints at Rome, who were composed of believing Jews and Gentiles, between whom there were differences of opinion upon minor matters. Though these Jews had heartily received Christ as their promised Messiah and Saviour, they clung to the idea that the Levitical law, with its distinction of clean and unclean meats and the observance of certain fasts and festivals, was still binding upon them. Not only did they contend zealously for the same, but they were strongly desirous of imposing them on their fellow Christians, whom they regarded as proselytes to Judaism. On the other hand, not only had the Gentile believers not been brought up under the Mosaic rites, but they were convinced that the ceremonial observances of Judaism had been annulled by the new and better dispensation which had been inaugurated by the Lord Jesus. This difference of opinion, with each party holding firm convictions thereon, meanaced the unity of their fellowship and the exercise of brotherly love unto each other. The one needed to beware of looking upon the other as being lax and of a latitudinarian spirit, while the latter must refrain from viewing the former as being bigoted and superstitious.

Nothing vital was at stake—any more than there is today when the wearing of jewellery and the use of tobacco are questions agitated in some Christian circles. But since the peace of the Roman assembly was being threatened, and a spirit of intolerance had begun to obtain, through failure of each party to allow full liberty of conscience unto their brethren, it was needful that the apostle should deal with this situation and give such instruction unto each as would prevent these differences of opinion upon non-essentials of faith and practice leading to a serious breach of the peace. Accordingly Paul was guided by the Holy Spirit so to counsel them as to give forth at the same time teaching which is most valuable, essential and pertinent to similar cases in all generations. This he did by laying down broad and general principles which it behoves all Christians to be regulated by; nay, we cannot disregard them without sinning, since they are clothed with Divine authority. While human nature remains as it is, and while differently constituted minds do not view things uniformly, if Christian charity is to be exercised and harmony prevail among God's people, it is most necessary that they understand and practice those principles.

First, we are exhorted, "Let not him that eateth despise him that eateth not; and let not him which eateth not judge him that eateth: for God hath received him" (Romans 14:3). Therein both parties are forbidden to give place unto unbrotherly thoughts and sentiments. Second, they were asked, "Who art thou that judgest another man's servant? to his own Master he standeth or falleth. Yea, he shall be holden up: for God is able to make him stand.' (verse 4). This is tantamount to saying that it is the height of arrogance for any Christian to ascend the tribunal of judgment and pass sentence of condemnation upon a brother in Christ. Third, it is admitted that "one man esteemeth one day above another; another esteemeth every day alike," and then follows, "Let every man be fully persuaded in his own mind" (verse 5). *There* is the charter of Christian liberty: let none allow himself to be deprived of it. Those words cannot mean less than that every Christian has the God-given right to think for himself, to form his own opinion of what Scripture teaches, and to decide what he considers is most pleasing and honouring unto God.

Note well how emphatic and sweeping are the words of Romans 14:5. "Let every man": not only the preacher, but the private member too. "Be fully persuaded": not coerced, nor uncertain, as he will be if, instead of forming his own opinion, he heeds the confusion of tongues now abounding on every side. "In his own mind": neither blindly following the popular custom nor yielding to the *ipse dixit* of others. Where doubtful things are concerned each one should turn to the Scriptures for guidance and carefully examine them for himself, and then act according to his best judgment of what they require him to do. It is an obligation binding on each of us to be regulated by what appears to be the revealed will of God. This is what constitutes the very essence of practical Christianity: the personal recognition of Christ's property in me and authority over me, and in and over my brethren. I am neither to exercise dominion over them nor submit to theirs over me. Let us seek to help each other all we can, but let us leave Christ to *judge* us. He only has the capacity as He only has the right to do so. Perform what you are assured to be your duty and leave others to do likewise: thereby the rights of the individual are preserved and the peace of the community promoted.

Different opinions on minor matters are to be expected, but that is no reason why those holding the same should not dwell together in amity and enjoy communion in the great fundamentals of the faith. If one is satisfied that certain "days" should be observed, that he has *Divine* warrant to solemnly celebrate "Christmas" or "Easter," then let him do so. But if another is convinced that such "days" are of human invention and devoid of Divine authority, then let him ignore them. Let each one act from religious conviction and suffer not the fear of censure from or contempt of others to deter him; nor the desire to ingratiate himself in the esteem of his fellows induce him to act contrary to his conscience. Each Christian is responsible to believe and act according to the best light which he has from God and continue to examine His Word and pray for more light. The dictates of conscience are not to be trifled with, and the right of private judgment is ever to be exercised by me and respected in others. Thereby the Christian duty of mutual forbearance is alone maintained and a spirit of tolerance and charity exercised.

"I speak as to wise men: *judge ye* what I say" (1 Cor. 10:15). In those words the apostle called upon the saints to decide discreetly if what he had further to advance on the subject condemned them for continuing to feast in idol temples. He was treating with whether or not such an action came within the scriptural definition of idolatry. In terming them "wise men," he intimated that they were well able to weigh an argument, and therefore it was their duty to examine carefully and ponder prayerfully what he said. In his "judge ye" he signified his desire for them to be personally convinced, from the exercise of those spiritual "senses" which pertain to all the regenerate (Heb. 5:13). "Judge in yourselves: is it comely that a woman pray unto God [with her head] uncovered?" (1 Cor. 11:13). Not only would Paul have them obediently submit to the Divine requirements, but also perceive for themselves what would be becoming, appealing to their sense of propriety, adding, "doth not nature itself teach you?" Again, "Let the prophets speak two or three, and let the other judge" (1 Cor. 14:29). Once more they were called upon to exercise their own judgment – in this case whether the messages given out by those claiming to be "prophets" were really the oracles of God.

Now this right of private judgment, and the duty of each person to determine for himself what God's Word teaches, is categorically *denied by Rome*, which avers that "ignorance is the mother of devotion," and that the highest form of service is that of "blind obedience." The Papacy insists that the Church is absolutely infallible in all matters of Christian Faith. During Session IV the Council of Trent (1563) decreed that "No one, relying on his own skill, shall, in matters of faith and of morals pertaining to the edification of Christian doctrine, wresting the sacred Scripture to his own senses, presume to interpret the said sacred Scripture contrary to that sense which holy mother Church—whose it is to judge of the true sense and interpretation of the Holy Scriptures—hath held and doth hold; or even contrary to the unanimous consent of the Fathers." This was ratified and repeated in the *Dogmatic Decrees of the Vatican Council* (chapter ii): "We, renewing the said decree, declare this to be their sense, that in matters of faith and morals, appertaining to the building up of Christian doctrine, that is to be held as the true sense of Holy Scripture, which our holy mother Church hath held and holds, to whom it belongs to judge of the true sense of the Holy Scripture; and therefore that it is permitted to no one to interpret the sacred Scripture contrary to this sense."

Nor has the arch-deceiver and enslaver of souls receded one hair's breadth from that position since then. The following propositions were *denounced* by the Papacy: "It is profitable at all times and in all places for all sorts of persons to study the Scriptures, and to become acquainted with their spirit, piety, and mysteries" (Proposition 79). "The reading of the Holy Scriptures in the hands of a man of business and a financier (Acts 8:28) shows that it is intended for everybody" (Proposition 80). "The Lord's day ought to be sanctified by the reading of books of piety, and especially of the Scriptures. They are the milk which God Himself, who knows our hearts, has supplied for them" (Proposition 81). "It amounts to shutting the mouth of Christ to Christians, and to wresting from their hands the Holy Bible, or to keeping it shut from them, by depriving them of the means of hearing it." Those, together with many other similar postulates, were "condemned to perpetuity" as being "false and scandalous" in his "bull" (a Papal decree to which is affixed the Pope's seal)—Unigenitus by Clement XI, issued on September 8, 1713.

In 1824 the encyclical epistle of Pope Leo XII complained of the Bible Societies, "which," it said, "violate the traditions of the Fathers and the Council of Trent, in circulating the Scriptures in the vernacular tongues of all nations." "In order to avoid this pestilence," said this poor creature, "our predecessors have published several constitutions . . . tending to show how pernicious for the faith and for morals is this perfidious instrument," i.e. the Bible Society. In those countries ruled by the emissaries of the Vatican, God's Word has ever been, and still is, withheld from the people, and they are forbidden to read or hear it read under pain of the Pope's anathema. All known copies of it are seized and committed to the flames. At this very hour the Lord's people in Spain are being persecuted for their loyalty to the Bible. So would they be in all English-speaking countries today if the Romanists could secure full temporal power over them. The Lord mercifully grant that such a catastrophe may never again happen.

Ere passing from this aspect of our subject, let us briefly notice one verse to which appeal is made by Romanists in support of their contention that the laity have no right to form their own views of what God's Word teaches: "Knowing this first, that no prophecy of the scripture is of any private interpretation" (2 Peter 1:20). On the basis of those words it is insisted that the Bible must be *officially* interpreted, and that "holy mother Church" is alone authorized and qualified to discharge this duty and to render this service. But that verse affords not the slightest support of their arrogant claim. Those words, as their context clearly shows, treat of the *source* of prophecy and *not* its meaning. The very next sentence explains what is signified by verse 20: "*For* the prophecy came not in old time by the will of man: but holy men of God spake as they were moved by the Holy Spirit." Thus, verse 20 manifestly imports, Be assured at the outset that what the prophets delivered proceeded not from their own minds. The Greek word for "private" is never again so rendered elsewhere in the New Testament, but is translated scores of times "his own." Consequently the "interpretation" has reference to what was *delivered by* the prophets and not to the explication of it: had the "interpretation" which the prophets delivered issued from themselves, then they *had been* "by the will of man," which the next verse expressly denies.

Taking verses 20 and 21 together, nothing could more emphatically affirm the absolute inspiration of the prophets. They spoke from God, and not from themselves. The *force,* then, of verse 20 is that no prophetic utterance was of human origination. It is the Divine authorship of their words, and not the explanation of their messages, that is here in view—the act of *supplying* the prophecy, and not the explaining of it when supplied. So far from lending any colour to the view that there inheres somewhere in the Church and its ministers an authority to fix the sense of Holy Writ, this very verse, as it is rendered in the Authorized Version, obviously refutes the same, because for any man—be it the Roman pontiff or a Protestant prelate—to determine the meaning of God's Word *would be* of "private interpretation"! Alas, that is the very thing which has happened throughout Christendom, for each church, denomination, party, or "circle of fellowship" puts its own meaning on the Word, and in many instances contrary to the Truth itself. Let the Christian reader be fully persuaded that there is nothing whatever in 2 Peter 1:20, which forbids him weighing the words of Scripture, exercising his own judgment, and, under the guidance and grace of the Holy Spirit, deciding what they signify.

Not only is private judgment a right which God has conferred upon each of His children, but it is their bounden *duty* to exercise the same. The Lord requires us to make full use of this privilege, and to employ all lawful and peaceful means for its maintenance. Not only are we responsible to reject all erroneous teaching, but we are not to be the serfs of any ecclesiastical tyranny. "Be not ye called Rabbi: for one is your Master, even Christ; and all ye are brethren. And call no man your father upon the earth: for one is your Father, which is in heaven" (Matt. 23:8, 9). Those words contain very much more than a prohibition against according ecclesiastical titles unto men; yea, it is exceedingly doubtful whether such a concept is contained therein; rather is Christ forbidding us to be in spiritual *bondage* to anyone. In verse 2 He had stated, "The scribes and the Pharisees sit in Moses' seat": that is, they have arrogated to themselves the power of religious legislation and demand entire subjection from their adherents. In the verses that follow, our Lord reprehended them for usurping authority and setting up themselves as demagogues; in view of which the Lord Jesus bade His disciples maintain their spiritual liberty and refuse all allegiance or subservience to any such tyrants.

"But be ye not called Rabbi: for one is your Master, even Christ; and all ye are brethren" (Matt. 23:8). In every generation there are those of an officious spirit who aspire to leadership, demanding deference from their fellows. Such men, especially when they are endowed with natural gifts above the average, are the kind who become the founders of new sects and parties, and insist upon unqualified subjection from their followers. *Their* interpretation of the Scriptures must not be challenged, their dicta are final. They must be owned as "rabbis" and submitted to as "fathers." Everyone must believe precisely what *they* teach, and order all the details of his life by the rules of conduct which they prescribe, or else be branded as a heretic and denounced as a gratifier of the lusts of the flesh. There have been, and still are, many such self-elevated little popes in Christendom, who deem themselves to be entitled to implicit credence and obedience, whose decisions must be accepted without question. They are nothing but arrogant usurpers, for Christ alone is the Rabbi or Master of Christians; and since all of His disciples be "brethren" they possess equal rights and privileges.

"Call no man your father upon the earth: for one is your Father, which is in heaven" (verse 9). This dehortation has ever been needed by God's people, for they are the most part simple and unsophisticated, trustful and easily imposed upon. In those verses the Lord Jesus was enforcing the duty of private judgment, bidding believers suffer none to be the dictators of their fatih or lords of their lives. No man is to be heeded in spiritual matters any further than he can produce a plain and decisive "thus saith the Lord" as the foundation of his appeal. To be in subjection to any ecclesiastical authority that is not warranted by Holy Writ, or to comply with the whims of men, is to renounce your Christian freedom. Suffer none to have dominion over your mind and conscience. Be regulated only by the teaching of God's Word, and firmly refuse to be brought into bondage to "the commandments and doctrines of men," with their "Touch not, taste not, handle not" (Col. 2:21, 22). Instead, "stand fast therefore in the liberty wherewith Christ hath made us free" (Gal. 5:1); yet "not using your liberty for a cloak of maliciousness, but as the servants of God" (1 Peter 2:16)—yielding unreservedly to *His* authority. Rather than conform to the rules of the Pharisees, Christ was willing to be regarded as a Sabbath-breaker!

"Not for that we have dominion over your faith, but are helpers of your joy: for by faith ye stand" (2 Cor. 1:24). Weigh well those words my reader, and remember they were written by one who "was not a whit behind the very chief of the apostles," and here he disclaims all authority over the faith of these saints! In the previous verse he had spoken of "sparing" them, and here "lest it should be thought that he and his fellow ministers assumed to themselves any tyrannical power over the churches or lorded it over God's heritage, these words are subjoined" (John Gill). The word "faith" may be understood here as either the grace of faith or the object thereof. Take it of the former: ministers of the Gospel can neither originate, stimulate, nor dominate it: the Holy Spirit is the

Author, Increaser, and Lord of it. Take it as the object of faith—that which is believed: ministers have no Divine warrant to devise any new articles of faith, nor to demand assent to anything which is not plainly taught in the Bible. "If any man speak, let him speak as the oracles of God" (1 Peter 4:11), neither withholding anything revealed therein nor adding anything of his own thereto.

Paul's work was to instruct and persuade, not to lord it over his converts and compel their belief. He had written his first letter to the saints in answer to the queries they had sent him, and at the beginning of this second epistle explains why he had deferred a further visit to them, stating that he was prepared to stay away until such time as they had corrected the evils which existed in their assembly. He refused to oppress them. "Faith rests not on the testimony of man, but on the testimony of God. When we believe the Scriptures, it is not man, but God whom we believe. Therefore faith is subject not to man, but to God alone . . . The apostles were but the organs of the Holy Spirit: what they spake as such they could not recall or modify. They were not the lords, so to speak, of the Gospel . . . Paul therefore places himself alongside of his brethren, not over them as a lord, but as a joint believer with them in the Gospel which he preached, and a helper of their joy, co-operating with them in the promotion of their spiritual welfare" (C. Hodge). If Paul would not, then how absurd for any man to attempt to exercise a spiritual dominion in matters of faith or practice!

"The elders which are among you I exhort . . . Feed the flock of God which is among you . . . not for filthy lucre, but of a ready mind; neither as being lords over God's heritage, but being ensamples to the flock" (1 Peter 5:1-3). These are part of the instructions given unto ministers of the Gospel as to how they are to conduct themselves in the discharge of their holy office, and we would earnestly commend them to the attention of every pastor who reads this article. They are Divinely forbidden to abuse their position and to assume any absolute authority or rule imperiously over the saints. Their task is to preach the Truth and enjoin obedience to Christ, and not unto themselves. They are not to act arbitrarily or in a domineering spirit, for though they be set over believers in the Lord (1 Thess. 5:12) and are to "rule" and therefore to be submitted unto in their lawful administration of the Word and the ordinances (Heb. 13:17), yet they are not to arrogate to themselves dominion over the consciences of men nor impose any of their own inventions; but instead, teach their flock to observe all things whatsoever Christ has commanded (Matt. 28:20).

The minister of the Gospel has no right to dictate unto others, or insist in a dogmatic manner that people must receive what he says on *his* bare assertion. Such a spirit is contrary to the genius of Christianity, unsuited to the relation which he sustains to his flock, and quite unbecoming a follower of Christ. No arbitrary control has been committed to any cleric. True ministerial authority or church rule is not a dictatorial one, but is a spiritual administration under Christ. Instead of lording it over God's heritage, preachers are to be "ensamples to the flock": personal patterns of good works, holiness, and self-sacrifice; models of piety, humility, charity. How vastly different from the conduct enjoined by Peter has been the arrogance, intolerance, and tyrannical spirit of his self-styled successors! Nor are they the only ones guilty thereof. Love of power has been as common a sin in the pulpit as love of money, and many of the worst evils which have befallen Christendom have issued from a lusting after dominion and ecclesiastical honours.

Such is poor human nature that good men find it hard to keep from being puffed up and misusing any measure of authority when it be committed unto them, and from not doing more harm than good with the same. Even James and John so far forgot themselves that, on one occasion, they asked Christ to grant them the two principal seats of power and honour in the day of His glory (Mark 10:35-37). Mark well this part of His reply: "Ye know that they which are accounted to rule over the Gentiles exercise lordship over them; and their great ones exercise authority upon them"—they love to bear sway, and, like Haman, have everybody truckle to them. "But so shall it *not be* among you" says Christ to His minsters—eschew any spirit of domineering, mortify the love of being flattered and held in honour because of your office. "But whosoever will be great among you shall be your minister; and whosoever of you will be the chiefest, shall be servant of all"—those who are to be accounted the greatest in Christ's spiritual kingdom are the ones characterized by a meek and lowly heart, and those who will receive a crown of glory in the day to come are those who most sought the good of others. "For even the Son of man came not to be ministered unto, but to minister, and to give His life a ransom for many"—then make self-abnegation and not self-exaltation your constant aim.

"Prove *all* things: hold fast that which is good" (1 Thess. 5:21). This is yet another verse which, by clear and necessary implication, teaches the privilege and right of private judgment, and makes known the duty and extent to which it is to be exercised. Linking it with what has been before us in the preceding paragraphs, it shows that if it be unwarrantable for the servants of Christ to usurp an absolute power, it is equally wrong for those committed to their care to submit thereto. Church government and discipline are indeed necessary and scriptural, yet not a lordly authority but a rule of holiness and love, wherein a spirit of mutual forbearance obtains. God does not require the minds and consciences of His children to be enslaved by any ecclesiastical dominion. Each one has the right to exercise his own judgment and have a say and vote upon all matters pertaining to his local assembly; and if he does not, then he fails in the discharge of his responsibility. Well did one of the old divines say on Psalm 110:1, "Christ is Lord to employ, to command, whom and what He will. To Him alone must we say, 'Lord, save me, I perish.' To Him only we must say, 'Lord, what wilt Thou have me to do?' To Him only must we go for instruction—'Thou hast the words of eternal life.'"

It scarcely needs to be said that the right of private judgment certainly does not mean that we are at liberty to bring the Word of God to the bar of human reason and sentiment, so that we may reject whatever does not commend itself to our intelligence or appeal to our inclinations. The Bible does not submit itself unto *our* opinion or give us the option of picking and choosing from its contents: rather is it our critic (Heb. 4:12). The Law of the Lord is perfect and, the best of us being very imperfect, it is madness to criticize it. But when we hear preaching from it, we must *try* what is said whether or not it accords with the Word, and whether the interpretation be valid or strained. It is a fundamental truth that "Christ Jesus came into the world to save sinners," yet even in the days of the apostles there were those who, while acknowledging Him as the only Saviour, taught that there was no salvation apart from circumcision.

Accordingly the church met at Jerusalem "for to *consider* of this matter" (Acts 15:4-11). So must *we* "consider" all we hear and read, whether it agrees with the Divine Rule, taking nothing for granted.

"*Prove* all things." This is not optional but obligatory: we are Divinely commanded to do so. God's Word is the only standard of truth and duty, and everything we believe and do must be tested by it. Thousands have sought to evade this duty by joining Rome and allowing that system to determine everything for them. Nor are the majority of the members of non-popish churches much better, being too indolent to search and study the Bible for themselves, believing whatever their preachers tell them. Beware, my reader, of allowing *any* influence to come between your soul and God's Word. How early did the Holy Spirit have occasion to say to one of the primitive churches which had given way to a spirit of partisanship and bigotry, "Who then is Paul? and who is Apollos?" When the mind rests upon the human instrument, not only is spiritual progress in the Truth immediately arrested, but the living power of what Truth is already attained dies out of the enslaved heart, being displaced by dogmas received on human authority. Divine Truth then degenerates into a party distinction, for which many zealously contend in naught but a sectarian spirit.

The origin of all sectarianism is subjection to men, human authority supplanting the authority of God, the preacher becoming the dictator. We must not suffer any to arrogate the place and office of the Holy Spirit. No human system can feed the soul: it has to come into immediate and quickening contact with the living and powerful Word of God in order to be spiritually nourished. Even where real Christians are concerned, many had their religious beliefs formed before they were converted, receiving them from their parents or the churches they attended, and not directly from God and His Word. Therefore they too need to heed this Divine injunction: "*Prove all things:* hold fast that which is good." Bring your beliefs to the test of the Scriptures, and you are likely to discover that it is much harder and more painful to *unlearn* some things than it is to learn new ones. Very few think for themselves, and fewer still are really willing to "*buy* the Truth" and set aside their former opinions, no matter what may be the cost. Much grace is needed for that! Since the eternal interests of our souls are involved, it is the height of folly for us to depend upon the judgment of others, for the ablest ministers are fallible and liable to err.

"These were more noble than those in Thessalonica, in that they received the word with all readiness of mind, and searched the scriptures daily whether those things *were so*" (Acts 17:11). Those Bereans sat in judgment upon the teaching of the apostles! They are commended for doing so! Not only was it their privilege and duty, but it is recorded to their honour. But mark *how* they discharged this duty. They brought all that they heard from the spoken discourse to the test of the written Word. They did not judge by their own preconceptions, views, prejudices, feelings, or partialities, but by God's Word. If what they heard was in accord therewith, they were bound to receive and submit to it; but if it was contrary thereto, they were equally bound to refuse and reject the ministry that taught it. That is recorded as an example to us! It reveals *how* we are to exercise this privilege of private judgment. The apostles claimed to be sent of God, but were they really preaching the Truth? The Bereans gave them a ready hearing, but took the trouble to examine and try their teaching by the

Scriptures, and searched them daily whether they were so. Do thou likewise, and remember that Christ commended the Ephesian saints because they *had tried* those who said they were apostles and "found them liars" (Rev. 2:2).

The right of private judgment does not mean that each Christian may be a law unto himself, and still less lord over himself. We must beware of allowing liberty to degenerate into licence. No, it means the right to form our own views from the Scriptures, to be in bondage to no ecclesiastical authority, to be subject unto God alone. Two extremes are to be guarded against: slavery to human authority and tradition; the spirit of self-will and pride. On the one hand we are to avoid blind credulity, on the other hand an affectation of independence or the love of novelty, which disdains what others believe, in order to obtain a cheap notoriety of originality. Private judgment does not mean private *fancy*, but a deliberate conviction based on Holy Writ. Though I must not resign my mind and conscience to others, or deliver my reason and faith over blindfold to any church, yet I ought to be very slow in rejecting the approved judgment of God's servants of the past. There is a happy medium between limiting myself to what the Puritans and others taught, and disdaining the help they can afford me. Self-conceit is to be rigidly restrained. Private judgment is to be exercised humbly, soberly, impartially, with a willingness to receive light from any quarter. Ponder the Word for yourself, but mortify the spirit of haughty self-sufficiency; and be ready to avail yourself of anything likely to afford you a better understanding of the Truth. Above all, daily beg the Holy Spirit to be your teacher. "Prove all things": when listening to your favorite preacher, or reading these articles! Accord your brethren the same right and privilege you claim for yourself.

THE DOCTRINE OF MORTIFICATION

Introduction

It is the studied judgment of this writer, and he is by no means alone therein, that *doctrinal preaching* is the most pressing need of the churches today. During the past fifty years a lot has been said about and much prayer has been made for a God-sent *revival*, but it is to be feared that that term is often used very loosely and unintelligently. Unless we are mistaken, if the question were put, A "revival" *of what?* a considerable variety of answers would be given. Personally, we would say a revival of old-fashioned piety, of practical godliness, of fuller conformity to the holy image of Christ. The "revival" we need is a deliverance from that spiritual apathy and laxity which now characterizes the average Christian, a return to self-denial and closer walking with God, a quickening of our graces, and the becoming more fruitful in the bringing forth of good works. Whether or not Scripture predicts such a revival we know not. Two things we are sure of: that whatever the future may hold for this world, God will maintain a testimony unto Himself (Psalm 145:4; Matt. 28:20) and preserve a godly seed on earth, until the end of human history (Psalm 72:5; Isaiah 27:3; Matt. 16:18). Second, that there must be a return to doctrinal preaching before there will be any improvement in practice.

Both the teaching of God's Word and the testimony of ecclesiastical history testify clearly to the deep importance and great value of doctrinal instruction, and the lamentable consequences of a prolonged absence of the same. Doctrinal preaching is designed to enlighten the understanding, to instruct the mind, to inform the judgment. It is that which supplies motives to gratitude and furnishes incentives unto good works. There can be no soundness in the Faith if the fundamental articles of the Faith be not known and, in some measure at least, understood. Those fundamental articles are denominated "the first principles of the oracles of God" (Heb. 5:12) or basic truths of Scripture, and are absolutely necessary unto salvation. The Divine inspiration and authority of the Holy Scriptures, the ever-blessed Trinity in unity (John 17:3), the two natures united in the one person of the Lord Jesus Christ (1 John 2:22, and 4:3), His finished work and all-sufficient sacrifice (Heb. 5:14), the fall, resulting in our lost condition (Luke 19:10), regeneration (John 3:3), gratuitous justification (Gal. 5:4)—these are some of the principal pillars which support the temple of Truth, and without which it cannot stand. Of old God complained, "My people are destroyed [cut off] for lack of knowledge" (Hosea 4:6), and declared, "Therefore My people are gone into captivity, because they have no knowledge: and their honourable men are famished, and their multitude dried up with thirst" (Isaiah 5:13). When He promised "I will give you pastors according to Mine heart," He described the same as those "which shall feed you with knowledge and understanding" (Jer. 3:15), and that knowledge is communicated first and foremost by a setting forth of the glorious doctrines of Divine revelation. Doctrinal Christianity is both the ground and the motive of practical Christianity, for it is *principle* and not *emotion* or impulse which is the dynamic of the spiritual life. It is *by the Truth* that men are illuminated and directed: "O send out Thy light and Thy truth: let them lead me; let them bring me unto Thy holy hill, and to Thy tabernacles" (Psalm 43:3). We are saved by a knowledge of the Truth (John 17:3; 1 Tim. 2:4), and by faith therein (2 Thess. 2:13). We are made free by the Truth (John 8:32). We are sanctified by the Truth (John 17:17). Our growth in grace is determined by our growth in the knowledge of God and the Lord Jesus Christ (2 Peter 1:2 and 3:18). It is mercy and truth that preserve us (Psalm 61:7; Proverbs 21:28)—"understanding shall keep thee" (Prov. 2:11).

Pertinently is the inquiry made, "If the foundations be destroyed, what can the righteous do?" (Psalm 11:3). The Hebrew word for "foundations" occurs only once more in the Old Testament, namely in Isaiah 19:10, where it is rendered "and they shall be broken in *the purposes* thereof." As it is from our purposes that our plans and actions proceed, so it is from the "first principles" of the Word that its secondary truths are derived; and upon them both, precepts are based. "The principles of religion are the foundations on which the faith and hope of the righteous are built" (Matthew Henry). While those foundations cannot be totally and finally removed, yet God may suffer them to be so relatively and temporarily. In such case the righteous should not give way to despair, but instead betake themselves unto prayer. "Some thing the righteous ones may do, and should do, when men are attempting to undermine and sap the foundation articles of religion: they should go to the throne of grace, to God in His holy temple, who knows what is doing, and plead with Him to put a stop to the designs and attempts of such subverters of foundations; and they should endeavour to build one another up on their most holy faith" (J. Gill).

During the past century there was an increasingly marked departure from doctrinal preaching. Creeds and confessions of faith were disparaged and regarded as obsolete. The study of theology was largely displaced by engaging the mind with science, psychology and sociology. The cry was raised, "Give us Christ, and not Christianity," and many superficial minds concluded that such a demand was both a spiritual and a pertinent one. In reality it was an absurdity, an imaginary distinction without any vital difference. A scriptural concept of Christ in His theanthropic person, His mediatorial character, His official relations to God's elect, His redemptive work for them, can be formed only as He is contemplated in His essential Godhead, His unique humanity, His covenant headship, and as the Prophet, Priest and King of His Church. Sufficient attention has not been given to that repeated expression "the doctrine of Christ" (2 John, 9), which comprehends the whole teaching of Scripture concerning His wondrous person and His so-great salvation. Nor has due weight been given to those words "the mystery of Christ" (Col. 4:3), which refer to the deep things revealed of Him in the Word of Truth.

The most conclusive evidences for the Divine origin of Christianity, as well as the chief glory, appear in its doctrines, for they cannot be of human invention. The ineffable and incomprehensible Trinity in unity, the incarnation of the Son of God, the death of the Prince of life, that His obedience and sufferings satisfied Divine justice and expiated our offences, the Holy Spirit making the believer His temple, and our union with Christ, are sublime and lofty truths, holy and mysterious, which far surpass the highest flight of finite reason. There is perfect harmony in all the parts of the doctrine of Christ. Therein a full discovery is made of the manifold wisdom of God, the duties required of us, the motives which prompt thereto. It is in perceiving the distinct parts and aspects of Truth, their relation to one another, their furtherance of a common cause, their magnifying of the Lord of glory, that the excellence and beauty of the whole are apparent. It is because many apprehend only detached fragments of the same that some things in it appear to be inconsistent to them. What is so much needed is a view and grasp of the whole—acquired only by diligent and persevering application.

There is much preaching, but sadly little *teaching*. It is the task of the teacher to declare all the counsel of God, to show the relation of one part of it to another, to present the whole range of Truth: thereby will the hearer's mental horizon be widened, his sense of proportion promoted, and the beautiful harmony of the whole be demonstrated. It is his business not only to avow but to evince, not simply to affirm but to establish what he affirms. Of the apostle we read that he "*reasoned* with them out of the Scriptures, opening and alleging, that Christ must needs have suffered, and risen again from the dead" (Acts 17:2, 3). He was eminently qualified for such a task both by nature and by grace. He was not only a man of God, but a man of genius and learning. He made considerable use of his reasoning faculty. He did not ask his hearers to believe anything that he averred without evidence, but furnished *proof* of what he taught. He usually preached on the basic and essential doctrines of the Gospel, which he felt ought to be verified by plain and conclusive reasoning.

"And he *reasoned* in the synagogue every Sabbath, and persuaded the Jews and the Greeks" (Acts 18:4, 19). Because such reasoning may be abused, it does not follow that it should have no place in the pulpit. To reason fairly is to draw correct consequences from right principles, or to adduce clear and convincing arguments in support thereof. In order to reason lucidly and effectively upon the truth of a proposition, it is usually necessary to explain it, then to produce arguments in support of it, and finally to answer objections against it. That is the plan Paul generally follows, as is evident from both the Acts and his Epistles. When he preached upon the existence of God, the first and fundamental truth of all religion, he reasoned simply yet impressively: "Forasmuch then as we are the offspring of God, we *ought not to think that* the Godhead is like unto gold, or silver, or stone, graven by art and man's device" (Acts 17:29); "For the invisible things of Him from the creation of the world are clearly seen" (Romans 1:20). When he enforced the doctrine of human depravity, he *proved* it first by a lengthy description of the character and conduct of the whole heathen world, and then by quotations from the Old Testament, and concluded "we have before *proved* both Jews and Gentiles, that they are all under sin" (Romans 3:19).

It is the teacher's task to explain, to prove, and then to apply, for hearts are reached through the understanding and conscience. When he appeared before Felix, the apostle "reasoned of righteousness, temperance, and judgment to come" so powerfully that the Roman governor "trembled" (Acts 24:25). But alas, solid reasoning, exposition of Scripture, doctrinal preaching, are now largely things of the past. Many were (and still are) all for what they term *experience*, rather than a knowledge of doctrine. And today we behold the deplorable effects of the same, for our generation lacks even a theoretical knowledge of the Truth. That which was termed experimental and practical preaching displaced theological instruction, and thus the grand fundamentals of the Gospel were brought into contempt. No wonder that popery has made such headway in the countries once Protestant. It may be that that satanic system may yet prevail more awfully. If it does, none will be able to overthrow it by any *experiences* of their own. Nothing but sound doctrinal preaching will be of any use.

No wonder, either, that practical godliness is also at such a low ebb, for the root which produces it has been unwatered and has withered. "Where there is not the *doctrine* of Faith, the *obedience* of Faith cannot be expected . . . On the other hand, doctrine without practice, or a mere theoretical and speculative knowledge of things, unless reduced to practice, is of no avail . . . Doctrine and practice should go together, and in order both to know and to do the will of God, instruction in Doctrine and practice is necessary; and the one bringing first light will lead to the other" (J. Gill). That is the order in 2 Timothy 3:16, "All scripture is given by inspiration of God, and is profitable [first] for doctrine, [and then] for reproof, for correction, for instruction in righteousness." Thus Paul exhorted Timothy, "Take heed unto thyself, and unto the doctrine; continue in them: for in doing this thou shalt both save thyself, and them that hear thee" (1 Tim. 4:16). So too he enjoined Titus, "This is a faithful saying, and these things [namely the doctrines of verses 3-7] I will that thou affirm constantly, that [in order that] they which have believed in God might be careful to maintain good works" (3:8).

Alas, very, very few now preach the doctrine of Christ in all its parts and branches, in all its causes and effects, in all its bearings and dependences. Yet there can be no better furniture for the spiritual mind than right and clear apprehensions thereof. Our preservation from error lies therein; our spiritual fruitfulness depends thereon. Doctrine is the mould into which the mind is cast (Romans 6:17), from which it receives its impressions. As the nature of the seed sown determines what will be the harvest, so the substance of what is preached is seen in the lives of those who sit regularly under it. Where are the purity, the piety, the zeal, that close walking with God and uprightness before men, which were so pronounced in Christendom during the sixteenth and seventeen centuries? Yet the preaching of the Reformers and Puritans was principally *doctrinal,* and, under God, it produced such a love of the Truth that thousands willingly suffered persecution and great privations, and hazarded their lives, rather than repudiate the doctrines and ordinances of Christ. To say it matters not what a man believes so long as his practice is good is utterly erroneous. Indifference to the Truth betrays a heart that is not right with God.

It also requires to be pointed out that those men whose ministry was most owned and used of God during last century were those who followed in the steps of the Puritans. C. H. Spurgeon, Caesar Malan, Robert Murray McCheyne, and the great leaders of the Scottish Free Church disruption, gave a prominent place to doctrinal instruction in all of their preaching. An observant eye will soon perceive that there is a distinct *spirit* which attends different types of preaching, manifesting itself more or less plainly in the regular attenders thereof. There is a solidity and soberness, a stability and godly fear seen in real Calvinists, which are not found among Arminians. There is an uprightness of character in those who espouse the Truth which is lacking in those who imbibe error. Where the sovereignty of God is denied there will be no holy awe of Him. Where the total depravity of man is not insisted upon, pride and self-sufficiency will obtain. Where the impotence of the natural man is not stressed there will be no dependence upon the Holy Spirit. Where the holy demands of God be not maintained there will be the absence of its effects on the heart and life.

Thus may we judge and determine the Truth of preaching: "Whatsoever doctrine both depress and humble man and advance the glory of God, is true. It answers the design of the Gospel, which all centres in this: that man is to be laid low, and God to be exalted as the chief cause. It pulls man down from his own bottom, and transfers all the glory man would challenge into the hands of God: it lays man in the dust at God's footstool. That doctrine which crosses the main design of the Gospel, and encourages pride in man, is not a spark from heaven. No flesh must glory in God's presence (1 Cor. 1:29). The doctrine of justification by works is thrown down by the apostle with this very argument as a thunderbolt: 'Where is boasting then? It is excluded . . . by the law of faith' (Romans 3:27), that is by the doctrine of the Gospel. Boasting would be introduced by ascribing regeneration to nature, as much as it is excluded by denying justification by works. The doctrine of the Gospel would contradict itself to usher in boasting with one hand whilst it thrust it out with the other. Our Saviour gave this rule long ago, that the glorifying of God is the evidence of truth in persons: 'he that seeketh His glory that sent him, the same is true' (John 7:18). By the same reason also in things and doctrines" (Charnock, 1660).

Turning from the general to the particular. In taking up our present subject

144

(D.V.) we shall endeavour to make good a half-promise given by us seventeen years ago, for we stated then in these pages that if we were spared we hoped to devote a series of articles to this important truth. Some of our readers may be inclined to challenge the accuracy of our present title, considering that the duty of mortification pertains far more to the practical side of things than to the doctrinal. The objection would be well taken if the popular distinction were valid, but like so many of the expressions now in vogue this one will not stand the test of Scripture. The term "doctrine" has a much wider meaning in the Word of God than is usually accorded it today. It includes very much more than the "five points" of Calvinism. Thus we read of "the doctrine which is *according to godliness*" (1 Tim. 6:3), which is very much more than a species of intellectual proposition intended for the instructing of our brains, namely the enunciation of spiritual facts and holy principles, for the warming of the heart and the regulating of our lives.

"The doctrine which is according to godliness" at once defines the *nature* of Divine doctrine, intimating as it does that its design or end is to inculcate a right temper of mind and deportment of life Godwards: it is pure and purifying. The objects which are revealed to faith are not bare abstractions which are to be accepted as true, nor even sublime and lofty concepts to be admired: they are to have a powerful effect upon our daily walk. There is no doctrine revealed in Scripture for a merely speculative knowledge, but all is to exert a powerful influence upon conduct. God's design in all that He has revealed to us is to the purifying of our affections and the transforming of our characters. The doctrine of grace teaches us to deny ungodliness and worldly lusts, and to live soberly, righteously, and godly in this present world (Titus 2:11, 12). By far the greater part of the doctrine (John 7:16) taught by Christ consisted not of the explication of mysteries, but rather that which corrected men's lusts and reformed their lives. Everything in Scripture has in view the promotion of *holiness*.

If it be an absurdity to affirm that it matters not what a man believes so long as he does that which is right, equally erroneous is it to conclude that if my creed be sound it matters little how I act. "If any provide not for his own, and specially for those of his own house, he hath denied the faith, and is worse than an infidel" (1 Tim. 5:8), for he shows himself to be devoid of natural affection. Thus it is possible to deny the Faith *by conduct* as well as by words. A neglect of performing our duty is as real a repudiation of the Truth as is an open renunciation of it, for the Gospel, equally with the Law, requires children to honour their parents. Observe how that awful list of reprehensible characters mentioned in 1 Timothy 1:9,10, are said to be "contrary to sound doctrine"—opposed to its salutary nature and spiritual tendency: i.e. that conduct which the standard of God enjoins. Observe too how that the spirit of covetousness or love of money is designated an *erring "from* the faith" (1 Tim. 6:10): it is a species of heresy, a departure from the doctrine which is according to godliness—an awful example of which we have in the case of Judas. Mortification, then, is clearly one of the practical doctrines of Holy Writ, as we hope to show abundantly in what follows.

Romans 8:13 supplies the most comprehensive description of our subject to be found in any single verse of the Bible, setting forth as it does the greatest number of its principal features: "For if ye live after the flesh, ye shall die; but if ye through the Spirit do mortify the deeds of the body, ye shall live." This is a most solemn and searching verse, and one which has little place in modern ministry, be it oral or written. If Arminians have sadly wrested it, many Calvinists have refused to face its plain affirmations and implications. Five things in it claim our best attention. First, the persons addressed. Second, the awful warning here set before them. Third, the duty enjoined upon them. Fourth, the effectual Helper provided. Fifth, the promise made to them. The better to focus our minds, and to enable us to grapple with the difficulties which not a few have found in the verse, ere seeking to fill in our outline we will ask a number of pertinent questions.

What is the relation between our text and the context? Why are both of its members in the hypothetical form—"if"? Does the "ye" in each half of the verse have reference to the same persons, or are there two entirely different classes in view? If the latter be the case, then by what valid principle of exegesis can we account for such? Why not change one of them to "any" or "they"? What is meant by "live after the flesh"? Is it possible for a real Christian to do so? If not, and it is unregenerate persons who are mentioned, then why say they "shall die," seeing that they are dead already spiritually? Are the terms "die" and "live" here used figuratively and relatively, or literally and absolutely? What is imported by "mortify" and why "the deeds of the body" rather than "the lusts of the flesh"? If the "ye" perform that task, then how "through the Spirit"? If He be the prime Worker, then why is the mortifying predicated of them? If there be conjoint action, then how are the two factors to be adjusted? In what manner will the promise "ye shall live" be made good, seeing they already be alive spiritually? We know of no commentator who has made any real attempt to grapple with these problems.

The whole context makes it quite evident *what* particular classes of people are here addressed. First, it is those who are in Christ Jesus, upon whom there is now no condemnation (verse 1). Second, it is those who have been made free from the law of sin and death, and had the righteousness of Christ imputed to them (verses 2-4). Third, it is those who give proof that they are the beneficiaries of Christ, by walking not after the flesh, but after the spirit (verse 4). In what immediately follows a description is given of two radically different classes: they who are after the flesh, carnally minded; they whose legal standing is not in the flesh, but in the spirit, who are spiritually minded because indwelt by the Spirit of God (verses 5-11). Fourth, concerning the latter—"we" as opposed to the "they" of verse 8—the apostle draws a plain and practical conclusion: "Therefore, brethren, we are debtors, not to the flesh, to live after the flesh" (verse 12)—the endearing appellation there used by Paul leaves us in no doubt as to the particular type of characters he was addressing. Manton had a most able sermon on this verse, and we will, mostly in our own language, epitomize his exposition.

Man would fain be at his own disposal. The language of his heart is "our lips are our own: who is lord over us?" (Psalm 12:4). He affects supremacy and claims the right of dominion over his own actions. But his claim is invalid, He was made by Another and for Another, and therefore he is a "debtor." Negatively, not to the flesh, which is mentioned because that corrupt principle is ever demanding subjection to it. Positively, he is debtor to the One who gave him being. Christians are debtors both as creatures and as new creatures, being entirely dependent upon God alike for their being and their well-being, for their existence and preservation. As our Maker, God is our Owner, and being our Owner He is therefore our Governor, and by consequence our Judge. He has an absolute propriety in us, an unchallengeable power over us, to command and dispose of us as He pleases. We have nothing but what we receive from Him. We are accountable to Him for our time and our talents. Every benefit we receive increases our obligation to Him. We have no right to please ourselves in anything. This debt is indissoluble: as long as we are dependent upon God for being and support, so long as we are bound to Him. Sin has in no wise cancelled our obligation, for though fallen man has lost his power to obey, the Lord has not lost His power to command.

By virtue of his spiritual being, the saint is still more a debtor to God. First, because of his redemption by Christ, for he is not his own, but bought with a price (1 Cor. 6:9). The state *from which* he was redeemed was one of woeful bondage, for he was a slave of Satan. Now when a captive was ransomed he became the absolute property of the purchaser (Lev. 25:45,46). The *end* which Christ had in view proves the same thing: He has "redeemed us to God" (Rev. 5:9). Second, because of his regeneration. The new nature then received inclines to God: we are created in Christ Jesus unto good works (Eph. 2:10). Having brought us from death unto life, renewed us in His image, bestowed upon us the status and privileges of sonship, we owe ourselves, our strength and our service unto God as His beneficiaries. The new creature is diverted from its proper use if we live after the flesh. Third, because of our own dedication (Romans 12:1). A genuine conversion involves the renunciation of the world, the flesh and the devil, and the giving up of ourselves unto the Lord (2 Cor. 8:5). Since our obedience to God is a *debt*, there can be no merit in it (Luke 17:10); but if we pay it not, we incur the debt of punishment (Matt. 6:12,15). Since the flesh has no right to command, the gratification of it is the yielding to a tyrannous usurper (Romans 6:12,14). When solicited by the flesh, the believer should reply, "I am the Lord's."

"For if ye live after the flesh, ye shall die; but if ye through the Spirit do mortify the deeds of the body, ye shall live." Here are two sharply contrasted propositions, each one being expressed conditionally. Two eventualities are plainly set forth. Two suppositions are mentioned, and the inevitable outcome of each clearly stated. Both parts of the verse affirm that if a certain course of conduct be steadily followed (for it is far from being isolated actions which are referred to) a certain result would inevitably follow. This hypothetical form of presenting the Truth is quite a common one in the Scriptures. Servants of Christ are informed that "*If* any man's [literally "any one's," i.e. of the "ministers" of verse 5, the "labourers" of verse 9] work abide which he hath built thereon, he shall receive a reward. *If* any man's ["one's," "minister's"] work shall be burned, he shall suffer loss" (1 Cor. 3:14, 15). Other well-known examples are, "for if I yet pleased men, I should not be the servant of Christ," and "For if I build again the things which I destroyed [renounced], I make myself a transgressor" (Gal. 1:10; 2:18). "How shall we escape, if we neglect so great salvation?" (Heb. 2:3, and cf. 10:26). Our text, then, is parallel with, "For he that soweth to his flesh shall of the flesh reap corruption: but he that soweth to the spirit shall of the spirit reap life everlasting" (Gal. 6:8).

There are two things which the people of God are ever in need of: faithful warnings, kindly encouragements—the one to curb their sinful propensities, the other to animate their spiritual graces to the performing of duty, especially when they be cast down by the difficulties of the way or are mourning over their failures. Here too a balance needs to be carefully preserved. Inexperienced believers have little realization of the difficulties and perils before them, and the hearts of older ones are so deceitful that each alike needs to be plainly and frequently corrected, and exhorted to pay attention to the danger-signals which God has set up along our way. It is both striking and solemn to note how often the Saviour sounded the note of warning, not only unto the wicked, but more especially unto His disciples. He bade them, "Take heed what ye hear" (Mark 4:24); "Beware of false prophets" (Matt. 7:15); "Take heed therefore that the light which is in thee be not darkness" (Luke 11:35); "Remember Lot's wife" (Luke 17:32); "Take heed to yourselves, lest at any time your hearts be overcharged with surfeiting, and drunkenness, and cares of this life" (Luke 21:34). To one He had healed, "Sin no more, lest a worse thing come unto thee" (John 5:14).

The word "flesh" is used in Scripture in a number of senses, but throughout Romans 8 it signifies that corrupt and depraved nature which is in us when we enter this world. That evil nature or principle is variously designated. It is termed "sin" (Romans 7:8), "warring against the law of my mind" (verse 23). In James 4:5, "the *spirit* that dwelleth in us lusteth to envy," to indicate that it is not a tangible or material entity. But more commonly it is called "the flesh" (John 3:6; Romans 7:25; Gal. 5:17). It is so termed because it is transmitted from parent to child as the body is, because it is propagated by natural generation, because it is strengthened and drawn forth by carnal objects, because of its base character and degeneracy. It was not in man when he left the hand of his Creator and was pronounced by Him "very good." Rather was it something that he acquired by the fall. The principle of sin as a foreign element, as a thing *ab extra*, as an invading agent, entered into him, vitiating the whole of his natural being—as frost enters into and ruins vegetables, and as blight seizes and mars fruit.

The "flesh" is the open, implacable, inveterate, irreconcilable enemy of holiness, yea, it is "enmity against God" (Romans 8:7)—an "enemy" may be reconciled, not so "enmity" itself. Then what an evil and abominable thing is the flesh: at variance with the Holy One, a rebel against His Law! It is therefore our enemy, yea, it is far and away the worst one the believer has. The Devil and the world without do all their mischief to the souls of men by the flesh within them. "The flesh is the womb where all sin is conceived and formed, the anvil upon which all is wrought, the false Judas that betrays us, the secret enemy within that is ready on all occasions to open the gates to the besiegers" (Thomas Jacomb, 1622-87). We must distinguish sharply between *being* in the flesh and *living after* the flesh. Thus, "For when we were in the flesh" (Romans 7:5) has reference to Christians in their unregenerate condition, as "they that are in the flesh cannot please God" speaks of the unsaved; whereas "But ye are not in the flesh, but in the spirit" (8:8,9) is predicated of believers. "In the flesh" imports a person's standing and state before God; living after the flesh describes his course and conversation. The one inevitably follows and corresponds to the other: a person's character and conduct agree with his condition and case.

The flesh is radically and wholly evil: as Romans 7:18, declares, there is "no good thing" in it. It is beyond reclamation, being incapable of any improvement. It may indeed put on a religious garb, as did the Pharisees, but beneath is nothing but rottenness. Fire may as soon be struck out of ice as holy dispositions and motions be produced by indwelling sin. As the "flesh" continually opposes that which is good, so it ever disposes the soul unto what is evil. To "walk after" or to "live after the flesh" (both terms have the same force) is for a person to conduct himself as do all the unregenerate, who are dominated, motivated and actuated by nothing but their fallen nature. To "live after the flesh" refers not to a single act, nor even to a habit or a series of acts in one direction; but rather to the whole man being governed and guided by this vile principle. That is the case with all who are out of Christ: their desires, thoughts, speech and deeds all proceed from this corrupt fount. It is by the flesh that the whole of their souls are set in motion and their entire course steered. All is directed by some fleshly consideration. They act *from* self, or base principle; they act *for* self, or base end. The glory of God is nothing to them, the flesh is all in all.

The flesh is a dynamical, active, ambitious principle, and therefore it is spoken of as a *lusting* thing. Thus we read of "the lusts of the flesh," yea, of "the wills of the flesh" (Eph. 2:3—margin) for its desires are vehement and imperious. "But [indwelling] sin, taking occasion [being aggravated] by the commandment ["thou shalt not covet"], wrought in me all manner of concupiscence" [or "lust"] (Romans 7:8). Education and culture may result in a refined exterior; family training and other influences may lead to an espousal of religion, as is the case with the great majority of the heathen; selfish considerations may even issue in voluntarily undergoing great austerities and deprivations, as the Buddhist to attain unto Nirvana, the Mohammedan to gain paradise, the Romanist to merit heaven—but the love of God prompts none of them, nor is His glory their aim. Though the Christian be "not in the flesh" as to his status and state, yet the flesh as an evil principle (unchanged) is still in him, and it "lusteth against the spirit" (Gal. 5:17) or new nature, and therefore are we exhorted, "Let not sin [i.e. the flesh] therefore reign in your mortal body, that ye should obey it in the lusts thereof" (Romans 6:12).

It requires to be pointed out that there is a *twofold* walking or living after the flesh: the one more gross and manifest, the other more indiscernible. The first breaks forth into open and bodily lusts and acts, such as gluttony, drunkenness, moral uncleanness: this is "the filthiness of the flesh." The second is when the flesh exerts itself in internal heart lusts, which are more or less concealed from our fellows, which lie smouldering and festering within our soul, such as pride, unbelief, self-love, envy, covetousness; this is the filthiness "of the spirit" (2 Cor. 7:1). In Galatians 5:18,19, the apostle gives a catalogue of the lustings of the flesh in *both* of these respects. He does so to expose a common fallacy. It is generally assumed that walking or living "according to the flesh" is limited to the first form mentioned, and the second one is little considered or regarded. So long as men abstain from gross intemperance, open profanity, brutish sensuality, they think that all is well with them, whereas they may be quite free from all gross practices and still be guilty of living after the flesh. Yea, such *is* the case with all in whose hearts there are inordinate affections after the world, a spirit of self-exaltation, covetousness, malice, hatred, uncharitableness, and many other reprehensible lusts.

Our text makes crystal clear to us the fundamental and vital importance of the duty here enjoined, for our performance or non-performance thereof is literally a matter of life and death. Mortification is not optional, but imperative. The solemn alternatives are plainly stated: neglect ensures everlasting misery, compliance therewith is assured eternal felicity. The whole verse is manifestly addressed unto saints, and they are faithfully warned, "If ye live after the flesh ye shall die": that is, die eternally, for as in 5:12,21; 7:23; 8:6, "death" includes all the penal consequences of sin both here and hereafter; so in our text "die" manifestly signifies "shall suffer the second death," which is "the lake which burneth with fire and brimstone" (Rev. 21:8). The express reason is here advanced why Christians should not live after the flesh: they are not debtors to it to do so (verse 12): if they surrender to its dominion, the wages of sin will most certainly be paid them. "The flesh belongs to the world, and the man who is yielding to its promptings is in the world, living like the world, and must perish with the world" (J. Stifler).

It was by yielding to the lusts of the flesh that Adam brought death upon himself and all his posterity. And if I live after the flesh, that is, am governed and guided by my old nature, acting habitually according to its inclinations—for it is a persistent and continuous course of conduct which is here mentioned—then, no matter what be my profession, I shall perish in my sin. It is the gratifying and serving of the flesh, instead of the will of God, which eternally ruins souls. "It may be asked whether one who has received the grace of God in truth can live after the flesh. To live in a continued course of sin is contrary to the grace of God; but flesh may prevail and greatly influence the life and conversation for a while. How long this may be the case of a true believer under backsliding, through the power of corruptions and temptations, cannot be known; but certain it is that it shall not be always thus with him" (John Gill).

The whole of our verse pertains to professing Christians, and at the present moment. The Apostle did not simply say, "If ye have lived after the flesh," for that is the case with every unregenerate soul. But if ye now live after the flesh, "ye shall die"—in the full meaning of that word. It is a general statement of a universal truth. We fully agree with the explanation furnished by B.W. Newton, who was a decided Calvinist. "An expression of this kind is addressed to us for two reasons. First, because in the professing church the apostle knew there were and would be false professors. So whenever collective bodies are addressed, he always uses words implying uncertainty and doubt, for tares will be among the wheat. And second, true believers themselves (though grace can preserve them) have now nevertheless always a tendency in them to the same paths. Therefore descriptions like this, which are true to the full of those who merely profess, may yet be rightly applied to all who are wandering into those paths." Examples of the one are found in such passages as Galatians 4:20, and 6:8; Ephesians 5:5-7; Col. 3:5, 6. Of the second it must be borne in mind that a backsliding Christian had turned aside from the narrow way of denying self, and that if he follows the course of self-pleasing to the bitter end, destruction awaits him."

See here the *faithfulness* of God in so plainly warning of the terrible doom awaiting all who live after the flesh. Instead of thinking hardly of God for His threatenings, we should be grateful for them. See the *justice* of God. To be pleasing self is to continue in the apostasy of mankind, and therefore the original sentence (Genesis 2:17) is in force against them. It is contempt of God, and the heinousness of the sin is measured by the greatness of Him who is affronted (1 Samuel 2:25). Moreover, they refuse the remedy, and therefore are doubly guilty. See here the *wisdom* of God in appointing the greater punishment to curb the greatness of the temptation. The pleasures of sin are but for a season, but the paths of sin are for evermore: if the latter were soundly believed and seriously considered, the former would not so easily prevail with us. Behold the *holiness* of God: a unmortified soul is unfit for His presence. Vessels of glory must first be seasoned with grace. Conformity to Christ fits for heaven, and where that be lacking there can be no entrance.

"For if ye live after the flesh, ye shall die: but if ye through the Spirit do mortify the deeds of the body, ye shall live" (Romans 8:13). The whole of this verse pertains and belongs to believers, who are "debtors, not to the flesh, to live after the flesh" (verse 12); but, instead, debtors to Christ who redeemed them, and therefore to live unto His glory; debtors to the Holy Spirit who regenerated and indwells them, and therefore to live in subjection to His absolute control. In our last, we sought to supply answers to the several questions raised by us in the second paragraph on the former part of our text; we turn now to consider those relating to its latter half.

On this occasion we will state very briefly what is signified by "mortify," leaving till later a fuller explanation of the precise nature of this duty. First, from its being here placed in apposition with "live after the flesh," its negative sense is more or less obvious. To "live after the flesh" is to be completely controlled by indwelling sin, to be thoroughly under the dominion of our inbred corruptions. Hence, mortification consists in a course of conduct which is just the reverse. It imports: Comply not with the demands of your old nature, but rather subdue them. Serve not, cherish not your lusts, but starve them: "make not provision for the flesh, to fulfil the lusts thereof" (Romans 13:14). The natural desires and appetites of the physical body require to be disciplined, so that they are our servants and not our masters; it is our responsibility to moderate, regulate and subordinate them unto the higher parts of our being. But the cravings of the body of sin are to be promptly refused and sternly denied. The spiritual life is retarded just in proportion as we yield subservience to our evil passions.

The imperative necessity for this work of mortification arises from the continued presence of the evil nature in the Christian. Upon his believing in Christ unto salvation he was at once delivered from the condemnation of the Divine law, and freed from the reigning power of sin; but "the flesh" was not eradicated from his being, nor were its vile propensities purged or even modified. That fount of filthiness still remains unchanged unto the end of his earthly career. Not only so, but it is ever active in its hostility to God and holiness: "The flesh lusteth against the Spirit [or new nature], and the Spirit against the flesh"

(Gal. 5:17). Thus there is a ceaseless conflict in the saint between indwelling sin and inherent grace. Consequently there is a perpetual need for him to mortify or put to death not only the actings of indwelling corruption but also the principle itself. He is called upon to engage in ceaseless warfare and not suffer temptation to bring him into captivity to his lusts. The Divine prohibition is "have no fellowship with the unfruitful works of darkness [enter into no truce, form no alliance with], but rather reprove them" (Eph. 5:11). Say with Ephraim of old, "What have I to do any more with idols?" (Hosea 14:8).

No real communion with God is possible while sinful lusts remain unmortified. Allowed evil draws the heart away from God, and tangles the affections, discomposes the soul, and provokes the Holy One to close His ears against our prayers: "Son of man, these men have set up their idols in their heart, and put the stumblingblock of their iniquity before their face: should I be enquired of at all by them?" (Ezek. 14:3). God cannot in any wise delight in an unmortified soul: for Him to do so would be denying Himself or acting contrary to His own nature. He has no pleasure in wickedness, and cannot look with the slightest approval on evil. Sin is a mire, and the more miry we are the less fit for His eyes (Psalm 40:2). Sin is leprosy (Isaiah 1:6), and the more it spreads the less converse will the Lord have with us. Deliberately to keep sin alive is to defend it against the will of God, and to challenge combat with the Most High. Unmortified sin is against the whole design of the Gospel—as though Christ's sacrifice was intended to indulge us in sin, rather than redeem us from it. The very end of Christ's dying was the death of sin: rather than sin should not die, He laid down His life.

Though risen with Christ, their life hid with Him in God, and they certain to appear with Christ in glory, the saints are nevertheless exhorted to mortify their members which are upon the earth (Col. 3:1-5). It may appear strange when we note what particular members the apostle specified. It was not vain thoughts, coldness of heart, unwary walking, but the visible and most repulsive members of the old man: "fornication, uncleanness, inordinate affection, evil concupiscence"; and in verse 8 he bids them again, "put off all these; anger, wrath, malice, blasphemy, filthy communication" and lying. Startling and solemn it is to find that believers require calling upon to mortify such gross and foul sins as those: yet it is no more than is necessary. The best Christians on earth have so much corruption within them, which habitually disposes them unto these iniquities (great and heinous as they are), and the Devil will so suit his temptations as will certainly draw their corruptions into open acts, unless they keep a tight hand and close watch over themselves in the constant exercise of mortification. None but the Holy One of God could truthfully aver, "the prince of this world cometh, and hath nothing in Me" (John 14:30) which could be enkindled by his fiery darts.

As the servants of God urge upon the wicked that they slight not any sin because in their judgment it is but a trivial matter, saying, "Is it not a little one? and my soul shall live" (Gen. 19:20); so the faithful minister will press it upon all of God's people that they must not disregard any sin because it is great and grievous, and say within themselves, "Is it not a great one? and my soul shall never commit it." As we presume upon the pardoning mercy of God in the committing of the least sins, so we are apt to presume upon our own strength to preserve us from the committing of great and crying sins. It is because of their self-confidence and carelessness that sometimes the most gracious and experienced suddenly find themselves surprised by the most awful lapses. When the preacher bids his hearers beware that they murder not, blaspheme not, turn not apostates from their profession of the faith, none but the self-righteous will say with Hazael, "But what, is thy servant a dog, that he should do this great thing?" (2 Kings 8:13). There is no crime, however enormous, no abomination, however vile, but what any of us are capable of committing, if we do not bring the cross of Christ into our hearts by a daily mortification.

But why "mortify the deeds of *the body*"? In view of the studied balancing of the several clauses in this antithetical sentence, we had expected it to read "mortify the flesh." In the seventh chapter and the opening verses of the eighth the apostle had treated of indwelling sin as the fount of all evil actions; and here he insists on the mortifying of both the root and the branches of corruption, referring to the duty under the name of the fruits it bears. The "deeds of the body" must not be restricted to mere outward works, but be understood as including also the springs from which they issue. As Owen rightly said, "The axe must be laid to the root of the tree." In our judgment "the body" here has a twofold reference. First, to the evil nature or indwelling sin, which in Romans 6:6, and 7:24, is likened unto a body, namely "the body of the sins of the flesh" (Col. 2:11). It is a body of corruption which compasses the soul: hence we read of "your members which are upon the earth" (Col. 3:5). The "deeds of the body" are the works which corrupt nature produces, namely our sins. Thus the "body" is here used objectively of "the flesh."

Second, the "body" here includes the house in which the soul now dwells. *It* is specified to denote the degrading malignity which there is in sin, reducing its slaves to live as though they had no souls. It is mentioned to import the tendency of indwelling sin, namely to please and pamper the baser part of our being, the soul being made the drudge of the outward man. The body is here referred to for the purpose of informing us that though the soul be the original abode of "the flesh" the physical frame is the main instrument of its actions. Our corruptions are principally manifested in our external members: it is *there* that indwelling sin is chiefly found and felt. Sins are denominated "the deeds of the body" not only because they are what the lusts of the flesh tend to produce, but also because they are executed by the body (Romans 6:12). Our task then is not to transform and transmute "the flesh," but to slay it: to refuse its impulses, to deny its aspirations, to put to death its appetites.

But who is sufficient for such a task—a task which is not a work of nature but wholly a spiritual one? It is far beyond the unaided powers of the believer. Means and ordinances cannot of themselves effect it. It is beyond the province and ability of the preacher: omnipotence must have the main share in the work. "If ye through the Spirit do mortify," that is "the Spirit of God, the Spirit of Christ" of Romans 8:9—the Holy Spirit; for He is not only the Spirit of holiness in His nature, but in His operations too. He is the principal efficient cause of mortification. Let us marvel at and adore the Divine grace which has provided such a Helper for us! Let us recognize and realize that we are as truly indebted to and dependent upon the Spirit's operations as we are upon the Father's electing and the Son's redeeming us. Though grace be wrought in the hearts of the regenerate, yet it lies not in their power to act it. He who imparted the grace must renew, excite, and direct it.

Believers may employ the aids of inward discipline and rigour, and practice outward moderation and abstinence, and while they may for a time check and suppress their evil habits, unless the Spirit puts forth His power in them there will be no true mortification. And *how* does He operate in this particular work? In many different ways. First, at the new birth He gives us a new nature. Then by nourishing and preserving that nature. In strengthening us with His might in the inner man. In granting fresh supplies of grace from day to day. By working in us a loathing of sin, a mourning over it, a turning from it. By pressing upon us the claims of Christ, making us willing to take up our cross and follow Him. By bringing some precept or warning to our mind. By sealing a promise upon the heart. By moving us to pray.

Yet let it be carefully noted that our text does not say, "If the Spirit do mortify," or even "If the Spirit through you do mortify," but, instead, "If *ye* through the Spirit": the believer is not passive in this work, but active. It must not be supposed that the Spirit will help us without our concurrence, as well while we are asleep as waking, whether or not we maintain a close watch over our thoughts and works, and exercise nothing but a slight wish or sluggish prayer for the mortification of our sins. Believers are required to set themselves seriously to the task. If on the one hand we cannot discharge this duty without the Spirit's enablement, on the other hand He will not assist if we be too indolent to put forth earnest endeavours. Then let not the lazy Christian imagine he will ever get the victory over his lusts.

The Spirit's grace and power afford no licence to idleness, but rather call upon us to the diligent use of means and looking to Him for His blessing upon the same. We are expressly exhorted, "let us cleanse ourselves from all filthiness of the flesh and spirit, perfecting holiness in the fear of God" (2 Cor. 7:1), and that makes it plain that the believer is not a cipher in this work. The gracious operations of the Spirit were never designed to be a substitute for the Christian's discharge of duty. Though His help be indispensable, yet it releases us not from our obligations. "Little children, keep yourselves from idols" (John 5:21) emphasizes our accountability and evinces that God requires much more than our waiting upon Him to stir us unto action. Our hearts are terribly deceitful, and we need to be much upon our guard against cloaking a spirit of apathy under an apparent jealous regard for the glory of the Spirit. Is no self-effort required to escape the snares of Satan by refusing to walk in those paths which God has prohibited? Is no self-effort called for in separating ourselves from the companionship of the wicked?

Mortification is a task to which every Christian must apply himself with prayerful diligence and resolute earnestness. The regenerate have a spiritual nature within that fits them for holy action, otherwise there would be no difference between them and the unregenerate. They are required to improve the death of Christ, to embitter sin to them by His sufferings. They are to use the grace received in bringing forth the fruits of righteousness. Nevertheless, it is a task which far transcends our feeble powers. It is only "through the Spirit" that any of us can acceptably or effectually (in any degree) "mortify the deeds of the body." He it is who presses upon us the claims of Christ: reminding us that inasmuch as He died *for* sin, we must spare no efforts in dying *to* sin—striving against it (Heb. 11:4), confessing it (1 John 1:9), forsaking it (Prov. 28:13). He it is who preserves us from giving way to despair, and encourages us to renew the conflict. He it is who deepens our longings after holiness, and moves us to cry, "Create in me a clean heart, O God" (Psalm 51:10).

"If ye through the Spirit do mortify the deeds of the body." Mark, my reader, the lovely balance of truth which is here so carefully preserved: while the Christian's responsibility is strictly enforced, the honour of the Spirit is as definitely maintained and Divine grace is magnified. Believers are the agents in this work, yet they perform it by the strength of Another. The duty is theirs, but the success and the glory are His. The Spirit's operations are carried on in accordance with the constitution which God has given us, working within and upon us as moral agents. The same work is, in one point of view, God's; and in another ours. He illumines the understanding, and makes us more sensible of indwelling sin. He makes the conscience more sensitive. He deepens our yearnings after purity. He works in us both to will and to do of God's good pleasure. Our business is to heed His convictions, to respond to His holy impulses, to implore His aid, to count upon His grace.

"If ye through the Spirit do mortify the deeds of the body, *ye shall live*." Here is the encouraging promise set before the sorely tried contestant. God will be no man's debtor: yea, He is a rewarder of them that diligently seek Him (Heb. 11:6). If then, by grace, we concur with the Spirit, denying the flesh, striving after holiness, richly shall we be recompensed. The promise unto this duty is opposed unto the death threatened in the clause foregoing: as "die" there includes all the penal consequences of sin, so "shall live" comprehends all the spiritual blessings of grace. If by the Spirit's enablement and our diligent use of the Divinely appointed means we sincerely and constantly oppose and refuse the solicitations of indwelling sin, then—but only then—we shall live a life of grace and comfort here, and a life of eternal glory and bliss hereafter. As we have shown in the November article on 1 John 2:25, "eternal life" is the believer's present possession (John 3:36; 10:28) and also his future goal (Mark 10:30; Gal. 6:8; Titus 1:2). He now has a title and right to it; he has it by faith, and in hope; he has the seed of it in his new nature. But he has it not yet in full possession and fruition.

"The promises of the Gospel are not made to the work, but to the worker; and to the worker not for his work, but according to his work, for the sake of Christ's work. The promise of life, then, is not made to the work of mortification, but to him that mortifies his flesh; and that not for his mortification, but because he is in Christ, of which this mortification is the evidence. That they who mortify the flesh shall live is quite consistent with the truth that eternal life is the free gift of God; and in the giving of it, there is no respect to the merit of the receiver. This describes the character of all who receive eternal life; and it is of great importance. It takes away all ground of hope from those who profess to know God and in works deny Him" (Robert Haldane). The conditionality of the promise, then, is neither that of causation nor uncertainty, but of coherence and connection. A life of glory proceeds not from mortification as the effect from the cause, but follows merely upon it as the end does the use of means. The highway of holiness is the only path which leads to heaven.

THE POWER OF GOD

"Twice have I heard this; that power belongeth unto God" (Psalm 62:11). In our first article upon this glorious theme, we practically confined our attention to the omnipotence of God as it is seen in and through the old creation. Here we propose to contemplate the exercise of His might in and on the new creation. That God's people are much slower to perceive the latter than the former is plain from Ephesians 1:19, where the apostle prayed that the saints might know "*what is* the exceeding greatness of His power to us-ward who believe, according to the working of His mighty power." Very striking indeed is this. When Paul speaks of the Divine power in creation he mentions "His power and Godhead" (Romans 1:20); but when he treats of the work of grace and salvation, he calls it "the exceeding greatness of His power."

God proportions His power to the nature of His work. The casting out of demons is ascribed to His "finger" (Luke 11:20); His delivering of Israel from Egypt to His "hand" (Exodus 13:9); but when the Lord saves a sinner it is His "holy *arm*" which gets Him the victory (Psalm 98:1). It is to be duly noted that the language of Ephesians 1:19, is so couched as to take in the *whole* work of Divine grace in and upon the elect. It is not restrained to the past—"who have believed according to"; nor to the time to come—"the power that shall work in you"; but, instead, it is "the exceeding greatness of His power to us-ward *who believe.*" It is the "effectual working" of God's might from the first moment of illumination and conviction till their sanctification and glorification.

So dense is the darkness which has now fallen upon the people (Isaiah 60:2), that the vast majority of those even in the "churches" deem it by no means a hard thing to become a Christian. They seem to think it is almost as easy to purify a man's heart (James 4:8) as it is to wash his hands; that it is as simple a matter to admit the light of Divine Truth into the soul as it is the morning sun into our chambers by opening the shutters; that it is no more difficult to turn the heart from evil to good, from the world to God, from sin to Christ, than to turn a ship round by the help of the helm. And this in the face of Christ's emphatic statement, "With men this is impossible" (Matt. 19:26).

To mortify the lusts of the flesh (Col. 3:5), to be crucified daily to sin (Luke 9:23), to be meek and gentle, patient and kind—in a word, *to be Christ-like*—is a task altogether beyond our powers; it is one on which we would never venture, or, having ventured on, would soon abandon, but that God is pleased to perfect His strength in our weakness, and is "mighty to save" (Isaiah 63:1). That this may be the more clearly evident to us, we shall now consider some of the features of God's powerful operations in the saving of His people.

1. *In Regeneration*

Little as real Christians may realize it, a far greater power is put forth by God in the new creation than in the old, in refashioning the soul and conforming it to the image of Christ than in the original making it. There is a greater distance between sin and righteousness, corruption and grace, depravity and holiness, than there is between nothing and something, or nonentity and being; and the greater the distance there is, the greater the power in producing something. The miracle is greater according as the *change* is greater. As it is a more signal display of power to change a dead man to life than a sick man to health, so it is a far more wonderful performance to change unbelief to faith and enmity to love than simply to create out of nothing. There we are told, "the gospel of Christ ... is *the power of God* unto salvation to every one that believeth" (Romans 1:16).

The Gospel is the instrument which the Almighty uses when accomplishing the most wondrous and blessed of all His works, i.e. the picking up of wretched worms of the earth and making them "*meet* to be partakers of the inheritance of the saints in light" (Col. 1:12). When God formed man out of the dust of the ground, though the dust contributed nothing to the act whereby God made him, it had in it no principle *contrary* to His design. But in turning the heart of a sinner toward Himself, there is not only the lack of any principle of assistance from him in this work, but the whole strength of his nature unites to combat the power of Divine grace. When the Gospel is presented to the sinner, not only is his understanding completely ignorant of its glorious contents, but the will is utterly perverse against it. Not only is there no desire for Christ, but there is inveterate hostility against Him. Nothing but the almighty power of God can overcome the enmity of the carnal mind. To turn back the ocean from its course would not be such an act of power as to change the turbulent bent of man's wicked heart.

2. *In convicting us of sin*

"For ye were sometimes darkness" (Eph. 5:8). Such was the Christian's fearful state before grace laid hold of him. He was not only *in* darkness, but he himself *was* "darkness." He was utterly devoid of a single ray of spiritual light. The "light of reason" of which men boast so much, and the "light of conscience" which others value so highly, were utterly worthless as far as giving any intelligence in the things of God was concerned. It was to this awful fact that Christ referred when He said, "If therefore the light that *is* in thee *be darkness*, how great is that darkness!" (Matt. 6:23). Yes, *so* "great" is that darkness that men "call evil good, and good evil;...put darkness for light, and light for darkness;...put bitter for sweet, and sweet for bitter!" (Isaiah 5:20). So "great" is that darkness that spiritual things are "foolishness" unto them (1 Cor. 2:14). So "great" is that darkness that they are completely *ignorant of it* (Eph. 4:18), and utterly blind to their actual state. Not only is the natural man unable to deliver himself from this darkness, but he has no desire whatever for such deliverance, for being spiritually dead he has no consciousness of any *need for* deliverance.

It is because of their fearful state that, until the Holy Spirit actually regenerates, *all* who hear the Gospel are totally incapacitated for any *spiritual* understanding of it. The majority who hear it imagine that *they* are already saved, that they are real Christians, and no arguments from the preacher, no power on earth, can ever convince them to the contrary. Tell them, "There is a generation that are pure in their own eyes, and yet is not washed from their filthiness" (Prov. 30:12), and it makes no more impression than does water on a duck's back. Warn them that, "Except ye repent, *ye* shall all likewise perish"

(Luke 13:3), and they are no more moved than are the rocks by the ocean's spray. No, they suppose that they have nothing to repent of, and know not that *their* repentance needs "to be repented of" (2 Cor. 7:10). They have far too high an opinion of their religious profession to allow that *they* are in any danger of hell. Thus, unless a mighty miracle of grace is wrought within them, unless Divine power shatters their complacency, there is no hope at all for them.

For a soul to be *savingly convicted* of sin is a greater wonder than for a putrid fountain to send forth sweet waters. For a soul to be brought to realize that "*every* imagination of the thoughts of his heart was only evil continually" (Gen. 6:5) requires the power of omnipotence to produce. By nature man is independent, self-sufficient, self-confident: what a miracle of grace has been wrought when he now feels and owns his helplessness! By nature a man thinks well of himself; what a miracle of grace has been wrought when he acknowledges, "in me . . . dwelleth no good thing" (Romans 7:18)! By nature men are "*lovers* of themselves" (2 Tim. 3:2); what a miracle of grace has been wrought when men *abhor* themselves (Job 42:6)! By nature man thinks he is doing Christ a favour to espouse His Gospel and patronize His cause; what a miracle of grace has been wrought when he discovers that he is utterly unfit for *His* holy presence, and cries, "Depart from me; for I am a sinful man, O Lord" (Luke 5:8). By nature man is proud of his own abilities, accomplishments, attainments; what a miracle of grace has been wrought when he can truthfully declare, "I count *all* things but loss for the excellency of the knowledge of Christ Jesus . . . and do count them but dung, that I may win Christ" (Phil. 3:8).

3. *In casting out the Devil*

"The whole world lieth in wickedness" (1 John 5:19), bewitched, fettered, helpless. As we go over the Gospel narratives and read of different ones who were possessed of demons, thoughts of pity for the unhappy victims stir our minds, and when we behold the Saviour delivering these wretched creatures we are full of wonderment and gladness. But does the Christian reader realize that we too were once in that same awful plight? Before conversion we were the slaves of Satan, the Devil wrought in us his will (Eph. 2:2), and so we walked according to the prince of the power of the air." What ability had we to deliver ourselves? Less than we have to stop the rain from falling or the wind from blowing. A picture of man's helplessness to deliver himself from Satan's power is drawn by Christ in Luke 11:21: "When a strong man armed keepeth his palace, his goods are in peace." The "strong man" is Satan; his "goods" are the helpless captives.

But blessed be His name, "the Son of God was manifested, that He might destroy the works of the devil" (1 John 3:8). This too was pictured by Christ in the same parable: "But when a stronger than he shall come upon him, and overcome him, he taketh from him all his armour wherein he trusted, and divideth the spoils" (Luke 11:22). Christ is mightier than Satan, He overcomes him in the day of His power (Psalm 110:3), and emancipates "His own" who are bound (Isaiah 61:1). He still comes by His Spirit to "set at liberty them that are bruised" (Luke 4:18), therefore is it said of God, "who hath delivered us from the power of darkness, and hath translated us into the kingdom of His dear Son" (Col. 1:13). The Greek word for "delivered" signifies freeing by violence, a plucking or snatching out of a power that otherwise would not yield its prey.

4. *In producing repentance*

Man without Christ cannot repent: "Him hath God exalted with His right hand to be a Prince and a Saviour, for to give repentance" (Acts 5:31). Christ gave it as a "prince," and therefore to none but His subjects, those who are in His kingdom, in whom He rules. Nothing can draw men to repentance but the regenerating power of Christ, which He exercises at God's right hand; for the acts of repentance are hatred of sin, sorrow for it, determination to forsake it, and earnest and constant endeavour after its death. But sin is so transcendently dear and delightful to a man out of Christ that nothing but an infinite power can draw him to these acts mentioned. Sin is more precious to an unregenerate soul than anything else in heaven or earth. It is dearer to him than liberty, for he gives himself up to it entirely, and becomes its servant and slave. It is dearer to him than health, strength, time, or riches, for he spends all these upon sin. It is dearer to him than his own soul. Shall a man lose his sins or his soul? Ninety-nine out of a hundred vote for the latter, and lose their souls on that account.

Sin is a man's self. Just as "I" is the central letter of "sin," so sin is the centre, the moving-power, the very life of self. Therefore did Christ say, "If any man will come after Me, let him *deny himself*" (Matt. 16:24). Men are "lovers of their own selves" (2 Tim. 3:2), which is the same as saying that their hearts are wedded to sin. Man "drinketh iniquity like water" (Job 15:16); he cannot exist without it, he is ever thirsting for it, he must have his fill of it. Now since man so dotes on sin, what is going to turn his delight into sorrow, his love for it into loathing of it? Nothing but almighty power.

Here, then, we may mark the folly of those who cherish the delusion that they can repent whenever they get ready to do so. But evangelical repentance is not at the beck and call of the creature. It is the gift of God: "If God peradventure will give them repentance to the acknowledging of the truth" (2 Tim. 2:25). Then what insanity is it that persuades multitudes to defer the effort to repent till their death-beds? Do they imagine that when they are so weak that they can no longer turn their bodies they will have strength to turn their souls from sin? Far sooner could they turn themselves back to perfect physical health. What praise, then, is due to God if He has wrought a saving repentance in us.

5. *In working faith in His people*

Saving faith in Christ is not the simple matter that so many vainly imagine. Countless thousands suppose it is as easy to believe in the Lord Jesus as in Caesar or Napoleon, and the tragic thing is that hundreds of preachers are helping forward this lie. It is as easy to believe on Him as on them in a *natural*, historical, intellectual way; but not so in a spiritual and saving way. I may believe in all the heroes of the past, but such belief effects no change in my life! I may have unshaken confidence in the historicity of George Washington, but does my belief in him abate my love for the world and cause me to hate even the garment spotted by the flesh? A supernatural and saving faith in Christ purifies the life. Is *such* a faith easily attained? No, indeed! Listen to Christ Himself: "How can ye believe, which receive honour one of another, and seek not the honour that cometh from God only?" (John 5:44). And again, we read, "They could not believe" (John 12:39).

Faith in Christ is receiving Him as He is offered or presented to us by God (John 1:12). Now God presents Christ to us not only as Priest, but as King; not only as Saviour, but as "Prince" (Acts 5:21)—note that "Prince" *precedes* "Saviour," as taking His "yoke" upon us goes before finding "rest" to our souls (Matt. 11:29)! Are men as willing for Christ to rule as to save them? Do they pray as earnestly for purity as for pardon? Are they as anxious to be delivered from the *power* of sin as they are from the fires of hell? Do they desire holiness as much as they do heaven? Is the dominion of sin as dreadful to them as its wages? Does the filthiness of sin grieve them as much as the guilt and damnation of it? The man who divides what God has joined together when He offers Christ to us *has not* "received" Him at all.

Faith is the gift of God (Eph. 2:8, 9). It is wrought in the elect by "the operation of God" (Col. 2:12). To bring a sinner from unbelief to saving faith in Christ is a miracle as great and as wondrous as was God's raising Christ from the dead (Eph. 1:19, 20). Unbelief is far, far more than entertaining an erroneous conception of God's way of salvation: it is a species of hatred against Him. So faith in Christ is far more than the mind assenting to all that is said of Him in the Scriptures. The demons do that (James 2:19), but it does not save them. Saving faith is not only the heart being weaned from every other object of confidence as the ground of my acceptance before God, but it is also the heart being weaned from every other object that competes with Him for my affections. Saving faith is that "which worketh by love" (Gal. 5:6), a love which is evidenced by keeping His commandments (John 14:23); but by nature all men hate his commandments. Therefore where there is a believing heart which is devoted to Christ, esteeming Him above self and the world, a mighty miracle of grace has been wrought in the soul.

6. *In communicating a sense of pardon*

When a soul has been sorely wounded by the "arrows of the Almighty" (Job 6:4), when the ineffable light of the thrice holy God has shone into our dark hearts, revealing their unspeakable filthiness and corruption; when our innumerable iniquities have been made to stare us in the face, until the convicted sinner has been made to realize he is fit only for hell, and sees himself even now on the very brink of it; when he is brought to feel that he has provoked God so sorely that he greatly fears he has sinned beyond all possibility of forgiveness (and unless *your* soul has passed through such experiences, my readers, you have never been born again), then nothing but Divine power can raise that soul out of abject despair and create in it a hope of mercy. To lift the stricken sinner above those dark waters that have so terrified him, to bestow the light of comfort as well as the light of conviction into a heart filled with worse than Egyptian darkness, is an act of Omnipotence. God only can heal the heart which He has wounded and speak peace to the raging tempest within.

Men may count up the promises of God and the arguments of peace till they are as old as Methuselah, but it will avail them nothing until a Divine hand shall pour in "the balm of Gilead." The sinner is no more able to *apply to himself* the Word of Divine comfort when he is under the terrors of God's law, and writhing beneath the strokes of God's convicting Spirit, than he is able to resurrect the mouldering bodies in our cemeteries. To "restore the *joy of salvation*" was in David's judgment an act of sovereign power equal to that of creating a clean heart (Psalm 51:10). All the Doctors of Divinity put together are as incapable of healing a wounded spirit as are the physicians of medicine of animating a corpse. To silence a tempestuous conscience is a mightier performance than the Saviour's stilling the stormy winds and raging waves, though it is not to be expected that any will grant the truth of this who are in themselves *strangers* to such an experience. As nothing but infinite power can remove the guilt of sin, so nothing but infinite power can remove the despairing sense of it.

7. *In actually converting a soul*

"Can the Ethiopian change his skin, or the leopard his spots?" (Jer. 13:23). No, indeed; though he may paint or cover them over. So one out of Christ may restrain the outward acts of sin, but he cannot *mortify* the inward principle of it. To turn water into wine was indeed a miracle, but to turn fire into water would be a greater one. To create a man out of the dust of the ground was a work of Divine power, but to re-create a man so that a sinner becomes a saint, a lion is changed into a lamb, an enemy transformed into a friend, hatred is melted into love, is a far greater wonder of Omnipotence. The miracle of conversion, which is effected by the Spirit through the Gospel, is described thus: "For the weapons of our warfare [i.e. the preachers] are not carnal, but mighty *through God* to the pulling down of strongholds; casting down imaginations, and every high thing that exalteth itself against the knowledge of God, and bringing into captivity every thought to the obedience of Christ" (2 Cor. 10:4, 5).

Well has it been said, "To dispossess a man, then, of his self-esteem and self-sufficiency, to make room for God in the heart where there was none but for sin, as dear to him as himself, to hurl down pride of nature, to make stout imaginations stoop to the cross, to make designs of self-advancement sink under a zeal for the glory of God and an overruling design for His honour, is not to be ascribed to any but to an outstretched arm wielding the sword of the Spirit. To have a heart full of the fear of God that was just before filled with contempt of Him, to have a sense of His power, an eye to His glory, admiring thoughts of His wisdom; to have a hatred of his habitual lustings that had brought him in much sensitive pleasure; to loathe them; to live by faith in and *obedience* to the Redeemer, who before was so heartily under the dominion of Satan and self, is a triumphant act of infinite power that can 'subdue all things' to itself" (S. Charnock).

8. *In preserving His people*

"Who are kept *by the power of God* through faith . . . ready to be revealed in the last time" (1 Peter 1:5). "Kept *from what?* Ah, what mortal is capable of returning a full answer? A whole article might profitably be devoted to this one aspect of our subject. Kept from the dominion of sin which still dwells within us. Kept from being drawn out of the narrow way by the enticements of the world. Kept from the horrible heresies which ensnare thousands on every side. Kept from being overcome by Satan, who ever seeks our destruction. Kept from departing from the living God so that we do not make shipwreck of the faith.

Kept from turning His grace into lasciviousness. Weak as water in ourselves, yet enabled to endure as seeing Him who is invisible. This "is the Lord's doing, and it is marvellous in our eyes."

Sin is a mighty monarch which none of his subjects can withstand. There was more in Adam while innocent to resist sin than in any other since, for sin has an ally within the fallen creature that is ever ready to betray him into temptation from without. But sin had no such advantage over Adam, nevertheless it overwhelmed him. The non-elect angels were yet better able to withstand sin than Adam was, having a more excellent nature and being nearer to God, yet sin prevailed against them, and threw them out of heaven into hell. Then what a *mighty* power is required to subdue it! Only He who "led captivity captive" can make His people more than conquerors.

"As the providence of God is a manifestation of His power in a continued creation, so the preservation of grace is a manifestation of His power in a continued regeneration. God's strength abates and modifies the violence of temptations, His staff supports His people under them, His might defeats the power of Satan. The counterworkings of indwelling corruptions, the reluctancies of the flesh against the breathings of the spirit, the fallacies of the senses and the rovings of the mind would quickly stifle and quench grace if it were not maintained by the same all-powerful blast that first inbreathed it. No less power is seen in perfecting it, than implanting it (2 Peter 1:3); no less in fulfilling the work of faith, than in ingrafting the word of faith (2 Thess. 1:11)."—S. Charnock.

The preservation of God's people in this world greatly glories the power of God. To preserve those with so many corruptions within and so many temptations without magnifies His ineffable might more than if He were to translate them to heaven the moment they believed. In a world of suffering and sorrow, to preserve the *faith* of His people amid so many and sore testings, trials, buffetings, disappointments, betrayals by friends and professed brethren in Christ, is infinitely more wonderful than if a man should succeed in carrying an unsheltered candle alight across an open moor when a hurricane was blowing. To the glory of God the writer bears witness that but for *omnipotent* grace he had become an infidel years ago as the result of the treatment he had received from those who posed as preachers of the Gospel. Yes, for God to supply strength to His fainting people, and enable them to "hold the beginning of their confidence stedfast unto the end" (Heb. 3:14), is more marvellous than though He were to keep a fire burning in the midst of the ocean.

How the contemplation of the power of God should deepen our confidence and trust in Him: "Trust ye in the Lord for ever: *for* in the Lord Jehovah is everlasting *strength*" (Isaiah 26:4). The power of God was the ground of Abraham's assurance (Heb. 11:19), of the three Hebrews' in Babylon (Daniel 3:17), of Christ's (Heb. 5:7). Oh, to bear constantly in mind that "*God is able* to make all grace abound toward us" (2 Cor. 19:8). Nothing is so calculated to calm the mind, still our fears, and fill us with peace, as faith's appropriation of God's sufficiency. "If God be for us, who *can* be against us?" (Romans 8:31). His infallible promise is, "Fear thou not; for I am with thee: be not dismayed; for I am thy God: I will strengthen thee; yea, I will help thee; yea, I will uphold thee with the right hand of My righteousness" (Isaiah 41:10). He who brought a nation through the Red Sea without any ships, and led them across the desert for forty years where was neither bread nor water, still lives and reigns!

THE SUPREMACY OF GOD

In one of his letters to Erasmus, Luther said, "Your thoughts of God are too human." Probably that renowned scholar resented such a rebuke, the more so since it proceeded from a miner's son; nevertheless, it was thoroughly deserved. We, too, though having no standing among the religious leaders of this degenerate age, prefer the same charge against the vast majority of the preachers of our day, and against those who, instead of searching the Scriptures for themselves, lazily accept their teachings. The most dishonouring and degrading conceptions of the rule and reign of the Almighty are now held almost everywhere. To countless thousands, even among those professing to be Christians, the God of Scripture is quite unknown.

Of old, God complained to an apostate Israel, "Thou thoughtest that I was altogether as thyself" (Psalm 1:21). Such must now be His indictment against the apostate Christendom. Men imagine that the Most High is moved by sentiment, rather than actuated by principle. They suppose that His omnipotency is such an idle fiction that Satan is thwarting His designs on every side. They think that if He has formed any plan or purpose at all, then it must be like theirs, constantly subject to change. They openly declare that whatever power He possesses must be restricted, lest He invade the citadel of man's "free will" and reduce him to a "machine." They lower the all-efficacious Atonement, which has actually redeemed everyone for whom it was made, to a mere "remedy," which sin-sick souls may use if they feel disposed to; and then enervate the invincible work of the Holy Spirit to an "offer" of the Gospel which sinners may accept or reject as they please.

The supremacy of the true and living God might well be argued from the infinite distance which separates the mightiest creatures from the almighty Creator. He is the Potter, they are but the clay in His hands, to be moulded into vessels of honour, or to be dashed into pieces (Psalm 2:9) as He pleases. Were all the denizens of heaven and all the inhabitants of earth to combine in open revolt against Him, it would occasion Him no uneasiness, and would have less effect upon His eternal and unassailable throne than has the spray of the Mediterranean's waves upon the towering rock of Gibraltar. So peurile and powerless is the creature to affect the Most High that Scripture itself tells us that when the Gentile heads unite with apostate Israel to defy Jehovah and His Christ "He that sitteth in the heavens shall *laugh*" (Psalm 2:4).

The absolute and universal supremacy of God is plainly and positively affirmed in many scriptures. "Thine, O Lord, is the greatness, and the power, and the glory, and the victory, and the majesty: for all that is in the heaven and in the earth is Thine; Thine is the kingdom, O Lord, and Thou art exalted as head above all ... and Thou reignest over all" (1 Chron. 29:11, 12)—note "reignest" now, not "will do so in the millennium." "O Lord God of our fathers, art not Thou God in heaven? and rulest not Thou over all the kingdoms of the heathen? and in Thine hand is there not power and might, so that none [not even the Devil himself] is able to withstand Thee?" (2 Chron. 20:6). Before Him presidents and popes, kings and emperors, are less than grasshoppers.

"But He is in one mind, and who can turn Him? and what His soul desireth, *even that* He doeth" (Job 23:13). Ah, my reader, the God of Scripture is no make-believe monarch, no mere imaginary sovereign, but King of kings, and Lord of lords. "I know that Thou canst do every thing, and that *no* thought of Thine can be hindered" (Job 42:2, margin), or, as another translator, "no purpose of Thine can be frustrated." All that He has designed He does. All that He has decreed He perfects. All that He has promised He performs. "But our God is in the heavens: He hath done *whatsoever* He hath pleased" (Psalm 115:3). And why has He? Because "there is no wisdom nor understanding nor counsel against the Lord" (Prov. 21:30).

God's supremacy over the works of His hands is vividly depicted in Scripture. Inanimate matter, irrational creatures, all perform their Maker's bidding. At His pleasure, the Red Sea divided and its waters stood up as walls (Exodus 14); the earth opened her mouth, and guilty rebels went down alive into the pit (Num. 14). When He so ordered, the sun stood still (Joshua 10); and on another occasion went *backward* ten degrees on the dial of Ahaz (Isaiah 38:8). To exemplify His supremacy, He made ravens carry food to Elijah (1 Kings 17), iron to swim on top of the waters (2 Kings 6:5), lions to be tame when Daniel was cast into their den, fire to burn not when the three Hebrews were flung into its flames. Thus "Whatsoever the Lord pleased, that did He in heaven, and in earth, in the seas, and all deep places" (Psalm 135:6).

The absolute and universal supremacy of God is affirmed with equal plainness and positiveness in the New Testament. There we are told that God "worketh *all* things after the counsel of His own will" (Eph. 1:11)—the Greek for "worketh" means "to work effectually." For this reason we read, "For of Him, and through Him, and to Him, are all things: to whom be glory for ever. Amen" (Romans 11:36). Men may boast that they are free agents, with wills of their own, and are at liberty to do as they please, but Scripture says to those who boast, "We will go into such a city, and continue there a year, and buy and sell . . . Ye ought to say, *if the Lord* will" (James 4:13, 15)!

Here then is a sure resting-place for the heart. Our lives are neither the product of blind fate nor the result of capricious chance, but every detail of them was ordained from all eternity, and is now ordered by the living and reigning God. Not a hair of our heads can be touched without His permission. "A man's heart deviseth his way: *but the Lord* directeth his steps" (Prov. 16:9). What assurance, what strength, what comfort this should give the real Christian! "My times are in *Thy* hand" (Psalm 31:15). Then let me *"rest in the Lord,* and wait patiently for Him" (Psalm 37:7).

HEART WORK

As well might a poor man expect to be rich in this world without industry, or a weak man to become strong and healthy without food and exercise, as a Christian to be rich in faith and strong in the Lord without earnest endeavour and diligent effort. It is true that all our labours amount to nothing unless the

Lord blesses them (Psalm 127:1), as it also is that apart from Him we can do nothing (John 15:5). Nevertheless, God places no premium upon sloth, and has promised that "the soul of the diligent shall be made fat" (Prov. 13:4). A farmer may be fully persuaded of his own helplessness to make his fields productive, he may realize that their fertility is dependent upon the sovereign will of God, and he may also be a firm believer in the efficacy of prayer; but unless he discharges *his own duty his barns will be empty*. So it is spiritually.

God has not called His people to be drones, nor to maintain an attitude of passiveness. No, He bids them work, toil, labour. The sad thing is that so many of them are engaged in the wrong task, or, at least, giving most of their attention to that which is incidental, and neglecting that which is essential and fundamental. "Keep thy heart with all diligence" (Prov. 4:23): *this* is the great task which God has assigned unto each of His children. But oh, how sadly is the heart neglected! Of all their concerns and possessions, the *least* diligence is used by the vast majority of professing Christians in the keeping of their hearts. As long as they safeguard their other interests—their reputations, their bodies, their positions in the world—the heart may be left to take its own course.

As the heart in our physical body is the centre and fountain of life, because from it blood circulates into every part, conveying with it either health or disease, so it is with us spiritually. If our heart be the residence of impiety, pride, avarice, malice, impure lusts, then the whole current of our lives will largely be tainted with these vices. If they are admitted there and prevail for a season, then our character and conduct will be proportionately affected. Therefore the citadel of the heart needs above all things to be well guarded, that it may not be seized by those numerous and watchful assailants which are ever attacking it. This spring needs to be well protected that its waters be not poisoned.

The man is what his heart is. If *this* be dead to God, then nothing in him is alive. If *this* be right with God, all will be right. As the mainspring of a watch sets all its wheels and parts in motion, so as a man "thinketh in his heart, so is he" (Prov. 23:7). If the heart be right, the actions will be. As a man's heart is, such is his state now and will be hereafter: if it be regenerated and sanctified there will be a life of faith and holiness in this world, and everlasting life will be enjoyed in the world to come. Therefore, "Rather look to the cleansing of thine heart, than to the cleansing of thy well; rather look to the feeding of thine heart, than to the feeding of thy flock; rather look to the defending of thine heart, than to the defending of thine house; rather look to the keeping of thine heart, than to the keeping of thy money" (Peter Moffat, 1570).

"Keep thy heart with all diligence, for out of it are the issues of life" (Prov. 4:23). The "heart" is here put for our whole inner being, the "hidden man of the heart" (1 Peter 3:4). It is that which controls and gives character to all that we do. To "keep"—garrison or guard—the heart or soul is the great work which God has assigned us: the enablement is His, but the duty is ours. We are to keep the imagination from vanity, the understanding from error, the will from perverseness, the conscience clear of guilt, the affections from being inordinate and set on evil objects, the mind from being employed on worthless or vile subjects; the whole from being possessed by Satan. This is the work to which God has called us.

Rightly did the Puritan John Favel say, "The keeping and right managing of the heart in every condition is the great business of a Christian's life." Now to "keep" the heart right implies that it has been *set right*. Thus it was at regeneration, when it was given a new spiritual bent. True conversion is the heart turning from Satan's control to God's, from sin to holiness, from the world to Christ. To *keep* the heart right signifies the constant care and diligence of the renewed to preserve his soul in that holy frame to which grace has reduced it and daily strives to hold it. "Hereupon do all events depend: the heart being kept, the whole course of our life here will be according to the mind of God, and the end of it will be the enjoyment of Him hereafter. This being neglected, life will be lost, both here as unto obedience, and hereafter as to glory" (John Owen in *Causes of Apostasy*).

1. To "keep" the heart means *striving to shut out from it all that is opposed to God*. "Little children, keep yourselves from idols" (1 John 5:21). God is a jealous God and will brook no rival; He claims the throne of our hearts, and requires to be loved by us supremely. When we perceive our affections being inordinately drawn out unto any earthly object, we are to fight against it, and "resist the devil." When Paul said, "All things are lawful unto me, but all things are not expedient: all things are lawful for me, but I will not be *brought under the power* of any" (1 Cor. 6:12), he signified that he was keeping his heart diligently, that he was jealous lest *things* should gain that esteem and place in his soul which was due alone unto the Lord. A very small object placed immediately before the eye is sufficient to shut out the light of the sun, and trifling things taken up by the affections may soon sever communion with the Holy One.

Before regeneration our hearts were deceitful above all things, and desperately wicked (Jer. 17:9): that was because the evil principle, the "flesh," had complete dominion over them. But inasmuch as "the flesh" remains in us after conversion, and is constantly striving for the mastery over "the spirit," the Christian needs to exercise a constant watchful jealousy over his heart, mindful of its readiness to be imposed upon, and its proneness unto a compliance with temptations. All the avenues to the heart need to be carefully guarded so that nothing hurtful enters therein, particularly against vain thoughts and imaginations, and especially in those seasons when they are apt to gain an advantage. For if injurious thoughts are suffered to gain an inroad into the mind, if we accustom ourselves to give them entertainment, then in vain shall we hope to be "spiritually minded" (Romans 8:6). All such thoughts are only making provision to fulfil the lusts of the flesh.

Thus, for the Christian to "keep" his heart with all diligence means for him to pay close attention to the direction in which his affections are moving, to discover whether the things of the world are gaining a firmer and fuller hold over him or whether they are increasingly losing their charm for him. God has exhorted us, "Set your affections on things above, not on things on the earth" (Col. 3:2), and the heeding of this injunction calls for constant examination of the heart to discover whether or not it is becoming more and more dead unto this deceitful and perishing world, and whether heavenly things are those in which we find our chief and greatest delight. "Take heed to thyself, and keep thy soul diligently, lest thou forget the things which thine eyes have seen, and lest they depart from thy heart" (Deut. 4:9).

2. To "keep" the heart means *striving to bring it into conformity with the*

Word. We are not to rest content until an actual image of its pure and holy teachings is stamped upon it. Alas, so many today are just *playing* with the solemn realities of God, allowing them to flit across their fancy, but never embracing and making them their own. Why is it, dear reader, that those solemn impressions you had when hearing a searching sermon or reading a searching article so quickly faded away? Why did not those holy feelings and aspirations which were stirred within you last? Why have they borne no fruit? Was it not because you failed to see that your heart was duly affected by them? You failed to "hold fast" that which you had "received and heard" (Rev. 3:3), and in consequence your heart became absorbed again in "the care of this life" or "the deceitfulness of riches," and thus the Word was choked.

It is not enough to hear or read a powerful message from one of God's servants, and to be deeply interested and stirred by it. If there be no diligent effort on your part, then it will be said that "your goodness is as a morning cloud, and as the early dew it goeth away" (Hosea 6:4). What, then, is required? This: earnest and persevering prayer that God will fasten the message in your soul as a nail in a sure place, so that the Devil himself cannot catch it away. What is required? This: "Mary kept all these things, and pondered them in her heart" (Luke 2:19). Things which are not duly pondered are soon forgotten: meditation stands to reading as mastication does to eating. What is required? This: that you promptly put into practice what you have learned, walk according to the light God has given, or it will quickly be taken from you (Luke 8:18).

Not only must the outward actions be regulated by the Word, but the heart must also be conformed thereto. It is not enough to abstain from murder, the causeless anger must be put away. It is not enough to abstain from the act of adultery, the inward lust must be mortified too (Matt. 5:28). God not only takes note of and keeps a record of all our external conduct, but He "weighteth the spirits" (Prov. 16:2). Not only so, He requires *us* to scrutinize the springs from which our actions proceed, to examine our motives, to ponder *the spirit* in which we act. God requires truth—that is sincerity, reality—in "the inward parts" (Psalm 51:6). Therefore does He command us, "Keep thy heart with all diligence, for out of it are the issues of life."

3. To "keep" the heart means *to preserve it tender unto sin.* The unregenerate man makes little or no distinction between sin and crime; as long as he keeps within the law of the land, and maintains a reputation for respectability among his fellows, he is, generally speaking, quite satisfied with himself. But it is far otherwise with one who has been born again: he has been awakened to the fact that he has to do with *God,* and must yet render a full account unto Him. He makes conscience of a hundred things which the unconverted never trouble themselves about. When the Holy Spirit first convicted him he was made to feel that his whole life had been one of rebellion against God, of pleasing himself. The consciousness of this pierced him to the quick: his inward anguish far exceeded any pains of body or sorrow occasioned by temporal losses. He saw himself to be a spiritual leper, and hated himself for it, and mourned bitterly before God. He cried, "Hide Thy face from my sins, and blot out all mine iniquities. Create in me a clean heart, O God; and renew a right spirit within me" (Psalm 51:9, 10).

Now it is the duty of the Christian, and part of the task which God has set him, to see to it that this sense of the exceeding sinfulness of sin be not lost. He is to labour daily that his heart be duly affected by the heinousness of self-will and self-love. He is steadfastly to resist every effort of Satan to make him pity himself, think lightly of wrongdoing, or excuse himself in the same. He is to live in the constant realization that the eye of God is ever upon him, so that when tempted he will say with Joseph, "How then can I do this great wickedness, and sin against God?" (Gen. 39:9). He is to view sin in the light of the cross, daily reminding himself that it was *his* iniquities which caused the Lord of glory to be made a curse for him; employing the dying love of Christ as a motive why he must not allow himself in anything that is contrary to the holiness and obedience which the Saviour asks from all His redeemed.

Ah, my Christian reader, it is no child's play to "keep the heart with all diligence." The easy-going religion of our day will never take its devotees (or rather its *victims!*) to heaven. The question has been asked, "Who shall ascend into the hill of the Lord? or *who* shall stand in His Holy place?" and plainly has the question been answered by God Himself: "He that hath clean hands, and a pure heart," etc. (Psalm 24:3, 4). Equally plain is the teaching of the New Testament, "Blessed are the pure in heart: for *they* shall see God" (Matt. 5:8). A "pure heart" is one that hates sin, which makes conscience of sin, which grieves over it, which strives against it. A "pure heart" is one that seeks to keep undefiled the temple of the Holy Spirit, the dwelling-place of Christ (Eph. 3:17).

4. To "keep" the heart means *to look diligently after its cleansing.* Perhaps some of our readers often find themselves sorrowfully crying, "Oh, the vileness of my heart!" Thank God if He *has* discovered this to you. But, dear friend, there is no sufficient reason why your "heart" should *continue* to be vile. You might lament that your garden was overgrown with weeds and filled with rubbish; but need it remain so? We speak not now of your sinful *nature*, the incurable and unchangeable "flesh" which still indwells you; but of your *"heart,"* which God bids you "keep." You *are* responsible to purge your mind of vain imaginations, your soul of unlawful affections, your conscience of guilt.

But, alas, you say, "I have no control over such things: they come unbidden and I am powerless to prevent them." So the Devil would have you believe! Revert again to the analogy of your garden. Do not the weeds spring up unbidden? Do not the slugs and other pests seek to prey upon the plants? What, then? Do you merely bewail your helplessness? No, you resist them, and take means to keep them under. Thieves enter houses uninvited, but whose fault is it if the doors and windows be left unfastened? Oh, heed not the seductive lullabies of Satan. God says, "Purify your hearts, ye double minded" (James 4:8); that is, one mind for Him, and another for self! one for holiness, and another for the pleasures of sin.

But *how* am I to "purify" my heart? By vomiting up the foul things taken into it, shamefacedly owning them before God, repudiating them, turning from them with loathing; and it is written, "If we confess our sins, He is faithful and just to forgive us our sins, and to *cleanse* us from all unrighteousness." By daily renewing our exercise of repentance, and *such* repentance as is spoken of in 2 Corinthians 7:11; "for behold this selfsame thing, that ye sorrowed after a godly sort, what carefulness it wrought in you, yea, what clearing of yourselves, yea, what indignation, yea, what fear, yea, what vehement desire, yea, what zeal, yea, what revenge! In all things ye have approved yourselves to be clear in this matter." By the daily exercise of faith (Acts 15:9), appropriating afresh the cleansing blood of Christ, bathing every night in that "fountain" which has been opened "for sin and uncleanness" (Zech. 13:1). By treading the path of God's commandments: "Seeing ye have purified your souls in obeying the truth through the Spirit" (1 Peter 1:22).

We now point out what is obvious to every Christian reader, namely that such a task calls for Divine aid. Help and grace need to be earnestly and definitely sought of the Holy Spirit each day. We should bow before God, and in all simplicity say, "Lord, Thou requirest me to keep my heart with all diligence, and I feel utterly incompetent for such a task; such a work lies altogether beyond my poor feeble powers; therefore I humbly ask Thee in the name of Christ graciously to grant unto me supernatural strength to do as Thou hast bidden me. Lord, work in me both to will and to do of Thy good pleasure."

"Man looketh on the outward appearance, but the Lord looketh on the heart" (1 Samuel 16:7). How prone we are to be occupied with that which is evanescent, rather than with the things that abide; how ready to gauge things by our senses instead of by our rational powers. How easily we are deceived by that which is on the surface, forgetting that true beauty lies within. How slow we are to adopt God's way of estimating. Instead of being attracted by comeliness of physical features we should value moral qualities and spiritual graces. Instead of spending so much care, time and money on the adorning of the body we ought to devote our best attention to the developing and directing of the faculties of our souls. Alas, the vast majority of our fellows live as though they had no souls, and the average professing Christian gives little serious thought to the same.

Yes, the Lord "looketh on the heart": He sees its thoughts and intents, knows its desires and designs, beholds its motives and motions, and deals with us accordingly. The Lord discerns what qualities are in our hearts: what holiness and righteousness, what wisdom and prudence, what justice and integrity, what mercy and kindness. When such graces are lively and flourishing, then is fulfilled that verse, "My beloved is gone down into his garden, to the beds of spices, to feed in the gardens, and to gather lilies" (Song of Sol. 6:2). God esteems nothing so highly as holy faith, unfeigned love, and filial fear; in His sight a "meek and quiet spirit" is of "great price" (1 Peter 3:4).

The sincerity of our profession largely depends upon the care and conscience we have in keeping our hearts. A very searching example of this is found in 2 Kings 10:31, "But Jehu took no heed to walk in the law of the Lord God of Israel with all his heart." Those words are more solemn because of what is said of him in the previous verse: "And the Lord said unto Jehu, Because thou hast done well in executing that which is right in Mine eyes, and hast done unto the house of Ahab according unto all that was in Mine heart, thy children of the fourth generation shall sit on the throne of Israel." Jehu was partial in his reformation, which showed his heart was not right with God; he abhorred the worship of Baal which Ahab had fostered, but he tolerated the golden calves which Jeroboam had set up. He failed to put away all the evil.

Ah, my reader, true conversion is not only turning away from gross sin, it is the heart forsaking *all* sin. There must be no reserve, for God will not allow any idol, nor must we. Jehu went so far, but he stopped short of the vital point; he put away evil, but he did not do that which was good. He heeded not the law of the Lord to walk in it *"with all his heart."* It is greatly to be feared that those who are heedless are graceless, for where the principle of holiness is planted in the heart it makes its possessor circumspect and desirous of pleasing God in all things—not from servile fear, but from grateful love; not by constraint, but freely; not occasionally, but constantly.

"Keep thine heart with all diligence." Guard it jealously as the dwelling place of Him to whom you have given it. Guard it with the utmost vigilance, for not only is there the enemy without seeking entrance, but there is a traitor within desirous of dominion. The Hebrew for "with all diligence" literally rendered is "above all"; above all the concerns of our outward life, for, careful as we should be as to that, it is before the eyes of men, whereas the heart is the object of *God's* holy gaze. Then "keep" or preserve it more sedulously than your reputation, your body, your estate, your money. With all earnestness and prayer, labour that no evil desire prevails or abides there, avoiding all that excites lust, feeds pride, or stirs up anger, crushing the first emotions of such evils as you would the brood of a scorpion.

Many people place great expectations in varied circumstances and conditions. One thinks he could serve God much better if he were more prospered temporally; another if he passed through the refining effects of poverty and affliction. One thinks his spirituality would be promoted if he could be more retired and solitary; another if only he could have more society and Christian fellowship. But, my reader, the only way to serve God better is to be content with the place in which He has put you, and therein *get a better heart!* We shall never enter into the advantages of any situation, nor overcome the disadvantages of any condition, until we fix and water the root of them in ourselves." Make the tree good, *and* the fruit good" (Matt. 12:33): get the heart right, and you will soon be superior unto all "circumstances."

"But how can I get my heart right? Can the Ethiopian change his skin or the leopard his spots?" Answer: you are creating your own difficulty by confounding "heart" with "nature"; they are quite distinct. It is important to recognize this, for many are confused thereon. There has been such an undue emphasis upon the "two natures in the Christian" that often it has been lost sight of that the Christian is *a person* over and above his two natures. The Scriptures make the distinction clear enough. For example, God does not bid us keep our "nature," but He does our "hearts." We do not believe with our "nature," but we do with our "hearts" (Romans 10:10). God never tells us to "rend" our nature (Joel 2:13), "circumcise" our nature (Deut. 10:6) or "purify" our nature (James 4:8), but He does our "hearts"! The "heart" is the very centre of our responsibility, and to deny that we are to improve and keep it is to repudiate human accountability.

It is the Devil who seeks to persuade people that they are not responsible for the state of their hearts, and may no more change them than they can the stars in their courses. And the "flesh" within finds such a lie very agreeable to its case. But he who has been regenerated by the sovereign grace of God cannot, with the Scriptures before him, give heed unto any such delusion. While he has to deplore how sadly neglected is the great task which God has set before him, while he has to bemoan his wretched failure to make his heart what it ought to be, nevertheless he wants to do better; and after his duty has been pressed upon him he will daily seek grace better to discharge his duty, and instead of being totally discouraged by the difficulty and greatness of the work required he will cry the more fervently to the Holy Spirit for His enablement.

The Christian who means business will labour to have a "willing" heart (Exodus 35:5), which acts spontaneously and gladly, not of necessity; a "perfect" heart (1 Chron. 29:9), sincere, genuine, upright; a "tender" heart (2 Chron. 34:26), yielding and pliable, the opposite of hard and stubborn; a "broken" heart (Psalm 34:18), sorrowing over all failure and sin; a "united" heart (Psalm 86:11), all the affections centred on God; an "enlarged" heart (Psalm 119:32), delighting in *every* part of Scripture and loving all God's people; a "sound" heart (Prov. 14:30), right in doctrine and practice; a "merry" heart (Prov. 15:15), rejoicing in the Lord alway; a "pure" heart (Matt. 5:8), hating all evil; an "honest and good heart" (Luke 8:15), free from guile and hypocrisy, willing to be searched through and through by the Word; a "single" heart (Eph. 6:5), desiring only God's glory; a "true" heart (Heb. 10:22), genuine in all its dealings with God.

The Time of Heart Work

The duty of keeping the heart with the utmost diligence is binding upon the Christian at all times; there is no period or condition of life in which he may be excused from this work. Nevertheless, there are distinctive seasons, critical hours, which call for more than a common vigilance over the heart, and it is a few of these which we would now contemplate, seeking help from above to point out some of the most effectual aids unto the right accomplishment of the task God has assigned us. General principles are always needful and beneficial, yet details have to be furnished if we are to know how to apply them in particular circumstances. It is this lack of definiteness which constitutes one of the most glaring defects in so much modern ministry.

1. *In times of prosperity.* When providence smiles upon us and bestows temporal gifts with a lavish hand, then has the Christian urgent reason to keep his heart with all diligence, for that is the time we are apt to grow careless, proud, earthly. Therefore was Israel cautioned of old, "And it shall be, when the Lord thy God shall have brought thee into the land which He sware unto thy fathers, to Abraham, to Isaac, and to Jacob, to give thee great and goodly cities, which thou buildest not, and houses full of good things, which thou filledst not, and wells digged, which thou diggedst not, vineyards and olive trees, which thou plantedst not; when thou shalt have eaten and be full; *then beware* lest thou forget the Lord" (Deut. 6:10-12). Alas that they heeded not that exhortation.

Many are the warnings furnished in Scripture. Of Uzziah it is recorded, "When he was strong, his heart was lifted up to his destruction" (2 Chron. 21:16). To the king of Tyre God said, "Thine heart is lifted up, because of thy riches" (Ezek. 28:5). Of Israel we read, "And they took strong cities, and a fat land, and possessed houses full of all goods, wells digged, vineyards and oliveyards, and fruit trees in abundance: so they did eat, and were filled, and became fat, and delighted themselves in Thy great goodness. *Nevertheless* they were disobedient, and rebelled against Thee, and cast Thy law behind their backs, and slew Thy prophets which testified against them to turn them to Thee" (Neh. 9:25, 26). And again, "Of their silver and their gold have they made them idols" (Hosea 8:4).

Sad indeed are the above passages, the more so because we have seen such a tragic repetition of them in our own days. Oh the earthly-mindedness which prevailed, the indulging of the flesh, the sinful extravagance, which were seen among professing Christians while "times were good!" How practical godliness waned, how the denying of self disappeared, how covetousness, pleasure and wantonness possessed the great majority of those calling themselves the people of God. Yet great as was their sin, far greater was that of most of the preachers, who, instead of warning, admonishing, rebuking, and setting before their people an example of sobriety and thrift, criminally remained silent upon the crying sins of their hearers, and themselves encouraged the reckless spending of money and the indulgence of worldly lusts. How, then, is the Christian to keep his heart from these things in times of prosperity?

First, by seriously pondering the dangerous and ensnaring temptations which attend a prosperous condition, for very, very few of those who live in the prosperity and pleasures of this world escape eternal perdition. "It is easier [said Christ] for a camel to go through the eye of a needle, than for a rich man to enter into the kingdom of heaven" (Matt. 19:24). What multitudes have been carried to hell in the cushioned chariots of earthly wealth and ease, while a comparative handful have been shipped to heaven by the rod of affliction. Remember, too, that many of the Lord's own people have sadly deteriorated in seasons of worldly success. When Israel was in a low condition in the wilderness, then were they "holiness unto the Lord" (Jer. 2:3); but when fed in the fat pastures of Canaan they said, "We are lords; we will come no more unto Thee" (verse 31).

Second, diligently seek grace to heed that word, "If riches increase, set not your heart upon them" (Psalm 62:10). Those riches may be given to try you; not only are they most uncertain things, often taking to themselves wings and flying swiftly away, but at best they cannot satisfy the soul, and only perish with the using. Remember that God values no man a jot more for these things: He esteems us by inward graces, and not by outward possessions: "In every nation he that feareth Him, and worketh righteousness, is accepted with Him" (Acts 10:35). Third, urge upon your soul the consideration of that awful day of reckoning, wherein according to our receipt of mercies so shall be our accountings of them: "For unto whomsoever much is given, of him shall be much required" (Luke 12:48). Each of us must yet give an account of our stewardship.

2. *In Times of adversity.* When providence frowns upon us, overturning our cherished plans, and blasting our outward comforts, then has the Christian urgent need to look to his heart, and keep it with all diligence from replying against God or fainting under His hand. Job was a mirror of patience, yet his heart was discomposed by trouble. Jonah was a man of God, yet he was peevish under trial. When the food supplies gave out in the wilderness, they who had been miraculously delivered from Egypt, and who sang Jehovah's praises so heartily at the Red Sea, murmured and rebelled. It takes much grace to keep the heart calm amid the storms of life, to keep the spirit sweet when there is much

to embitter the flesh, and to say, "The Lord gave, and the Lord taketh away; blessed be the name of the Lord." Yet this is a Christian duty!

To help thereunto, first consider, fellow Christian, that despite these cross providences God is still faithfully carrying out the great design of electing love upon the souls of His people, and orders these very afflictions as means sanctified to that end. Nothing happens by chance, but all by Divine counsel (Eph. 1:11), and therefore it is that "all things work together *for good* to them that love God, to them who are the called according to His purpose" (Romans 8:28). Ah, beloved, it will wonderfully calm your troubled breast and sustain your fainting heart to rest upon that blessed fact. The poor worldling may say, "The bottom has dropped out of everything," but not so the saint, for the eternal God is *his* refuge, and underneath him are still the "everlasting arms."

It is ignorance or forgetfulness of God's loving designs which makes us so prone to chafe under His providential dealings. If faith were more in exercise we should "count it all joy" when we fall into divers temptations, or trials (James 1:2). Why so? Because we should discern that those very trials were sent to wean our hearts from this empty world, to tear down pride and carnal security, to refine us. If, then, my Father has a design of love unto my soul, do I well to be angry with Him? Later, if not now, you will see that those bitter disappointments were blessings in disguise, and will exclaim, "It is good for me that I have been afflicted" (Psalm 119:71).

"God is not the author of confusion" (1 Cor. 14:33); no, the Devil causes that, and he has succeeded in creating much in the thinking of many, by confounding the "heart" with the "nature." People say, "I was born with an evil heart, and I cannot help it." It would be more correct to say, "I was born with an evil nature, which I am responsible to subdue." The Christian needs clearly to recognize that *in addition to* his two "natures"—the flesh and the spirit—he has a heart which God requires him to "keep." We have already touched upon this point, but deem it advisable to add a further word thereon. I cannot change or better my "nature," but I may and must my "heart." For example, "nature" is slothful and loves ease, but the Christian is to redeem the time and be zealous of good works. Nature hates the thought of death, but the Christian should bring his heart to desire to depart and be with Christ.

The popular religion of the day is either a head or a hand one: that is to say, the labouring to acquire a larger and fuller intellectual group of the things of God or a constant round of activities called "service for the Lord." But the *heart* is neglected! Thousands are reading, studying, talking "Bible courses," but for all the *spiritual* benefits their souls derive they might as well be engaged in breaking stones. Lest it be thought that such a stricture is too severe, we quote a sentence from a letter recently received from one who has completed no less than eight of these "Bible study courses": "There was nothing in that 'hard work' which ever called for self-examination, which led me really to know God, and appropriate the Scriptures to my deep need." No, of course there was not: their compilers—like nearly all the speakers at the big "Bible conferences"—studiously avoid all that is unpalatable to the flesh, all that condemns the natural man, all that pierces and searches the conscience. Oh, the tragedy of this *head* "Christianity."

Equally pitiable is the *hand* religion of the day, when young "converts" are put to teaching a Sunday school class, urged to "speak" in the open air, or take up "personal work." How many thousands of beardless youths and young girls are now engaged in what is called "winning souls for Christ," when *their own* souls are spiritually starved! They may "memorize" two or three verses of Scripture a day, but that does not mean their souls are being fed. How many are giving their evenings to helping in some "mission," when they need to be spending the time in "the secret of the Most High"! And how many bewildered souls are using the major part of the Lord's day in rushing from one meeting to another instead of seeking from God that which will fortify them against the temptations of the week! Oh, the tragedy of this *hand* "Christianity."

How subtle the Devil is! Under the guise of promoting growth in "the knowledge of the Lord," he gets people to attend a ceaseless round of meetings, or to read an almost endless number of religious periodicals and books; or under the pretence of "honouring the Lord" by all this so-called "service" he induces the one or the other to *neglect* the great task which *God* has set before us: "keep thy heart with all diligence; for out of it are the issues of life" (Prov. 4:23). Ah, it is far easier to speak to others than it is constantly to use and improve all holy means and duties to preserve the soul from sin, and maintain it in sweet and free communion with God. It is far easier to spend an hour reading a sensational article upon "the signs of the times" than it is to spend an hour in agonizing before God for purifying and rectifying grace!

This work of keeping the heart is *of supreme importance*. The total disregard of it means that we are mere formalists. "My son, give Me thine heart" (Prov. 23:26): until *that* be done, God will accept nothing from us. The prayers and praises of our lips, the labour of our hands, yea, and a correct outward walk, are things of no value in *His* sight while the heart be estranged from Him. As the inspired apostle declared, "Though I speak with the tongues of men and of angels, and have not *love*, I am become as sounding brass, or a tinkling cymbal. And though I have the gift of prophecy, and understand all mysteries, and all knowledge; and though I have all faith, so that I could remove mountains, and have not *love*, I am nothing: And though I bestow all my goods to feed the poor, and though I give my body to be burned, and have not *love*, it profiteth nothing" (1 Cor. 13:1-3). If the heart be not right with God, we cannot *worship* Him, though we may go through the form of it. Watch diligently, then, your love for *Him*.

God cannot be imposed upon, and he who takes *no* care to order his heart aright before Him is a hypocrite. "And they come unto thee as the people cometh, and they sit before thee as My people, and they hear thy words, but they will not do them; for with their mouth they show much love, *but their heart* goeth after their covetousness. And, lo, thou art unto them as a very lovely song of one that hath a pleasant voice, and can play well on an instrument" (Ezek. 33:31, 32). Here are a company of formal hypocrites, as is evident from the words "as My people": like them, but not of them. And what constituted them impostors? Their outside was very fair—high professions, reverent postures, much seeming delight in the means of grace. Ah, but their *hearts* were not set on God, but were commanded by their lusts, went after covetousness.

But lest a real Christian should infer from the above that He is a hypocrite too, because many times his heart wanders, and he finds—strive all he may—that he cannot keep his mind stayed upon God when praying, reading His Word, or engaged in public worship, to him we answer that the objection carries its own refutation. You say "strive all I may"; ah, if you *have,* then the blessing of the upright is yours, even though God sees well to exercise you over the affliction of a wandering mind. There remains still much in the understanding and affections to humble you, but if you are *exercised* over them, strive against them, and *sorrow over* your very imperfect success, then that is quite enough to clear you of the charge of reigning hypocrisy.

The keeping of the heart is supremely important because "out of it are the issues of life"; it is the source and fountain of all vital actions and operations. The heart is the warehouse, the hand and tongue are but the shops; what is in *these* comes from *thence*—the heart contrives and the members execute. It is in the heart that the principles of the spiritual life are formed: "A good man out of the good treasure of his heart bringeth forth that which is good; and an evil man out of the evil treasure of his heart bringeth forth that which is evil" (Luke 6:45). Then let us diligently see to it that the heart be well stored with pious instruction, seeking to increase in grateful love, reverential fear, hatred of sin, and benevolence in all its exercises, that from within these holy springs may flow and fructify our whole conduct and conversation.

This work of keeping the heart is *the hardest of all.* "To shuffle over religious duties with a loose and heedless spirit will cost no great pains; but to set thyself before the Lord, and tie up thy loose and vain thoughts to a constant and serious attendance upon Him: this will cost something! To attain a facility and dexterity of language in prayer, and put thy meaning into apt and decent expressions, is easy; but to get thy heart broken for sin whilst thou art confessing it, be melted with free grace, whilst thou art blessing God for it, be really ashamed and humbled through the apprehensions of God's infinite holiness, and to *keep* thy heart in *this* frame, not only in, but after duty, will surely cost thee some groans and travailing pain of soul. To repress the outward acts of sin, and compose the external acts of thy life in a laudable and comely manner, is no great matter—even carnal persons by the force of common principles can do this; but to kill the root of corruption within, to set and keep up an holy government over thy thoughts, to have all things lie straight and orderly in the heart, this is *not* easy" (John Flavel).

Ah, dear reader, it is far, far easier to speak in the open air than to uproot pride from your soul. It calls for much less toil to go out and distribute tracts than it does to cast out of your mind unholy thoughts. One can speak to the unsaved much more readily than he can deny self, take up his cross daily, and follow Christ in the path of obedience. And one can teach a class in the Sunday School with far less trouble than he can teach himself how to strengthen his own spiritual graces. To keep the heart with all diligence calls for frequent examination of its frames and dispositions, the observing of its attitude towards God, and the prevailing directions of its affections; and that is something which no empty professor can be brought to do! Give liberally to religious enterprises he may, but give himself unto the searching, purifying and keeping of his heart he will not.

This work of keeping the heart is *a constant one.* "The keeping of the heart is such a work as is never done till life be done: this labour and our life end together. It is with a Christian in this business, as it is with seamen that have sprung a leak at sea; if they tug not constantly at the pump, the water increases upon them, and will quickly sink them. It is in vain for them to say the work is hard, and we are weary; there is no time or condition in the life of a Christian, which will suffer an intermission of this work. It is in the keeping watch over our hearts, as it was in the keeping up of Moses's hands, while Israel and Amalek were fighting below (Exodus 17:12); no sooner do Moses' hands grow heavy and sink down, but Amalek prevails. You know it cost David and Peter many a sad day and night for intermitting the watch over their own hearts but a few minutes" (J. Flavel).

Consequences of Heart Work

Having sought to show that the keeping of the heart is the great work assigned the Christian, in which the very soul and life of true religion consists, and without the performance of which all other duties are unacceptable to God, let us now point out some of the corollaries and consequences which necessarily follow from this fact.

1. The labours which many have taken in religion are lost. Many great services have been performed, many wonderful works wrought by men, which have been utterly rejected by God, and shall receive no recognition in the day of rewards. Why? Because they took no pains to keep their hearts with God in those duties; this is the fatal rock upon which thousands of vain professors have wrecked to their eternal undoing—they were diligent about the externals of religion, but regardless of their hearts. How many hours have professors spent in hearing, reading, conferring and praying, and yet as to the supreme task God has assigned have done nothing. Tell me, vain professor, when did you spend five minutes in a serious effort to keep, purge, improve it? Think you that such an easy religion can save you? If so, we must *inverse* the words of Christ and say, "Wide is the gate and broad is the way that leadeth unto life, and many there be that go in thereat."

2. If the keeping of the heart be the great work of the Christian, then how few *real* Christians are there in the world. If everyone who has learned the dialect of Christianity and can talk like a Christian, if every one who has natural gifts and abilities and who is helped by the common assisting presence of the Spirit and pray and teach like a Christian, if all who associate themselves with the people of God, contribute of their means to His cause, take delight in public ordinances, and pass as Christians were real ones, then the number of the saints would be considerable. But, alas, to what a little flock do they shrink when measured by *this* rule: how few make conscience of keeping their hearts, watching their thoughts, judging their motives. Ah, there is no human applause to induce men to engage in this difficult work, and were hypocrites to do so they would quickly discover what they do not care to know. This heart work is left in the hands of a few hidden ones. Reader, are *you* one of them?

3. Unless real Christians spend more time and pains about their hearts than they have done, they are never likely to grow in grace, be of much use to God, or be possessors of much comfort in this world. You say, "But my heart seems so listless and dead." Do you wonder at it, when you keep it not in daily communion with Him who is the fountain of life? If your body had received no

more concern and attention than your soul, what state would it now be in? Oh, my brother, or sister, has not your zeal run in the wrong channels? God may be enjoyed even in the midst of earthly employments: "Enoch walked with God, and begat sons and daughters" (Gen. 5:19)—he did not retire into a monastery, nor is there any need for you to do so.

4. It is high time the Christian reader set to this heart work in real earnest. Do not you lament, "They made me the keeper of the vineyards; but mine own vineyard have I not kept" (Song of Sol. 1:16)? Then away with fruitless controversies and idle questions; away with empty names and vain shows; away with harsh censuring of others—turn upon yourself. You have been a stranger long enough to this work; you have trifled about the borders of religion too long: the world has deterred you from this vitally necessary work too long. Will you now resolve to look better after your heart? Haste you to your closet.

Advantages of Heart Work

The heart of man is his worst part before it be regenerate, and his best part afterwards; it is the seat of principles and the source of actions. The eye of God is, and the eye of the Christian ought to be, principally fixed upon it. The great difficulty after conversion is to keep the heart with God. Herein lies the very pinch and stress of religion; here is that which makes the way to life a narrow way, and the gate of heaven a straight one. To afford some direction and help in this great work, these articles have been presented. We realize their many defects, yet trust that God will be pleased to use them. No other subject can begin to compare with it in practical importance.

The general neglect of the heart is the root cause of the present sad state of Christendom; the remainder of this article might readily be devoted unto the verifying and amplifying of that statement; instead, we merely point out briefly one or two of the more prominent features. Why is it that so many preachers have withheld from their congregations that which was, so obviously, most needed? Why have they "spoken smooth things" instead of wielding the sword of the Spirit? Because their own hearts were not right with God: *His* holy fear was not upon them. An "honest and good heart" (Luke 8:15) will cause a servant of Christ to preach what he sees to be the most essential and profitable truths of the Word, however displeasing they may be unto many of his people. He will faithfully rebuke, exhort, admonish, correct and instruct, whether his hearers like it or not.

Why have so many church members departed from the faith and given heed to seducing spirits? Why have multitudes been led away by the error of the wicked, turning the grace of God into lasciviousness? Why have so many others been attracted to companies of notional professors, which, despite their proud boasts of being the only people gathered together in (or unto) the name of Christ, are, for the most part, people who have only an acquaintance with the letter of Scripture and are strangers to practical godliness? Ah, the answer is not far to seek: it was because they had no *heart* acquaintance with the things of God. It is those who are sickly and diseased who fall easy victims unto the quacks; so it is those whose hearts are never rooted and grounded in the Truth who are tossed about with every wind and doctrine. The study and guarding of the heart is the best antidote against the infectious errors of the times. And this leads us to point out some of the *advantages* of keeping the heart. For much of what follows we are indebted to the Puritan, John Flavel.

1. The pondering and garrisoning of the heart is a great help to the understanding of the deep things of God. An honest and experienced heart is a wonderful aid to a weak head. Such a heart will serve as a commentary upon a great portion of the Scriptures. When such a one reads the Psalms of David or the Epistles of Paul, he will find there many of his own difficulties stated and solved: he will find them speaking the language of his own heart—recounting *his* experiences, expressing *his* sorrows and joys. By a close and regular study of the heart he will be far better fitted to understand the things of God than graceless rabbis and inexperienced doctors—not only will they be clearer, but far sweeter unto him. A man may discourse orthodoxly and profoundly of the nature and effects of faith, of the preciousness of Christ, and the sweetness of communion with God, who never felt the impressions or efficacy of them upon his own spirit. But how dull and dry will these *notions* be unto those who have *experienced them.*

Ah, my reader, experience is the great schoolmaster. Much in Job and Lamentations will seem dull and uninteresting until you have had deeper exercises of soul. The seventh chapter of Romans is not likely to appeal much unto you until you make more conscience of indwelling sin. Many of the later Psalms will appear too extravagant in their language until you enjoy closer and sweeter fellowship with God. But the more you endeavour to keep your heart, and bring it into subjection unto God, to keep it from the evil solicitations of Satan, the more *suited to your own case* will you find many chapters of the Bible. It is not simply that you have to be in the "right mood" to appreciate, but that you have to pass through certain exercises of heart ere you can discover their appropriateness. Then it is that you will have "felt" and "tasted" for yourself the things of which the inspired writers treat. Then it is that you will have the key which unlocks many a verse that is fast closed unto masters of Hebrew and Greek.

2. Care in keeping the heart supplies one of the best evidences of sincerity. There is no external act which distinguishes the sound from the unsound professor, but before this trial no hypocrite can stand. It is true that when they think death to be very near many will cry out of the wickedness and fear in their hearts, but that signifies nothing more than does the howling of an animal when it is in distress. But if you are tender of your conscience, watchful of your thoughts, and careful each day of the workings and frames of your heart, this strongly argues the sincerity of it; for what but a real hatred of sin, what but a sense of the Divine eye being upon you, could put anyone upon these secret duties which lie out of the observation of all creatures? If, then, it be such a desirable thing to have a fair testimony of your integrity, and to know of a truth that you fear God, then study, watch, keep the heart.

The true comfort of our souls much depends upon this, for he that is negligent in keeping his heart is generally a stranger to spiritual assurance and the sweet comforts flowing from it. God does not usually indulge lazy souls with inward peace, for He will not be the patron of any carelessness. He has united together our diligence and comfort, and they are greatly mistaken who suppose that the beautiful child of assurance can be born without soul pangs. Diligent self-examination is called for: first the looking into the Word, and then the looking into our hearts, to see how far they correspond. It is true that the Holy Spirit indwells the Christian, but He cannot be discerned by His essence; it is His operations that manifest Him, and these are known by the graces he produces in the soul; and those can only be perceived by diligent search and honest scrutiny of the heart. It is in the heart that the Spirit works.

3. Care in keeping the heart makes blessed and fruitful the means of grace and the discharge of our spiritual duties. What precious communion we have with God when He is approached in a right frame of soul: then we may say with David, "My meditation of Him shall be sweet" (Psalm 104:34). But when the heart be indisposed, full of the things of this life, then we miss the comfort and joy which should be ours. The sermons you hear and the articles you read (if by *God's* servants) will appear very different if you bring a *prepared* heart to them! If the heart be right you will not grow drowsy while hearing or reading of the riches of God's grace, the glories of Christ, the beauty of holiness, or the needs-be for a scripturally ordered walk. It was because the heart was neglected that you got so little from attending to the means of grace!

The same holds good of prayer. What a difference there is between a deeply exercised and spiritually burdened heart pouring out itself before God in fervent supplication and the utterance of verbal petitions by rote! It is the difference between reality and formality. He who is diligent in heart work and perceives the state of his own soul is at no loss in knowing *what* to ask God for. So he who makes it a practice of walking with God, communing with God, meditating upon God, spontaneously worships Him in spirit and in truth: like David, he will say, "My heart is inditing a good matter" (Psalms 45:1). The Hebrew there is very suggestive: literally it is "my heart is boiling up a good matter"; it is a figurative expression, taken from a living spring, which is bubbling up fresh water. The formalist has to rack his mind and, as it were, laboriously pump up something to say unto God; but he who makes conscience of heart work finds his soul like a bottle of new wine—ready to burst, giving vent to sorrow or joy as his case may be.

4. Diligence in keeping the heart will make the soul stable in the hour of temptation. The care or neglect of the conscience largely determines our attitude toward and response unto solicitations of evil. The careless heart falls an easy prey to Satan. His main attacks are made upon the heart, for if he gains *that* he gains all, for it commands the whole man! Alas, how easy a conquest is an *unguarded* heart; it is no more difficult for the Devil to capture it than for a burglar to enter a house whose windows and doors are unfastened. It is the watchful heart that both discovers and suppresses the temptation before it comes in its full strength. It is much like a large stone rolling down a hill—it is easy to stop at first, but very difficult after it has gained full momentum. So, if we cherish the first vain imagination as it enters the mind, it will soon grow into a powerful lust which will not take a nay.

Acts are preceded by desires, and desires by thoughts. A sinful object first presents itself to the imagination, and unless *that* be nipped in the bud the affections will be stirred and enlisted. If the heart does not repel the evil imagination, if instead it dwells on it, encourages it, feeds on it, then it will not be long before the consent of the will is obtained. A very large and important part of heart work lies in observing its first motions, and checking sin *there*. The motions of sin are weakest at the first, and a little watchfulness and care then prevents much trouble and mischief later. But if the first movings of sin in the imagination be not observed and resisted, then the careless heart is quickly brought under the full power of temptation, and Satan is victorious.

5. The diligent keeping of the heart is a great aid to the improving of our graces. Grace never thrives in a careless soul, for the roots and habits of grace are planted in the heart, and the deeper they are radicated there the more thriving and flourishing grace is. In Ephesians 3:17, we read of being "rooted and grounded in love": love in the heart is the spring of every gracious word of the mouth and of every holy act of the hand. But is not *Christ* the "root" of the Christian's graces? Yes, the originating root, but grace is the derivative root, planted and nourished by Him, and according as *this* thrives under Divine influences, so the fruits of grace are more healthy and vigorous. But in a heart which is not kept diligently those fructifying influences are choked. Just as in an uncared-for garden the weeds crowd out the flowers, so vain thoughts that are not dis-allowed, and lusts which are not mortified, devour the strength of the heart. "My soul shall be satisfied as with marrow and with fatness; and my mouth shall praise Thee with joyful lips: *when* I remember Thee upon my bed, and meditate on Thee in the night watches" (Psalm 55:5, 6).

6. The diligent care of the heart makes Christian fellowship profitable and precious. Why is it that when Christians meet together there are often sad jarrings and contentions? It is because of unmortified passions. Why is their conversation so frothy and worthless? It is because of the vanity and earthiness of their hearts. It is not difficult to discern by the actions and converse of Christians what frames their spirits are under. Take one whose mind is truly stayed upon God; how serious, heavenly and edifying is his conversation: "The mouth of the righteous speaketh wisdom, and his tongue talketh of judgment: the law of his God *is in his heart*" (Psalm 37:30, 31). If each of us was humbled every day before God and under the evils of his own heart, we should be more pitiful and tender toward others (Gal. 6:1).

7. A heart well kept fits us for any condition God may cast us into, or any service He has to use us in. He who has learnt to keep his heart lowly is fit for prosperity; and he who knows how to apply Scripture promises and supports is fit to pass through any adversity. So he who can deny the pride and selfishness of his heart is fit to be employed in any service for God. Such a man was Paul; he not only ministered to others, but looked well to his own vineyard (see 1 Cor. 9:27). And what an eminent instrument he was for God: he knew how to abound and how to suffer loss. Let the people defy him, it moved him not, except to indignation; let them stone him, he could bear it.

8. By keeping our hearts diligently we should the soonest remove the scandals and stumbling-blocks out of the way of the world. How the worthy name of our Lord is blasphemed because of the wicked conduct of many who bear His name. What prejudice has been created against the Gospel by the inconsistent lives of those who preach it. But if we keep *our* hearts, we shall not add to the scandals caused by the ways of loose professors. Nay, those with whom we come in contact will see that we "have been with Jesus." When the majestic beams of holiness shine from a heavenly walk, the world will be awed and respect will

again be commanded by the followers of the Lamb.

Though the keeping of the heart entails such hard labour, do not such blessed gains supply a sufficient incentive to engage diligently in the same? Look over the eight special benefits we have named, and weigh them in a just balance; they are not trivial things. Then guard well your heart, and watch closely *its love for God.* Jacob served seven years for Rebekah, and they seemed unto him but a few days, for the love that he had unto her. The labour of *love* is always delightful. If God has your heart, the feet will run swiftly in the way of His commandments: duty will be a delight. Then let us earnestly pray, "So teach us to number our days, that we may *apply our hearts* unto wisdom" (Psalm 90:12)—as we "apply" our hands unto manual tasks.

Let me now close the whole of these articles with a word or two of consolation to all serious Christians who have sought to give themselves faithfully and closely to this heart work, but who are groaning in secret over their apparent lack of success therein, and who are fearful that their experience falls short of a saving one. First, this argues that your heart *is* honest and upright. If you are mourning over heart conditions and sins, that is something no hypocrite does. Many a one is now in hell who had a better head than mine; many a one now in heaven complained as of bad a heart as thine.

Second, God would never leave you under so many heart burdens and troubles if He intended not your benefit thereby. You say, Lord, why do I go mourning, all the day having sorrow of heart? For long have I been exercised over its hardness, and not yet it is broken. Many years have I been struggling against vain thoughts, and still I am plagued by them. When shall I get a better heart? Ah, God would thereby show you what your heart by nature is, and have you take notice of how much you are beholden to free grace! So, too, He would keep you humble, and not let you fall in love with yourself!

Third, God will shortly put a blessed end to these cares, watchings and heartaches. The time is coming when your heart shall be as you would have it, when you will be delivered from all fears and sorrows, and never again cry, "O my hard, vain, earthly, filthy heart." Then shall all darkness be purged from your understanding, all vanity from your affections, all guilt from your conscience, all perversity from your will. Then shall you be everlastingly, delightfully, ravishingly entertained and exercised upon the supreme goodness and infinite excellency of God. Soon shall break that morning without clouds, when all the shadows shall flee away; and then we "shall be *like Him,* for we shall see Him as He is" (1 John 3:2). Hallelujah!

THE CHRISTIAN'S ARMOUR
Ephesians 6:10-18

In the passage which is to be before us the apostle gathers up the whole previous subject of the epistle into an urgent reminder of the solemn conditions under which the Christian's life is lived. By a graphic figure he shows that the Christian's life is lived on the battlefield, for we are not only pilgrims but soldiers; we are not only in a foreign country, but in the enemy's land. Though the redemption which Christ has purchased for His people be free and full, yet, between the beginning of its application to us and the final consummation of it, there is a terrible and protracted conflict through which we have to pass. This is not merely a figure of speech, but a grim reality. Though salvation is free, yet it is not obtained without great effort. The fight to which God's children are called in this life is one in which Christians themselves receive many sore wounds, and thousands of professors are slain. Now, as we shall see in the verses which follow, the apostle warns us that the conflict has to do with more than human foes; the enemies we have to meet are superhuman ones, and therefore in order to fight successfully against them we need supernatural strength.

We must remember that the Christian belongs to the spiritual realm as well as the natural, and so he has spiritual as well as natural foes; hence he needs spiritual strength as well as physical. Therefore the apostle begins here by saying, "Finally, my brethren, be strong in the Lord, and in the power of His might" (verse 10). The word "finally" denotes that the apostle had reached his closing exhortation, and the words "be strong" link up with what immediately precedes as well as with what now follows. Some of you will remember that the whole of the fifth chapter and the opening verses of the sixth chapter are filled with exhortations, and in order for the Christian to obey them he needs to be "strong in the Lord, and in the power of His might."

"Finally, my brethren [after all the Christian duties I have set before you in the previous verses], "be strong in the Lord, and in the power of His might." The words "be strong" mean to muster strength for the conflict, and be strong "in the Lord" signifies that we must seek strength from the only source from which we can obtain it. Note carefully, it is not "be strong *from* the Lord," nor is it "be strengthened *by* the Lord." No, it is "be strong *in* the Lord." Perhaps you will get the thought if I use this analogy: just as a thumb that is amputated is useless, and just as a branch cut off from the vine withers, so a Christian whose fellowship with the Lord has been broken is in a strengthless, fruitless, useless state. Thus, "be strong in the Lord" means, first of all, see to it that you maintain a live practical relationship to and remain in constant communion with the Lord. It is deeply important that we should, ere we proceed farther, grasp the exhortation found in verse 10; otherwise there will be no strength for the conflict.

"Be strong in the Lord, *and* in the power of His might." At first sight there seems to be a needless repetition there; but it is not so. A soldier not only needs strength of body; he also needs *courage*, and that is what is in view in verse 10—the last clause brings in the thought of boldness. "Be strong": in faith, in hope, in wisdom, in patience, in fortitude, in every Christian grace. To be strong in grace is to be weak in sin. It is vitally essential to remember that we need to have our strength and courage renewed daily. Be strong in the Lord: seek His strength at the beginning of each day. God does not impart strength to us

181

182

wholesale: He will not give us strength on Monday morning to last through the week. No, there has to be the renewing of our strength and that strength has to be drawn from the Lord by the actings of faith, appropriating from *His* "fulness."

"Put on the whole armour of God, that ye may be able to stand against the wiles of the devil" (verse 11). Our first need is to stir up ourselves to *resist* temptation by a believing reliance upon God's all-sufficient grace, that is obtaining from Him the strength which will enable us to go forth and fight against the foe. Our second greatest need is to be *well armed* for the conflict into which we must daily enter. *This* is the relation between verses 10 and 11: "Be strong in the Lord" and "Put on the whole armour of God": first, stir up yourselves to resist temptation, seeking strength at the beginning of the day for the conflict; then see to it that you take unto yourselves, put on, the whole armour of God.

The Christian is engaged *in a warfare.* There is a fight before him, hence armour is urgently needed. It is impossible for us to stand against the wiles of the Devil unless we avail ourselves of the provision which God has made for enabling us to stand. Observe that it is called the "armour *of God*": just as the strength we need comes not from ourselves, but must be supplied by the Lord, so our means of defence lie not in our own powers and faculties, but only as they are quickened by God. It is called the "armour of God" because *He* both provides and bestows it, for we have none of our own; and yet, while this armour is of God's providing and bestowing, *we* have to put it on! God does not fit it on us; He places it before us; and it is *our* responsibility, duty, task, to *put on* the whole armour of God.

Now it is very important that we should recognize that this term "armour" is a figurative one, a metaphor, and refers not to something which is material or carnal. It is a figurative expression denoting the Christian's *graces,* and when we are told to "put on" the armour it simply means we are to call into exercise and action our graces. Those who wish to approve themselves of being in possession of grace must see to it that they have all the graces of a saint. "Put on the whole armour of God, that [in order that] ye may be able to stand against the wiles of the devil." There is no standing against him if we are not armoured. On the other hand, there is no failing and falling before him if our graces are healthy and active.

"For we wrestle not against flesh and blood, but against principalities, against powers, against the rulers of the darkness of this world, against spiritual wickedness in high places (verse 12). The opening "for" has the force of "because": the apostle is advancing a reason, which virtually amounts to an argument, so as to enforce the exhortation just given. Because we wrestle not against flesh and blood, but against principalities, not against puny human enemies no stronger than ourselves, but against the powers and rulers of the darkness of this world, the panoply of God is essential. That is brought in to emphasize the terribleness of the conflict before us. It is no imaginary one, and no ordinary foes we have to meet; but spiritual, superhuman, invisible ones. Those enemies seek to destroy faith and produce doubt. They seek to destroy hope and produce despair. They seek to destroy humility and produce pride. They seek to destroy peace and produce bitterness and malice. They seek to prevent our enjoyment of heavenly things by getting us unduly occupied with earthly things. Their attack is not upon the body, but upon the soul.

"Wherefore take unto you the whole armour of God, that ye may be able to withstand in the evil day, and having done all, to stand" (verse 13). The opening "wherefore" means that, in view of the fact that we wrestle against these powerful, superhuman, invisible foes, who hate us with a deadly hatred and are seeking to destroy us, therefore appropriate and use the provision which God has made, so that we may stand and withstand. The first clause of verse 13 explains the opening words of verse 11. Verse 11 says "put on," make use of all proper weapons for repulsing the attacks, and verse 13 says "take unto you the whole armour of God"; we "put on" by taking it "unto us," that is, by appropriation, by making it our own. "That ye may be able to withstand": to *withstand* is the opposite of yielding, of being tripped up, thrown down, by the Devil's temptations; it means that we stand our ground, resist the Devil. "That ye may be able to withstand in the evil day, and having done all, to stand": the *"stand"* is the opposite of a slothful sleep, or a cowardly flight.

I want you to notice that we are not told to *advance.* We are only ordered to *"stand."* God has not called His people to an aggressive war upon Satan, to invade his territory, and seek to wrest from him what is his; He has told us to occupy the ground which He has allotted us. I want you to see what would have been implied had this verse said, "Take unto you the whole armour of God, and advance upon the devil, storm his strongholds, liberate his prisoners." But not so; the Lord has given no charge or commission to the rank and file of His people to engage in what is now called "personal work," "soulwinning," "rescuing the perishing." All such feverish activities of the flesh as we now behold in the religious world find no place in this Divine exhortation. This is the third time in these verses that the Spirit of God has repeated that word "stand"—not advance, not rush hither and thither, like a crazy person. "Stand therefore" is *all* God has told us to do in our conflict with the Devil.

"Stand, therefore, having your loins girt about with truth." Now that brings before us the first of the seven pieces of the Christian's armour mentioned in this passage. First, let me warn you against the carnalization of this word, thinking of something that is external, visible, or tangible. The figure of the "girdle" is taken from a well-known custom in oriental countries, where the people all wear long, flowing outer garments reaching to the feet, which would impede the actions when walking, working or fighting. The first thing a person does there when about to be active is to gird up around his waist that outer garment which trails to the ground. When the garment is not girded and hangs down, it indicates that the person is at rest. To "gird up" is therefore the opposite of sloth and ease. Be girdled about with a girdle of truth: I believe there is a double reference or meaning here in the word "truth." But first of all I want to take up *what* it is that we need to "gird."

The breastplate is for the heart, the helmet for the head; what, then, is the "girdle" for? In that form from which the figure is borrowed, the reference is to *the waist* or loins. But what does that metaphor denote? Plainly the centre or mainspring of all our activities. And what is that? Obviously *the mind* is the mainspring of action: first the thought, and then the carrying out of it. 1 Peter 1:13, helps us here: "gird up the loins *of your mind.*" "Let your loins be girt about with truth": it is not so much our embracing the truth as the truth embracing us. Thus, the spiritual reference is to *the holiness in and regulation of the thoughts of the mind.* The mind "girded up" means a mind which is disciplined; the opposite of one where the thoughts are allowed to run loose and wild. Again, the "loins" are the place of strength, so is the mind. If we allow our thoughts and imaginations to run wild, we will have no communion with God, and no power against Satan.

"Having your loins girt about with truth." I think the word "truth" has reference, in the first place, to the Word of God: "Thy word is *truth*" (John 17:17). *That* is what must regulate the mind, control the thoughts, subdue the imaginations: there must be a knowledge of, faith in, love for, subjection to, God's Word. "Stand, therefore, having your loins [your mind] girt about with *truth.*" Now that suggests to us the characteristic quality of the adversary against whom we are called upon to arm. Satan is a liar, and we can only meet him with the Truth. Satan prevails over ignorance by means of guile or deceit; but he has no power over those whose minds are regulated by the Truth of God.

I think the word "truth" here has a second meaning. Take for example Psalm 51:6, God "desireth truth in the inward parts": "truth" there signifies reality, sincerity. Truth is the opposite of hypocrisy, pretence, unreality. That is why the girdle of truth comes first, because *it* being lacking, everything else is vain and useless. The strength of every grace lies in *the sincerity* of it. In 1 Timothy 1:5, we read "faith unfeigned," which means true, genuine, real faith; in contrast with a faith which is only theoretical, notional, lifeless, inoperative—a faith which utterly withers before the fires of testing.

The girdle of truth (corresponding to the military belt of the warrior) signifies, then, the mind being regulated by real sincerity; and this alone will protect us against Satan's temptations unto slackness and guile and hypocrisy. Only as this is "put on" by us shall we be able to "*stand* against the wiles of the devil": to "stand" is to "resist" that he does not throw us down.

The second part or piece of the Christian's armour is mentioned in verse 14: "and having on the breastplate of righteousness." First of all, notice the connecting "and," which intimates that there is a very close relation between the mind being girded with truth and the heart protected with the breastplate of righteousness. All of these seven pieces of armour are *not* so connected, but the "and" here between the first two denotes that they are inseparably united. Now, obviously, the breastplate of righteousness is that protection which we need for *the heart.* This verse is closely parallel to Proverbs 4:23, "Keep thine heart with all diligence," understanding by the "heart" the affections and conscience.

As there was a double reference in the word "truth," first to the Word of God and second to the sincerity of spirit, so I believe there is a double reference here in "the breastplate of *righteousness.*" I think it refers both to that righteousness which Christ wrought out for us and that righteousness which the Spirit works in us—both the righteousness which is imputed and the righteousness which is imparted—which is what we need if we are to withstand the attacks of Satan. We might compare 1 Thessalonians 5:8: "Let us, who are of the day, be sober, putting on the breastplate of faith and love." I have been quite impressed of late in noting how frequently that word "sober" occurs in the Epistles, either in its substantive or verbal form. Soberness is that which should characterize and identify the people of God. It is the opposite of that superficial flightiness which is one of the outstanding marks of worldlings today. It is the opposite of levity, and also of that feverish restlessness of the flesh by which so many are intoxicated religiously and every other way.

This second piece of armour, as I have said, is inseparably connected with the girdle of truth, for sincerity of mind and holiness of heart must go together. To put on the breastplate of righteousness means to maintain the power of holiness over our affections and conscience. A verse that helps us to understand this is Acts 24:16, "Herein do I exercise myself, to have always a conscience void of offence toward God and men." There you have an illustration of a man taking unto himself, putting on, the "breastplate of righteousness."

We pass on to the third piece of armour. "And your feet shod with the preparation of the gospel of peace" (verse 15). This is perhaps the most difficult of the seven pieces of armour to understand and define; and yet, if we hold fast the first thought, that the Holy Spirit is using a figure of speech here, that the reference is to that which is internal rather than external, spiritual rather than material, and also that He is following a logical order, there should not be much difficulty in ascertaining what is meant by the sandals of peace. Just as the girdle of truth has to do with the *mind*, the breastplate of righteousness with the *heart*, so the shoes for the feet area figure of that which concerns the *will*. At first sight that may sound far-fetched, and yet if we will think for a moment it should be obvious that what the feet are to the body the will is to the soul. The feet carry the body from place to place, and the will is that which *directs* the activities of the soul; what the will decides, that is what we *do.*

Now the will is to be regulated by the peace of the Gospel. What is meant by that? This: in becoming reconciled to God and in having good will to our fellows the Gospel is the means or instrument that God uses. We are told in Psalm 110:3, "Thy people shall be willing in the day of Thy power": that means far more than that they shall be ready to hearken to and believe the glad tidings of the Gospel. There is brought over into the Gospel substantially everything which was contained in both the moral and ceremonial Law. The Gospel is not only a message of good news, but a Divine commandment and rule of conduct: "For the time is come that judgment must [not "shall"—now, not in the future] begin at the house of God: and if it first begin at us, what shall the end of them be that *obey not* the gospel of God?" (1 Peter 4:17).

The Gospel requires us to deny ourselves, take up the cross daily, and follow Christ in the path of unreserved obedience to God. "Your feet shod with the preparation of the gospel of peace" signifies that you must with alacrity and readiness respond to God's revealed will. The *peace* of "the gospel" comes from walking in subjection to its terms and by fulfilling the duties which it prescribes. Just so far as we are obedient to it we experimentally enjoy its peace. Thus, this third piece of armour is for fortifying the will against Satan's temptations unto self-will and disobedience, and this by subjection to the Gospel. Just as the feet are the members which convey the body from place to place, so the will directs the soul; and just as the feet must be adequately shod if we are to walk properly and comfortably, so the will must be brought into subjection unto the revealed will of God if we are to enjoy His peace. Let there be that complete surrender daily, the dedicating of ourselves to God, and then we will be impervious unto

Satan's attacks and temptations to disobedience.

You will take notice when we come to the fourth piece of armour that the "and" is lacking. The first three were joined together, for that which is denoted by those figurative terms is inseparably linked together—the mind, the heart, the will: there you have the complete inner man. "Above all, taking the shield of faith, wherewith ye shall be able to quench all the fiery darts of the wicked" (verse 16). I think the words "above all" have a double force. First, literally, understanding them as a preposition of place, meaning over all, shielding as a canopy, protecting the mind, the heart and the will. There must be faith in exercise if those three parts of our inner being are to be guarded. Second, "above all" may be taken adverbially, signifying chiefly, pre-eminently, supremely. It is *an essential* thing that you should take the shield of faith, for Hebrews 11:6, tells us, "But without faith it is impossible to please Him." Yes, even if there were sincerity, love, and a pliable will, yet without faith we could not please Him. Therefore, "above all" take unto you the shield of faith.

Faith is all in all in resisting temptation. We must be fully persuaded of the Divine inspiration of the Scriptures if we are to be awed by their precepts and cheered by their encouragements; we will never heed properly the Divine warnings or consolations unless we have explicit confidence in their Divine authorship. The whole victory is here ascribed to *faith "above all"*; it is not by the breastplate, helmet or sword, but by the shield of faith that we are enabled to quench all the fiery darts of the wicked. It seems to be a general principle in the Spirit's arrangement of things in Scripture to put the most vital one in the centre; we have seven pieces of armour, and the shield of faith is the fourth. So in Hebrews 6:4-6, we have five things mentioned, and in the middle is "made partakers of the Holy Spirit."

Faith is the life of all the graces. If faith be not in exercise, love, hope, patience cannot be. Here we find faith intended for the defence of the whole man. The shield of the soldier is something he grips, and raises or lowers as it is needed. It is for the protection of his entire person. Now the figure which the Holy Spirit uses here in connection with Satan's attacks is taken from one of the devices of the ancients in their warfare, namely the use of darts which had been dipped in tar and set on fire, in order to blind their foes: *that* is what lies behind the metaphor of "quench all the fiery darts of the wicked"; it has in view Satan's efforts to prevent our looking upward! When these darts were in the air the soldiers had to bow their heads to avoid them, holding their shields above. And Satan is constantly seeking to prevent our looking upward.

The attacks of the Devil are likened to "fiery darts," first, because of the *wrath* with which he shoots them. There is intense hatred in Satan against the child of God. Again, the very essence of his temptations is to *inflame* the passions and distress the conscience. He aims to kindle covetousness, to excite worldly ambition, to ignite our lusts. In James 3:6, we read, "the tongue is set on fire of hell"—that means the Devil's "fiery darts" have affected it. Thirdly, his temptations are likened unto "fiery darts" because of *the end* to which they lead if not quenched; should Satan's temptations be followed out to the end they would land us in the lake of fire. The figure of "darts" denotes that his temptations are swift, noiseless, dangerous.

Now taking the shield of faith means appropriating the Word and acting on it.

The shield is to protect *the whole* person, wherever the attack be made, whether on spirit, or soul, or body; and there is that in the Word which is exactly suited unto each, but *faith* must lay hold of and employ it. Now in order to use the shield of faith effectually the Word of Christ needs to dwell in us "richly" (Col. 3:16). We must have right to hand a word which is pertinent for the particular temptation presented. For example, if tempted unto covetousness, we must use "Lay not up for yourselves treasure on earth"; when solicited by evil companions, "If sinners entice thee, consent thou not"; if tempted to harshness, "Be kindly affectioned one to another." It is because the *details* of Scripture have so little place in our meditations that Satan trips us so frequently.

Like most of the other terms used, "faith" here also has a double signification. The faith which is to be our "shield" is both an objective and a subjective one. It has reference, first, to the Word of God without, the authority of which is ever binding upon us. It points, secondly, to our confidence in that Word, the heart going out in trustful expectation to the Author of it, and counting upon its efficacy to repulse the Devil.

"And take the helmet of salvation" (verse 17). This is the fifth piece of the Christian's armour. First of all we may note the link between the fourth and fifth pieces as denoted by the word "and," for this helps us to define *what* the "helmet of salvation" is; it is *linked with faith*! Hebrews 11:1, tells us, "faith is the substance of things hoped for," and if we compare 1 Thessalonians 5:8, we get a confirmation of that thought: "But let us, who are of the day, be sober, putting on the breastplate of faith and love; and for an helmet the *hope* of salvation." Here in Thessalonians, then, we have "hope" directly connected with "the helmet." Incidentally, this verse is one of many in the New Testament which puts salvation in the future rather than in the past! Hope always looks forward, having to do with things to come; as Romans 8:25, tells us, "If we hope for that we see not, then do we with patience wait for it." Now faith and hope are inseparable: they are one in birth, and one in growth; and, we may add, one in decay. If faith languish, hope is listless.

By the helmet of salvation, then, I understand the heart's expectation of the good things promised, a well-grounded assurance that God *will* make good to His people those things which His Word presents for future accomplishment. We might link up with this 1 John 3:3—scriptural hope *purifies*. It delivers from discontent and despair, it comforts the heart in the interval of waiting. Satan is unable to get a Christian to commit many of the grosser sins which are common in the world, so he attacks along other lines. Often he seeks to cast a cloud of gloom over the soul, or produce anxiety about the future. Despondency is one of his favourite weapons, for he knows well that "the joy of the Lord" is our "strength" (Neh. 8:10), hence his frequent efforts to dampen our spirits. To repulse these, we are to "take the helmet of salvation": that is, we are to exercise *hope*—anticipate the blissful future, look forward unto the eternal rest awaiting us; look away from earth to heaven!

"And the sword of the Spirit, which is the word of God" (verse 17). God has provided His people with an offensive weapon as well as defensive ones. At first sight that may seem to clash with what we said about Christians *not* being called upon to be aggressive against Satan, seeking to invade his territory and wrest it from him. But this verse does not clash to the slightest degree. 2 Corinthians 7:1, gives us the thought: "Having therefore these promises, dearly beloved, let us cleanse ourselves from all filthiness of the flesh and spirit": *that* is the active, aggressive side of the Christian's warfare. We are not only to resist our lusts but to subdue and overcome them.

It is significant to note *how late* the "sword of the Spirit" is mentioned in this list. Some have thought that it should have come first, but it is not mentioned until the sixth. Why? I believe there is a twofold reason. First, because all the other graces that have been mentioned are necessary to make a right use of the Word. If there is not a sincere mind and a holy heart we shall only handle the Word dishonestly. If there is not practical righteousness, then we shall only be handling the Word theoretically. If there is not faith and hope we shall only misuse it. All the Christian graces that are figuratively contemplated under the other pieces of armour must be in exercise *before* we can profitably handle the Word of God. Second, it teaches us that even when the Christian has attained unto the highest point possible in this life he still needs *the Word*. Even when he has upon him the girdle of truth, the breastplate of righteousness, his feet shod with the shoes of the preparation of the Gospel of peace, and has taken unto himself the shield of faith and the helmet of salvation, he still needs the Word!

The last piece of armour is given in verse 18: "Praying always with all prayer and supplication in the Spirit, and watching thereunto with all perseverance and supplication for all saints." *Prayer* is that which alone gives us the necessary strength *to use* the other pieces of armour! After the Christian has taken unto himself those six pieces, before he is thoroughly furnished to go forth unto the battle and fitted for victory, he needs the help of his General. For this, the apostle bids us pray "always" with all supplication in the Spirit. We are to fight upon our knees! Only prayer can keep alive the different spiritual graces which are figured by the various pieces of armour. "Praying always": in *every* season—in times of joy as well as sorrow, in days of adversity as well as prosperity. Not only so, but *"watching thereunto* with all perseverance": that is one of the essential elements in prevailing prayer—persistence. Watch yourself that you do not let up, become slack or discouraged. Keep on! The eighteenth verse is as though the apostle said, "Forget not to seek unto *the God of* this 'armour' and make humble supplication for His assistance; for only He who has given us these arms can enable us to make a successful use of them." Some have called it the "all verse." "Praying always with all prayer . . . with all perseverance, and supplication *for all saints"*—think not only of yourself, but also of your fellow soldiers who are engaged in the same conflict!

SAVING FAITH

"He that believeth and is baptized shall be saved; but he that believeth not shall be damned" (Mark 16:16). These are the words of Christ, the risen Christ, and are the last that He uttered ere He left this earth. None more important were ever spoken to the sons of men. They call for our most diligent attention. They are of the greatest possible consequence, for in them are set forth the terms of eternal happiness or misery: life and death, and the conditions of both. Faith is the principal saving grace, and unbelief the chief damning sin. The law which threatens death for every sin has already passed sentence of condemnation upon all, because all have sinned. This sentence is so peremptory that it admits of but one exception—all shall be executed if they believe not.

The condition of life as made known by Christ in Mark 16:16, is double: the principal one, faith; the accessory one, baptism; we term it accessory because it is not absolutely necessary to life, as faith is. Proof of this is found in the fact of the omission in the second half of the verse: it is *not* "he that is not baptized shall be damned," but "he that believeth not." Faith is so indispensable that, though one be baptized, yet believeth not, he shall be damned. As we have said above, the sinner is already condemned; the sword of Divine justice is drawn even now, and waits only to strike the fatal blow. Nothing can divert it but saving faith in Christ. My reader, continuance in unbelief makes hell as certain as though you were already in it. While you remain in unbelief, you have no hope and are "without God in the world" (Eph. 2:12).

Now if believing be so necessary, and unbelief so dangerous and fatal, it deeply concerns us to *know* what it is *to* believe. It behoves each of us to make the most diligent and thorough inquiry as to the nature of saving faith. The more so because all faith in Christ does not save; yea, all faith in Christ does not save. Multitudes are deceived upon this vital matter. Thousands of those who sincerely believe that they have received Christ as their personal Saviour, and are resting on His finished work, are building upon a foundation of sand. Vast numbers who have not a doubt that God *has* accepted them in the Beloved, and that they are eternally secure in Christ, will only be awakened from their pleasant dreamings when the cold hand of death lays hold of them; and then it will be too late. Unspeakably solemn is this, Reader, will *that* be your fate? Others just as sure that they were saved as you are now in hell.

1. *Its Counterfeits*

There are those who have a faith which is so like to that which is saving that they themselves may take it to be the very same, and others too may deem it sufficient, yea, even others who have the spirit of discernment. Simon Magus is a case in point. Of him it is written, "Then Simon himself *believed* also: and when he was baptized, he continued with Philip" (Acts 8:13). Such a faith had he, and so expressed it, that Philip took him to be a Christian, and admitted him to those privileges which are peculiar to them. Yet, a little later, the apostle Peter said to him, "Thou hast neither part nor lot in this matter: for thy heart is not right in the sight of God . . . I perceive that thou art in the gall of bitterness, and in the bond of iniquity" (Acts 8:21, 23).

A man may believe *all* the truth contained in Scripture so far as he is acquainted with it, and he may be familiar with far more than are many genuine Christians. He may have studied the Bible for a longer time, and so his faith may grasp much which they have not yet reached. As his knowledge may be more extensive, so his faith may be more comprehensive. In this kind of faith he may go as far as the apostle Paul did when he said, "This I confess unto thee, that after the way which they call heresy, so worship I the God of my fathers, believing *all* things which are written in the law and in the prophets" (Acts 24:14). But this is no proof that his faith is saving. An example to the contrary is seen in Agrippa: "King Agrippa, believest thou the prophets? I know that thou *believest"* (Acts 26:27).

Call the above a mere historical faith if you will, yet Scripture also teaches that people may possess a faith which is more than the product of mere nature, which is of the Holy Spirit, and yet which is a *non-saving* one. This faith which we now allude to has two ingredients which neither education nor self-effort can produce: spiritual light and a Divine power moving the mind to assent. Now a man may have both illumination and inclination from heaven, and yet not be regenerated. We have a solemn proof of this in Hebrews 6:4. There we read of a company of apostates, concerning whom it is said, "It is impossible ... to renew them again unto repentance." Yet of *these* we are told that they were "enlightened," which means that they not only perceived it, but were inclined toward and embraced it; and both because they were "partakers of the Holy Spirit."

People may have Divine faith, not only in its originating power, but also in its foundation. The ground of their faith may be the Divine testimony, upon which they rest with unshaken confidence. They may give credit to what they believe not only because it appears reasonable or even certain, but because they are fully persuaded it is the Word of Him who cannot lie. To believe the Scriptures on the ground of their being *God's* Word is a Divine faith. Such a faith had the nation of Israel after their wondrous exodus from Egypt and deliverance from the Red Sea. Of them it is recorded, "The people feared the Lord, and *believed* the Lord, and His servant Moses" (Exodus 14:31), yet of the great majority of them it is said that their carcasses fell in the wilderness, and He swore that they should *not* enter into His rest (Heb. 3:17, 18).

It is indeed searching and solemn to make a close study of Scripture upon this point and discover how much is said of unsaved people in a way of having faith in the Lord. In Jeremiah 13:11, we find God saying, "For as the girdle cleaveth to the loins of a man, so have I caused to *cleave* unto *Me* the whole house of Israel and the whole house of Judah, saith the Lord," and to "cleave" unto God is the same as to "trust" Him: see 2 Kings 18:5,6. Yet of that very same generation God said, "This evil people, which refuse to hear My words, which walk in the imagination of their heart, and walk after other gods, to serve them, and to worship them, shall even be as this girdle, which is good for nothing" (Jer. 13:10).

The term "stay" is another word denoting firm trust. "And it shall come to pass in that day, that the remnant of Israel, and such as are escaped of the house of Jacob, shall no more again stay upon him that smote them, but shall *stay* upon the Lord" (Isaiah 10:20); "Thou wilt keep him in perfect peace, whose mind is *stayed* upon Thee" (Isaiah 26:3). And yet we find a class of whom it is recorded, "They call themselves of the holy city, and *stay themselves upon* the God of Israel" (Isaiah 48:2). Who would doubt that *this* was a saving faith? Ah, let us not be too hasty in jumping to conclusions: of this same people God said, "Thou art obstinate, and thy neck is an iron sinew, and thy brow brass" (Isaiah 48:4).

Again, the term *"lean"* is used to denote not only trust, but dependence on the Lord. Of the spouse it is said, "Who is this that cometh up from the wilderness, *leaning upon* her beloved?" (Song of Sol. 8:5). Can it be possible that *such* an expression as this is applied to those who are *unsaved?* Yes, it is, and by none other than God Himself: "Hear this, I pray you, ye heads of the house of Jacob, and princes of the house of Israel, that *abhor* judgment, and *pervert all* equity . . . The heads thereof judge for reward, and the priests thereof teach for hire, and the prophets thereof divine for money: yet will they *lean upon the Lord,* and say, Is not the Lord among us? none evil can come upon us" (Micah 3:9, 11). So thousands of carnal and wordly people are leaning upon Christ to uphold them, so that they cannot fall into hell, and are confident that no such "evil" can befall *them.* Yet is their confidence a horrible presumption.

To *rest upon* a Divine promise with implicit confidence, and that in the face of great discouragement and danger, is surely something which we would not expect to find predicated of a people who were unsaved. Ah, truth *is* stranger than fiction. This very thing is depicted in God's unerring Word. When Sennacherib and his great army beseiged the cities of Judah, Hezekiah said, "Be strong and courageous, be not afraid nor dismayed for the king of Assyria, nor for all the multitude that is with him: for there be more with us than with him: with him is an arm of flesh; but with us is the Lord our God" (2 Chron. 32:7, 8); and we are told that "the people *rested themselves upon* the words of Hezekiah." Hezekiah had spoken the words of God, and for the people to rest upon them was to rest on God Himself. Yet less than fifteen years after this same people did "worse than the heathen" (2 Chron. 33:9). Thus, resting upon a promise of God is not, of itself, any proof of regeneration.

To *rely upon* God on the ground of His "covenant" was far more than resting upon a Divine promise; yet unregenerate men may do even this. A case in point is found in Abijah, king of Judah. It is indeed striking to read and weigh what he said in 2 Chronicles 13 when Jeroboam and his hosts came against him. First, he reminded all Israel that the Lord God had given the kingdom to David and his sons for ever "by *a covenant* of salt" (verse 5). Next, he denounced the sins of his adversary (verses 6-9). Then he affirmed the Lord to be "our God" and that He was with him and his people (verses 10-12). But Jeroboam heeded not, but forced the battle upon them. "Abijah and his people slew them with a great slaughter" (verse 17), "because they *relied upon* the Lord God of their fathers" (verse 18). Yet of this same Abijah it is said, "he walked in all the sins of his father," etc. (1 Kings 15:3). Unregenerate men may rely upon Christ, rest on His promise, and plead His covenant.

"The people of Nineveh [who were heathen] *believed* God" (Jonah 3:5). This is striking, for the God of heaven was a stranger to them, and His prophet a man whom they knew not—why then should they trust his message? Moreover, it was not a promise, but a threatening, which they believed. How much easier, then, is it for a people now living under the Gospel to apply to themselves a promise, than the heathen a terrible threat! "In applying a threatening we are like to meet with more opposition, both from within and from without. From within, for a threatening is like a bitter pill, the bitterness of death is in it; no wonder if that hardly goes down. From without, too, for Satan will be ready to raise opposition: he is afraid to see men startled, lest the sense of their misery denounced in the threatening should rouse them up to seek how they may make an escape. He is more sure of them while they are secure, and will labour to keep them off the threatening, lest it should awaken them from dreams of peace and happiness, while they are sleeping in his very jaws.

"But now, in applying a promise, an unregenerate man ordinarily meets no opposition. Not from within, for the promise is all sweetness; the promise of pardon and life is the very marrow, the quintessence, of the Gospel. No wonder if they be ready to swallow it down greedily. And Satan will be so far from opposing, that he will rather encourage and assist one who has no interest in the promise *to* apply it; for this he knows will be the way to fix and settle them in their natural condition. A promise misapplied will be *a seal upon the sepulchre*, making them sure in the grave of sin, wherein they lay dead and rotting. Therefore if unregenerate men may apply a threatening, which is in these respects more difficult, as appears may be the case of the Ninevites, why may they not be apt to apply [appropriate] a Gospel promise when they are not like to meet with such difficulty and opposition?" (David Clarkson, 1680, for some time co-pastor with J. Owen; to whom we are indebted for much of the above).

Another most solemn example of those having faith, but not a saving one, is seen in the stony-ground hearers, of whom Christ said, "which for a while *believed*" (Luke 8:14). Concerning this class the Lord declared that they hear the Word and with joy receive it (Matt. 13:20). How many such have we met and known: happy souls with radiant faces, exuberant spirits, full of zeal that others too may enter into the bliss which they have found. How difficult it is to distinguish such from genuine Christians—the good-ground hearts. The difference is not apparent; no, it lies *beneath* the surface—they have no *root* in themselves (Matt. 13:21): deep digging has to be done to discover this fact! Have you searched yourself narrowly, my reader, to ascertain whether or not "the root of the matter" (Job 19:28) be in you?

But let us refer now to another case which seems still more incredible. There are those who are willing to take Christ as their Saviour, yet who are most reluctant to submit to Him as their Lord, to be at His command, to be governed by His laws. Yet there are some unregenerate persons who acknowledge Christ as their Lord. Here is the scriptural proof for our assertion: "Many will say to Me in that day, *Lord, Lord,* have we not prophesied in Thy name? and in Thy name have we cast out devils? and in Thy name done many wonderful works? And then will I profess unto them, I never knew you: depart from Me, ye that work iniquity" (Matt. 7:22, 23). There is a *large* class ("many") who profess subjection to Christ as Lord, and who do many mighty works in His name: thus a people who can show you their faith by their works, and yet it is not a saving one!

It is impossible to say how far a non-saving faith may go, and how very closely it may resemble that faith which is saving. Saving faith has Christ for its object; so has a non-saving faith (John 2:23, 24). Saving faith is wrought by the Holy Spirit; so also is a non-saving faith (Heb. 6:4). Saving faith is produced by the Word of God; so also is a non-saving faith (Matt. 13:20, 21). Saving faith will make a man prepare for the coming of the Lord; so also will a non-saving faith: of both the foolish and wise virgins it is written, "Then *all* those virgins arose, and *trimmed* their lamps" (Matt. 25:7). Saving faith is accompanied with joy; so also is a non-saving faith (Matt. 13:20).

Perhaps some readers are ready to say that all of this is very unsettling and, if really heeded, most distressing. May God in His mercy grant that this article may have just those very effects on many who read it. If you value your soul, dismiss it not lightly. If there be such a thing (and there *is*) as a faith in Christ which does not save, then how easy it is to be *deceived* about *my* faith! It is not without reason that the Holy Spirit has so plainly cautioned us at this very point. "A deceived heart hath turned him aside" (Isaiah 44:20). "The pride of thine heart hath deceived thee" (Obad. 3). "Take heed that *ye* be not deceived" (Luke 21:8). "For if a man think himself to be something, when he is nothing, he deceiveth himself" (Gal. 6:3). At no point does Satan use this cunning and power more tenaciously, and more successfully, than in getting people to believe that they have a saving faith when they have not.

The Devil deceives more souls by this one thing than by all his other devices put together. Take this present article as an illustration. How many a Satan-blinded soul will read it and then say, It does not apply to *me;* I know that *my* faith *is* a saving one! It is in this way that the Devil turns aside the sharp point of God's convicting Word, and secures his captives in their unbelief. He works in them a false sense of security, by persuading them that they *are* safe within the ark, and induces them to ignore the threatenings of the Word and appropriate only its comforting promises. He dissuades them from heeding that most salutary exhortation, "Examine yourselves, whether ye be in the faith; *prove* your own selves" (2 Cor. 13:5). Oh, my reader, heed that word *now.*

In closing this first article we will endeavour to point out some of the particulars in which this non-saving faith is defective, and wherein it comes short of a faith which does save. First, with many it is because they are willing for Christ to save them from hell, but are not willing for Him to save them from *self.* They want to be delivered from the wrath to come, but they wish to retain their self-will and self-pleasing. But He will not be dictated unto: you must be saved on *His* terms, or not at all. When Christ *saves,* He saves from *sin*—from its power and pollution, and therefore from its guilt. And the very essence of sin is the determination to have my *own* way (Isaiah 53:6). Where Christ saves, He subdues this spirit of self-will, and implants a genuine, a powerful, a lasting, desire and determination to please *Him.*

Again, many are never saved because they wish to divide Christ; they want to take Him as Saviour, but are unwilling to subject themselves unto Him as their Lord. Or if they are prepared to own Him as Lord, it is not as an *absolute* Lord. But this cannot be: Christ will either be Lord of all or He will not be Lord at all. But the vast majority of professing Christians would have Christ's sovereignty limited at certain points; it must not encroach too far upon the liberty which some worldly lust or carnal interest demands. His peace they covet, but His *"yoke"* is unwelcome. Of all such Christ will yet say, "But these Mine enemies, *which would not* that I should *reign over them,* bring hither, and slay them before Me" (Luke 19:27).

Again, there are multitudes who are quite ready for Christ to justify them, but not to sanctify. Some kind, some degree, of sanctification they will tolerate, but to be sanctified *wholly,* their "whole spirit and soul and body" (1 Thess. 5:23), they have no relish for. For their hearts to be sanctified, for pride and covetousness to be subdued, would be too much like the plucking out of a right eye. For the constant mortification of *all* their members they have no taste. For Christ to come to them as Refiner, to burn up their lusts, consume their dross, to dissolve utterly their old frame of nature, to melt their souls, so as to make them run in a new mould, they like not. To deny self utterly, and take up their cross daily, is a task from which they shrink with abhorrence.

Again, many are willing for Christ to officiate as their Priest, but not for Him to legislate as their King. Ask them, in a general way, if they are ready to do whatsoever Christ requires of them, and they will answer in the affirmative, emphatically and with confidence. But come to particulars: apply to each one of them those specific commandments and precepts of the Lord which *they* are ignoring, and they will at once cry out "Legalism"! or "We cannot be perfect in everything." Name nine duties and perhaps they are performing them, but mention a tenth and it at once makes them angry, for you have come too close home to *their* case. After much persuasion, Naaman was induced to bathe in the Jordan, but he was unwilling to abandon the house of Rimmon (2 Kings 5:18). Herod heard John gladly and did "many things" (Mark 6:20), but when John referred to Herodias it touched him to the quick. Many are willing to give up their theatre-going, and card-parties, who refuse to go forth unto Christ outside the camp. Others are willing to go outside the camp, yet refuse to *deny* their fleshly and worldly lusts. Reader, if there is a *reserve* in your obedience, you are on the way to hell.

2. *Its Nature*

"There is a generation that are pure in their own eyes, and yet is not washed from their filthiness" (Prov. 30:12). A great many suppose that such a verse as this applies only to those who are trusting in something other than Christ for their acceptance before God, such as people who are relying upon baptism, church membership or their own moral and religious performances. But it is a great mistake to limit such scriptures unto the class just mentioned. Such a verse as "There is a way which seemeth right unto a man, but the end thereof are the ways of death" (Prov. 14:12) has a far wider application than merely to those who are resting on something of or from themselves to secure a title to everlasting bliss. Equally wrong is it to imagine that the only *deceived* souls are they who have no faith in Christ.

There is in Christendom today a very large number of people who have been taught that nothing the sinner can do will ever merit the esteem of God. They have been informed, and rightly so, that the highest moral achievements of the natural man are only "filthy rags" in the sight of the thrice holy God. They have heard quoted so often such passages as, "By grace are ye saved through faith; and that not of yourselves: it is the gift of God: not of works, lest any man should boast" (Eph. 2:8, 9), and "Not by works of righteousness which we have done, but according to His mercy He saved us" (Titus 3:5), that they have become thoroughly convinced that heaven cannot be attained by any doing of the creature. Further, they have been told so often that *Christ alone* can save any sinner that this has become a settled article in their creed, from which neither man nor devil can shake them. So far, so good.

That large company to whom we are now referring have also been taught that while Christ is the only way unto the Father, yet He becomes so only as faith is personally exercised in and upon Him: that He becomes our Saviour only when we believe on Him. During the last twenty-five years, almost the whole emphasis of "gospel preaching" has been thrown upon faith in Christ, and evangelistic efforts have been almost entirely confined to getting people to "believe" on the Lord Jesus. Apparently there has been great success; thousands upon thousands have responded; have, as they suppose, accepted Christ as their own personal Saviour. Yet we wish to point out here that it is as serious an error to suppose that all who "believe in Christ" are saved as it is to conclude that only those are deceived (and are described in Proverbs 14:12, and 30:12) who have no faith in Christ.

No one can read the New Testament attentively without discovering that there *is* a "believing" in Christ *which does not save*. In John 8:30, we are told, "As He spake these words, many *believed* on Him." Mark carefully, it is not said "many believe *in* Him," but "many believed *on* Him." Nevertheless one does not have to read much farther on in the chapter to discover that those very people were unregenerate and unsaved souls. In verse 44 we find the Lord telling these very "believers" that *they* were of their father the Devil; and in verse 59 we find them taking up stones to cast at Him. This has presented a difficulty unto some; yet it ought not. They created their own difficulty, by supposing that all faith in Christ necessarily saves. It does not. There *is* a faith in Christ which saves, and there is also a faith in Christ which *does not* save.

"Among the chief rulers also many *believed on* Him." Were, then, those men saved? Many preachers and evangelists, as well as tens of thousands of their blinded dupes, would answer, "Most assuredly." But let us note what immediately follows here: "but because of the Pharisees they did not confess Him, lest they should be put out of the synagogue: for they loved the praise of men more than the praise of God" (John 12:42, 43). Will any of our readers now say that those men were *saved*? If so, it is clear proof that you are utter strangers to any saving work of God in your own souls. Men who are afraid to hazard for Christ's sake the loss of their worldly positions, temporal interests, personal reputations, or anything else that is dear to them, are yet in their sins—no matter how they may be trusting in Christ's finished work to take them to heaven.

Probably most of our readers have been brought up under the teaching that there are only two classes of people in this world, believers and unbelievers. But such a classification is most misleading, and is utterly erroneous. God's Word divides earth's inhabitants into *three* classes: "Give none offence, neither to [1] the Jews, nor [2] to the Gentiles, nor [3] to the church of God" (1 Cor. 10:32). It was so during Old Testament times, more noticeably so from the days of Moses onwards. There were first the "gentile" or heathen nations, outside the commonwealth of Israel, which formed by far the largest class. Corresponding with that class today are the countless millions of modern heathen, who are "lovers of pleasure more than lovers of God." Second, there was the nation of Israel, which has to be subdivided into two groups, for, as Romans 9:6, declares, "They are *not* all Israel, which are of Israel." By far the larger portion of the nation of Israel were only the nominal people of God, in outward relation to Him: corresponding with this class is the great mass of professors bearing the name of Christ. Third, there was the spiritual remnant of Israel, whose calling, hope and inheritance were heavenly: corresponding to them this day are the genuine Christians, God's "*little* flock" (Luke 12:32).

The same threefold division among men is plainly discernible throughout John's Gospel. First, there were the hardened leaders of the nation, the scribes and Pharisees, priests and elders. From start to finish they were openly opposed to Christ, and neither His blessed teaching nor His wondrous works had any melting effects upon them. Second, there were the common people who "heard Him gladly" (Mark 12:37), a great many of whom are said to have "believed on Him" (see John 2:23; 7:31; 8:30; 10:42; 12:11), but concerning whom there is nothing to show that they were saved. They were not outwardly opposed to Christ, but they never yielded their hearts to Him. They were impressed by His Divine credentials, yet were easily offended (John 6:66). Third, there was the insignificant handful who "received Him" (John 1:12) into their hearts and lives; received Him as their Lord and Saviour.

The same three classes are clearly discernible (to anointed eyes) in the world today. First, there are the vast multitudes who make no profession at all, who see nothing in Christ that they should desire Him; people who are deaf to every appeal, and who make little attempt to conceal their hatred of the Lord Jesus. Second, there is that large company who are attracted by Christ in a natural way. So far from being openly antagonistic to Him and His cause, they are found among His followers. Having been taught much of the Truth, they "believe in Christ," just as children reared by conscientious Mohammedans believe firmly and devoutedly in Mohammed. Having received much of instruction concerning the virtues of Christ's precious blood, they trust in its merits to deliver them from the wrath to come; and yet there is nothing in their daily lives to show that they are *new* creatures in Christ Jesus! Third, there are the "few" (Matt. 7:13, 14) who deny themselves, take up the cross daily, and follow a despised and rejected Christ in the path of loving and unreserved obedience unto God.

Yes, there is a faith in Christ which saves, but there is a faith in Christ which does not save. From this statement probably few will dissent, yet many will be inclined to weaken it by saying that the faith in Christ which does not save is merely a historical faith, or where there is a believing *about* Christ instead of a believing *in* Him. Not so. That there are those who mistake a historical faith about Christ for a saving faith in Christ we do not deny; but what we would here emphasize is the solemn fact that there are *also* some who have *more* than a historical faith, more than a mere head-knowledge about Him, who yet have a faith which comes short of being a quickening and saving one. Not only are there some with this non-saving faith, but today there are vast numbers of such all around us. They are people who furnish the antitypes of those to which we called attention in the last article: who were represented and illustrated in Old Testament times by those who believed in, rested upon, leaned upon, relied upon the Lord, but who were, nevertheless, unsaved souls.

What, then, does saving faith consist of? In seeking to answer this question our present object is to supply not only a scriptural definition, but one which, at the same time, differentiates it from a non-saving faith. Nor is this any easy task, for the two things often have much in common: that faith in Christ which does not save has in it more than one element or ingredient of that faith which *does* vitally unite the soul to Him. Those pitfalls which the writer must now seek to avoid are undue discouraging of real saints on the one hand by raising the standard higher than Scripture has raised it, and encouraging unregenerate professors on the other hand by so lowering the standards as to include them. We do not wish to withhold from the people of God their legitimate portion; nor do we want to commit the sin of taking the children's bread and casting it to the dogs. May the Holy Spirit Himself deign to guide us into the Truth.

Much error would be avoided on this subject if due care were taken to frame a scriptural definition of *unbelief*. Again and again in Scripture we find believing and not believing placed in antithesis, and we are afforded much help toward arriving at a correct conception of the real nature of saving faith when we obtain a right understanding of the character of unbelief. It will at once be discovered that saving faith is far more than a hearty assenting unto what God's Word sets before us, when we perceive that unbelief is much more than an error or judgment or a failure to assent unto the Truth. Scripture depicts unbelief as a virulent and violent *principle of opposition to God*. Unbelief has both a passive and active, a negative and positive, side, and therefore the Greek noun is rendered both by "unbelief" (Romans 11:20; Heb. 4:6, 11), and "disobedience" (Eph. 2:2; 5:6) and the verb by "believed not" (Heb. 3:18; 11:30) and "obey not" (1 Peter 3:1; 4:17). A few concrete examples will make this plainer.

Take first the case of Adam. There was something more than a mere negative failing to believe God's solemn threat that in the day he should eat of the forbidden fruit he would surely die: by one man's *disobedience* many were made sinners (Romans 5:12). Nor did the heinousness of our first parent's sin consist in listening to the lie of the serpent, for 1 Timothy 2:14, expressly declares "Adam *was not* deceived." No, he was determined to have his own way, no matter what God had prohibited and threatened. Thus, the very first case of unbelief in human history consisted not only in negatively failing to take to heart which God has so clearly and so solemnly said, but also in a deliberate defiance of and rebellion against Him.

Take the case of Israel in the wilderness. Concerning them it is said, "They could not enter in [the promised land] because of unbelief" (Heb. 3:19). Now exactly what do those words signify? Do they mean that Canaan was missed by them because of their failure to appropriate the promise of God? Yes, for a "promise" of entering in was "left" them, but it was not "mixed with faith in them that heard it" (Heb. 4:1, 2)—God had declared that the seed of Abraham should inherit that land which flowed with milk and honey, and it was the privilege of that generation which was delivered from Egypt to lay hold of and apply that promise to themselves. But they did not. Yet that is not all! There was something far worse: there was another element in their unbelief which is usually lost sight of nowadays—they were openly disobedient against God. When the spies brought back a sample of the goodly grapes, and Joshua urged them to go up and possess the land, they would not. Accordingly Moses declared, "notwithstanding ye would not go up, but *rebelled* against the commandment of the Lord your God" (Deut. 1:26). Ah, *there* is the positive side of their unbelief; they were self-willed, disobedient, defiant.

Consider now the case of that generation of Israel which was in Palestine when the Lord Jesus appeared among them as "a minister of the circumcision for the truth of God" (Romans 15:8). John 1:11, informs us, "He came unto His own, and His own received Him not," which the next verse defines as "they believed" Him not. But is that all? Were they guilty of nothing more than a failure to assent to His teaching and trust to His person? Nay, verily, that was merely the *negative* side of their unbelief? Positively, they "hated" Him (John 15:25), and would "not come to" Him (John 5:40). His holy demands suited not their fleshly desires, and therefore they said, "We will not have this man to reign over us" (Luke 19:14). Thus their unbelief, too, consisted in the spirit of self-will and open defiance, a determination to please themselves at all costs.

Unbelief is not simply an infirmity of fallen human nature, it is a heinous crime. Scripture everywhere attributes it to love of sin, obstinacy of will, hardness of heart. Unbelief has its root in a depraved nature, in a mind which is enmity against God. Love of sin is the immediate cause of unbelief: "And this is the condemnation, that light is come into the world, and men loved darkness rather than light, because their deeds were evil" (John 3:19). "The light of the Gospel is brought unto a place or people: they come so near it as to discover its end or tendency; but as soon as they find that it aims to part them and their sins, they will have no more to do with it. They like not the terms of the Gospel, and so perish in and for their iniquities" (John Owen). If the *Gospel* were more clearly and faithfully preached, fewer would profess to believe it!

Saving faith, then, is the opposite of damning belief. Both issue from the heart that is alienated from God, which is in a state of rebellion against Him; saving faith from a heart which is reconciled to Him and so has ceased to fight against Him. Thus an essential element or ingredient in saving faith is a yielding to the authority of God, a submitting of myself to His rule. It is very much more than my understanding assenting and my will consenting to the fact that Christ is a Saviour for sinners, and that He stands ready to receive all who trust Him. To be received by Christ I must not only come to Him renouncing all my own righteousness (Romans 10:3), as an empty-handed beggar (Matt. 19:21), but I must also forsake my self-will and rebellion against Him (Psalm 12:11, 12; Prov. 28:13). Should an insurrectionist and seditionist come to an earthly king seeking his sovereign favour and pardon, then, obviously, the very law of his coming to him for forgiveness requires that he should come on his knees, laying aside his hostility. So it is with a sinner who really comes savingly to Christ for   pardon; it is against the law of faith to do otherwise.

Saving faith is a genuine *coming to Christ* (Matt. 11:28; John 6:37, etc.). But let us take care that we do not miss the clear and inevitable implication of this term. If I say "I *come* to the U.S.A." then I necessarily indicate that I *left* some other country to get here. Thus it is in "coming" to Christ; something has to be left. Coming to Christ not only involves the abandoning of every false object of confidence, it also includes and entails the forsaking of all other competitors for my heart. "For ye were as sheep going astray; but are now *returned* unto the Shepherd and Bishop of your *souls* (1 Peter 2:25). And what is meant by "ye *were* [note the past tense—they are no longer doing so] as sheep going *astray*"? Isaiah 53:6, tells us: "All we like sheep have gone astray; we have turned every one to *His own* way." Ah, *that* is what must be forsaken before we can truly "come" to Christ—that course of self-will must be abandoned. The prodigal son could not *come* to his Father while he remained in the far country. Dear reader, if you are still following a course of self-pleasing, you are only deceiving yourself if you think you have come to Christ.

Nor is the brief definition which we have given above of what it means really to "come" to Christ any forced or novel one of our own. In his book *Come and Welcome to Jesus Christ*, John Bunyan wrote: "Coming to Christ is attended with an honest and sincere forsaking all for Him [here he quotes Luke 14:26,

27]. By these and like expressions elsewhere, Christ describeth the true comer: he is one that casteth all behind his back. There are a great many pretended comers to Jesus Christ in the world. They are much like the man you read of in Matthew 21:30, that said to his father's bidding, 'I go, sir: and went not.' When Christ calls by His Gospel, they say, 'I come, Sir,' but they still abide by their pleasure and carnal delights." C. H. Spurgeon, in his sermon on John 6:44, said, "Coming to Christ embraces in it repentance, self-abnegation, and faith in the Lord Jesus, and so sums within itself all those things which are the necessary attendants of those great steps of heart, such as the belief of the truth, earnest prayers to God, the submission of the soul to the precepts of His Gospel." In his sermon on John 6:37, he says, "To come to Christ signifies to turn from sin and to trust in Him. Coming to Christ is a leaving of all false confidences, a renouncing of all love to sin and a looking to Jesus as the solitary pillar of our confidence and hope."

Saving faith consists of the complete surrender of my whole being and life to the claims of God upon me: "But first gave their own selves to the Lord" (2 Cor. 8:5).

It is the unreserved acceptance of Christ as my absolute Lord, bowing to His will and receiving His yoke. Possibly someone may object, Then why are Christians exhorted as they are in Romans 12:1? We answer, All such exhortations are simply a calling on them to *continue as they began:* "As ye have therefore received Christ Jesus the Lord, so walk ye in Him" (Col. 2:6). Yes, mark it well that Christ is "received" as *Lord.* Oh, how far, far below the New Testament standard is this modern way of begging sinners to receive Christ as their own personal "Saviour." If the reader will consult his concordance, he will find that in *every passage* where the two titles are found together it is *always* "Lord and Saviour, and never vice versa: see Luke 1:46, 47; 2 Peter 1:11; 2:20; 3:18.

Until the ungodly are sensible of the exceeding sinfulness of their vile course of self-will and self-pleasing, until they are genuinely broken down and penitent over it before God, until they are willing to forsake the world for Christ, until they have resolved to come under His government, for such to depend upon Him for pardon and life is not faith, but blatant presumption, it is but to add insult to injury. And for any such to take His holy name upon their polluted lips and profess to be His followers is the most terribly blasphemy, and comes perilously nigh to committing that sin for which there is no forgiveness. Alas, alas, that modern evangelism is encouraging and producing just such hideous and Christ-dishonouring monstrosities.

Saving faith is a believing on Christ with the *heart:* "If thou shalt confess with thy mouth the Lord Jesus, and shalt believe in thine heart that God raised Him from the dead, thou shalt be saved. For with the heart man believeth unto righteousness" (Romans 10:9, 10). There is no such thing as a saving *faith* in Christ where there is no real *love* for Him, and by "real love" we mean a love which is evidenced by *obedience.* Christ acknowledges none to be His friends save those who do whatsoever He commands them (John 15:14). As unbelief is a species of rebellion, so saving faith is a complete subjection to God: Hence we read of "the obedience of faith" (Romans 16:26). Saving faith is to the soul what health is to the body: it is a mighty principle of operation, full of life, ever working, bringing forth fruit after its own kind.

3. *Its Difficulty*

Some of our readers will probably be surprised to hear about the *difficulty* of saving faith. On almost every side today it is being taught, even by men styled orthodox and "fundamentalists," that getting saved is an exceedingly simple affair. So long as a person believes John 3:16, and "rests on it," or "accepts Christ as his personal Saviour," that is *all* that is needed. It is often said that there is nothing left for the sinner to do but direct his faith toward the right object: just as a man trusts his bank or a wife her husband, let him exercise the same faculty of faith and trust in Christ. So widely has this idea been received that for anyone now to condemn it is to court being branded as a heretic. Notwithstanding, the writer here unhesitatingly denounces it as a most God-insulting lie of the Devil. A natural faith is sufficient for trusting a human object; but a supernatural faith is required to trust savingly in a Divine object.

While observing the methods employed by present-day "evangelists" and "personal workers," we are made to wonder what place the Holy Spirit has in their thoughts; certainly they entertain the most degrading conception of that miracle of grace which He performs when He moves a human heart to surrender truly unto the Lord Jesus. Alas, in these degenerate times few have any idea that saving faith *is* a miraculous thing. Instead, it is now almost universally supposed that saving faith is nothing more than an act of the human will, which any man is capable of performing: all that is needed is to bring before a sinner a few verses of Scripture which describe his lost condition, one or two which contain the word "believe," and then a little persuasion, for him to "accept Christ," and the thing is done. And the awful thing is that so very, very few see anything wrong with this—blind to the fact that such a process is only the Devil's drug to lull thousands into a false peace.

So many have been *argued into* believing that they are saved. In reality, their "faith" sprang from nothing better than a superficial process of logic. Some "personal worker" addresses a man who has no concern whatever for the glory of God and no realization of his terrible hostility against Him. Anxious to "win another soul to Christ," he pulls out his New Testament and reads to him 1 Timothy 1:15. The worker says, "You are a sinner," and his man assenting he is at once informed, "Then that verse includes *you*." Next John 3:16, is read, and the question is asked, "Whom does the word 'whosoever' include?" The question is repeated until the poor victim answers, "You, me, and everybody." Then he is asked, "Will you believe it; believe that God loves you, that Christ died for you?" If the answer is "Yes," he is at once assured that he is now saved. Ah, my reader, if *this* is how you were "saved," then it was with "*enticing* words of man's wisdom" and *your* "faith" stands only "in the wisdom of men" (1 Cor. 2:4, 5), and not in the power of God!

Multitudes seem to think that it is about as easy for a sinner to purify his heart (James 4:8) as it is to wash his hands; to admit the searching and flesh-withering light of Divine truth into the soul as the morning sun into his room by pulling up the blinds; to turn from idols to God, from the world to Christ, from sin to holiness, as to turn a ship right round by the help of her helm. Oh, my reader, be not deceived on this vital matter; to mortify the lusts of the flesh, to be crucified unto the world, to overcome the Devil, to die daily unto sin and live unto righteousness, to be meek and lowly in heart, trustful and obedient, pious and patient, faithful and uncompromising, loving and gentle; in a word, to be a Christian, *to be Christ-like,* is a task far, far beyond the poor resources of fallen human nature.

It is because a generation has arisen which is ignorant of the *real nature* of saving faith that they deem it such a simple thing. It is because so very few have any scriptural conception of *the character* of God's great salvation that the delusions referred to above are so widely received. It is because so very few realize *what* they need saving from that the popular "evangel" (?) of the hour is so eagerly accepted. Once it is seen that saving faith consists of very much more than believing that "Christ died for me," that it involves and entails the complete surrender of my heart and life to His government, few will imagine that they possess it. Once it is seen that God's salvation is not only a legal but also an experimental thing, that it not only justifies but regenerates and sanctifies, fewer will suppose they are its participants. Once it is seen that Christ came here to save His people not only from hell, but from sin, from self-will and self-pleasing, then fewer will desire His salvation.

The Lord Jesus did not teach that saving faith was a simple matter. Far from it. Instead of declaring that the saving of the soul was an easy thing, which many would participate in, He said: "Strait is the gate, and narrow is the way, which leadeth unto life, and few there be that find it" (Matt. 7:14). The only path which leads to heaven is a hard and laborious one. "We must through *much tribulation* enter into the kingdom of God" (Acts 14:22): an entrance into that path calls for the utmost endeavours of soul—"*Strive* to enter in at the strait gate" (Luke 13:24).

After the young ruler had departed from Christ, sorrowing, the Lord turned to His disciples and said, "How *hard* is it for them that trust in riches to enter into the kingdom of God! It is easier for a camel to go through the eye of a needle, than for a *rich* man to enter into the kingdom of God" (Mark 10:24, 25). What place is given to such a passage as this in the theology (if "theology" it is fit to be called) which is being taught in the "Bible institutes" to those seeking to qualify for evangelistic and personal work? None at all. According to their views, it is just as easy for a millionaire to be saved as it is for a pauper, since *all* that either has to do is "rest on the finished work of Christ." But those who are wallowing in wealth think not of God: "According to their pasture, so were they filled; they were filled, and their heart exalted; therefore have they forgotten Me!" (Hosea 13:6).

When the disciples heard these words of Christ's "they were astonished out of measure, saying among themselves, Who then can be saved?" Had our moderns heard them, they had soon set their fears at rest, and assured them that anybody and everybody could be saved if they believed on the Lord Jesus. But not so did Christ reassure them. Instead, He immediately added, "With men it is *impossible,* but not with God" (Mark 10:27). Of himself, the fallen sinner can no more repent evangelically, believe in Christ savingly, come to Him effectually, than he can create a world. "With men it is impossible" rules out of court all special pleading for the power of man's will. Nothing but a *miracle of grace* can lead to the saving of any sinner.

And *why* is it impossible for the natural man to exercise saving faith? Let the answer be drawn from the case of this young ruler. He departed from Christ sorrowing, "for he had great possessions." He was wrapped up in them. They were his idols. His heart was chained to the things of earth. The demands of Christ were too exacting: to part with all and follow Him was more than flesh and blood could endure. Reader, what are *your* idols? To him the Lord said, "One thing thou lackest." What was it? A yielding to the imperative requirements of Christ; a heart surrendered to God. When the soul is stuffed with the dregs of earth, there is no room for the impressions of heaven. When a man is satisfied with carnal riches, he has no desire for spiritual riches.

The same sad truth is brought out again in Christ's parable of the "great supper." The feast of Divine grace is spread, and through the Gospel a general call is given for men to come and partake of it. And what is the response? This: "They all with one consent began to make excuse" (Luke 14:18). And why should they? Because they were more interested in other things. Their hearts were set upon land (verse 18), oxen (verse 19), domestic comforts (verse 20). People are willing to "accept Christ" on their own terms, but not on His. What His terms *are* is made known in the same chapter: giving Him the supreme place in our affections (verse 26), the crucifixion of self (verse 27), the abandonment of every idol (verse 33). Therefore did He ask, "which of you, intending to build a tower [figure of a hard task of setting the affections on things *above*], sitteth not down first, and *counteth the cost*?" (Luke 14:28).

"How can ye believe, which receive honour one of another, and seek not the honour that cometh from God only?" (John 5:44). Do these words picture the exercise of saving faith as the simple matter which so many deem it? The word "honour" here signifies approbation or praise. While those Jews were making it their chief aim to win and hold the good opinion of each other, and were indifferent to the approval of God, it was impossible that they should come to Christ. It is the same now: "Whosoever therefore will be [desires and is determined to be] a friend of the world is the enemy of God" (James 4:4). To come to Christ effectually, to believe on Him savingly, involves turning our backs upon the world, alienating ourselves from the esteem of our godless (or religious) fellows, and identifying ourselves with the despised and rejected One. It involves bowing to His yoke, surrendering to His lordship, and living henceforth for *His* glory. And *that* is no small task.

"*Labour* not for the meat which perisheth, but for that meat which endureth unto everlasting life, which the Son of man shall give unto you" (John 6:27). Does this language imply that the obtaining of eternal life is a simple matter? It does not; far from it. It denotes that a man must be in deadly earnest, subordinating all other interests in his quest for it, and be prepared to put forth strenuous endeavours and overcome formidable difficulties. Then does this verse teach salvation by works, by self-efforts? No, and yes. No in the sense that anything we do can *merit* salvation—eternal life is a "gift." Yes in the sense that wholehearted seeking after salvation and a diligent use of the prescribed means of grace are demanded of us. Nowhere in Scripture is there any promise to the dilatory. (Compare Hebrews 4:11).

"No man can come to me, except the Father which hath sent Me draw him" (John 6:44). Plainly does this language give the lie to the popular theory of the day, that it lies within the power of man's will to be saved any time he chooses to be. Flatly does this verse contradict the flesh-pleasing and creature-honouring idea that anyone can receive Christ as his Saviour the moment he decides to do so. The reason why the natural man cannot come to Christ till the Father "draw" him is because he is the bondslave of sin (John 8:34), serving divers lusts (Titus 3:3), the captive of the Devil (2 Tim. 2:26). Almighty power must break his chains and open the prison doors (Luke 4:18) ere he *can* come to Christ. Can one who loves darkness and hates the light reverse the process? No, no more than a man who has a diseased foot or poisoned hand can heal it by an effort of will. Can the Ethiopian change his skin or the leopard his spots? No more can they do good who are accustomed to do evil (Jer. 13:23).

"And if the righteous with difficulty is saved, the ungodly and sinner where shall they appear?" (1 Peter 4:18, Bag. Int.). Matthew Henry said, "It is as much as the best can do to secure the salvation of their souls; there are so many sufferings, temptations, and difficulties to be overcome; so many sins to be mortified; the gate is so strait, and the way so narrow, that it is as much as the righteous man can do to be saved. Let the absolute necessity of salvation balance the difficulty of it. Consider your difficulties are the greatest at first: God offers His grace and help; the contest will not last long. Be but faithful to the death and God will give you the crown of life (Rev. 2:10)." So also John Lillie, "After all that God has done by sending His Son, and the Son by the Holy Spirit, it is only with difficulty, exceeding difficulty, that the work of saving the righteous advances to its consummation. The entrance into the kingdom lies through much tribulation—through fightings without and fears within—through the world's seductions, and its frowns—through the utter weakness and continual failures of the flesh, and the many fiery darts of Satan."

Here then are the reasons why saving faith is so difficult to put forth. (1) By nature men are entirely ignorant of its real character, and therefore are easily deceived by Satan's plausible substitutes for it. But even when they are scripturally informed thereon, they either sorrowfully turn their backs on Christ, as did the rich young ruler when he learned His terms of discipleship, or they hypocritically profess what they do not possess. (2) The power of self-love reigns supreme within, and to *deny* self is too great a demand upon the unregenerate. (3) The love of the world and the approbation of their friends stands in the way of a complete surrender to Christ. (4) The demands of God that He should be loved with *all* the heart and that we should be "holy in all manner of conversation" (1 Peter 1:15) repels the carnal. (5) Bearing the reproach of Christ, being hated by the religious world (John 15:18), suffering persecution for righteousness' sake, is something which mere flesh and blood shrinks from. (6) The humbling of ourselves before God, penitently confessing *all* our self-will, is something which an unbroken heart revolts against. (7) To fight the good fight of faith (1 Tim. 6:12) and overcome the Devil (1 John 2:13) is too arduous an undertaking for those who love their own ease.

Multitudes desire to be saved from hell (the natural instinct of *self*-preservation) who are quite unwilling to be saved from *sin*. Yes, there are tens of thousands who have been deluded into thinking that they have "accepted Christ as their Saviour," whose lives show plainly that they *reject* Him as their Lord. For a sinner to obtain the pardon of God he must *"forsake his way"*

(Isaiah 55:7). No man can turn *to God* until he turns *from idols* (1 Thess. 1:9). Thus insisted the Lord Jesus, "Whosoever he be of you that forsaketh not all that he hath, he cannot be My disciple" (Luke 14:33).

The terrible thing is that so many preachers today, under the pretence of magnifying the grace of God, have represented Christ as the Minister of *sin;* as One who has, through His atoning sacrifice, procured an indulgence for men to continue gratifying their fleshly and worldly lusts. Provided a man professes to believe in the virgin birth and vicarious death of Christ, and claims to be resting upon Him alone for salvation, he may pass for a real Christian almost anywhere today, even though his daily life may be no different from that of the moral worldling who makes no profession at all. The Devil is chloroforming thousands into hell by this very delusion. The Lord Jesus asks, "Why call ye Me, Lord, Lord, and *do not* the things which I say?" (Luke 6:46); and insists, "Not every one that saith unto Me, Lord, Lord, shall enter into the kingdom of heaven; but he that *doeth* the will of My Father which is in heaven" (Matt. 7:21).

The hardest task before most of us is not to learn, but to unlearn. Many of God's own children have drunk so deeply of the sweetened poison of Satan that it is by no means easy to get it out of their systems; and while it remains in them it stupefies their understanding. So much is this the case that the first time one of them reads an article like this it is apt to strike him as an open attack upon the sufficiency of Christ's finished work, as though we were here teaching that the atoning sacrifice of the Lamb needed to be plussed by something from the creature. Not so. Nothing but the merits of Immanuel can ever give any sinner title to stand before the ineffably holy God. But what we are now contending for is, *When* does God impute to any sinner the righteousness of Christ? Certainly not while he is opposed to Him.

Moreover, we do not honour the work of Christ until we correctly define *what* that work was designed to effect. The Lord of glory did not come here and die to procure the pardon of our sins, and take us to heaven while our hearts still remain cleaving to the earth. No, He came here to prepare a way to heaven (John 10:4; 14:4; Heb. 10:20-22; 1 Peter 2:21), to call men into that way, that by His precepts and promises, His example and spirit, He might form and fashion their souls to that glorious state, and make them willing to abandon all things for it. He lived and died so that His Spirit should come and quicken the dead sinners into newness of life, make them new creatures in Himself, and cause them to sojourn in this world as those who are not of it, as those whose hearts have already departed from it. Christ did not come here to render a change of heart, repentance, faith, personal holiness, loving God supremely and obeying Him unreservedly, as unnecessary, or salvation as possible *without* them. How passing strange that any suppose He did!

Ah, my reader, it becomes a searching test for each of our hearts to face honestly the question, Is *this* what I really long for? As Bunyan asked (in his *The Jerusalem Sinner Saved*), "What are thy desires? Wouldest thou be saved? Wouldest thou be saved with a *thorough* salvation? Wouldest thou be saved from guilt, and from filth too? Wouldest thou be the *servant* of the Saviour? Art thou indeed weary of the service of thy old master, the Devil, sin, and the world? And have these desires put thy soul to flight? Dost thou fly to Him that is a Saviour from the wrath to come, for life? If these be thy desires, and if they be unfeigned, fear not."

"Many people think that when we preach salvation, we mean salvation from going to hell. We do mean that, but we mean a great deal more: we preach salvation from *sin;* we say that Christ is able to save a man; and we mean by that that He is able to save him from sin and to make him holy; to make him a new man. No person has any right to say 'I am saved,' while he continues in sin as he did before. How can you be saved from sin while you are living in it? A man that is drowning cannot say he is saved from the water while he is sinking in it; a man that is frost-bitten cannot say, with any truth, that he is saved from the cold while he is stiffened in the wintry blast. No, man, Christ did not come to save thee *in* thy sins, but to save thee *from* thy sins, not to make the disease so that it should not kill thee, but to let it remain in itself mortal, and, nevertheless, to remove it from thee, and thee from it. Christ Jesus came then to heal us from the plague of sin, to touch us with His hand and say 'I will, be thou clean' " (C. H. Spurgeon, on Matt. 9:12).

They who do not yearn after holiness of heart and righteousness of life are only deceiving themselves when they suppose they desire to be saved by Christ. The plain fact is, all that is wanted by so many today is merely a soothing portion of their conscience, which will enable them to go on comfortably in a course of self-pleasing which will permit them to continue their worldly ways without the fear of eternal punishment. Human nature is the same the world over; that wretched instinct which causes multitudes to believe that paying a papist priest a few dollars procures forgiveness of all their past sins, and an "indulgence" for future ones, moves other multitudes to devour greedily the lie that, with an unbroken and impenitent heart, by a mere act of the will, they may "believe in Christ," and thereby obtain not only God's pardon for past sins but an "eternal security," no matter what they do or do not do in the future.

Oh, my reader, be not deceived; God frees none from the condemnation but those "which are *in Christ Jesus*" (Romans 8:1), and "if any man be in Christ, he is a *new creature*: old things are [*not* "ought to be"] passed away; behold, *all* things *are* become new (2 Cor. 5:17). Saving faith makes a sinner come to Christ with a real soul-thirst, that he may drink of the living water, even of His sanctifying Spirit (John 7:38, 39). To love our enemies, to bless them that curse us, to pray for them that despitefully use us, is very far from being easy, yet *this* is only one part of the task which Christ assigns unto those who would be *His* disciples. *He* acted thus, and He has left us an example that we should follow His steps. And *His* "salvation," in its *present* application, consists of revealing to our hearts the imperative need for our measuring up to His high and holy standard, with a realization of our own utter powerlessness so to do; and creating within us an intense hunger and thirst after such personal righteousness, and a daily turning unto Him and trustful supplication for needed grace and strength.

4. Its Communication

From the human viewpoint, things are now in a bad state in the world. But from the spiritual viewpoint things are in a far worse state in the religious realm. Sad is it to see the anti-Christian cults flourishing on every side; but far more grievous is it, for those who are taught of God, to discover that much of the so-called "Gospel" which is now being preached in many "fundamentalist churches" and "gospel halls" is but a satanic delusion. The Devil knows that his captives are quite secure while the grace of God and the finished work of Christ are "faithfully" proclaimed to them, so long as the only way in which sinners *receive* the saving virtues of the Atonement is unfaithfully concealed. While God's peremptory and unchanging demand for repentance is left out, while Christ's own terms of discipleship (i.e. how to become a Christian: Acts 11:26) in Luke 14:26, 27, 33, are withheld, and while saving faith is frittered down to a mere act of the will, blind laymen will continue to be led by blind preachers, only for both to fall into the ditch.

Things are far, far worse even in the "orthodox" sections of Christendom than the majority of God's own children are aware. Things are rotten even at the very foundation, for with very rare exceptions God's way of salvation is no longer being taught. Tens of thousands are "ever learning" points in prophecy, the meaning of the types, the significance of the numerals, how to divide the "dispensations," who are, nevertheless, "never able to come to the knowledge of the truth" (2 Tim. 3:7) of salvation itself—unable because unwilling to pay the price (Prov. 23:23), which is a full surrender to God Himself. As far as the writer understands the present situation, it seems to him that what is needed today is to press upon the serious attention of professing Christians such questions as: *When* is it that God *applies* to a sinner the virtues of Christ's finished work? *What is it* that I am called upon to do in order to appropriate myself to the efficacy of Christ's atonement? What is it that gives me an actual entrance into the good of His redemption?

The questions formulated above are only three different ways of framing the same inquiry. Now the popular answer which is being returned to them is, "Nothing more is required from any sinner than that he simply *believe on* the Lord Jesus Christ." In the preceding articles of this series we have sought to show that such a reply is misleading, inadequate, faulty, and that because it ignores all the other scriptures which set forth what God requires from the sinner: it leaves out of account God's demand for repentance (with all that that involves and includes), and Christ's clearly defined terms of discipleship in Luke 14. To restrict ourselves to any one scripture term of a subject, or set of passages using that term, results in an erroneous conception of it. They who limit their ideas of regeneration to the one figure of the new birth lapse into serious error upon it. So they who limit their thoughts on how to be saved to the one word "believe" are easily misled. Diligent care needs to be taken to collect *all* that Scripture teaches on any subject if we are to have a properly balanced and accurate view thereof.

To be more specific. In Romans 10:13, we read, "For whosoever shall call upon the name of the Lord shall be saved." Now does this mean that all who have, with their lips, cried unto the Lord, who have in the name of Christ besought God to have mercy on them, have been saved by Him? They who reply in the affirmative are only deceived by the mere sound of words, as the deluded Romanist is when he contends for Christ's bodily presence in the bread, because He said "this *is* My body." And how are we to show the papist is misled? Why, by comparing Scripture *with Scripture.* So here. The writer well remembers being on a ship in a terrible storm off the coast of Newfoundland. All the hatches were battened down, and for three days no passenger was allowed on the decks. Reports from the stewards were disquieting. Strong men paled. As the winds increased and the ship rolled worse and worse, scores of men and women were heard calling upon the name of the Lord. Did He save them? A day or two later, when the weather changed, those same men and women were drinking, cursing, card-playing!

Perhaps someone asks, "But does not Romans 10:13 say what it means?" Certainly it does, but no verse of Scripture yields its meaning to lazy people. Christ Himself tells us that there are many who call Him "Lord" to whom He will say "Depart from Me" (Matt. 7:22, 23). Then what is to be done with Romans 10:13? Why, diligently compare it with *all* other passages which make known what the sinner must do ere God will save him. If nothing more than the fear of death or horror of hell prompts the sinner to call upon the Lord, he might just as well call upon the trees. The Almighty is not at the beck and call of any rebel who, when he is terrified, sues for mercy. "He that turneth away his ear from hearing the law, even his prayer shall be abomination" (Prov. 28:9)! "He that covereth his sins shall not prosper: but whoso confesseth and *forsaketh them* shall have mercy" (Prov. 28:13). The only "calling upon His name" which the Lord heeds is that which issues from a broken, penitent, sin-hating heart, which thirsts after holiness.

The same principle applies to Acts 16:31, and all similar texts: "Believe on the Lord Jesus Christ, and thou shalt be saved." To a casual reader, that seems a very simple matter, yet a closer pondering of those words should discover that more is involved than at first sight appears. Note that the apostles did not merely tell the Philippian jailer to "rest on the finished work of Christ," or "trust in His atoning sacrifice." Instead, it was a *Person* that was set before him. Again, it was not simply "Believe on the Saviour," but *"the Lord Jesus Christ."* John 1:12 shows plainly that to "believe" is to "receive," and to be saved a sinner must receive One who is not only Saviour but "Lord," yea, who must be received *as* "Lord" *before* He becomes the Saviour of that person. And to receive "Christ Jesus *the Lord"* (Col. 2:6) necessarily involves the renouncing of our own sinful lordship, the throwing down of the weapons of our warfare against Him, and the submitting to His yoke and rule. And before any human rebel is brought to do *that,* a miracle of Divine grace has to be wrought within him. And this brings us more immediately to the present aspect of our theme.

Saving faith is not a native product of the human heart, but a spiritual grace communicated from on high. "It is the gift of God" (Eph. 2:8). It is "of the operation of God" (Col. 2:12). It is by "the power of God" (1 Cor. 2:5). A most remarkable passage on this subject is found in Ephesians 1:16-20. There we find the apostle Paul praying that the saints should have the eyes of their understanding enlightened, that they might know "what is the exceeding greatness of His power to us-ward who believe, according to the working of His mighty power, which He wrought in Christ when He raised Him from the dead." Not the strong power of God, or the greatness of it, but the "exceeding greatness of His power to us-ward." Note too the standard of comparison: we "believe *according to* the working of His mighty power, which He wrought in Christ when He raised Him from the dead."

God put forth His *"Mighty power"* when He resurrected Christ. There was a mighty power seeking to hinder, even Satan and all his hosts. There was a mighty difficulty to be overcome, even the vanquishing of the grace. There was a mighty result to be achieved, even the bringing to life of One who was dead. None but God Himself was equal to a miracle so stupendous. Strictly analogous is that miracle of grace which issues in saving faith. The Devil employs all his arts and power to retain his captive. The sinner is dead in trespasses and sins, and can no more quicken himself than he can create a world. His heart is bound fast with the grave-clothes of worldly and fleshly lusts, and only Omnipotence can raise it into communion with God. Well may every true servant of the Lord emulate the apostle Paul and pray earnestly that God *will* enlighten His people concerning this wonder of wonders, so that instead of attributing their faith to an exercise of their own will they may freely ascribe all the honour and glory unto Him to whom alone it justly belongs.

If only the professing Christians of this untoward generation could begin to obtain some adequate conception of the *real condition* of every man by nature, they might be less inclined to cavil against the teaching that nothing short of a miracle of grace can ever qualify any sinner to believe unto the saving of his soul If they could only see that the heart's attitude towards God of the most refined and moral is not a whit different from that of the most vulgar and vicious; that he who is most kind and benevolent toward his fellow creatures has no more real desire after Christ than has the most selfish and brutal; then it would be evident that Divine power must operate to change the heart. Divine power was needed to create, but much greater power is required to regenerate a soul: creation is only the bringing of something out of nothing, but regeneration is the transforming not only of an unlovely object, but of one that *resists* with all its might the gracious designs of the heavenly Potter.

It is not simply that the Holy Spirit approaches a heart in which there is no love for God, but He finds it filled with enmity against Him, and incapable of being subject to His law (Romans 8:7). True, the individual himself may be quite unconscious of this terrible fact, yea, ready indignantly to deny it. But that is easily accounted for. If he has heard little or nothing but the love, the grace, the mercy, the goodness of God, it would indeed be surprising if he hated *Him*. But once the *God of Scripture* is made known to him in the power of the Spirit, once he is made to realize that God is the Governor of this world, demanding unqualified submission to all His laws; that He is inflexibly just, and "will by no means clear the guilty"; that He is sovereign, and loves whom He pleases and hates whom He wills; that so far from being an easy-going, indulgent Creator, who winks at the follies of His creatures, He is ineffably holy, so that His righteous wrath burns against all the workers of iniquity—then will people be conscious of indwelling enmity surging up against Him. And nothing but the almighty power of the Spirit can overcome that enmity and bring any rebel truly to love the God of Holy Writ.

Rightly did Thomas Goodwin the Puritan say, "A wolf will sooner marry a lamb, or a lamb a wolf, than ever a carnal heart be subject to the law of God, which was the ancient husband of it (Romans 7:6). It is the turning of one contrary into another. To turn water into wine, there is some kind of symbolizing, yet that is a miracle. But to turn a wolf into a lamb, to turn fire into water, is a yet greater miracle. Between nothing and something there is an infinite distance, but between sin and grace there is a greater distance than can be between nothing and the highest angel in heaven . . . To destroy the power of sin in a man's soul is as great a work as to take away the guilt of sin. It is easier to say to a blind man, 'See,' and to a lame man, 'Walk,' than to say to a man that lies under the power of sin, 'Live, be holy,' for there is that that will not be subject."

In 2 Corinthians 10:4, the apostle describes the character of that work in which the true servants of Christ are engaged. It is a conflict with the forces of Satan. The weapons of their warfare are "not carnal"—as well might modern soldiers go forth equipped with only wooden swords and paper shields as preachers think to liberate the Devil's captives by means of human leaning, worldly methods, touching anecdotes, attractive singing, and so on. No, "their weapons" are the "word of God" and "all prayer" (Eph. 6:17, 18); and even these are only mighty "through God," that is by His direct and special blessing of them to particular souls. In what follows, a description is given of where the might of God is seen, namely in the powerful *opposition* which it meets with and vanquishes; "to the pulling down of strong holds, casting down imaginations, and every high thing that exalteth itself against the knowledge of God, and bringing into captivity every thought to the obedience of Christ."

Herein lies the power of God when He is pleased thus to put it forth in the saving of a sinner. The heart of that sinner is fortified against Him: it is steeled against His holy demands, His righteous claims. It is determined not to submit to His law, nor to abandon those idols which it prohibits. That haughty rebel has made up his mind that he *will not* turn away from the delights of this world and the pleasure of sin and give God the supreme place in his affections. But God has determined to overcome his sinful opposition, and transform him into a loving and loyal subject. The figure here used is that of a besieged town—the heart. Its "strongholds"—the reigning power of fleshly and worldly lusts—are "pulled down"; self-will is broken, pride is subdued, and the defiant rebel is made a willing captive to "the obedience of Christ"! "Mighty through God" points to this miracle of grace.

There is one other detail pointed by the analogy drawn in Ephesians 1:19, 20, which exemplifies the mighty power of God, namely "and set Him [Christ] at His own right hand in the heavenly places." The members of Christ's mystical body are predestinated to be conformed to the glorious image of their glorified Head: in measure, now; perfectly, in the day to come. The ascension of Christ was contrary to *nature*, being opposed by the law of gravitation. But the power of God overcame that opposition, and translated His resurrected Son bodily into heaven. In like manner, His grace produces in His people that which is contrary to nature, overcoming the opposition of the flesh, and drawing their hearts unto things above. How we would marvel if we saw a man extend his arms and suddenly leave the earth, soaring upward into the sky. Yet still more wonderful is it when we behold the power of the Spirit causing a sinful creature to rise above temptations, worldliness and sin, and breathe the atmosphere of heaven; when a human soul is made to disdain the things of earth and find its satisfaction in things above.

The historical order in connection with the Head in Ephesians 1:19, 20, is also the experimental order with regard to the members of His body. Before setting His Son at His own right hand in the heavenlies, God raised Him from the dead;

so before the Holy Spirit fixes the heart of a sinner upon Christ He first quickens him into newness of life. There must be *life* before there can be sight, believing, or good works performed. One who is physically dead is incapable of doing anything; so he who is spiritually dead is incapable of any spiritual exercises. First the giving of life unto dead Lazarus, then the removing of the grave-clothes which bound him hand and foot. God must regenerate before there can be a "new creature in Christ Jesus." The washing of a child follows its birth.

When spiritual life has been communicated to the soul, that individual is now able to see things in their true colours. In God's light he sees light (Psalm 36:9). He is now given to perceive (by the Holy Spirit) what a lifelong rebel he has been against his Creator and Benefactor: that instead of making God's will his rule he has gone his own way; that instead of having before him God's glory he has sought only to please and gratify self. Even though he may have been preserved from all the grosser outward forms of wickedness, he now recognizes that he is a spiritual leper, a vile and polluted creature, utterly unfit to draw near, still less to dwell with, Him who is ineffably holy; and such an apprehension makes him feel that *his* case is hopeless.

There is a vast difference between hearing or reading of what conviction of sin is and being made to feel it in the depths of one's own soul. Multitudes are acquainted with the theory who are total strangers to the experience of it. One may read of the sad effects of war, and may agree that they are indeed dreadful; but when the enemy is at one's own door, plundering his goods, firing his home, slaying his dear ones, he is far more sensible of the miseries of war than ever he was (or could be) previously. So an unbeliever may hear of what a dreadful state the sinner is in before God, and how terrible will be the sufferings of hell; but when the Spirit brings home to his own heart its actual condition, and makes him feel the heat of God's wrath in his own conscience, he is ready to sink with dismay and despair. Reader, do *you* know anything of such an experience?

Only thus is any soul prepared truly to appreciate Christ. They that are whole need not a physician. The one who has been savingly convicted is made to realize that none but the Lord Jesus can heal one so desperately diseased by sin; that He alone can impart that spiritual health (holiness) which will enable him to run in the way of God's commandments; that nothing but His precious blood can atone for the sins of the past and naught but His all-sufficient grace can meet the pressing needs of the present and future. Thus there must be discerning faith before there is coming faith. The Father "draws" to the Son (John 6:44) by imparting to the mind a deep realization of our desperate need of Christ, by giving to the heart a real sense of the inestimable worth of Him, and by causing the will to receive Him on His own terms.

5. *Its Evidences*

The great majority of those who read this article will, doubtless, be they who profess to be in possession of a saving faith. To all such we would put the questions. Where is your proof? What effects has it produced in you? A tree is known by its fruits, and a fountain by the waters which issue from it; so the nature of your faith may be ascertained by a careful examination of what it is bringing forth. We say "*a careful examination*," for as all fruit is not fit for eating nor all water for drinking, so all works are not the effects of a faith which saves. Reformation is not regeneration, and a changed life does not always indicate a changed heart. Have you been saved from a dislike of God's commandments and a disrelish of His holiness? Have you been saved from pride, covetousness, murmuring? Have you been delivered from the love of this world, from the fear of man, from the reigning power of every sin?

The heart of fallen man is thoroughly depraved, its thoughts and imaginations being only evil continually (Gen. 6:5). It is full of corrupt desires and affections, which exert themselves and influence man in all he does. Now the Gospel comes into direct opposition with these selfish lusts and corrupt affections, both in the root and in the fruit of them (Titus 2:11, 12). There is no greater duty that the Gospel urges upon our souls than the mortifying and destroying of them, and this indispensably, if we intend to be made partakers of its promises (Romans 8:13; Col. 3:5, 8). Hence the first real work of faith is to cleanse the soul from these pollutions, and therefore we read, "They that are Christ's have crucified the flesh with the affections and lusts" (Gal. 5:24). Mark well, it is not that they "ought to" do so, but that they have *actually*, in some measure or degree.

It is one thing really to *think* we believe a thing, it is quite another actually to do so. So fickle is the human heart that even in natural things men know not their own minds. In temporal affairs what a man really believes is best ascertained by his practice. Suppose I meet a traveller in a narrow gorge and tell him that just ahead is an impassable river, and that the bridge across it is rotten: if he declines to turn back, am I not warranted in concluding that he does not believe me? Or if a physician tells me a certain disease holds me in its grip, and that in a short time it will prove fatal if I do not use a prescribed remedy which is sure to heal, would he not be justified in inferring that I did not trust his judgment were he to see me not only ignoring his directions but following a contrary course? Likewise, to believe there is a hell and yet run unto it; to believe that sin continued in will damn and yet live in it—to what purpose is it to boast of *such* a faith?

Now, from what was before us in the last article, it should be plain beyond all room for doubt that when God imparts saving faith to a soul radical and real effects will follow. One cannot be raised from the dead without there being a consequent walking in newness of life. One cannot be the subject of a miracle of grace being wrought in the heart without a noticeable change being apparent to all who know him. Where a supernatural root has been implanted, supernatural fruit must issue therefrom. Not that sinless perfection is attained in the life, nor that the evil principle, the flesh, is eradicated from our beings, or even purified. Nevertheless, there is now a yearning after perfection, there is a spirit resisting the flesh, there is a striving against sin. And more, there is a growing in grace, and a *pressing forward* along the "narrow way" which leads to heaven.

One serious error so widely propagated today in "orthodox" circles, and which is responsible for so many souls being deceived, is the seemingly Christ-honouring doctrine that it is "His blood which *alone* saves any sinner." Ah, Satan is very clever; he knows exactly what bait to use for every place in which he fishes. Many a company would indignantly resent a preacher's telling them that getting baptized and eating the Lord's supper were God's appointed means for saving the soul; yet most of these same people will readily accept the lie that it is *only* by the blood of Christ we can be saved. That is true Godwards, but it is not true manwards. The work of the Spirit in us is *equally* essential as the work of Christ for us. Let the reader carefully ponder the whole of Titus 3:5.

Salvation is twofold: it is both legal and experimental, and consists of justification and sanctification. Moreover, I owe my salvation not only to the Son but to all three persons in the Godhead. Alas, how little is this realized today, and how little is it preached. First and primarily I owe my salvation to God the Father, who ordained and planned it, and who chose me unto salvation (2 Thess. 2:13). In Titus 2:4, it is the Father who is denominated "God our Saviour." Secondly and meritoriously I owe my salvation to the obedience and sacrifice of God the Son Incarnate, who performed as my Sponsor everything which the law required, and satisfied all its demands upon me. Thirdly and efficaciously I owe my salvation to the regenerating, sanctifying and preserving operations of the Spirit: note that *His* work is made just as prominent in Luke 15:8-10, as is the Shepherd's in Luke 15:4-7! As Titus 3:5, so plainly affirms, God "*saved* us *by* the washing of regeneration and renewing of the Holy Spirit"; and it is the presence of *His* "fruit" in my heart and life which furnishes the immediate evidence of my salvation.

"With the heart man believeth unto righteousness" (Romans 10:10). Thus it is the heart which we must first examine in order to discover evidences of the presence of a saving faith. And first, God's Word speaks of "*purifying* their hearts by faith" (Acts 15:9). Of old the Lord said, "O Jerusalem, wash thine heart from wickedness, that thou mayest be saved" (Jer. 4:14). A heart that is being purified by faith (cf. 1 Peter 1:22), is one fixed upon a pure Object. It drinks from a pure Fountain, delights in a pure Law (Romans 7:22), and looks forward to spending eternity with a pure Saviour (1 John 3:3). It loathes all that is filthy—spiritually as well as morally—yea, hates the very garment spotted by the flesh (Jude 23). Contrariwise, it loves all that is holy, lovely and Christlike.

"The pure in heart shall see God" (Matt. 5:8). Heart purity is absolutely essential to fit us for dwelling in that place into which there shall in no wise enter anything "that defileth, neither worketh abomination" (Rev. 21:27). Perhaps a little fuller definition is called for. Purifying the heart by faith consists of, first, the purifying of the understanding, by the shining in of Divine light, so as to cleanse it from error. Second, the purifying of the conscience, so as to cleanse it from guilt. Third, the purifying of the will, so as to cleanse it from self-will and self-seeking. Fourth, the purifying of the affections, so as to cleanse them from the love of all that is evil. In Scripture the "heart" includes all these four faculties. A deliberate purpose to continue in any one sin cannot consist with a pure heart.

Again, saving faith is always evidenced by a *humble* heart. Faith lays the soul low, for it discovers its own vileness, emptiness, impotency. It realizes its former sinfulness and present unworthiness. It is conscious of its weaknesses and wants, its carnality and corruptions. Nothing more exalts Christ than faith, and nothing more debases a man. In order to magnify the riches of His grace, God has selected faith as the fittest instrument, and this because it is that which causes us to go entirely out from ourselves unto Him. Faith, realizing we are nothing but sin and wretchedness, comes unto Christ as an empty-handed beggar to receive all from Him. Faith empties a man of self-conceit, self-confidence, and self-righteousness, and makes him seem nothing, that Christ may be all in all.

The strongest faith is always accompanied by the greatest humility, accounting self the greatest of sinners and unworthy of the least favour (see Matt. 8:8-10).

Again, saving faith is always found in a *tender* heart. "A new heart also will I give you, and a new spirit will I put within you: and I will take away the stony heart out of your flesh, and I will give you an heart of flesh" (Ezek. 36:26). An unregenerate heart is hard as stone, full of pride and presumption. It is quite unmoved by the sufferings of Christ, in the sense that they act as no deterrent against self-will and self-pleasing. But the real Christian *is* moved by the love of Christ, and says, How can I sin against His dying love for me. When overtaken by a fault, there is passionate relenting and bitter mourning. Oh, my reader, do *you* know what it is to be melted before God, for you to be heart-broken with anguish over sinning against and grieving such a Saviour? Ah, it is not the absence of sin but the grieving over it which distinguishes the child of God from empty professors.

Another characteristic of saving faith is that it "worketh by love" (Gal. 5:6). It is not inactive, but energetic. That faith which is "of the operation of God" (Col. 2:12) is a mighty principle of power, diffusing spiritual energy to all the faculties of the soul and enlisting them in the service of God. Faith is a principle of life, by which the Christian lives unto God; a principle of motion, by which he walks to heaven along the highway of holiness; a principle of strength, by which he opposes the flesh, the world, and the Devil. "Faith in the heart of a Christian is like the salt that was thrown into the corrupt fountain, that made the naughty waters good and the barren land fruitful. Hence it is that there followeth an alteration of life and conversation, and so bringeth forth fruit accordingly: 'A good man out of the good treasure of the heart bringeth forth good fruit'; which treasure is faith" (John Bunyan in *Christian Behaviour*).

Where a saving faith is rooted in the heart it grows up and spreads itself in all the branches of obedience, and is filled with the fruits of righteousness. It makes its possessor act for God, and thereby evidences that it is a living thing and not merely a lifeless theory. Even a newborn infant, though it cannot walk and work as a grown man, breathes and cries, moves and sucks, and thereby shows it is alive. So with the one who has been born again; there is a breathing unto God, a crying after Him, a moving toward Him, a clinging to Him. But the infant does not long remain a babe; there is growth, increasing strength, enlarged activity. Nor does the Christian remain stationary: he goes "from strength to strength" (Psalm 84:7).

But observe carefully, faith not only "worketh" but it "worketh *by love*." It is at this point that the "works" of the Christian differ from those of the mere religionist. "The papist works that he may merit heaven. The Pharisee works that he may be applauded, that he may be seen of men, that he may have a good esteem with them. The slave works lest he should be beaten, lest he should be damned. The formalist works that he may stop the mouth of conscience, that will be accusing him, if he does nothing. The ordinary professor works because it is a shame to do nothing where so much is professed. But the true believer works because he *loves*. This is the principal, if not the only, motive that sets him a-work. If there were no other motive within or without him, yet would he be working for God, acting for Christ, because he loves Him; it is like fire in his bones" (David Clarkson).

Saving faith is ever accompanied by *an obedient walk*. "Hereby we do know that we know Him, if we keep His commandments. He that saith, I know Him, and keepeth not His commandments, is a liar, and the truth is not in him" (1 John 2:3, 4). Make no mistake upon this point: infinite as are the merits of Christ's sacrifice, mighty as is the potency of His priestly intercession, yet they avail not for any who continue in the path of disobedience. He acknowledges none to be His disciples save them who do homage to Him as their Lord. "Too many professors pacify themselves with the idea that they possess imputed righteousness, while they are indifferent to the sanctifying work of the Spirit. They refuse to put on the garment of obedience, they reject the white linen which is the righteousness of the saints. They thus reveal their self-will, their enmity to God, and their non-submission to His Son. Such men may talk what they will about justification by faith, and salvation by grace, but they are rebels at heart; they have not on the wedding-dress any more than the self-righteous, whom they so eagerly condemn. The fact is, if we wish for the blessings of grace, we must in our hearts submit to the *rules* of grace without picking and choosing" (C.H. Spurgeon on "The Wedding Garment").

Once more: saving faith is *precious*, for, like gold, it will endure trial (1 Peter 1:7). A genuine Christian fears no test; he is willing, yea, wishes, to be tried by God Himself. He cries, "Examine me, O Lord, and prove me; try my reins and my heart" (Psalm 26:2). Therefore he is willing for his faith to be tried by others, for he shuns not the touchstone of Holy Writ. He frequently tries for himself, for where so much is at stake he must be *sure*. He is anxious to know the worst as well as the best. That preaching pleases him best which is most searching and discriminating. He is loath to be deluded with vain hopes. He would not be flattered into a high conceit of his spiritual state without grounds. When challenged, he complies with the apostle's advice in 2 Corinthians 13:5.

Herein does the real Christian differ from the formalist. The presumptuous professor is filled with pride, and, having a high opinion of himself, is quite sure that *he* has been saved by Christ. He disdains any searching tests, and considers self-examination to be highly injurious and destructive of faith. That preaching pleases him best which keeps at a respectable distance, which comes not near his conscience, which makes no scrutiny of his heart. To preach to him of the finished work of Christ and the eternal security of all who believe in Him strengthens his false peace and feeds his carnal confidence. Should a real servant of God seek to convince him that his hope is a delusion, and his confidence presumptuous, he would regard him as an enemy, as Satan seeking to fill him with doubts. There is more hope of a murderer being saved than of *his* being disillusioned.

Another characteristic of saving faith is that it gives the heart victory over all the vanities and vexations of things below. "For whatsoever is born of God *overcometh the world*: and this is the victory that overcometh the world, even our faith" (1 John 5:4). Observe that this is not an ideal after which the Christian strives, but an actuality of present experience. In this the saint is conformed to His Head: "Be of good cheer; I have overcome the world" (John 16:33). Christ overcame it for His people, and now He overcomes it in them. He opens their eyes to see the hollowness and worthlessness of the best which this world has to offer, and weans their hearts from it by satisfying them with spiritual things. So little does the world attract the genuine child of God that he longs for the time to come when God shall take him out of it.

Alas, that so very few of those now bearing the name of Christ have any real experimental acquaintance with these things. Alas, that so many are deceived by a faith which is not a saving one. "He only is a Christian who *lives for Christ*. Many persons think they can be Christians on easier terms than these. They think it is enough to trust in Christ while they do not live for Him. But the Bible teaches us that if we are partakers of Christ's death we are also partakers of His life. If we have any such appreciation of His love in dying for us as to lead us to confide in the merits of His death, *we shall be* constrained to consecrate our livess to His service. And this is the only evidence of the genuineness of our faith" (Charles Hodge on 2 Corinthians 5:15).

Reader, are the things mentioned above actualized in your own experience? If they are not, how worthless and wicked is your profession! "It is therefore exceedingly absurd for any to pretend that they have a good heart while they live a wicked life, or do not bring forth the fruit of universal holiness in their practice. Men that live in the ways of sin, and yet flatter themselves that they shall go to heaven, expecting to be received hereafter as holy persons, without a holy practice, act as though they expected to make a fool of their Judge. Which is implied in what the apostle says (speaking of men's doing good works and living a holy life, thereby exhibiting evidence of their title to everlasting life), 'Be not deceived; God is not mocked: for whatsoever a man soweth, that shall he also reap' (Gal. 6:7). As much as to say, Do not deceive yourselves with an expectation of reaping life everlasting hereafter, if you do not sow to the Spirit here; it is in vain to think that God will be made a fool of by you" (Johathan Edwards in *Religious Affections*).

That which Christ requires from His disciples is that they should magnify and glorify Him in this world, and that by living holily to Him and suffering patiently for Him. Nothing is as honouring to Christ as that those who bear His name should, by their holy obedience, make manifest the power of His love over their hearts and lives. Contrariwise, nothing is so great a reproach to Him, nothing more dishonours Him, than that those who are living to please self, and who are conformed to this world, should cloak their wickedness under His holy name. A Christian is one who has taken Christ for his example in all things; then how great the insult which is done Him by those claiming to be Christians whose daily lives show they have no respect for His godly example. They are a stench in His nostrils; they are a cause of grievous sorrow to His real disciples; they are the geratest hindrance of all to the progress of His cause on earth; and they shall yet find that the hottest places in hell have been reserved for them. Oh that they would either abandon their course of self-pleasing or drop the profession of that name which is above every name.

Should the Lord be pleased to use this article in shattering the false confidence of some deluded souls, and should they earnestly inquire how they are to obtain a genuine and saving faith, we answer, Use the means which God has prescribed. When faith be His gift, He gives it in His own way; and if we desire to receive it, then we must put ourselves in that way wherein He is wont to communicate it. Faith is the work of God, but He works it not immediately, but through the channels of His appointed means. The means prescribed cannot effect faith of themselves. They are no further effectual than in instruments in the hands of Him who is the principal cause. Though He has not tied Himself to them, yet He has confined us. Though He be free, yet the means are necessary to us.

The first means is *prayer*. "A new heart also will I give you, and a new spirit will I put within you" (Ezek. 36:26). Here is a gracious promise, but in what way will He accomplish it, and similar ones? Listen, "Thus saith the Lord God; I will yet for this *be enquired of* by the house of Israel, to do it for them" (Ezek. 36:37). Cry earnestly to God for a new heart, for His regenerating Spirit, for the gift of saving faith. Prayer is a universal duty. Though an unbeliever sin in praying (as in everything else), it is not a sin for him to pray.

The second means is the *written Word* heard (John 17:20; 1 Cor. 3:5) or read (2 Tim. 3:15). Said David, "I will never forget Thy precepts: for *with them* Thou hast quickened me" (Psalm 119:93). The Scriptures are the Word of God; through them He speaks. Then read them, asking Him to speak life, power, deliverance, peace, to your heart. May the Lord deign to add His blessing.

www.ingramcontent.com/pod-product-compliance
Lightning Source LLC
Chambersburg PA
CBHW060742100426
42813CB00027B/3025